q369.1109 Bott

Bottoms, Bill.

The VFW.

24.95

The VFW

An Illustrated History of the Veterans of Foreign Wars of the United States

Woodbine House • 1991

For information regarding bulk sales of this book, please contact:
Woodbine House
5615 Fishers Lane
Rockville, MD 20852
800–843–7323

The VFW Cross of Malta Emblem is used by authorization of the Veterans of Foreign Wars of the United States

Photo credits: pp. 4, 6, 29, 31, 33, 36, 39, 44, 57, 65, 69, 73, 75, 82, 99, 101 (bottom), 103, 105, 111, 114, 132, 135, 138, 141, 146, 152, 153, 155, 159, 160, 165, 175, 215, 217, 218, 219, 223 (bottom), 229, 230, 233, 244, 246, 247, 248, 253, 298, 302, 303, 306, 308, 314, 317, 324, 326 courtesy of *VFW Magazine*; pp. 182, 184, 188, 189, 191, 192, 193, 196, 197, 198, 199, 200, 201, 204, 206, 208, 209, 210, 234, 296, 299 courtesy of VFW National Home.

Library of Congress Cataloging-in-Publication Data

Bottoms, Bill.
    The VFW : an illustrated history of the Veterans of Foreign Wars of the United States / Bill Bottoms.
       p. cm.
    Includes index.
    ISBN 0–933149–34–4 : $24.95
    1. Veterans of Foreign Wars of the United States—History.
I. Title.
E181.V473B68 1991
369'.11'0973—dc20   89–40627
                                                     CIP

Manufactured in the United States of America

1 2 3 4 5 6 7 8 9 10

This Book is Presented to:

_____

A Gift From:

_____

Date:

_____

*"**The VFW is not really an organization, it is a concept—an idea—an endless devotion—a center of patriotic concern and love of fellow man such as the world has never seen.**"*

*Dr. Kenneth Wells, co-founder and past President of the Freedoms Foundation of Valley Forge
and present President of Family Foundation of America.*

TABLE OF CONTENTS

ACKNOWLEDGEMENTS

No undertaking of this magnitude is ever completed without the assistance of a great many people—too many for me to acknowledge in the space available. I shall therefore settle for naming the major contributors without whom this book could never have been written. As there is no easy way to indicate the importance of the assistance these people provided in assembling this chronicle, I shall attempt to list them in the order their assistance was first asked for and given.

William E. Ryan, Ed.D, then of Briar Cliff College, Sioux City, Iowa. Without his patience and understanding I would never have entered this crazy world of writers.

The late Walter E. Fankhauser, Past State Commander, Department of Iowa (1976–1977). When he appointed me as his Chief of Staff, I became more deeply involved in an organization that retains my interest and loyalty yet today.

Ralph R. (Rod) Johnson, my friend, colleague and Past State Commander, Department of Iowa (1985–1986), who gave me my first insight into the problems suffered by the Vietnam veterans.

Past Commander-in-Chief and current Adjutant General Howard E. Vander Clute, Jr., whose initial and continued support of this project and whose advice gave me direction and understanding.

Former Assistant Adjutant General for Administration Edward Burnham, who acted as VFW editor for the book and whose knowledge of this organization is unsurpassed. To you Ed, my special thanks.

Helen Putnam Blackwell, daughter of James C. Putnam, who is recognized as the first Commander-in-Chief of the VFW.

As you read through these many pages of our history, you will begin to understand better that the information contained in this book had to be gathered from many sources and many different locations. To simplify the acknowledgements, I have attempted to classify the next group of contributors by position and location.

VFW National Headquarters

Wade LaDue, former Director of Public Relations

Vern J. Paul, Assistant Director of Public Affairs

Gary Bloomfield, Managing Editor of the *VFW Magazine*

Staff members: Glenna Murray, Betty Bachand, Jan Krashin, Judy Nick, Carole Atkinson

The Washington Office

Larry Rivers, Executive Director of the Washington Office

James R. (Bob) Currieo, Director of VFW/PAC

James McGill, Director of National Legislative Service
William G. Smith, Director of Public Affairs

The VFW National Home

Joseph Epling, former Assistant Director/Operations
Sue Woodard, Administrative Coordinator
Department Adjutants and Quartermasters

VFW Ladies Auxiliary

Glenn Grossman, National Auxiliary Secretary/Treasurer
Brenda Hampton, Public Relations Director

Comrades

William L. Selby, Past Post Commander, Buckeye Post 1598
James W. Bishop, Sr., Buckeye Post 1598
The late Fred E. Long, James L. Noble Post 3
Paul Savage, Past Department Commander, Michigan
J.B. Virgil, Past Department Commander, Europe

Leaders of Other Veterans Organizations

Prosper J.G.A. Ego, President, Foundation of the Ex-servicemen of the Netherlands
Gen. Hsu Li-nung, Chairman, Vocational Assistance Commission for
Retired Servicemen, Republic of China, Taiwan
Gen. Joon-Yeol So, President, and Col. Kyoo-Tek Ahn of Korean Veterans Association

Marjorie S. Bottoms, my wife, should be on both ends of this chronological list. She has ably assisted me from my first conception of this idea, through my mumblings and grumblings, and finally my elation at the completion of this project some three years later. To her, first and last, I owe my appreciation.

My sincere appreciation also goes to the knowledgeable staff at Woodbine House; especially to Susan Stokes, my editor, and Fran Marinaccio, Robin Dhawan, and Jim Peters.

To each of you who offered and gave your assistance, but could not be mentioned because of space restrictions, I give my personal thanks.

Finally, to each of you comrades, both past and present, without whom there would have been nothing to record, thank you.

FOREWORD

By Bob Dole, U.S. Senator (R) Kansas

For more than ninety years, the Veterans of Foreign Wars has been the guiding flame for our nation's defenders. Since the end of the Spanish-American War, the VFW has successfully secured the rights of those men and women who risked their lives in defense of our country and our ideals. The VFW's achievements are as diverse as the needs of veterans throughout the twentieth century.

With more than 2 million members worldwide, the VFW is an active, positive force in the community, as well as a powerful voice for all veterans. The VFW's efforts in education activities, health services, and youth programs are constant reminders to all Americans that patriotism doesn't stop when the uniform is taken off.

For nearly a century, the VFW has been an important voice and counselor to all veterans. The VFW's participation in our democratic process was a major factor in the enactment of the G.I. Bill, and in the expansion of programs and benefits that our veterans have earned through their service to the United States. The VFW was also a primary force in establishing the Senate Veterans Affairs Committee and in elevating the Veterans Administration to Cabinet level. Each year, the VFW Commander-in-Chief appears before the Veterans Committees of the House and Senate to report on the state of the VFW and express the concerns, views, and goals of our nation's veterans. I'm proud to say that a former National Commander, Norm Staab, hails from my hometown of Russell, Kansas.

As the VFW approaches its centennial year, its role continues to grow and evolve, but its basic commitment to those who have so bravely served our country remains strong and intact. Just as VFW Post 6240 in Russell, Kansas, was there for me when I needed them after I was injured in Italy during World War II, the VFW is there today whenever there is a community that needs help, or a veteran with a problem to solve.

This is the story of the VFW—a story of pride and patriotism for our nation. As a veteran, as a member of the VFW, and as an American—I commend it to you all.

INTRODUCTION

Only in fairy tales do success stories begin as simply and clearly as "once upon a time." Real-life success stories are apt to be complicated by reasons and causes that make identification of a clear-cut beginning impossible. So it is with the story of the organization now known as the Veterans of Foreign Wars of the United States (VFW). The VFW was conceived in war, nurtured by time, and birthed by compassion. In this respect, it was similar to many earlier veteran's groups. But from its uncertain beginnings, the VFW has grown to be the largest, most powerful group of overseas veterans the world has ever known. This is no small distinction, considering the vast numbers of veterans who have banded together over the centuries.

History acknowledges that there were veteran's groups during the time of Caesar's Legions. Writings on the walls of caves indicate their existence, in a less formal sense, thousands of years before. Man's desire to record feats of conquest and valor and his need to communicate with others who shared these experiences led to the formation of these quasi-military associations. It would be impossible to number or name all the veteran's groups that have existed. Most were like spring flowers, blooming brightly for a short while, then fading away. To understand why the Veterans of Foreign Wars has endured, however, it helps to examine the reasons some of its immediate predecessors failed.

The three largest and most notable American veteran's groups to precede the VFW were: The Society of Cincinnati, the Grand Army of the Republic (GAR), and the United Confederate Veterans (UCV). Like all true veteran's groups, each of these organizations had its origin in the hardship

and need of ex-servicemen. Each succeeded in accomplishing some of its aims, but also made costly mistakes that later groups—including the VFW—could learn from.

The Society of Cincinnati, the first group founded, ran into trouble almost from the outset. Its intentions were laudable: to help Revolutionary War veterans recover some form of compensation for their service (many had not been paid in five years). Unfortunately, the society and its members quickly found themselves at odds with their fellow citizens. The trouble stemmed from the society's membership policy. According to the founding statement, the former officers of the American Army meant to ". . . combine themselves into one Society of Friends, to endure as long as they shall endure, or any of their eldest male posterity, and in failure thereof, the collateral branches, who may be judged worthy of becoming its supporters and members." In the absence of male descendants, some state societies admitted female family members. The citizens of the new republic, having just thrown out the British and King George, were not about to accept this threat of a possible hereditary class system once again.

One of the most outspoken critics of the Society of Cincinnati was South Carolina Supreme Court Judge Aedunas Burke. In a pamphlet published in French and German as well as English, Burke charged that the society's members had designs "planted in a fiery, hot ambition, and a thirst for power." He feared that if the society were not opposed, "the United States would be disunited into two ranks of men, patricians, or nobles, and the rabble." John Adams, Sam Adams, and Benjamin Franklin also condemned the society. The State of Massachusetts investigated the society and Rhode Island disfranchised members in its state.

The public outcry effectively hamstrung the Society of Cincinnati. Even though George Washington was its first Commander-in-Chief, eligible officers who feared antagonizing the public stayed out of its ranks by the hundreds. As a result, the highest membership attained during the society's embryo years amounted to about 1500. (After being revived in 1900, the society's membership peaked at 2500 in 1970.) Basically Republican in its politics and favoring the rich, it was endowed with large permanent funds collected by requiring each prospective member to pay an application fee equal to one month's salary. To its credit, the society did establish a fund to aid indigent officers and officers' widows.

The second major veteran's group to appear, the Grand Army of the Republic (GAR), took notable steps forward in its membership requirements. It was founded in 1866 by Dr. B.F. Stephenson, a Springfield, Illinois, surgeon, with the assistance of Congressman John A. Logan and Governor Richard J. Oglesby, also of Illinois. From the start, it welcomed all Union veterans of the Civil War, regardless of rank—which made it the first American veteran's organization to disregard rank as a condition of membership. The GAR also guaranteed its own demise, however, by restricting membership to veterans of the Civil War only.

Before attrition began to take its toll, the GAR was quite successful in achieving its purpose of "defense of the late soldiery of the United States morally, socially, and politically." The first veteran's organization to recognize the power of the ballot, the GAR attacked anti-veteran politicians and issues with gusto. One of its first victories came in 1868 when it helped to secure May 30th (Memorial Day) as a day in which the nation would pause and remember those who had died in the Civil War. Later, Radical Republican politicians (those who favored a harsh reconstruction policy in the South) passed favorable veteran pension legislation in return for GAR votes,

and the GAR helped keep a Republican in the White House. On one occasion, they also helped boot a Republican out of office. After two-term President Grover Cleveland vetoed private pension bills, the GAR turned against him and squelched his bid for a third term in office.

Although the GAR built itself into a political power that no other veteran's organization has ever been able to duplicate, that power was short-lived. Because the GAR had been founded as a one-war organization, its political power waned as large numbers of veterans eligible for membership died. In 1890 the GAR reached its peak membership—408,489. But by 1900 it had ceased to be a dominant force in politics. The GAR's last encampment was held in Indianapolis, Indiana, in 1949, 83 years after its founding.

The final American veteran's group of any stature to appear before the VFW's founding was the United Confederate Veterans (UCV). Perhaps because it was founded in 1889 when its Union counterpart was still going strong, it too made the mistake of restricting membership to veterans of the Civil War. Furthermore, its members proudly adopted the policy of accepting no financial assistance from the federal government and little from its own state governments. Consequently, although it had been formed by the merger of nine smaller Confederate veteran's organizations, the UCV never attained the clout or size of the GAR. Today the UCV is mostly remembered for its struggle to persuade book publishers to print impartial accounts of the Civil War and its vote in support of including 30,152 Confederate graves in the Federal Cemetery System. By 1903, the UCV could claim only 47,000 active and 35,000 inactive members out of 246,000 living Confederate veterans. The last UCV encampment was held in Norfolk, Virginia, on May 30, 1951.

Before consigning the GAR and the UCV back to the history books, it is important to note that both had the opportunity to live on after their last Civil War—era member had died and both spurned the chance. At the conclusion of the Spanish American War in 1898, both groups were asked to reverse their membership policies and admit veterans of that conflict. Had either organization agreed to do so, it is possible that the course of history may have been drastically changed. Perhaps the Spanish American War veterans would not have been compelled to form their own organizations to plead their cause; perhaps the Veterans of Foreign Wars would never have been founded. But then again, underlying the philosophy of the VFW is the belief that only those who have experienced the hardships and sufferings of war are qualified to speak for others who have had the same experiences. And the Spanish American War was a war unlike any other in which the United States had taken part.

Historians claim this war was the result of Spain's treatment of the Cuban people. For years the Spanish rulers had tyrannized the Cubans—arresting and shooting them with little or no provocation, censoring the Cuban press, and levying ruinous excise taxes that bled the island of nearly half its annual income. Then in 1895, the Cubans revolted. In the savage struggle that followed, thousands of Cuban women and children perished outright or while in concentration camps. Americans recoiled at the inhuman treatment of the Cubans and bewailed the loss of $100 million in trade with the island. When the Battleship *Maine* and 260 sailors and marines on board her blew up under mysterious circumstances in Cuba's Havana Harbor, America had an added excuse for war, a rallying point. To the incantation, "Remember the Maine," the nation, feeling the righteousness of its cause, went to war in May 1898.

While the words "went to war" are technically correct, they are also a little misleading. They imply that the United States had a well-organized course of action that it was ready to put into motion, when in truth the nation fumbled, stumbled, and bungled its way to victory. True, the U.S. Navy displayed classroom tactics and efficiency that would have done credit to any navy of long-standing fame. In Manila Harbor, the Philippines, the American flotilla attacked and handily defeated the Spanish Naval Contingent after Commodore George Dewey leaned across the

The explosion of the Battleship Maine *in April 1898 set into action a series of events that eventually resulted in the formation of the VFW.* (National Archives)

rail of his ship's bridge and uttered the now famous words, "You may fire when ready, Gridley." In Santiago Harbor, Cuba, the American Squadron under Admiral William Thomas Sampson routed the Spanish Fleet and blockaded the survivors in the harbor—a feat which destroyed Spain's credibility as a world naval power. But the Army, as future President Theodore Roosevelt declared, "progressed from blunder to blunder."

Although it took the United States Army less than a year to defeat Spanish troops in both the Cuban and Philippine theaters, victory was possible only because the Spanish soldiers were hampered by even worse leadership and equipment than were the Americans. In fact, the U.S. Army was a marginal force at best.

In the thirty-three years since the Civil War, a tight-fisted Congress had virtually destroyed the awesome power that had been the Union Army. Much of the Army's equipment had been sold at auction or was obsolete and in dire need of repair. Most qualified personnel had left the service and were now working at higher-paying jobs in the civilian sector. With its ranks thinned to just over 28,000 soldiers at the start of the war, the U.S. Army was a ridiculous entity. Fortunately, when President William McKinley issued a call for volunteers, thousands of determined, able-bodied men responded. But from the arrival of the first recruit until the war's end, the problems only multiplied.

For any country conducting its first military operation outside its own borders, the logistics of supply would have been extremely difficult. For an army without qualified personnel, adequate equipment, and sufficient funding, trying to maintain operations in two theaters of war 12,000 miles apart was a nightmare. Consequently, a large majority of the regulars and volunteers from east of the Mississippi River were trained in the East and sent to Puerto Rico and Cuba. Those from west of the river were sent to the Philippine Theater.

On both sides of the Mississippi, training did little to prepare recruits for war. At one training station in the West, recruits could be seen practicing close order

American civilians volunteering for service in the war against Spain (National Archives)

drill wearing straw hats, derbies, and even a cape or two. Many recruits learned the rudiments of the manual of arms with broom handles or crudely whittled-out wooden rifles. The uniforms they were issued to wear in the tropical climates of Cuba and the Philippines were woolen and suitable for use in the coldest areas of the United States. Some recruits spent their whole enlistments in these often-called "Concentration Camps" and were treated so badly by incompetent noncoms and officers that their only desire was to get discharged as rapidly as possible. Hundreds died of typhoid, dysentery, and other intestinal ailments brought about by grossly unsanitary conditions and putrid beef. This beef had been improperly canned and knowingly sold to the Army by unscrupulous contractors. Other recruits received scarcely any training before being sent into combat. The First Colorado Voluntary Infantry Regiment, for example, was inserted into combat in the Philippines just three months after muster. Considering the time required to transport them to the theater of operations, their training could not have lasted more than a few days.

Besides poorly trained and equipped soldiers, other problems plagued the Army. The ships used to carry the troops to war were coastal vessels, not designed to venture any great distance from the shore. Because they were intended for short trips, they lacked adequate ventilation for those sleeping below deck and enough sanitary facilities on any level. They also had little or no area for food preparation.

Food was a problem not only for troops en route to combat, but also for soldiers in combat. Large quantities of their rations were unfit for consumption.

The 71st New York Volunteers boarding the Vigilancia *bound for Cuba* (National Archives)

Much of the rest was so poorly packaged that it soon spoiled and became infested with maggots. Ironically, even food which remained edible was often fated to remain on the docks. Means of transporting it to the front were seldom available. During one period, while front line troops were pursuing the enemy in Luzon Province, Philippine Islands, the food situation was so critical that rations were distributed only every other day.

Even graver than the lack of an adequate food supply was the lack of a competent Army medical department. Most of the Army's doctors were what was known as "Contract Surgeons"—civilians in the military who had no status, authority, or recognition. These Contract Surgeons were largely ignorant about the treatment of deadly tropical diseases such as yellow fever—an ignorance shared by active duty medical personnel. So degraded was the status of the "Contract Surgeon" that years later they were nearly refused membership in the Army of the Philippines, a forerunner of the VFW. Only a motion by General Irving Hale, who had commanded the First Colorado, won them a place in that veteran's organization.

To compound the physicians' ignorance about tropical diseases, there was also a critical shortage of medications and other medical supplies. As a result, medical personnel had to resort to stopgap measures such as pouring cooking sugar into wounds to arrest the flow of blood.

In the end, less than one percent of the American servicemen shipped overseas died. This survival rate speaks only to the excellent condition of the men, however, not to the conduct of the campaign or the Army's care of them. Significantly, of the 2,430 American casualties in the Spanish American War, only 385 were combat deaths.

With little other than "guts" and determination, these "Boys in Blue" gave the United States its first taste of empire. At the peace treaty of December 1898 in Paris, Spain ceded Puerto Rico and Guam to the United States. A stipulation in the treaty also allowed the U.S to purchase the Philippines for $20 million.

Cuba, independent of Spain, remained under U.S. military control for three years.

When the first American troops began returning home in the latter part of 1898, they were rightfully proud of the service they had given their country. They had performed the duty requested of them, even without the instruments of war that fighting men have the right to expect their countries to furnish. Overseas, out of touch with the realities of life at home, these men believed in their hearts that their nation would be grateful to them.

But they were wrong. And because they were wrong, the stage would be set for the appearance of a new kind of veteran's organization—one whose avowed purpose was that such criminal ingratitude would never again rear its head.

In time, at least the nation's future veterans would be grateful.

"When Johnny comes marching home again. . . ."

CHAPTER ONE

THE BEGINNING
1898–1899

When Johnny came marching home after the Spanish American War, he did not receive quite the hero's welcome he expected. Instead, the American veteran found the situation more as the sage Teddy Roosevelt had predicted it would be in his farewell address to his Rough Riders. "The world will be kind to you for ten days," Colonel Roosevelt told his troops. "Everything you do will be all right. After that you will be judged by a stricter code, and if you prove worthless, you will be considered as spoiled by going to war."

For many Spanish American War veterans, the grace period was even shorter than ten days. Many were mustered out of the service far from home and left to find their own transportation back. Most arrived home virtually penniless only to discover that their hero status was no help in finding employment. Often the jobs they had given up when they answered the president's call for volunteers had been taken by men who had stayed safely at home.

Treatment of veterans who were sick or wounded was especially shoddy. Yet, according to Dr. Nicholas Senn, Chief Surgeon of the United States Volunteers, the war had undermined the health of vast numbers of soldiers. As Dr. Senn wrote to a colleague about the soldiers of the Cuban Campaign: "The men left in excellent spirits. Most of them returned mere shadows of themselves. The pale and sunken faces, sunken eyes, the staggering gait and emaciated forms show only too plainly the effects of climate and disease. Many of them are wrecks for life, others are candidates for a premature grave and hundreds will require most careful attention and treatment before they regain the vigor they lost in Cuba."

But despite Dr. Senn's concern, even the most severely disabled veterans were denied hospital care or medications. Nor were there any government programs to help returnees rehabilitate themselves so they could resume their places in society. They were given two months' pay ($31.20 for a private), discharged, and sent home to their families.

Many veterans were embittered by the treatment they received. They had won property in two oceans, and, in the process, new-found status as a world power for the United States. The federal government now had an annual surplus of $46 million in revenue over expenditures and surely could have spared the funds to aid its needy war veterans. And yet, all the country offered veterans in return for their services was pain, sorrow, and an early grave. The war had caused no visible damage to property inside our borders, so it was difficult for officials and citizens to see

As commander of the Rough Riders, Colonel Theodore Roosevelt (far right) predicted that Spanish American War veterans would not receive a hero's welcome. (National Archives)

the need to spend more money on a war that was officially over.

Ironically, the veterans' victorious actions had only provided the country with a new mania, exploitation. With the war won, there was no further need for soldiers and even less need for ex-soldiers. With the depression of 1893 working toward its end, the average man was once again beginning to feel good about his prospects. Everyone knew life could only get better. Now was the time to get those riches everyone had always dreamed about. Now was the time for "grab-it-tude," not gratitude.

Even President William McKinley, a Civil War veteran whose concern for his men had taken him from private to major, succumbed to the "grab-it-tude" frenzy. Although early in his administration he had championed the cause of the workingman, he now channeled his energies into pursuing an expansionist foreign policy. Political strife racked the country.

With their motto of "Civilization," McKinley's administration and its backers sought to advance their conquest of the lands gained in the Spanish American War. Civil servants were sent to Cuba, Puerto Rico, and the Philippines, ostensibly to help these countries modernize their governments and their business and trade practices. In reality, however, much of their intent was to exploit the countries' assets. Although opponents of McKinley's administration cried "Imperialism" and protested that the United States should be reducing her overseas holdings, McKinley's backers ignored these objections. Worse, the needs of the men who had secured the new lands for their country were forgotten.

Politicians were not the only ones to turn their backs on the Spanish American War veterans. The two major organizations for Civil War veterans also rebuffed the nation's newest veterans. Both the North's Grand Army of the Republic (GAR) and the

The citizens of Philadelphia turned out to see the 16th Pennsylvania Volunteers come marching home, but then turned their backs on the veterans and their needs. (National Archives)

South's United Confederate Veterans (UCV) refused them a place in their ranks. This refusal to admit new blood was the same shortsightedness that had brought about the demise of every previous veteran's organization.

With no organization to plead their cause, the veterans were left to protest their treatment on their own. For more than a year, the cries of the lone veteran went unheeded. Then, within the space of several months, the seeds of a solution were planted in two locations—one to the east of the Mississippi River and one to the west. In both Columbus, Ohio, and Denver, Colorado, veterans began to band together to jointly attack their problems. Like the war with Spain, the veterans' fight for better treatment from their government would now be conducted on two fronts.

THE EAST

American troops in the Eastern theater—in Cuba—were the first to cease fighting the Spanish and return home. Among those returning in 1898 was the 17th Infantry Regiment, a Regular Army unit stationed at Columbus Barracks (later renamed Fort Hayes) in Columbus, Ohio.

As part of the Second Infantry Division, the 17th had played a major role in expelling the Spanish from Cuba. It took part in several of the larger engagements, including the capture of Santiago, on Cuba's southeast coast. During the assault on that city in mid-summer 1898, the 17th Infantry Regiment and other elements of the Second Division successfully took El

Caney Hill, while Colonel Teddy Roosevelt and his Rough Riders tackled the more famous San Juan Hill. Soon afterwards, Spanish troops throughout Cuba surrendered, and the 17th was sent home.

Following its return from Cuba, the 17th spent the next few months replacing both men and equipment. Once the regiment was back up to strength, it was shipped to the Philippines to replace a unit of volunteers. First, though, men who were sick or wounded were given two months' pay and discharged. No allowances were made for medication, hospital care, food, or transportation home. Since they were of no further use to the Army or the government, the men became the problem of Columbus, Ohio, their own hometowns, or their families.

Among the first to grapple with the problems of these disabled soldiers was a small group of their former comrades. Unlike most members of the 17th Infantry Regiment, these compassionate men were not career soldiers, but had been discharged upon their return to Columbus because their terms of enlistment had expired. It was their hope that they could help their less fortunate comrades by founding a veteran's organization.

Thirteen former members of the 17th Infantry Regiment combined their efforts to make this dream a reality. Of these thirteen, two men stood out as the leaders: James C. Putnam and James Romanis. Both men had been discharged as privates. They also shared a recent and firsthand knowledge of the horrors of war, a deep compassion for their fellow man, and the willingness to work to rectify what they saw as unfair treatment of veterans of the Spanish American War. Their approaches to solving these problems, however, differed widely.

Jim Putnam, otherwise known as "Bill" or "Ol' Putt," or just plain "Put(t)," didn't much care what people called him as long as they believed in whatever cause he was promoting at that moment. An extrovert, he was at home in any group and never shy about telling listeners how he viewed an issue. He had only been a resident of Columbus since his discharge, but it wasn't long before he became known to many of the

town's people as he pedalled his old Columbia bicycle around the streets searching for veterans with whom to chat about his beliefs. He was pursuing a long-time dream. "Putt" believed that a man who served his country in time of war was entitled to more than an earlier-than-normal grave. He was convinced that the only way for the veterans to be heard was through an organization whose sole interest was in helping them. Everyone said it would be a long, hard fight, but that suited him just fine. He came from a long line of fighters. (See Chapter 11 for more information on his personal life and ancestry.)

While the more flamboyant Putnam pedalled around Columbus in search of others interested in forming an organization to help needy veterans, James Romanis pursued the same goal from where he worked, a pharmacy just outside the gates of Columbus Barracks. Here he talked to many veterans who came to purchase relief from the pains and sickness they had acquired while serving in the tropics. Mostly

James Putnam

he talked to comrades with whom he had served, or others who asked his advice.

An introvert, Romanis was Putnam's opposite. Little is known about his life before he became involved in the veteran's movement. Afterwards, he devoted a majority of his time to the organization he helped found. His strength proved to be guiding the interior operations of the organization. Usually he worked in ways that were consistent with his lifestyle, quietly and shunning notoriety. But when it was necessary to promote his beloved organization, he could shake off his reserve and deliver eloquent, moving speeches. Just how much his efforts contributed to the eventual success of the organization will never be known. Until his death, however, he was a quiet, guiding force.

Perhaps it was because Romanis and Putnam each worked toward their common goal from different perspectives that they ultimately succeeded. No veteran's organization before theirs had ever survived its generation. The rules and practices that gave their organization its longevity did not even exist at its inception. Instead, they grew out of the beliefs and determination of its founders—and out of the founders' feeling that there was no equal to the bonds of loyalty forged between men in the crucible of war. Romanis and Putnam succeeded not by strengthening or changing these bonds, but by utilizing them for the common good.

The First Meeting

On the 25th and 26th of September 1899, James Romanis placed notices in the *Columbus Dispatch*. The first notice read: "There will be a meeting of the Seventeenth Infantry at 286 East Main Street, Friday evening September 29th at 7 p.m. standard time, for the purpose of effecting an organization. It is to the interest of all old Seventeenth men to be present at this meeting, as an association for mutual benefit in getting pension, claims, etc., is to be formed."

On the evening of the 29th, Francis Dubiel closed his clothing store and tailor shop earlier than the cus-

tomary 9 p.m. He and two others had offered their establishments as meeting places for the men of the Seventeenth; his was chosen because it would accommodate a larger crowd. Now, as the meeting time approached, Dubiel added a little more fuel to the old pot-bellied stove to ward off the chill of early evening. September that year seemed colder than usual.

As the men arrived, most took seats around the stove. Romanis sat on one of the counters, his legs dangling over the edge. Putnam sat silently with the group around the stove, puffing on his ever-present pipe. Dubiel escorted new arrivals to the back of his store, where the others were seated. The group was quiet. Perhaps they were aware that their miliary service had allowed them each to feel something that would never again be experienced by combat soldiers. They had fought in the last of the "romantic" wars; they had witnessed the final dashing cavalry and infantry charges, the colors carried at the head of the assaulting units, and much hand-to-hand combat on the ramparts. Talk of the new horseless carriages, mustache cups, and the daring knee-length bathing suits had been left outside. It was as if each man was aware that levity had no place in the business they would conduct this night. They waited patiently.

Shortly after seven o'clock, Romanis slid down from the counter and stood erect. Looking at the assembled group, he mentally called the role. Seated were James C. Putnam, George Kelly, Bert J. DuRant, Walker Waddington, John Malloy, Charles Click, John H. Clark, David Brown, George Beeckman, Andrew S. Grant, and Oscar S. Brookin, a former private who had been awarded the prestigious Congressional Medal of Honor for rescuing a wounded comrade while under intensive enemy fire. Francis Dubiel stood near the doorway leading to the front part of the store so he could greet any late arrivals. Romanis said softly, "We all know why we're here. Any of you that either Jim or I haven't talked to have read the ad. We've got a lot to talk about so we'd best be getting at it."

The group elected Dubiel temporary chairman and Romanis recording secretary. Parliamentary pro-

In 1931, James Romanis, Oscar Brookin, George Kelly, and John Malloy, four of the orginal members of the American Veterans of Foreign Service, returned to the organization's birthplace in Columbus, Ohio.

cedure was not one of their strengths, but they tried to keep a sense of order in their deliberations.

Without an agenda to follow, the subjects they discussed were many and varied. Ideas were not presented in any logical sequence. How and when they were interjected into the discussion depended upon who had the floor and his train of thought at that moment.

One of the first discussions centered around forming an association. All agreed that this was the primary step. With that consensus, they began to debate questions such as the association's purpose and membership requirements.

Since everyone present had served with the Seventeenth Infantry, it was natural that someone would suggest the association's membership should be drawn only from this regiment. But Putnam reminded them that this limiting idea had sounded the death knell for other organizations. "Most of you probably read in the paper a short time back about one of the GAR Units

selling their meeting hall because they didn't have enough members anymore to hold meetings." Several of the men nodded. "Some of you might remember that I approached them about taking us into membership in their organization and they refused. If we aren't careful we'll have the same problem somewhere down the line." He suggested they find a way to make their association endure forever, so that it would be "evergreen." Others suggested methods of ensuring their association's longevity, but no one came up with an immediate answer to their dilemma.

Romanis, the ever practical, brought up the subject of recruiting new members. The arguments waxed and waned until a late arrival came into the meeting. He was Simon Heiman, Dubiel's brother-in-law. Heiman had served in Puerto Rico with the 4th Ohio Volunteers.

Heiman's presence opened up a new avenue of membership requirements to be explored. At the insistence of Bert DuRant and Dubiel, a motion was made to allow men who had served honorably in any overseas outfit during the Spanish American War to join. It passed without a dissenting vote.

Throughout the debate on membership, there was never any thought about relaxing the requirement for honorable service on foreign soil. This requirement was paramount to their thinking that their association be a "Gold Chevron" order—composed solely of men who had earned the "Gold Chevron" signifying service outside the limits of the continental United States. As they said repeatedly, "Only those who have seen and felt what we have seen and felt can speak honestly and knowledgeably about our service and our feelings."

Further discussion eventually broadened the right to membership to everyone who had been awarded a Campaign Medal by our government for service in any war or conflict. The scope of this motion would allow survivors of the 1846 war with Mexico to join if they so desired. More importantly, its passage ensured the association's longevity by granting the right to membership to those who qualified in any future war. The association *would* be "evergreen."

Once the membership issue was settled, it was time to select a name for the organization. Putnam, DuRant, and George Kelly were given this task and the additional one of drawing up a constitution.

As the meeting was drawing to a close, someone in the group mentioned a former member of the "Old Seventeenth" who wanted to attend, but was stricken by the fever and financially destitute. The group, well aware that many of their comrades were down and out, dug into their personal funds to help. This scene would recur many times over the next twenty-three years—until the government finally acknowledged its debt to the men it ordered to war. Even then, the acknowledgement, in the form of pensions of $12 a month or $30 a month if the recipient was totally disabled, fell short of the Revolutionary War grants (passed by Congress on March 18, 1818) of $20 each month.

It was several hours into Saturday morning before the flow of conversation and ideas ground to a halt.

Most of the men worked on Saturday and needed to get home to sleep. Realizing that much still needed to be accomplished, the veterans scheduled another meeting for Saturday, October 7th.

The meeting had been an exhausting, but exhilarating one. As James Putnam recalled later, while speaking at the VFW National Encampment in 1933, "If you ever saw an enthusiastic meeting of veterans of foreign wars, it was that little meeting of those thirteen men. Men clasped each other's hands and shed tears, hugged each other and pandemonium broke loose. I am an old man of 63 now. Never in all my experience in veterans affairs have I seen such enthusiasm as was displayed in Francis Dubiel's clothing store that night."

Laying the Groundwork

The second meeting of "Old Seventeenth" men opened with Francis Dubiel again acting as temporary chairman and James Romanis as the secretary. First on the agenda was the approval of the constitution Putnam had written and endorsement of the name *American Veterans of Foreign Service* proposed by DuRant. Next came the election of officers. James Putnam was elected President. George Kelly and Bert DuRant were elected Vice Presidents; James Romanis, Secretary; Francis Dubiel, Treasurer; David Brown, Chaplain; and John Clark, John Malloy, and Oscar Brookin, Trustees. Walker Waddington and Andrew Grant held positions of Sergeants-at-Arms.

Two other decisions reached that night would greatly influence the future of the organization. The first was that all members of the American Veterans of Foreign Service (AVFS) would be considered equals. After all, they were an organization of previous military men, with the key word being "previous." No allowance was made for special treatment of those who had held superior rank during their previous service. This decision was understandable, considering that of the original thirteen who met in Dubiel's store, only one had been an officer. Until the founding of the Vietnam Veterans of America some

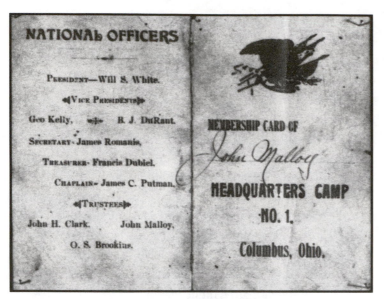

John Malloy's AVFS membership card

some discussion they settled on the Cross of Malta, the emblem which had decorated the banners of the Order of the Knights of St. John during the Crusades. The order had been famous for caring for its wounded comrades, a fact which was not lost on the American Veterans of Foreign Service. As Comrade James Putnam explained years later in a letter written to Commander-in-Chief Lyall Beggs, "Because it was the emblem of the Crusaders and as the American Veterans of Foreign Service were also crusaders, or a new departure in veteran's organizations, we decided it was a fitting emblem for such an organization."

The emblem consisted of an eight-pointed or Maltese Cross. Between the segments, the rays of the sun were cantoned, forming a star. Superimposed on the center was an American eagle with outstretched wings and claws. In the right claw of the eagle was an olive branch, and in the left a sheaf of arrows. From the bill of the eagle a streamer was suspended bearing the Latin inscription, "Pro Deo—Pro Patria" ("For God—For Country"), and over the head of the eagle thirteen stars were grouped. On the breast of the eagle was an American shield. Later the eagle would be encircled by the legend "Veterans of Foreign Wars of the United States."

Once the organization's foundation had been laid, its members moved rapidly to obtain national stature for their group. Early in October, following the

seventy years later, it would be the only major veteran's organization founded by enlisted men.

The second decision was to prepare for anticipated future expansion. To properly channel this hoped-for growth, a provision was made for the formation of additional units. They would be administered locally and be called "camps." The unit they had just founded in Columbus would be known as "Headquarters Camp Number One." All of the Columbus officers would hold dual positions, serving in national as well as local capacities.

The final noteworthy decision reached that night was to acquire a logo or emblem so that their deeds would not be forgotten with the passage of time. After

Letterhead of the American Veterans of Foreign Service

group's first meeting, David Brown, James Romanis, James C. Putnam, John Malloy, and Francis Dubiel had appeared before David Ramsey, a Notary Public in the Secretary of State's office, to request articles of incorporation for the organization. This they felt would allow them to expand on a national basis. The corporation would be chartered under the non-profit statutes provided by the state of Ohio. Because the new association had no funds, Putnam paid the incorporation fee with his own money.

On the incorporation application, the principal business location of the corporation was listed as Columbus, Franklin County, Ohio. The purpose for which the corporation had been formed was given as: "For social enjoyment of the membership of said association and their families and friends. The promotion of the mutual interests of all such and more especially to preserve the reminiscences of the camps and field beyond the borders of our native land."

The charter was granted on October 10, 1899, just days after the organization's second meeting. Within a few weeks, new camps were formed in Cincinnati, Hamilton, Marysville, Delaware, and Marion, Ohio; and in Sparta, Illinois, and Portsmouth, New Hampshire.

No sooner had its founders started the American Veterans of Foreign Service off on the right track than several of them found their commitment strained by family and job obligations. The first to fall victim to outside commitments was David Brown, national chaplain. The pressure of business forced him to resign on October 21, 1899. The next was President Putnam, who had resigned his job with the Columbus Fire Department and secured a position with the Pennsylvania Railroad. Although he would maintain a residence in Columbus until 1908, his new job required extensive traveling, thus precluding his continuing as president.

Putnam's resignation as president was effective December 1, 1899. As Putnam confided in a letter dated August 6, 1929, to then-National Historian J.I. Billman, he had "always led a roving, dare-devil existence and soon left for other parts." Since he was given Brown's position as national chaplain, however, Putnam was still able to serve his organization well. Via his railroad pass, his job allowed him to travel to other cities, where he could preach the gospel of the American Veterans of Foreign Service organization.

For reasons known only to the members of the organization at that time, a vice president did not succeed Putnam as president. Instead, Will White, a former captain who had served in Puerto Rico with the 4th Ohio Volunteer Infantry, was selected from the rank and file.*

Even considering the resignation of two of its national officers, the fledgling organization entered the twentieth century on a positive note. Membership was on the upswing both in Headquarters Camp and in the new camp in Cincinnati. And the possibility of adding several more camps in the near future was also very real.

THE WEST

Military historians maintain that the First Colorado Voluntary Infantry Regiment was one of the finest outfits to take to the field during the Spanish American War. Composed of the First and Second Regiments of the Colorado National Guard and brought up to strength with an infusion of cowboys, clerks, miners, and other raw recruits from the West,

---

*   There is some question about the date of White's elevation to the presidency of the organization. Four times are possible: December 1, 1899, later in December, January of 1900, and May of 1900. A majority of records available tend to indicate it was December 1, 1899 or very shortly thereafter.

it was commanded by its organizer, Colonel (later Brevet Major General) Irving Hale.

Like other National Guard units, the First Colorado was state controlled until federalized by the United States government. Once federalized, each member had to pass a rigorous physical examination and be sworn into federal service. Mustered at Camp Adams, now the Park Hill Division of Denver, on April 29, 1898, the regiment saw service as part of the Eighth Army in the Philippine Islands from July 16, 1898, to July 16, 1899. Although its members received only minimal training, the Regiment compiled an outstanding record.

To the accompaniment of the Regimental Band's rendition of "A Hot Time," the Regiment waded the Cingallon River and stormed the Spanish Fortress of San Antonio de Abad, forcing a withdrawal of the Spanish forces. It also raised the first American flag over Manila.

It was during the Fort San Antonio de Abad action that Colonel Hale was promoted to Brigadier General. The September 3rd order promoting him read in part: "For skill and courage in preparation for attack and leading his regiment in the assault on Fort San Antonio de Abad."

Most of the men of the First were scheduled for discharge during the first weeks of April, 1899. But their hopes of seeing their homes before summer were dashed on February 4th when the Philippine Insurrection broke out. A group of Filipinos, under the leadership of Emilio Aguinaldo, believed that the expulsion of the Spanish should have resulted in the total independence of the Philippines. To this end, Aguinaldo led his countrymen in a further revolt, this time against the American forces. The First Colorado was ordered to remain in the Philippines several months past their expected rotation date to help quell this insurrection.

Exactly one year to the day after their arrival in the Philippines, the First Colorado boarded the transport *Warren* for their trip home. Routed to Nagasaki and thence through the Inland Sea to Yokohama, Japan, they sailed via the Great Circle

General Irving Hale

route to San Francisco, where the regiment was mustered out September 8, 1899.

So proud of their soldiers were the people of Denver that they ignored the usual policy of leaving men who had "mustered out" to find their own way home from the mustering-out point. By public subscription of funds, they hired a special train to transport the men home to Denver.

On September 14th, the men of "Bike Battalion" (Companies B, I, K, and E) were greeted by 75,000 citizens of their capital city. After a joyous parade and stirring speeches of appreciation for the job the First had done in the Philippines, General Irving Hale ordered his men to fall out for the last time.

As Teddy Roosevelt had forewarned, problems began almost immediately for the former members of the First. Like their eastern counterparts, many discovered that the jobs they had held before the war had been taken by others. And those who were unable to work because of disease or crippling wounds belatedly found they had no prospects of rehabilitation or financial assistance from the federal government. Veterans' employment woes were further increased by the depression that gripped the nation. Not only had their old jobs been taken by others, but new ones were almost non-existent. Even veterans in good health had great difficulty providing for their families and themselves. While General Washington had seen that his Revolutionary War veterans were given preference in the hiring for federal jobs, no such advantage was available to the volunteers.

For General Hale, re-entry into civilian life was somewhat smoother than it was for his men. Because he had been wounded earlier that year in the fighting around Mecauyan, the Army decided it had no further need for his services and discharged him on October 1, 1899. But Hale had little difficulty securing employment after his separation. A large electrical company in Denver hired him as an engineer and general manager.

A born leader, Irving Hale was a man of tremendous energy and vision. His enthusiasm and loyalty toward his home state and the men who had served under his command made him a natural selection to lead many civic and organizational projects. After the First was disbanded, Hale kept in contact with his men. He talked to those he met on the streets and visited some of them in their homes. What he en-

Plaque installed in the Denver State Capitol to commemorate founding of the Army of the Philippines

countered touched him deeply. It seemed especially unjust to him that men who had suffered during wartime service were now destined by an uncaring government for further suffering and starvation. Hale helped many veterans from his personal funds. He soon became convinced, however, that the only way to right all the wrongs being imposed upon his returning veterans was to form an association.

On November 18th and 23rd, 1899, Hale and other former officers from the First discussed the possibility of forming a veteran's association. The second meeting was called to formulate plans for a reunion of all veterans of the Philippines in Denver on August 13, 1900. The date commemorated the second anniversary of the capture of Manila by American forces. At this meeting, the decision was also made to form a veteran's association. General Hale, acting as temporary chairman, appointed a committee to draft a constitution. He asked everyone present to pass the word to all members of the First that another meeting would be held December 12th, and that it would be to their advantage to attend.

Twenty-eight men answered his call. Present at the meeting in Room 33 of the State Capitol Building were: Frank C. Noble, Henry Lippincott, Charles E. Locke, W.A. Cornell, George Borstadt, W.B. Sawyer, J.O. Adams, Charles B. Lewis, Ben K. Duffy, George LaShell, E.L. Dale, L. Madison, J.C. Brinkley, Gus E. Hartung, John A. Briggs, Samuel R. Todd, Fred E. Franklin, A.G. Givens, Charles A. Wilkinson, O.M. Oleson, Charles H. Anderson, James K. Polks, L.H. Kemble, C.G. Springer, W.C. Harrison, David D. Thorton, P.G. Bridges, and Arthur K. Etz.

The first order of business was a report by the three-man committee Hale had previously appointed to draft a constitution. Former officers Henry Lippincott, Charles H. Anderson, and Charles B. Lewis all reported in favor of an "immediate formation of a permanent organization of officers and enlisted men, comprising the land forces of the United States who served honorably in the distant Philippines, to sustain the honor and supremacy of our beloved flag, and having for its objects: The perpetuation of the memory of the achievements of the participants in this striking and unique epoch of our country's history; the perpetuation of the memories of our departed companions in arms, many of whom are now sleeping their last sleep under the palms of the tropics, or in the sand of the deep seas; to cement and strengthen the bonds of friendship formed in camp and bivouac, on long lonely voyages to the Orient, in the trenches and on lonely outposts, in skirmish and battle among rice ridges and swamps of the Philippine Islands; to collect and preserve the relics, records, books and other historical data relating to the Spanish-American War and maintain and foster true patriotism and love of our country and its institutions." (Not stated in the report but underlying all the other reasons for forming the organization was the same one that had motivated the founders of the American Veterans of Foreign Service: to assist comrades-in-arms and their families who were in

need.) This report was unanimously adopted and parts of it were later used in other statements of the organization's philosophy.

The adoption of the committee's report was followed by the election of Hale as President and Frank Noble as Secretary. They were charged with contacting all former commanding officers of regiments that had comprised the Eighth Army to suggest they form local units. If all went according to plan, the units would be merged into a single association at the reunion in Denver the next year. The name the former men of the First chose for their new association was the *Colorado Society of the Army of the Philippines*.

Later in the meeting, Hale spoke of the hunger, sickness, and poverty he had seen on his visits to veterans around town. He described the helplessness and frustration their comrades were suffering because of their inability to find employment. He asked for suggestions and comments.

Former Lt. Colonel Henry Lippincott, who had served as Deputy Surgeon General of the United States Army and Chief Surgeon of the Pacific and Eighth Army Corps, maintained that the government should furnish medical care for those who needed it and provide pensions for veterans unable to support themselves and their families due to service-connected disabilities. His suggestions received unanimous approval from the gathering. Another well-supported suggestion concerned preference in hiring of federal employees. Since their jobs had been taken by men who did not fight in America's war with Spain, they felt that those who *did* fight should be considered first for federal jobs.

General Hale told the assembled group that he favored forming a separate association from the one they had just founded to help them press the government for assistance. Toward this end, he said, he had already communicated with the "Boys from Iowa" who had recently passed through Denver on their way home, and with General Frederick M. Funston, from Nebraska, who had been in town on business. Everyone he had contacted had heartily supported his proposed plan.

A roster of membership for the Colorado Society of the Army of the Pacific was started at this meeting. Each man signed only his name with no reference to past rank. "We are an association of civilians first and veterans second," Hale had counselled them. At the time of signing each paid $1.00 dues, the amount suggested by Dr. Charles Locke. In his words, "A dollar is plenty to pay for the boys who are not getting much."

The paper on which each man signed his name also carried the principles of the association. "We, the undersigned, agree to form an organization to be of mutual aid to our comrades and to perpetuate the memory of those who died in the service of their country and to keep alive the glorious deeds of bravery and courage performed in field of war. This organization will be non-political." (By "non-political," they meant that the organization would not favor one political party, not that it would stay out of politics entirely. They certainly did not want to rule out the possibility that their group could and would replace the Grand Army of the Republic as a political power.)

While many of the initial goals of the Colorado Society of the Army of the Philippines were similar to those of the American Veterans of Foreign Service, there were two important differences between the groups. First, as the name of the Army of the Philippines suggests, membership in the society was open only to veterans from one branch of service, the Army. This automatically excluded personnel of the Navy and Marine Corps. Second, it restricted eligibility to those who had served in the Philippine Theater of War and only in the Spanish American War. If these rules were left standing, the Society, like all previous veteran's organizations, would die out with its generation.

In time, the Colorado Society of the Army of the Philippines would not only adopt innovative membership rules that would assure its longevity, but it would also merge with the organization that first formulated those new rules—the American Veterans of Foreign Service. Together, these two organizations would form the nucleus of the present-day Veterans of Foreign Wars. For now, however, no one in the Army of the Philippines was much concerned about the possible demise of their organization. Perhaps it was because the twentieth century was dawning and all thoughts were on beginnings, not endings. Perhaps it was because the entire country was caught up in anxious expectation of greater and better things to come.

CHAPTER TWO

THE EARLY YEARS
1900–1914

As could be expected, the new century started off with much activity. It was as if everyone felt that they needed to get off to a fast start to get the most for themselves during the next hundred years. In Europe, activities during the early years would precipitate a war that threatened to tear the world asunder. But in the United States, the Spanish American War veterans worked on building harmony, not discord. In the space of thirteen years, the American Veterans of Foreign Service, the Colorado Society Army of the Philippines, and three newer veteran's organizations would all resolve their differences and merge into one association. United under the name of the Veterans of Foreign Wars of the United States, these veterans would go on to jointly pursue their dream of better treatment of *all* American veterans.

The watchword in the creation of the VFW was one sorely lacking in European politics of the day—*compromise*. Before the major re-organization of five veteran's organizations into one could take place, several minor mergers and changes in or-

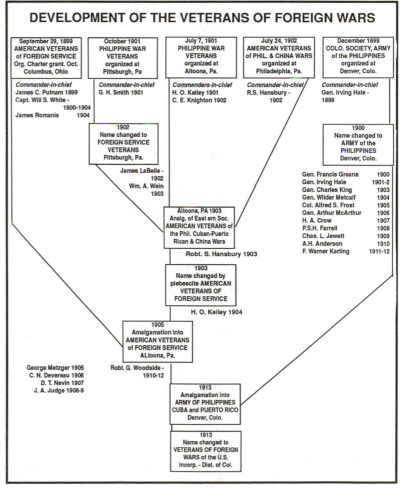

Figure 1

ganizational structure had to occur. Thousands of members of the existing organizations also had to concede that one large national organization could serve their interests better than the more specialized, but smaller ones to which they already belonged.

Since most of the changes needed to clear the way for the formation of the VFW occurred in the Eastern United States, this chapter focuses on developments in that area first. It then turns to a discussion of veterans' activities in the West, and finally, to a description of the creation of the VFW. See Figure 1 for an overview of the mergers and organizational name changes that preceded the final amalgamation and selection of the name "Veterans of Foreign Wars."

THE EAST: 1900–1914

The American Veterans of Foreign Service

From the first meeting of the American Veterans of Foreign Service, it was evident that its founders had far more than a local society in mind. But although their enthusiasm and aspirations were great, their planning often did not keep pace with their ideas. It took the pragmatism of Jim Romanis to turn the ideas into reality.

Romanis recognized from the start that the key to national recognition for the Society was a nationwide membership. Already the Society had provided for the formation of local units or "camps" outside of Columbus, Ohio. But for camps to be formed, there was an unwritten qualification related to size. One or two members could not do everything necessary to run a camp. Camps could therefore be established only in towns large enough to support a functional group.

Addressing this inadequacy was the crux of Romanis's membership-at-large plan. Under his plan, veterans were encouraged to become attached to a camp, but were still welcome in the organization if unable to do so. As long as he paid his membership dues of fifty cents every three months, any veteran with honorable and qualifying service could join. (In the aftermath of the depression, many prospective members could not come up with the required dues. At a time when 40 acres of poultry land was advertised in a Columbus newspaper for $175, fifty cents was a huge sum for many.) Romanis promoted his membership-at-large scheme by corresponding with prospective members both inside and outside the country. There are no records of the early years to show what percentage of the AVFS's total membership was made up of these at-large members, but it is believed to be considerable.

While Romanis concentrated on increasing membership, the Society took steps that would increase its visibility within the community. William Hamilton, a former member of the 17th U.S. Infantry, designed a membership badge which displayed on a shield the insignia of the infantry, cavalry, artillery, and engineers, as well as an anchor representing the Navy. In hopes that this badge would serve as a conversation piece and help attract members, the executive committee of the AVFS approved it on February 12, 1900.

Meanwhile, the entire membership was getting involved in community and civic functions. It was almost a statement of policy: "See us, acknowledge us, we are here." By February 1900, the town of Columbus was beginning to sit up and take notice of the new group. As a local newspaper reported, "The organization is increasing steadily and much good work benefitting the soldiers is being accomplished." As part of its community service, the organization assisted in Memorial Day services, occasionally attended church as a group, officiated in funeral services of ex-soldiers, marched in parades, helped other groups secure a War Memorial for Columbus, and welcomed Admiral Dewey on his visit to Columbus during the summer of 1900.

On July 24, 1900, the AVFS formed a women's auxiliary. Patterned after the Women's Relief Corps of the Grand Army of the Republic, the Auxiliary to the American Veterans of Foreign Service immediately set about supporting the programs of its parent organization. The Auxiliary members also oversaw social activities such as receptions and dances, often funding these events themselves through raffles.

By the end of the year, it was obvious that the AVFS did not intend to be taken lightly. Thanks to Romanis's membership-at-large recruiting program, the Society could now proudly claim members all over the United States, in the Philippines, and Alaska. Its members had also begun to work in the Congress, advocating for legislation that would provide pensions and hospital care for the disabled.

As yet, the AVFS was not in a position to challenge the GAR, the leading advocate of veterans' benefits. The Society still lacked the ability to weld the strength it was starting to acquire into political clout. Its members also lacked knowledge of parliamentary procedure and experience in running a fraternal organization. But the GAR had passed its peak of political power and was less effective with each passing day. Membership, too, was plummeting, as evidenced by this item in a February 1900 issue of the *Ohio State Journal:*

"A pathetic scene was witnessed at Lexington, Richland County, Ohio, a few days ago, in the final disbandment of a post of the Grand Army. It was known as the Conger Post No. 330, and was named after the late Colonel Conger. The report for the year ending May 1899, showed that the post had only 22 members, but since then death has dealt heavily with the members, only eight of whom are now living, over 35 [sic] percent having died. It surrendered its charter, and sold its property to the highest bidders. The tender sympathies of those present were appealed to when the old muskets and flags were sold in the presence of the aged members of the post. One flag and banner, presented to the post by Mrs. Conger, wife of the late Colonel Conger, were reserved by the eight members of the post."

The decline of the GAR would unquestionably open the door to new veterans' advocates. But whether or not the void left by the GAR could be filled by the AVFS or another organization comprised of Spanish American War veterans remained to be seen. At present, the AVFS was growing mainly on the strength of its officers' enthusiasm, and their confidence in the justice of their cause—little else.

For the next several years, the convictions of the Society's officers stood it in good stead. Under the direction of President Will White, the AVFS instituted a policy that continues in the VFW today— that of helping ex-servicemen even if they are not members of the organization. In early 1901, for example, the AVFS heard of the plight of Private Myron Hall, a veteran who had seen action during the battle of San Juan Hill but was not an AVFS member. While in Cuba, Hall had contracted an incurable disease, was discharged, and sent home to a Columbus alms house to die. Seeking better care for Hall, the AVFS arranged for his transfer to the Soldiers and Sailors Home at Sandusky, Ohio. Hall's note of appreciation to White and the organization appeared in the *Columbus Dispatch* on April 17, 1901:

April 15, 1901

Dear Comrade White,

I thought I would wait until I was settled before writing. I was transferred to a cottage today. The grounds on which the home is built are beautiful, as far as I have seen, and I like it very well. Everything is neat and clean. There is plenty to eat and good medical attendance.

Tell Mrs. White that the syrup she made for me is helping my cough. It is not nearly so bad. I wish to thank you, also the Comrades of the lodge for what they have done for me. And as soon as I can, will reimburse them. You do not know how much good you did me. I appreciate it, and in the future, I shall do all I can for the benefit of the lodge. I am getting along nicely, but I do not know what to do about that pension of mine. I wish you would see if it cannot be pushed.

> *Yours truly,*
> *Myron B. Hall*
> *Soldier's Home*

Another Columbus paper reported that when the AVFS learned of a comrade from the Fourth Ohio Volunteers who was in financial difficulties, "a liberal appropriation from the camp's treasury was allowed for his benefit."

In October 1901, the third National Encampment of the organization was held in Columbus. (The anniversary meetings held at the headquarters camp in Columbus in 1900 and 1901 were considered, in retrospect, to have been the first and second National Encampments.) Some attendees were housed in tents—a practice reminiscent of a GAR encampment—but most stayed in hotels. President Will White was re-elected for another year, but very little other business was brought up or acted upon. Members spent most of their time reminiscing and socializing at smokers or around campfires, sight-seeing, and exchanging greetings with city and state officials.

Buckeye Post 1598 was so numbered to commemorate Camp Lawton, which stood at 1598 North High Street in Columbus.

Much of the real business of 1901 was conducted in December. That month, the Society agreed that changes in the organizational structure were needed. The officers, who were serving in both local camp and national capacities, felt they were spending too much time on local matters to be able to carry out their primary job of expanding the organization. As a result, the separation of local and national offices—first discussed the previous year—was approved. A separate camp would be established to deal with local affairs, thus freeing the national officers to spend their time handling national duties.

In preparation for the new camp's establishment, the members held an election. John B. Davie, an architect, was elected camp president and Louis M.H. Potter was elected secretary. Both of these men were graduates of Ohio State University. At Romanis's suggestion, Davie designed a lapel button for the organization. This button is believed to have featured the Cross of Malta, which was adopted as the AVFS's official emblem at its second meeting. With Romanis's assistance, Davie also wrote the first ritual for the order. The women's auxiliary presented the camp with its first set of colors.

On December 1, 1901, the membership of Headquarters Camp One was transferred to the new camp—Camp Lawton.* Camp Lawton was named after Major General Henry W. Lawton, an Ohio-born soldier who rose from the ranks to command troops in both Cuba and the Philippines. Lawton was killed by a sniper while attacking San Mateo in the Philippine Islands. Long known for his bravery and his disdain of enemy fire, the general died as he would have wished, at the head of his troops. "I am shot," he exclaimed as he fell into the arms of a subordinate officer. A surgeon was

---

* There is some confusion about this date due to an article in the *Columbus Press-Post* of July 24, 1900, which announced that "A committee was appointed to draft suitable resolutions to Mrs. Lawton for the use of her hero husband's name for the camp." But a letter from James Romanis, the AVFS National Secretary, states that the Lawton Camp was not established until December 1901. To validate this statement, Romanis included a "Zanograph" copy of a membership card bearing that date.

rushed to the general's side, but his efforts were in vain.

General Lawton died a poor man. All over the country, when this fact was made known, collections were taken up to provide for his widow and their four children. The U.S. Army and organizations of both Spanish American and Union Army veterans directed the drive. And the fledgling AVFS chose to memorialize Lawton by naming their flagship camp after him.

Separation of local and national authority again became an issue during the years between Camp Lawton's formation and the final merger of the AVFS and other veteran's organizations into the Veterans of Foreign Wars. As many national officers became members of Camp Lawton, once again they had little time to devote to local activities. Consequently, Camp Lawton was disbanded and then re-formed. If Camp Lawton had remained in continuous operation, it could have become VFW Post Number One, by virtue of its early founding date. Instead, a former Army of the Philippines camp in Denver—the John S. Stewart Post—was given the distinction of being Post Number One, an honor it has never relinquished.

Following the initial restructuring of the AVFS in December 1901, Romanis authored a membership card, a certificate of membership, and a national constitution. Then, over the next few years, the Society worked hard to become a truly national organization, in fact as well as in name. In particular, the AVFS scrambled to fill the political void left by the declining GAR.

By the 1903 National Encampment held at Washington Court House, Ohio, October 11th and 12th, the AVFS felt ready to formally enter the political arena. At the suggestion of President James Romanis, the encampment appointed ten men to a legislative committee: George Kelly, Columbus, Ohio; John B. Davie, Milwaukee, Wisconsin; Samuel J. Browning, Kansas City, Missouri; James M. Young, Cincinnati, Ohio; Charles A. Jones, Cheyenne, Wyoming; Edwin C. Johnson, Portsmouth, New Hampshire; Lynn F. Smithers, Washington

Court House, Ohio; Daniel McKensie, Columbus, Ohio; and James Lee, Marysville, Ohio.

The proposal establishing the legislative committee directed its members to prepare a pension bill for foreign service veterans and present it to Congress during the next Congressional session. Many encampment delegates also make unscheduled but impassioned speeches to the committee about the dire need for equitable pension laws. To ensure support of the proposed bill, these delegates instructed the committee members to correspond with their Congressmen to "let them know how the AVFS stood on pensions and legislation for needy veterans."

In other business at the 1903 encampment, James Romanis was re-elected National President, Theopilus F. Malloy elected National Secretary, and Francis Dubiel returned to the office of National Treasurer. The convention delegates discussed the need to make the federal government take its supposed "soldier's preference" more seriously when filling job vacancies in its agencies. The Pension Bureau in particular needed to be persuaded to hire more veterans. Also approved on the convention floor was a resolution outlawing intoxicating liquors in AVFS meeting halls, anterooms, or encampments. Any camp that broke the rule would forfeit its charter.

The next year was one of growth and frustration for the AVFS. With the establishment of Camp W.S. Schley in Portsmouth, New Hampshire, the Society added its twenty-fourth camp to its roster. But even with its ever-increasing size, the Society's members were largely ineffective in pushing for federal employment and pensions for veterans.

At the National Encampment in Columbus, Ohio, on September 11 to 13, 1904, the delegates took stock of their accomplishments. Despite the Society's efforts to change hiring practices at the Pension Bureau, little had changed. Of the Bureau's 1,691 employees, only 462 were ex-soldiers, while 513 were long-time employees over 60 years old (in 1900, the average life expectancy was 47.3 years). Nor had the AVFS succeeded in increasing funding of pensions for disabled veterans. The Society intended to keep on trying, however, as one speaker made clear:

"With strenuous objections of the anti-military element being put forth yearly in an endeavor to cut the pension appropriation, it is certain that the veterans and widows of the veterans who earned their right to enrollment as pensioners, by reason of disabilities incurred in the defense of their flag, will not quietly stand back and see appropriations increased for the benefit of ones for whom it was never intended. Nor will this association remain quiet while such action is threatened.

"The election being over, it now remains for the Congressmen elected to redeem their ante-election pledges. A careful watch will be kept over their official action and it will be interesting to note later how many bear out their promises."

Speaking of the Civil Service Preference Clause the AVFS had brought to the attention of Congress several years before, another speaker noted, "At the time of its introduction, the bill had little or no organized support and was defeated by Congressman Grosvenor of Ohio, who saw fit to make a strong speech against it. Should it again come before the House, we doubt if any Congressman will have the temerity to oppose it." Through passage of this clause, AVFS members sought not only to "be hired over their civilian counterparts if their qualifications should be equal," but also to change retention policies so that government administrators could not arbitrarily replace veterans with other employees.

In new business at the 1904 National Encampment, the delegates voted to change the position of National Historian from an appointed one to an elected one. They also approved a resolution to change their officers' titles from civilian to military ones. In the ensuing election, the Columbus camp was able to place more of its comrades in the newly re-named national offices than any other group. Elected to national office were: National Commander, James Romanis, Columbus, Ohio; Senior Vice Commander, Thomas P. Edgar, Sparta, Illinois; Junior Vice Commander, Francis Dubiel, Columbus, Ohio; Adjutant General,

Following the 1904 Encampment, this announcement appeared in the Columbus Evening Dispatch.

THE COLUMBUS EVENING DISPATCH, THURSDAY, SEPTEMBER 15, 1904.

Columbus Men Elected by American Veterans of Foreign Service to Serve in Seven of the Ten Offices of the Organization.

JAMES ROMANIS.
Elected National Commander.

FRANCIS DUBIEL.
Elected Junior Vice Commander.

GEORGE KELLY.
Elected Adjutant General.

H. C. PRITNER.
Elected Chaplain.

Columbus men easily carried away the chief offices within the gift of the American Veterans of Foreign Services at its convention in Cincinnati, which adjourned Tuesday, after an interesting session lasting two days. James Romanis, despite his protests, was re-elected president for a third term. Before returning to Columbus, President Romanis is expected to visit Pittsburg, where the Eastern association of veterans is in session to discuss with them the proposition to amalgamate the organizations. The entire list of officers elected follows:: National commander, James Romanis, Columbus, Ohio; senior vice commander, Thomas P. Edgar, Sparta, Ill.; junior vice commander, Francis Dubiel, Columbus, Ohio; adjutant general, George Kelly, Columbus, Ohio; quartermaster general, Thomas Farrel, Columbus, Ohio; historian, T. F. Malloy, Columbus, Ohio;; judge advocate general, Fred Peastak, Newport, Ky.; inspector general, (three years) C. O. Johnson, Portsmouth, N. H.; (two years), Charles Cronin, Cincinnati, and (one year), W. A. Ward, Columbus, Ohio; chaplain, H. C. Printer,, Columbus, Ohio.

George Kelly, Columbus, Ohio; Quartermaster General, Thomas Farrel, Columbus, Ohio; Historian, T.F. Malloy, Columbus, Ohio; Judge Advocate General, Fred Peastak, Newport, Kentucky; Inspector General (three-year term) C.O. Johnson, Portsmouth, New Hampshire; (two-year term) Charles Cronin, Cincinnati, Ohio; (one-year term) W.A. Ward, Columbus, Ohio; Chaplain, H.C Printer, Columbus, Ohio.

Although James Romanis had once again been selected to fill the highest office in the AVFS, this was not to be his most important accomplishment of that year. Several weeks before the encampment, he had achieved an even greater coup by persuading a group of Spanish American War veterans based in Pennsylvania to send a representative to the AVFS's encampment. This veteran's group, which was coincidentally also known as the American Veterans of Foreign Service, had responded by sending their National Junior Vice Commander, Dr. George Metzger. When he appeared before the assembled delegates in Columbus, Metzger made an unexpected proposal. He suggested that the Columbus officers attend his group's National Encampment the following week in Allegheny, Pennsylvania, for the purpose of discussing a possible merger of the two veteran's groups. Without hesitation, the delegates voted to send their President, James Romanis, and empowered him to take any action he felt necessary to expedite the merger.

The Other American Veterans of Foreign Service

Where had this other organization called the American Veterans of Foreign Service come from?

The group could actually trace its roots to three distinct veteran's organizations formed in three separate locations. It was the result of a merger between groups known as the "Philippine War Veterans," the "Foreign Service Veterans," and the "American Veterans of Philippine and China Wars."

The first group founded, the Philippine War Veterans, had been established under the leadership and guidance of Philippine war veteran Captain Herbert O. Kelley. It was mustered in Altoona, Pennsylvania, on July 7, 1901. In 1902, C.E. Knighton succeeded Kelley as president.

The second veteran's group was organized in Pittsburgh in early October 1901. Its founder was a Philippine veteran, G.H. Smith. Smith's organization also chose the name "Philippine War Veterans." On April 27, 1902, Jacques LaBelle was elected Commander and the group reorganized under the name of "Foreign Service Veterans."

Of the three groups that eventually banded together to form the Pennsylvania branch of the American Veterans of Foreign Service, the last to appear was the American Veterans of Philippine and China Wars. It was founded by Captain Robert S. Hansbury in Philadelphia on July 24, 1902. As the name suggests, this group restricted its membership to veterans who had served in the Philippines or China between 1898 and 1902. Yet this association expanded more rapidly than the other two. In little over a year after its founding, the association had formed new camps in Allegheny, Altoona, and Pittsburgh, Pennsylvania; Boston, Massachusetts; Camden, New Jersey; Wilmington, Delaware; Bismark, North Dakota; Helena, Montana; Denver, Colorado; Chicago, Illinois; Montgomery, Alabama; Atlanta, Georgia; and Knoxville, Tennessee.

Although these three organizations had slightly different service requirements for membership, there were also several interesting similarities. Each decided to restrict membership to veterans (or the sons of veterans) who had earned a campaign medal. Each organization also had aspirations to be national in scope, and thus each organization's commander was, in fact, a Commander-in-Chief. In fact, with the exception of G.H. Smith, the original leaders of each unit would go on to head larger associations.

On September 10, 11, and 12, 1903, the Philippine War Veterans, Foreign Service Veterans, and American Veterans of the Philippine and China Wars met in Altoona, Pennsylvania. Each organization hoped to gain members and strength as a result of the meeting. They got their wish: by the last day of the convention, the delegates from each organization had voted to merge into one larger organization headed by Captain Robert Hansbury. The new organization gave Hansbury the title of "National Commander" not "President," making it the first veteran's organization to confer military rather than civilian titles on its officers. Subsequently, it also became the first organization to refer to local units as "posts" rather than "camps."*

The only sticking point during the merger negotiations was the new organization's name. Each smaller organization feared that its members' deeds would go unnoticed in a larger group unless the group's name reflected all members' contributions to the war. Consequently, the new organization ended up with a comprehensive but cumbersome name: The American Veterans of the Philippine, Cuban, Puerto Rican and China Wars.

Because the organization's name was recognized to be unwieldy, later in 1903 it was changed by plebescite to American Veterans of Foreign Service. Neither this group, nor the Columbus group, was aware that their associations would now be known by the same name.

The Road to Merger

Exactly how the two groups known as the American Veterans of Foreign Service first learned of each other is not known. Most likely, however, the Columbus branch was the first to hear that it had a namesake. This theory is supported by an article by Herbert O. Kelley, National Commander of the Pennsylvania branch, which appeared in the November 1904 issue of the *American Veteran of Foreign Service* magazine. In the article, Kelley makes it clear

that his group was unaware of the Columbus group until Romanis contacted them:

> "When the organization known throughout the eastern part of the country as the 'American Veterans of Foreign Service' was making arrangements during the past summer for its Annual Encampment, it was thought that it was the only organization of its kind in the country. Judge then the surprise when the National Officers were invited to the annual convention of the 'American Veterans of Foreign Service' which was to be held in Cincinnati one week previous to their own. At first it was conceived as a jest, but as subsequent events proved it was no joke, but a stern reality. . . ."

As mentioned earlier, Kelley's group responded to the Ohio group's invitation by dispatching National Junior Vice President George Metzger to the encampment in Cincinnati. At the conclusion of this encampment on September 12, 1904, James Romanis hurried to Allegheny, Pennsylvania. There Robert S. Hansbury, the out-going commander of the Pennsylvania-based American Veterans of Foreign Service, cordially welcomed him to his group's annual encampment. While the delegates listened attentively, Romanis voiced his ideas about merging the two AVFS branches. He proposed that both groups adopt the insignia of the Columbus group (the Cross of Malta) and that each group maintain its own administration for the ensuing year and then meet at a mutually agreed upon time to finalize the merger. Both suggestions were instantly accepted.

Upon his return to Columbus, Romanis immediately began trying to drum up support for the decisions reached in Altoona. From the start, he received able assistance from George Kelly, one of the organization's original thirteen founders. Over the

---

*   In 1904, all the officers were given military titles: the top three officers were to be known as Commander-in-Chief, Senior Vice Commander-in-Chief, and Junior Vice Commander-in-Chief, while others were dubbed Adjutant General, Quartermaster General, Inspector General, and Chaplain. A National Historian was also added to the list of elective officers.

next year, Kelly and Herbert O. Kelley, newly elected commander of the Pennsylvania branch, wrote many letters to one another to work out the details involved in bringing the groups together.

In the meantime, Romanis inaugurated a monthly magazine. Its purpose was to entertain AVFS members and to publicize and promote the impending merger. It was sent to and received its content from members of both branches of the AVFS. Appropriately named the *American Veteran of Foreign Service*, this magazine was the first publication ever attempted by the organization. Romanis, who was part owner of the Service Publishing Company, established, wrote for, edited, and oversaw the printing of this new publication.

Because Romanis was the publication's reporter and editor, to him fell the sad duty of reporting the death of one of the AVFS's original founders: six-term treasurer, present National Junior Vice Commander, comrade-in-arms, and close friend, Francis Dubiel. In his "In Memoriam" Romanis said of Dubiel: "This gentle spirit passed to its final reward—was transferred to that grandest of all armies beyond the skies—on the afternoon of Friday, Oct. 21, 1904, in the 43rd year of his life.

"Born and reared up to young manhood in Austrian-Poland, he immigrated to the United States about 1883 or 4 at the age of twenty-three. After his enlistment, he was assigned to the famous 8th U.S. Cavalry stationed in the southwest, participated in all its campaigns against the hostile Indians and accompanied the same regiment on its noted overland march from Texas to Ft. Meade, North Dakota. His term of enlistment having expired, he determined to settle down and enjoy, for a time at least, the more prosaic life of an American citizen, which proud title he had now attained by five years of faithful and honorable service as a soldier. But this uneventful mode of life became monotonous and irksome within a short time, for an ardent nature and martial spirit such as was his, and again he joined 'Old Glory' and donned the suit of blue, this time in the 'Old Fighting Seventeenth Infantry.' He served ten years in that regiment and was

a member of Company G when it went to Cuba. Here it was that 'Frank' became the victim of that fatal malady, chronic tropical malaria, that blighted his after life and cut it off while in the bloom of a young manhood that gave promise of many more happy years with his loved ones and friends.

"Dubiel was a man of good education and possessed an analytical as well as a logical mind, and was an excellent reasoner, speaking and writing the Greek, Latin, French and German fluently in addition to his native Polish and English. His word was always as good as his bond and he had a high disdain for anything that savored of hypocrisy or sham."

Over the next months, Romanis filled the *American Veteran of Foreign Service* with articles meant to persuade members of both branches that the upcoming merger would be in their best interest. One of the first pieces published was contributed for the November 1904 issue by Herbert O. Kelley. After summarizing the events that led to Romanis's proposal that the two branches merge, Kelley revealed his fervent wish that "Hopefully the next convention would see two organizations under one head, 'A new Grand Army of the Republic.' A 'Grand Army' in every sense of the word. The North, South, East and West, every section of the country would be represented, every branch of the service. Men of all rank, from the highest to the lowest, all enrolled under its banner." Following a description of the good work both branches of the AVFS had already accomplished, Kelley went on to explain how much more could be achieved once the branches united:

"When the boys came home [from the Spanish American War] they were greeted with even more enthusiasm than their departure invoked. But while thousands of hearts were gladdened at the sight of loved ones safely returned, there were many that ached from thinking of loved ones lying under the tropical skies, loved ones who had given their life for their country. . . .

"They are our dead, and it devolves upon us soldiers to see that their memory shall never die. This cannot be accomplished as in-dividuals but by united effort. Organized throughout the country we can care for each fallen comrade's grave and keep the memory of his achievements as green as the grass sur-rounding it and when death shall lay its hands on any one of us, our comrades will carry us to our last resting place, wrapped in the folds of that dear old flag, that every true American should be willing to sacrifice his all for. Long live the American Veterans of Foreign Ser-vice; may the time come when every eligible veteran shall be enrolled, then there will be a veteran army second only to the GAR."

To drive home his point that there was strength in numbers, Romanis also published remarks by several National Officers of the Columbus branch. In January 1905, Romanis printed excerpts from the Address of Welcome given at the 1904 Columbus Encampment by National Inspector General Charles J. Cronin, who was also Commander of Camp Harry C. Egbert in Cin-cinnati. These excerpts included an appeal to the members' sense of loyalty:

"Now that the war is over, we are enlisted in the battle of life, and find the dangers as great, and the need of organization greater.

"Travelers in Switzerland who make the climb to that west peak, of Mount Blanc, are viewed from the valley below through power-ful glasses, and as you watch the group slowly making their way along the dizzy heights, two or three lose their footing; drop suddenly out of sight and are gone. You are sure they have fallen to a horrible death down on the rocks below. You look again, No! they are not lost, one is restored to his place in the long line of climbers and slowly the others struggle up into the view and resume their upward march. What is the explanation? Before they came to those dangerous places they bound them-selves together with a strong rope. Those who

fell in the dangerous place were held by the strength of companions on either side.

"That, my comrades, is what we hope to do with this organization, to become so power-ful that we will obtain the same respect in the battles of life that we did in the war."

In the next month's issue of the *American Veteran of Foreign Service*, Romanis let National Junior Vice Commander Thomas P. Edgar take a stab at explain-ing the need to expand the Society's membership. Edgar began by asserting that he believed the American Veterans of Foreign Service was "the logi-cal successor" to "that great order of men known as the Grand Army of the Republic," then closed with some inspirational words about the Society's potential for growth. Since the AVFS's incorporation, he pointed out, "its membership has grown steadily and at this writing has assumed membership of many thousands and is increasing day to day. Among the most successful of the new camps organized is Camp Harry Clay Egbert, No. 23, of Cincinnati, Ohio whose membership in August, 1903 was something like ten members. Today it is one of the largest camps in the order, its membership ranging over the hundred mark. And so it is with all who have gone into the matter of organization; they increase daily, and I venture to say that within the next twelve months our order will have increased a goodly figure.

"You can assist in this increase and it is your duty to do everything in your power to bring it about. Devote a portion of your time to this end. Seek to in-still into your subject the importance of joining now. . . . In my experience in organizing, I have found the duty a pleasant one. Put your shoulder to the wheels of progress and let us see what we can attain when we make the effort."

Although Romanis gave the impending merger a great deal of emphasis, he also used the *American Veteran of Foreign Service* to present other issues of importance to veterans or to incite their opinions and comments. For example, after several years of wran-gling over the new regulations and proposed design and construction of a new Congressional Medal of

Honor, Romanis tendered the following article in the magazine's February 1905 issue:

> "The new Medal of Honor is universally concerned by the wearers of the old. It is described by these men, 'For Valor Crowned,' as being a bit of cheap metal washed over with gold, and they say that any old 25–cent souvenir of a World's Fair is just as valuable as it is. The metal of the old Medal of Honor badge is secured from cannon captured in the war of the rebellion. Its intrinsic worth is nil, but its association makes it valuable. It is prized above solid gold for this very reason. Very few of the wearers of the old Medal of Honor will turn theirs back to get the new one."

Even when Romanis's articles were not explicitly about the coming merger, they often had underlying messages about the need to expand. In the May 1905 issue of the *American Veteran of Foreign Service,* for example, Romanis complained that "A review of important legislation before Congress in the past session fails to disclose anything of importance bearing on military affairs, aside of the regular establishment." He charged that Congressmen too often introduced bills favorable to veterans and then did not push to get them passed since "the introduction of bills into the Senate or House appeared to be sufficient proof to the authors that they had proven their loyalty to those who urged such measures." The remedy, Romanis suggested, was for the American Veterans of Foreign Service to use its numerical strength to retaliate at the polls.

Romanis's final editorial on the subject of merger appeared in the August 1905 issue of the *American Veteran of Foreign Service.* In it, Romanis urged "the attendance of as many representatives as the strength of the organization will permit, in order to assure the centralization at such times of the best talent and stimulus the association affords from all its extreme and central points." Summing up, he told the AVFS members that "to assist yourself or your comrades, to

advance the association's interest, to make it better and stronger, to give it the guidance it deserves, if not for the pleasures of the visit, which will be many, you owe it to yourself and your comrades to meet with us in Altoona, September 13, 14, 15, 16, 1905."

The New American Veterans of Foreign Service

Just how many members of the American Veterans of Foreign Service heeded Romanis's call to attend the 1905 encampment was not recorded. But the September 12th *Altoona Times* reported that several hundred delegates and visitors were expected. Whatever the attendance, the paper obviously thought the event momentous enough to give it total coverage. Also on September 12th, it carried the following headlines:

"VETERANS COMING FOR CONVENTION"

"TWO BRANCHES TO MERGE"

"WESTERN AND EASTERN SECTIONS WILL COMPLETE ARRANGEMENTS FORMULATED LAST YEAR"

Each branch was scheduled to meet separately on the morning of the 13th to conclude the business of its old organization. Starting at 1:30 in the afternoon, they would meet together in the Knights of Pythias Hall to work out the details of the merger. H.O. Kelley, National Commander of the Eastern branch, would chair the joint meeting.

According to the September 14th *Altoona Times,* everything did not go quite as scheduled. Several events—including the organization's annual "military parade"—had to be postponed because the Columbus group did not arrive on time. When the delegates from the Columbus branch finally did arrive, it was without their Commander, James Romanis.

Why Romanis opted to remain away is unclear, but it may have been because he had learned of a movement to elect him Commander of the newly merged association. Some believed that after six years of the day-to-day pressures of running an organization, he simply longed for some time away from it. Others said that he probably wanted to retire now that the organization he had spent so much time and money promoting was no longer in danger of failing. Later, Romanis himself said, "The honors of a fraternal association should not be kept by one individual, but be passed around among the members." Whatever the reasons, Romanis reverted to his introverted personality and kept them to himself.

When the two groups finally sat down to discuss the proposed merger, it became clear that the delegates from both sides had basically the same feelings: they were in favor of consolidation, but feared the loss of their old group's identity. This made the process of total group acceptance tit for tat.

The official organization seal adopted by the new group was the seal of the Columbus branch, the Cross of Malta. The official uniform would be the Eastern branch's uniform, of khaki color and cotton material almost indistinguishable from the U.S. Army uniforms of that era.

Membership of committees was carefully divided up geographically. For example, the legislative committee was composed of: Bicker of McKeesport, KY; Harrell of Cincinnati, OH; Tadlow of Philadelphia, OH; Davie of Milwaukee, WI; Hickey of Washington, D.C.; and Halmon of Youngstown, Ohio.

After the outward trappings of the AVFS had been agreed upon, the delegates turned to questions of leadership. With Romanis out of the picture, H.O. Kelley of the Eastern Branch's Altoona Post seemed the logical choice to head the new organization. As mentioned earlier, he and George Kelly of Columbus had been largely responsible for bringing the groups together. With this in mind, the delegates elected Herbert O. Kelley to head the newly merged organization.

Before the encampment ended, the group made two more important decisions. The new AVFS decided to plan for a Ladies Auxiliary similar to that of the Columbus branch. In addition, an intermediate level of administration was set up between posts and the national organization. These additional headquarters were called "state departments." Their administrative control was to extend to the boundaries of the state they represented.

After the 1905 merger, it was quite some time before the AVFS once again made headlines. From 1905 to 1908, the organization worked mainly on structuring and consolidating this newly merged, larger group. Under Commanders-in-Chief Charles H. Devereaux, David T. Niven, and J. Alfred Judge, the division of clerical work, responsibility, and authority was realigned to meet the needs of the new association. The group did, however, take a stand on one outside issue: they advocated that commissary stores once again be allowed on military bases. (The commissary stores had been removed earlier in response to pressure put on the Congress by the business community and charges of fraud.)

Although the AVFS itself was not in the spotlight during this time, one of their former theaters of war was. In 1906, President Theodore Roosevelt sent troops back into Cuba to suppress a revolt. They remained there until 1909. This time, the men of the AVFS watched from the sidelines, many with a grateful sigh.

In August 1909, rumors of merger were heard once again when the AVFS and the Colorado-based Army of the Philippines simultaneously held encampments in Pittsburgh. But even though two AVFS Posts—the Logan Post of Buffalo and the Noble Post of Altoona—made resolutions in favor of merger and the AVFS as a whole voiced its approval, nothing was accomplished. Leaders would later pin the cause of failure on that old nemesis, fear that absorption into a larger group would threaten the identities of smaller groups.

Although the delegates nixed a merger, many of the two groups' meetings were held jointly in a spirit of comradeship. Since both groups had grown in size and popularity, it was becoming easier for them to attract nationally known speakers for their annual encampments. Addressing this joint AVFS and Philippines encampment were two active Army officers, Lt. General S.M.B. Young and Major General Frederick Grant. Grant, U.S. Army Commander of the Lakes, told the assembled group, "You are the natural successors to the GAR. They are rapidly passing away and it is up to you to keep up the military and patriotic spirit of the nation."

Like true heirs of the GAR, the AVFS began putting more pressure on elected representatives to get what President Theodore Roosevelt had called "a square deal." Specifically, they pushed for the passage of a bill that the 1910 Encampment approved and endorsed. This act, which would pension widows and minor children of deceased Spanish American War veterans, was presented to Congress by Major John A. Logan of Post No. 26. Introduced into the House of Representatives by Congressman Thomas Crago, a Philippine veteran and member of the AVFS, the bill passed the House only to die later in the hopper of a Senate committee.

Outpacing the AVFS's growth in political power was its growth in membership. In 1910 an AVFS membership report showed thirty-four posts in good standing with approximately 1,200 members. An additional 400 members were added to the rolls during the first term of Robert Woodside, who had replaced two-term Commander-in-Chief J. Alfred Judge at the 1910 Encampment. At the 1911 Encampment in Philadelphia, Nat Long, the AVFS National Organizer, informed the 500 delegates that the number of posts had increased over six times in the last three years.

By today's standards, these recruiting figures may seem low, but considering the difficulties of contacting prospective members, the AVFS did surprisingly well. In the early 1900s, the average age of the approximately 250,000 veterans eligible for membership was in the mid 20s. Many were unmarried and on the move with the rapidly expanding nation. Some were career military and stationed in one of America's forty-five states, its territories, or in foreign lands. To reach these far-flung veterans, the AVFS had to depend primarily on the U.S. mails, which, where they existed, were slow and often unreliable. Only 18 people per 1000 had a telephone. Door-to-door recruit-

ment was possible, but slow: transportation around the countryside was normally accomplished by riding a train, horse, bicycle, or "shank's mare" (walking). True, 460,000 automobiles would be sold during the century's first decade, but impassable roads often made them an impractical means of transportation. Certainly the phrase "You can't get there from here" took on new meaning when uttered by frustrated automobile travelers.

The 1912 National Encampment in Philadelphia was one of the most colorful in AVFS history. Speeches were heard from: the mayor of Philadelphia; representatives of the GAR; Commander of the Medal of Honor Legion, poet, and Indian scout Jack Crawford; and past and present officers of the AVFS. Over 5000 members of patriotic groups, the military, the AVFS, and its auxiliary took part in the parade. White-haired members of the GAR rode in open-topped carriages while Spanish War Veterans, their age beginning to show, puffed along behind the Indian War veterans. But in spite of their age, the Spanish American War veterans were still "The Boys" to the speakers who addressed them from the stage of the Lu Lu Temple. The delegates, satisfied with the performance of Commander-in-Chief Woodside, awarded him his third consecutive term.

THE WEST: 1900–1914

General Irving Hale, president of the infant Colorado Society Army of the Philippines, dreamed of building a national veteran's organization that would rival the GAR in size and power. This was a dream he shared with Jim Romanis, co-founder of the American Veterans of Foreign Service. But unlike his Eastern counterpart, whose dream was clouded only by minor procedural problems in getting his organization up and running, Hale needed to overcome two major obstacles—one natural, one man-made—that stood in the way of his goal.

Geographical factors presented the first stumbling block to growth of the Army of the Philippines. The East had many more towns large enough to support a camp, and veterans who lived outside of town had less distance to travel to camp meetings. To complicate matters, cowboys, sheep herders, and men who worked in the mining camps out west were continually moving about. Contacting prospective members was difficult, and their last known addresses were often unreliable. By the time a cowboy based at a line shack in the mountains got his mail, or a sheep herder came down to get his annual supplies, the reason for the letter or notice had usually been put to rest some months earlier. Thriving mining towns were known to vanish over night and later set up again in a different location. Beginning around 1904, many veterans who were unable to find employment boarded ships to Panama to work on the Canal. Once W.C. Gorgas, a U.S. Army sanitarian, eradicated yellow fever in the canal zone, more would follow.

The second major hindrance to recruitment of new members was one that the Army of the Philippines had imposed on itself: its restriction of membership to men who had served in one theater of one war. But perhaps because the Society had no trouble attracting members at first, Hale and his followers did not immediately recognize their mistake. Since Hale had been the organizer and commanding officer of the First Colorado Volunteer Infantry Regiment, it seemed only natural to the men that he take the lead in organizing a veteran's group to commemorate their services. As word of his group spread, men joined without question. Hale had always seen to their welfare and they were equally loyal to him.

On February 3, 1900, the organization approved the by-laws, which had been drawn up by a committee appointed by General Hale. According to these by-laws, membership was open to all officers and enlisted men with honorable records who had served in the Volunteer or Regular Army with the Army of the

Philippines. Officers elected were General Hale, president; Colonel Henry Lippincott, first vice-president representing the Regular Army; Hospital Steward Edgar Loose of Pueblo, second vice-president representing the state volunteers; Colonel Grove, third vice-president representing the general volunteers from the United States; Sergeant Ben Stapleton (for many years mayor of Denver), recording secretary; Corporal Harry W. McCauley, corresponding secretary; and Lieutenant Charles B. Lewis, treasurer.

During the February meeting, Hale also read aloud from letters he had received from other former leaders of the Army of the Philippines. Hale had written to these officers suggesting that they meet with the men formerly under their command to arouse interest in forming a national veteran's organization at a reunion next summer. In their replies, the officers were enthusiastic both about the coming reunion and the proposed organization for all veterans of the Philippine theater. The letters were from Generals Summers of Oregon, Reeves of Minnesota, Otis of California, and Greene of New York. Letters were also received from Colonels Metcalf of Kansas; Frost of South Dakota; Barnett of Pennsylvania; Eager of Nebraska; Ames of Minnesota; Little of Kansas; Looper of Iowa; Fife of Washington; Truman of North Dakota; Duboce of California; Childers of Tennessee; and others.

Thanks to Hale's outreach efforts, almost one thousand Philippine veterans, representing nineteen military units of the Eighth Army, attended the reunion in Denver starting August 13, 1900. They came from Colorado, Utah, Oregon, Iowa, Nebraska, the Dakotas, and all of the western states. A few men attended from Tennessee, Pennsylvania, and New York.

The reunion featured a parade of several thousand men, including a platoon of police and units of the Colorado National Guard, the Spanish American War veterans, the Grand Army of the Republic, the United Confederate Veterans, and the Regular Army. Generals Greene, Summers, and Metcalf led the parade mounted on horses. General Hale marched,

General Francis Greene, Commander,
Army of the Philippines, 1900

leading his First Colorado as he had done for so many years.

When Hale addressed the assembled group, he made it clear that this pomp and circumstance was only the prelude to the reunion's larger purposes: to enjoy a social gathering and form a permanent organization of the Army of the Philippines.

In the business session that followed, a constitution and by-laws were swiftly adopted for the national body. So too was a name for the new organization: "The National Association of the Army of the Philippines." The membership requirements approved were slightly broader than those of the Colorado Society of

the Army of the Philippines. Former members of the Navy who had served in the Philippine Campaign would now be admitted in addition to members of the Army, and sons of eligible veterans could also join. By allowing sons to join, the veterans hoped to give their organization continuity.

Although General Hale was the most popular and logical candidate to head the national association, he was not elected president. Instead the honor went to General Francis V. Greene of New York City. Historians believe he was elected to help attract more veterans from the East as members.

Even with an Easterner at its helm *and* the head start the reunion had given it in members, the Society found its recruiting efforts hampered by the requirement that members must have served in the Philippines. It formed new posts more slowly than the AVFS, which allowed all overseas veterans membership. Indeed, during the Army of the Philippine's first year as a national organization, no new posts were added to the two already in existence: the John S. Stewart Camp of Denver, mustered December 12, 1899 and recognized as the first camp of the Army of the Philippines, and Camp Merwin M. Carleton, mustered in St. Paul, Minnesota, in May 1900.

Of course, during the first few years of the century, the Army of the Philippines probably devoted itself more to internal structuring than to actual recruiting. Despite the membership restrictions, there *were* significant numbers of eligible veterans who would join a camp when given the opportunity. Gradually, these camps were added: Camp Malate, Pittsburgh, Pennsylvania (November, 1901); Camp A.R. Patterson, Minneapolis (January, 1902); and in 1903, Camp John M. Stotsenburg, Lincoln, Nebraska (January); Camp Luzon, Chicago (March); Camp La Loma, Uniontown, Pennsylvania (August); Camp Luzon, Waynesburg, Pennsylvania (August); Camp Noah P. Rahskopf, Aberdeen, South Dakota (November); and Camp Lawton, Detroit (November).

Only about 400 veterans attended the second reunion of the National Association of the Army of the Philippines, held in Salt Lake City, Utah, on August 13, 14, and 15, 1901.* As was customary in the organization's early years, this reunion was mostly social. The attendees spent much of their time telling war stories and sharing overseas experiences. The delegates did take time from their socializing to unanimously elect General Irving Hale president of the association. And during the business session, J.J. Meyers of Salt Lake City introduced a resolution dubbed the "Philippine Travel Bill." This resolution called on the United States Congress to enact legislation that would retroactively pay each veteran of the Philippine Campaign one day's pay and rations for every twenty miles he had had to travel from San Francisco to his home. It was designed to make amends to the returning veterans who had been mustered out of the Army at their port of entry or the military base nearest that point and then left to find their own transportation home.

General Hale opposed Meyers's resolution. He marshalled enough support to have the motion submitted to the executive committee for further study. This effectively kept the resolution off the convention floor until 1910. Hale's move, although backed by some of the most influential members of the association, caused the Salt Lake contingent to withdraw from the association.

By the time the association met for its third annual reunion in 1902, the country was gripped in a reckless, macho kind of patriotism embodied by President Teddy Roosevelt. His "walk softly but carry a big stick" and "square deal" philosophies made him more popular with the masses than any president of that era had been.

In his address to the association members and distinguished guests Major Generals Arthur MacArthur, John Bates, and Lloyd Wheaton, General Hale left no doubts that he too valued patriotism highly. He out-lined the reasons for the existence of the organization as: "first, loyal support of the government in its campaign to govern the Philippines and second, defense of the U.S. Army." He continued by saying, "The Army of the Philippines, like all military organizations rests upon a triple foundation—comradeship, patriotism and history. It binds together regular and volunteer regiments, their officers and men of all states. The greatest aim of this organization is to keep alive the Spirit of Patriotism and to help maintain and defend the honor of our country."

In a spirit of patriotism and comradeship, the convention invited a St. Louis-based group named the Philippine Island Veterans to affiliate with them, but the group did not respond to this offer. The 2000 in attendance roared their approval as the delegates elected Hale to lead the association for another year.

Only about half as many veterans as had attended the previous reunion attended the 1903 reunion in St. Paul, Minnesota. Of the one thousand veterans there, two hundred were voting delegates. Each delegate represented—according to the by-laws—ten members in good standing in their home camp. With twenty registered delegates, Camp Merwin M. Carleton of St. Paul had the largest attendance.

The relatively small crowd did not stop the St. Paul *Globe* from eulogizing the veterans in the over-wrought fashion of that era. One reporter wrote:

"Not since the close of the Civil War, has opportunity presented itself for the assembling of beardless majors and colonels who had won their titles in actual warfare.

"It was rather an inspiring sight to watch the crowd of young and vigorous men in that convention. Every man of the lot a veteran and entitled to the handle he has to his name."

Among the major items of business was a resolution asking that the Civil Service Rules be amended so that survivors of any American war would have the

---

* The Army of the Phillippines referred to its annual conventions as "reunions" rather than adopting the GAR term "encampments" as the AVFS did.

same preference for federal employment the disabled had. The association also voted to petition the government to furnish cemetery headstones for Spanish American War veterans. Neither of these resolutions was ever acted upon, but a third one was: at General Hale's urging, a resolution was passed allowing the civilian contract surgeons and dentists who had served with the Army in the Philippines to join the association.

General Hale refused renomination for the presidency, but remained a leader of the group. After accepting his refusal, the association elected General Charles King as its president for the ensuing year.

Over the next three or four years, the National Association of the Army of the Philippines made little progress in bettering the plight of Philippine veterans and their families. The national reunions, too, kept their reputations as being more fun than work.

At the 1904 reunion in St. Louis, most attendees were more interested in visiting the nearby World's Fair than in business. Still, the encampment drew a large number of distinguished guests, including Secretary of War William Howard Taft, first civil governor of the Philippines; General A.R. Chafee, Chief of Staff; Major General Arthur MacArthur, Governor General of the Philippines; and Brigadier General Frederick Funston, captor of Aguinaldo in the Philippines. General Wilder S. Metcalf was elected President for the 1904 to 1905 year.

At the 1905 reunion in Chicago, many of the veterans and their wives once again concentrated on enjoying their ample free time. And with the new nickelodeons springing up in every neighborhood in the city and vaudeville pushing hard to stay alive, they did not lack for entertainment.

During their serious moments, the delegates elected former Colonel Alfred S. Frost as their new national leader. Frost, a twenty-one-year member of the Regular Army, was the present Chief of Police in Evanston, Illinois. At the time of his election, the national organization could boast of having two state departments, thirty-seven camps in good standing,

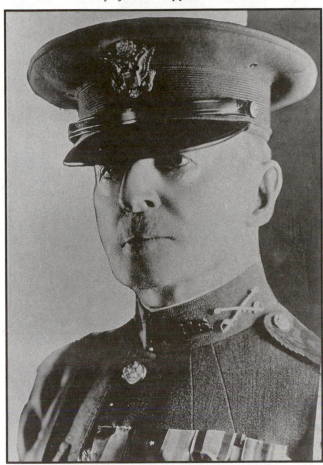

General Charles King, Commander, Army of the Philippines, 1903

and, in addition to its regular members, 179 life members and 310 members at large.

The Army of the Philippines selected Des Moines, Iowa, as its 1906 convention site. Chief among the resolutions passed was one changing all the officers' titles from civilian to military titles. This change was in keeping with the philosophy of the Army of the Philippines, which was more closely aligned with the military than was the AVFS. Considering that of the organization's first eleven leaders, there had been seven Generals of the Army, two Colonels, one Major, and a Captain, this closeness is understandable. Continuing the tradition of electing former officers as leaders, Major General Arthur MacArthur was elected to head the association for the 1906–07 year.

At the 1907 convention in Kansas City, Missouri, the veterans once again had "a gay time," as reported by the Denver *Post* on August 14. "They were given a smoker at Casino Hall, where they sang and told stories until the wee, small hours of the morning." According to the *Post,* they also enjoyed "a general outing at Fairmont Park."

With General MacArthur wielding the gavel, the 1907 convention attendees covered many items of business in addition to socializing. It was announced that 380 members had been added since the last reunion and that twenty-two states had members-at-large who lived in areas where there were not enough members to form a Post. The convention also raised the cost of life membership from $15 to $25, increased the Adjutant General's salary, boosted the charter fees from $10 to $15, and changed the titles of its local officers to military ones. As one of their last actions, the delegates elected Captain H.A. Crow Commander-in-Chief.

The next twelve months were busy ones for the members of the congressional (legislative) committee of the National Association. Under the direction of committee chairman Irving Hale, the members worked to obtain either the McKinley Medal or the Congressional Medal of Honor for those who had enlisted for the Spanish War and remained voluntarily to quell the Philippine Insurrection. They requested the Medal of Honor not out of an inflated sense of their fellow veterans' accomplishments, but because at the time there were few other medals authorized for deeds of gallantry in the field of battle. In fact, during a critical juncture in the Civil War, President Abraham Lincoln had offered the Medal of Honor to 864 members of a volunteer infantry regiment to induce their re-enlistment. Of these, 309 accepted the medal and re-enlisted. The balance, through a clerical error, also received the medal and went home. (In 1916 and 1917 a Congressional panel corrected these abuses and reinstated the honor that was intended to come with the medal.)

The congressional committee also worked on securing the Foreign Campaign Badge (issued under Army General Order Number 4, January 11, 1905, for service in Cuba, Puerto Rico, the Philippines and China). Although Congressman E.A. Hayes of California had introduced a bill which would award the badge to all officers and enlisted men who had served honorably overseas during this period, Congress was in no hurry to pass it. This, according to Hale, was largely the fault of individual members of the Army of the Philippines. At the 1908 reunion in Galesburg, Illinois, Hale spoke of the committee's displeasure:

> "The committee has done large amounts of work in trying to secure passage of the bill, issuing large numbers of circular letters to all camps, requesting them to pass and forward resolutions and individual letters to their Congressman and Senators. As stated in the last report, only six of the fifty-six camps responded to these requests and there seems to be in general, a surprising and discouraging apathy on the subject."

On a more positive note, the delegates learned that over the last year, 597 new members had been signed up inside the United States and an additional 133 were added to the camps at Cebu, Cavite, and Manila in the Philippine Islands. The Philippine additions were primarily due to Assistant Adjutant General G. Springer of Manila, who was also a Vice Commander of the national organization. It should be noted, however, that records do not show how many of the new members in the Philippines were actually overseas veterans. According to the rules of eligibility of the Army of the Philippines, sons of overseas members were also eligible to belong.

In other business at the 1908 convention, a proposal was made for the organization to erect a monument in Manila honoring Americans who had fallen in battle in the Philippines. The delegates elected Major P.J.H. Farrell of Chicago Commander-in-Chief for the 1908 to 1909 year and made President Theodore Roosevelt, Secretary of War William Taft, and Captain Ferrucio Vitole of the Italian Army honorary members of the association.

As discussed in the first half of this chapter, both the Army of the Philippines and the AVFS converged on Pittsburgh in 1909. Here the members of the Army of the Philippines gladly socialized with their comrades in the AVFS, but rejected all attempts to merge the two organizations. At the end of the convention, Colonel Charles L. Jewett picked up the reins of leadership for the Army of the Philippines.

In the ensuing months, the Army of the Philippines made little headway on any issue of importance. At the eleventh annual convention in the Chicago, for example, the delegates were faced with new versions of resolutions first proposed years before. Resolutions called for immediate enactment of the Philippine Travel Bill (the same bill they had discussed at their 1901 reunion) and the erection of a Philippine Monument. The latter resolution called for a bill to be submitted by the executive committee to Congress asking the government to pay for the monument. In new business, the delegates passed an amendment to the by-laws providing that a national historian would be appointed by the executive committee.

By the twelfth National Reunion in 1911, the travel pay issue had still not been resolved, although a bill authorizing this pay was before Congress. "In order to obtain satisfactory results," Commander-in-Chief A.H. Anderson told the audience, "it will be necessary for the organization to support this measure." Anderson also described another bill that would need organizational support. The idea for this bill—to provide pensions for widows and children of deceased soldiers and sailors of the War with Spain and the Philippine Insurrection—had been originated by the AVFS. But it was Pennsylvania Congressman Thomas A. Crago, a former member of the Army of the Philippines, who had introduced the measure into Congress as his first bill. (After the amalgamations in the East, Crago's post became affiliated with the AVFS, rather than the Army of the Philippines.)

A carry-over item from the preceding two reunions was the subject of amalgamation with other veteran's organizations. Interest in merging with the AVFS was apparently lukewarm. Commander-in-

Colonel Charles Jewett, Commander, Army of the Philippines, 1909

Chief Anderson reported to the delegates, "I have had some interviews with the Commander-in-Chief of the AVFS and he has proposed a certain plan of working the two orders in closer affiliation by means of a waiver of initiation fees of each in favor of the other and the only additional expense would be the per capita tax of each member affiliating with the other, but nothing has been done."

Next the question of merger with the United Spanish War Veterans was brought on the floor. The United Spanish War Veterans organization was just one of the multitude of veteran's groups formed by Spanish War returnees. While it is quite possible that there were other groups by the same name, this one was based in St. Louis. The debate grew heated with both the pros and cons forcefully arguing their views.

When the proposal was brought to a vote, its opponents won. Besides defeating the proposed merger, those opposed succeeded in securing passage of an amendment to the constitution that would complicate approval of any mergers contemplated in the future. The amendment, introduced by Camp Bumpus, read:

"This organization must and shall not amalgamate, affiliate, become part of, or enter into any agreement of whatsoever nature with any other organization of any description, except upon the individual consent of every member of this organization. This amendment, after its adoption shall not be amendable to reconsideration or be repealed except upon the individual consent of every member of this organization."

Coming as it did after Anderson's earlier revelation that recruitment of members was lagging, this amendment—and the sentiment behind it—seemed to border on the suicidal. According to Anderson, the response to his year-long efforts to increase membership through select mailings to eligible prospects had been disappointing. And coming as the amendment did just two years before the Army of the Philippines would agree to a major merger, the amendment was surprising. Surely F. Warner Karling, who was elected the new Commander-in-Chief in a close race, had no inkling that it would fall to him to guide his organization through that merger.

In fact, during Karling's first term, very little out of the ordinary happened. The legislative committee continued to push for passage of the Travel Pay Bill and the Widows and Orphans Bill, and the Congress continued to take no action.

At the 1912 reunion in Lincoln, Nebraska, Karling's main duty was to remind the camps that they needed to endorse all bills and joint resolutions as requested. He specifically referred to the Widows and Orphans Pension Bill. "Do not let it rest there," he begged the delegates, "but keep pounding away. The man to address your correspondence to is Representative J.L. Slayden of Texas, who seems to have a desire to hold us back. Everybody should write and let him know who we are and that it is just as necessary

as the pensions that are granted to the widow and orphans of the veterans of other wars." Karling also reported that the organization had been advised to bring the Travel Pay Bill before the Board of Claims of the War Department and that he had so instructed the National Judge Advocate.

Before the reunion ended, several representatives from the AVFS who were in attendance suggested a merger of the two organizations. The Army of the Philippines promptly invited these members to attend the next year's reunion in Denver to discuss the possibility further.

In fact, the entire AVFS National Encampment would end up meeting with the Army of the Philippines in Denver, thanks to the scheming of one man. That man, Gus Hartung, was the commander of the Denver-based John S. Stewart Camp of the Army of the Philippines. During the 1912 reunion, he proposed that the next reunion of the Army of the Philippines be held in Denver, and the delegates agreed. After the possibility of a merger was raised, Hartung contacted Robert Woodside, Commander-in-Chief of the AVFS, and suggested that the AVFS, too, hold its next convention in Denver. When Woodside accepted, the way was paved for the joint meeting of 1913.

DENVER, COLORADO: 1913

1913 was a turbulent year. Fights, riots, wars, retrenchment, advancement, splits, and mergers—overseas and at home—all boiled over from the same pot. On the other side of the Atlantic, nine Southern European countries had begun warring with one another. Another conflict was brewing in our hemisphere. In Tampico, Mexico, unarmed U.S. Fleet Marines who had gone ashore to purchase supplies were forcibly detained by Mexican authorities. When the United States naval officer in charge requested an apology, his request was ignored.

Amidst this turmoil, the American Veterans of Foreign Service and the National Association of the Army of the Philippines opened their joint convention in Denver, Colorado. Their problems—like those of the rest of the world—would be difficult to solve.

At the start of the convention, the possibility of merging the two groups may have been in the backs of some veterans' minds—most notably, in the minds of three leaders who had long favored this action: General Irving Hale and Gus Hartung of the Army of the Philippines, and AVFS Commander-in-Chief Robert Woodside. Officially, however, the reason both groups were holding their conventions in the same city was because Gus Hartung had invited both groups to meet there. The Stewart Camp had further promised to present a sterling silver facsimile of an army tin cup to the camp in each organization with the largest turnout at the reunion.

Publicly, the main reason the two conventions were held in Denver was to allow the approximately 500 members from each group in attendance to social-ize. According to the Denver *Post* of August 17th, the convention programs would be "given over chiefly to entertainment, including numerous sightseeing trips." It predicted that "one of the big features of the veterans' convention, will be the picnic tomorrow at Elitch's gardens. All the local men, accompanied by the visitors, will go to the resort for a special entertain-ment program, which will be followed by a picnic din-ner at twilight in the apple orchard. At night, 350 of the former soldiers will attend the garden theater."

In retrospect, the *Post's* prediction that the picnic and theater excursion would be "the big feature" of the convention appears ludicrous. Yet at the time the reporter wrote his article, no one could have predicted the course that the events of the next few days would take.

The convention opened with both groups meeting separately. Each group had a certain amount of old business to handle, and undoubtedly wanted to dis-cuss in private what they would and would not con-cede in a merger. Certainly the leaders in both associa-tions who favored the merger needed time to sway un-decided members to their way of thinking.

Throughout these meetings, the incalculable fac-tor present was the issue with Mexico. Each day the chances of a peaceful settlement grew dimmer. Al-though no actual battles erupted, the "pushing and shoving" that is part of any border incident steadily worsened until the AVFS felt compelled to send the following message to Secretary of War Lindley M. Garrison:

```
    The American Veterans of Foreign Ser-
vice in the 13th National Encampment send
heartiest greetings to you.
    At this moment we wish to renew our
allegiance and pledge our support to our
country in case war is declared against
Mexico.
    We are men who have seen service in
foreign lands and we are ready to give
our service and aid should our country
need us.
    /s/ Robert G. Woodside
    Commander-in-Chief
```

The convention got down to the business of merger on Tuesday, August 19th. It was a long day. Like the opening of Pandora's Box, all the blessings escaped, leaving only hope. Only the cool heads of their leaders prevented total rebellion by the hot heads in the rank and file.

Those who supported the merger cited the bless-ings of having one large, strong organization instead of two smaller, weaker ones. Citing these advantages were men from both sides: Irving Hale, F. Warner Karling, Robert Woodside, Rice Means, and Thomas Crago. There was strength in numbers, they claimed. There would be economy in administration, ad-vantages in recruiting, and increased political clout.

Opposition to union stemmed primarily from the feelings of "sectionalism" held by some of members and leaders of lesser stature. These objections were

Among the Past Commanders-in-Chief who attended the 1951 Encampment in New York were two of the strongest supporters of the 1913 merger. AVFS Commander Robert G. Woodside and Gus Hartung are seated second and third from the right, respectively.

mainly voiced by members of the Army of the Philippines.

While rivalry between the groups arose in part from local pride in their unit's "feats of arms," the main dissention came over choosing a name for the new group. Backers of each organization felt that theirs was the name which should be retained and were loath to relinquish it.

The bickering and arguments continued until shortly after midnight on August 20th. By now, both sides were near the point of revolt. Only the diplomacy of General Hale prevented it. He saved the merger by moving that the new association go by the name of "Army of the Philippines, Cuba and Puerto Rico" until a referendum could be held and a name be chosen by a vote of all members and all posts.

Rice Means, a young Denver attorney and veteran officer of the First Colorado, received a unanimous and wholly unexpected vote to be the new organization's Commander-in-Chief. Other officers elected by the delegates were: Robert G. Woodside of Pittsburgh, Senior Vice Commander; Lieutenant C.C.

Culver of the U.S. Army in Manila, First Junior Vice Commander; Major Charles T. Spear of St. Paul, Second Junior Vice Commander; Robert Cusick of Camden, N.J., Third Junior Vice Commander; John Fade of Baltimore, Fourth Junior Vice Commander; Charles J. Riley of San Francisco, Fifth Junior Vice Commander; A.V. Pray of Des Moines, Iowa, Paymaster General; Marvin J. O'Donnell of Kansas City, Judge Advocate General; Dr. Frank D. Husted of Philadelphia, Surgeon General; Chaplain J.S. Smith, U.S. Army, Chaplain; F. Warner Karling of Kansas City, Member of the Executive Committee for the long term; and C.J. Barbour of Pittsburgh, Member of the Executive Committee for one year.

Because of the heated discussions and lingering resentment over issues that had passed despite objections from substantial minorities, the delegates postponed most organizational changes to a later meeting or left them to the newly elected officers to make. One major change, however, was silently approved when the Army of the Philippines agreed to merge. Henceforth, membership in both groups would be open not just to veterans of the Philippine Campaign, but to veterans who served honorably in any war on foreign soil.

It was 12:30 a.m., August 20, 1913, when the delegates voted to accept the merger and its terms. At this time, the name "Army of the Philippines, Cuba and Porto Rico" [sic] was officially transferred to sixty-nine camps previously belonging to the American Veterans of Foreign Service and the Army of the Philippines. The two organizations were now officially united in name, if not yet in spirit.

THE AFTERMATH

The "in ranks" revolt had not ended just because the convention was over. If anything, the dissenters now had more time and the floor all to themselves when they continued their tirades. Even supporters of the merger had their problems. They had the questions of their "Stay-at-Home Comrades" to answer and the "Die-Hards" opposed to merger to convince. In many camps, the legality of the merger topped the list of the most discussed items.

In an attempt to take charge of the situation, on September 12, 1913, Commander-in-Chief Rice Means issued General Order Number One. In it, Means appealed to the members' loyalty and patriotism in asking them to set aside their dissatisfaction with the merger. He also announced that local units would henceforth by known as "posts" rather than "camps." The full text of the General Order read as follows:

I. The Commander-in-Chief hereby assumes command of the Army of the Philippines, Cuba and Puerto Rico, with headquarters at 613 Symes Bldg., Denver, Colorado.

The consolidation of the Army of the Philippines and the American Veterans of Foreign Service has been effected and is now a reality. By reason of such consolidation some of our comrades have not been entirely satisfied, but as their duties in the service of their country were performed with valor and fortitude, though sometimes contrary to their personal desires and wishes; so the Commander-in-Chief expects that personal dissatisfaction, if any existed, will be forgotten and every comrade will give his loyal support and hearty co-operation in the upbuilding of his organization. National Headquarters desires to increase our membership to double its present number, so let each comrade do his duty by bringing in as least one new member this year. Growth is as much desired as efficiency. The future of the Army of the Philippines, Cuba and Puerto Rico is bright with promise. With each comrade working for the upbuilding of our organization, the ensuing year will be a successful one.

II. The following appointments on the staff of the Commander-in-Chief are hereby announced: Adjutant General Gus Bing, 1843 Welton Street, Denver, Colorado; Inspector General and Chief of Staff Gus E.Hartung, 970 Gas and Electric Building, Denver, Colorado; National Historian Charles A. Martin, 1921 North Croskey Street, Philadelphia, Pennsylvania.

III. All local organizations will hereafter be termed "Posts" and will be numbered consecutively by original date of charter. All Post Adjutants are directed to furnish the Adjutant General immediately with the date of charter, together with the complete roster of members in good standing, together with the address of each.

IV. Attention is called to the fact that a twenty-cent additional per capita tax is now due and owing. Post Adjutants are directed to see that the proper amount is remitted to the Adjutant General immediately.

V. On the 15th day of October, 1913 and on the 15th day of each calendar month thereafter a copy of the official paper known as the "The Veteran" will be mailed to each comrade in good standing free of charge. Julian E. Duvall is hereby appointed Editor-in-Chief of the Veteran. Each post is requested to appoint an associate editor, who will furnish items of interest to the Editor-in-Chief at Norton, Kansas.

/s/ Rice Means
Commander-in-Chief

Despite Means's appeal, several camps on both sides of the Mississippi continued to protest the merger. In the West, conditions were ripe for revolt because the Camp Bumpus amendment forbidding amalgamation without the consent of every member was still in effect. Yet only two former Army of the Philippines Posts—in Boston and Chicago—refused point blank to join the new organization. The Boston post refused affiliation and then declared itself the original Army of the Philippines. The Luzon Post of Chicago also refused to merge, but eventually returned to the fold in 1926.

The main resistance to the merger was led by a group of AVFS members in Pennsylvania. This is surprising, considering that at the Denver meeting, AVFS members had been generally more amenable to merger than had Army of the Philippines members. After amalgamation, however, these dissenters decided that the merger was in violation of the state charter under which they were organized. It, they claimed, prohibited their merging with any unincorporated groups, such as the organization put together in Denver. Because they questioned the legality of the merger, this group continued publishing the newspaper of the American Veterans of Foreign Service, even though the newly combined groups were now publishing another paper.

To put the matter of amalgamation to a vote, this group called a convention in Newark, New Jersey, for November 21 and 22, 1913. Camps from New York, New Jersey, Pennsylvania, and the Canal Zone gathered to determine whether or not they would remain in the new organization. At this convention, Joseph Levy, their former Judge Advocate, presented the case for refusing the merger. Past Commander-in-Chief Robert Woodside, probably the AVFS's foremost proponent of the amalgamation, countered Levy's arguments by enumerating the advantages to be gained by the union.

The renegade group elected George F. Lumb of Harrisburg, Pennsylvania, as their Commander-in-Chief. Lumb's first act was to call for a vote on merging the camps present at the meeting into a new (separate) organization with a new name. Twenty-one posts and 493 delegate votes approved this action and seven posts and 85 delegate votes were against it. While twenty-one posts would represent approximately 66 percent of all the previous AVFS Posts, the number is misleading. In some of these posts, dissenters constituted only a small minority of the membership. Even so, the rebellion was serious enough to claim the attention of leaders like Robert Woodside.

The group's referendum, instead of clearing up the matter, resulted in further confusion. Seeing that nothing further could be accomplished at this meeting, Woodside called for another one—this time in Philadelphia. At this meeting, Woodside proposed a solution. An entirely new set of officers was elected, a new constitution drawn up, and a new society called "Veterans of Foreign Wars" was created. The society's constitution empowered it to "unite with a similar body at a future time," thereby legalizing its merger with the group formed in Denver.

Sticky as the question of legality was, there was an issue that was even more explosive that had to be solved before the situation could be considered stable. A name for the new organization formed in Denver, temporarily titled "Army of the Philippines, Cuba and Puerto Rico," had to be agreed upon.

In February 1914, Commander-in-Chief Rice Means sent all posts a message suggesting that they agree on a name that was so comprehensive that every veteran would realize that this new organization was not like the GAR or any other previous veteran's organizations. This one would not die out with the founding generation, but would be available to veterans as long as the United States was forced to fight wars. To reinforce this message, the chief had circulars sent to each post. In part they said:

"There must arise an organization which will embody the true patriotic sentiments of this nation. If an organization is a limited one, it must perforce die out. Other military organizations were organized to perpetuate the campaign of the War with Spain, a very brief time. Since that time our nation has become a world power. We have taken our place as the leading nation of the world. . . . But so sure as we assume our responsibility as a nation, foremost in the world, we must have conflicts or disputes which require the presence of our soldiers in foreign climes. Wars and conflict, by reason of our position, are inevitable.

"So I believe that whenever a man serves this, his country, in time of war, or in time of conflict with other people or tribes or other nations, he, in a true sense, is a patriot and a comrade of yours and mine. So it is incumbent upon us now to form an organization that will be everlasting, that cannot die out with

In 1914, the delegates convened in Pittsburgh to formally unite the VFW.
The Ladies Auxiliary was also formed at this convention.

your death and mine, but one that will live as long as our nation lives. It must be so broad in its provisions for eligibility to include every man who has served or who in the future will serve in any war in which the United States is engaged. . . ."

With bated breath, National Headquarters in Denver issued Commander-in-Chief Means's General Order Number 6, dated April 15, 1914. This order put the selection of the name to a vote of all posts and their members. The suggested names were: The Veteran Army and Navy of the United States; The Veteran Army and Navy of the Republic; and The Veterans of Foreign Wars of the United States. Thirty-one posts, which was a majority of those voting, chose the name Veterans of Foreign Wars of the United States.

Official approval of the selected name was later given at the 1914 Convention in Pittsburgh. This approval, coupled with the adoption of the constitution, made that convention the first annual convention of the Veterans of Foreign Wars of the United States. The opening words of the constitution further testify to the official place and time of the VFW's foundation:

CONSTITUTION

Adopted at Pittsburgh, Pa., September 15–16, 1914.

PREAMBLE

We, the officers and enlisted men and honorably discharged officers and enlisted men of the Army, Navy and Marine Corps of the United States of America, do unite to establish a permanent organization which shall be known as Veterans of Foreign Wars of the United States.

The founders left no doubt that they believed they had established a truly *permanent* organization. The first page of the October 1914 issue of *The Veteran* carried this announcement:

"We have entered into a new epoch in the history of veteran's organizations. Such societies have come and gone. Others are fading away, but ours is destined to live as long as our country lives—forever!

"Our house is built upon the rock of eternity, not upon the sands of time. The Veterans of Foreign Wars is a serviceman's organization."

CHAPTER THREE

THE LEARNING YEARS
1914–1929

For an organization to remain progressive, it must continually change with the times. It must constantly assess and reassess the needs and problems of its members and adjust its goals to address those problems. In the first fifteen years after the VFW's founding, its members did not lack for goals. But as yet, its members did not have the experience or knowledge that would enable them to successfully achieve all their goals. Just as the young of any species must do, the VFW had to learn to crawl before it could walk or run.

During this period, the VFW's goals focused primarily on the needs of two important groups—present-day veterans and their families, and servicemen who would be the nation's future veterans. For the benefit of the first group, the VFW advocated for veterans' entitlements such as job preference, vocational rehabilitation and training, pensions for disabled veterans and families of deceased veterans, and medical care for veterans with service-connected disabilities. For the benefit of the second group, the VFW worked for reforms in military preparedness to ensure that our armed forces would never again be sent into combat as poorly trained and equipped as were the troops in the Spanish American War.

The idea that veterans should be "entitled" to certain benefits by virtue of their service was not, of course, original with the VFW. In decades past, the Grand Army of the Republic had achieved notable success in obtaining benefits for its Civil War–era members. But when the VFW looked to the GAR for guidance in securing entitlements for its members, it found little help. The GAR had worked for and with veterans of a single generation, not the veterans of past, present, and future generations as the VFW intended to do. There were no guidelines or marked routes for advocating on the vast scale the VFW had in mind. Even with the concerted efforts of intelligent, dedicated men, learning how to pursue entitlements for *all* veterans would take much trial and error and many years.

The VFW's second proposed goal of seeking increased military preparedness set forth another hurdle which no veteran's association had previously attempted. No organization had ever before dared to challenge the government's stance on recruiting, training, and equipping its servicemen. Certainly no organization had ever had the gall to point out to the government that preparedness meant acting before, not during or after a problem arose. And although the VFW's early cries on the subject of preparedness were largely ignored, the VFW never relinquished its goal. Eventually, the VFW would make up for what it lacked in experience with stamina and determination.

During these learning years, many of the victories the VFW won were small. Many of its attempts to secure what it deemed fair treatment for the nation's veterans failed. Yet in each attempt, there was a victory. The victory was in learning that the VFW could influence legislation on behalf of its veterans.

Men such as Thomas Crago, United States Congressman from Pennsylvania, were the proximate cause of many of these victories. Crago, who was elected VFW Commander-in-Chief in 1914, was responsible for what is recognized as the greatest VFW victory of that time: the pension bill which provided for the widows of Spanish War veterans, which he authored and defended on the floor of the House. Through Crago and others like him, the organization learned how and when to apply its influence to gain the legislation necessary to accomplish its goals. In the near future, these hard-learned lessons would serve well both the VFW and a much larger group of veterans.

PRELUDE TO WAR

In 1915, the nation's need to prepare for war was palpable to the VFW. True, President Woodrow Wilson had vowed to keep the United States out of war, affirming in a 1914 speech that "the United States must be neutral in fact as well as in name. . . . We must be impartial in thought as well as in action." But all over the world, events appeared to be drawing the United States inexorably closer to war.

In Europe that year, Germany launched the world's first airship raid (on ports in eastern England), the first submarine raid (on Le Havre, France), and the first zeppelin raid (on London). Italy declared war on Austro-Hungary, and the two countries fought the first battle of Isonzo, and the second, and the third. . . .* And on May 7, 1915, more than 1,100 people, including 128 Americans, lost their lives when the Germans sank the British ship *Lusitania*.

Closer to home, the problems south of the border that had begun when Mexican authorities forcibly detained an unarmed contingent of U.S. Marines still festered. Early in 1915, President Wilson had responded to this provocation by sending a naval force to occupy the city of Vera Cruz. Then 7,000 U.S. Army troops under the command of General Frederick Funston arrived.

There were also signs that the discord in Europe was spilling over to our shores. Countering a British blockade of their ports, the Germans had announced that any ships attempting to enter specified British ports would be sunk. Although no American ship had been sunk, President Wilson notified Germany that they would be held accountable if any were.

On July 2, 1915, Erich Muenter, an instructor of German at Cornell University, planted a bomb that blew up the Senate Reception Room. On July 3rd, he fatally shot financier J. Pierpont Morgan, and then committed suicide July 6th. Although it was never legally proven, Muenter was widely suspected of being in league with Germany because he was a German-American. These feelings were influenced to some extent by a speech former President Theodore Roosevelt had recently given in which he questioned the loyalty of citizens such as Muenter who were "Hyphenated Americans": Irish-Americans, German-Americans, Italian-Americans. . . . "There can be no 50/50 Americanism in this country," he thundered. "There is room here for only 100 percent

---

* There would be nine battles of Isonzo before the end of 1916.

Americanism, only for those who are Americans and nothing else."

Also in 1915, the Secret Service revealed the contents of a briefcase belonging to the German Director of Propaganda in the United States. Inside were detailed plans for the sabotage of strategic targets inside this country.

As if the members of the VFW needed any further evidence that war was on the horizon, President Wilson issued a call for men to serve on the Mexican border. Because many VFW members responded, quite a few familiar faces were missing from the National Encampment in 1915. The VFW had, however, sent invitations to the convention to all Spanish War veterans and auxiliaries and encouraged them to join the organization. The same invitation had been extended to members of the Imperial Order of the Dragon, who had served in the China relief expedition of 1900 and were holding their annual convention on the same dates.

From the moment the National Encampment was gaveled to order in Detroit on August 16, much of the talk centered on the need for preparedness. According to the Detroit *News Tribune,* one of the first practical suggestions was offered by W.S. Voorsanger, a member from Pittsburgh. Voorsanger proposed a plan to create an "adequate veteran reserve" by "securing the enlistment in such reserve of several hundred thousand veterans of the campaigns of the last two decades."

Lt. Col. Robert S. Woodside further testified as to the need for a reserve corps. The August 16th *Denver Times* quoted him as saying, "The Veterans reserve corps is needed for the safety of the country. . . . The creation of a reserve force would stop a wasteful leak in our army administration." Although this suggestion was never adopted on a national level, many departments supplied their states with men who performed some of the duties a reserve corps might have provided. These men patrolled sea coasts and national boundaries and investigated and reported suspected subversive groups and saboteurs.

The convention also discussed what the Regular Army needed to do to boost its readiness. According to the August 16th *Denver Times,* Commander-in-Chief Thomas Crago recommended that the United States have "a first line army of 100,000 men, a second line army of the same number and equipment for 1,000,000 men." Said Crago, "The experience that Russia is now having shows the vital importance of equipment for war. . . . Those of us who have served in our wars know that proper equipment has not always been forthcoming until long after the men were ready for service."

The veterans' implied criticism of U.S. military policy was not actually targeted at President Wilson, but at America's pacifists and isolationists. These groups believed that the oceans separated us from the rest of the world's problems and we had no reason to get involved. Teddy Roosevelt, the nation's leading proponent of preparedness, had nicknamed this "peace at any price" group the "Flubdubs" and "Flapdoodle Patriots." He continually criticized Wilson for backing them—in part because Wilson had campaigned for president under the slogan "He Kept Us out of War." But although Wilson had great reservations about entering the war in Europe, that slogan was originally used without his knowledge or consent.

On August 18th, the National Encampment of 1915 adopted a resolution that made it clear where the VFW's grievances lay. While denouncing peace at any price advocates as decadent Americans, they pledged their united support to President Wilson and advocated community mass meetings to promote patriotism and preparedness. The text of that resolution follows:

> "Be it resolved. . . that the President of the United States be again assured of the united support of the members of this organization, in any crisis that may arise, whether in the field of performing active service, or in the camp as experienced instructors, or whatever duty may require—we pledge ourselves to give instant response to the call of duty.

A zealous advocate of military preparedness, in 1917 Theodore Roosevelt joined the VFW.

"We so maintain stoutly and unchangeably, that peace without honor is intolerable. Peace at any price is the swan song of the decadent and virtueless. With full understanding of the horrors of war, we realize the horrors of unpreparedness. We do not advocate preparedness for war, but preparedness against war; a preparedness which in the event of the catastrophe of war, will prevent the enormous initial sacrifice of human lives which has characterized every war in which the United States has been engaged throughout its past history.

"We respectfully urge upon the President of the United States, upon every thoughtful and patriotic citizen, the necessity of protecting American citizens, the enforcement of American humane doctrines, and the defense of our national honor. We dare not indulge ourselves in the enjoyment of the blessings of peace, while turning deaf ears to the cry of distress, or to the summons of a righteous cause.

"This encampment does hereby instruct all posts, as well as all individual members of the Veterans of Foreign Wars to assist in arranging community mass meetings of patriotism and preparedness, there to crystallize and concentrate the sentiment of this nation to a true understanding of our duties to other countries and to ourselves."

Before the convention ended, the delegates chose as their new Commander-in-Chief Gus Hartung, the former Army of the Philippines camp commander who had helped to orchestrate the final amalgamation in Denver. Prior to his election to the VFW's top office, Hartung had been the organization's Chief of Staff.

During Hartung's term in office, the VFW added twelve new posts and over a thousand members, bringing the total membership to about 5,000 members. Much of this growth was due to Hartung's fine Senior Vice Commander, Albert Rabing. Rabing, who believed that the Senior Vice Commander should be more than a figurehead, was tireless in his efforts to increase and consolidate the organization. He visited existing posts, instituted new ones, swore in members, made speeches, and generally saw that the VFW's name was kept in the public eye.

While Sr. Vice Commander-in-Chief Rabing concentrated on recruitment, Commander-in-Chief Hartung turned his attention to the mandate the 1915 convention had given him to work for preparedness. During his travels that year, he spoke out forcefully and often on the need for America to increase her military strength. In response to his message, more and more VFW members again donned the uniforms of their country's armed forces.

Finally, a stubborn Congress had to acknowledge that America's military strength was stretched to the limit. American troops in the Philippines were still mopping up remnants of the Insurrectionists who had been fighting our forces since shortly after the conclusion of the Spanish American War. In Mexico, an expedition led by General John J. Pershing was attempting to catch and punish the bandit Pancho Villa. And with rebel forces in Haiti and the Dominican Republic making violent attempts at overthrowing their governments, still more American soldiers had to be sent overseas to protect American citizens and property. In 1916, Congress at last increased military funding, opening the door for increased recruiting efforts.

One VFW member who helped to swell the ranks of America's armed forces was Adjutant General Robert S. Woodside. Woodside resigned his position to enter the Army's Officer Training Course at Fort Oglethorpe, Georgia. Here he had the good fortune to be instructed by a Regular Army captain named Dwight D. Eisenhower. Later, speaking of the VFW at the time of his resignation, Woodside would say, "We had no salaried officers because we could not afford to pay them. However we had a compact, loyal and active membership, ready to take advantage of the opportunity for the growth soon to present itself."

After Woodside's resignation, the VFW changed its policy of locating the national headquarters offices in a large city near the Adjutant General's or Commander-in-Chief's home. In 1916, the headquarters was moved to 32 Union Square in New York City. At the time, Commander-in-Chief Hartung strongly recommended that a permanent office be located in the nation's capital, but no action was taken. This was a learning error on the part of the organization. That year was an election year. With war imminent, both the Republican and Democratic parties were scrambling for votes. With a Washington office, the VFW could have capitalized on the candidates' hunger for votes by pressing for support of veterans' issues.

While the political contest between Woodrow Wilson and the Republican candidate, Charles E. Hughes, was brewing, the VFW held a different sort of contest: a nationwide essay contest. This contest,

"The American Creed" contest, was intended to bind more tightly the bonds of patriotism. At the end of the contest period, William Tyler Page, Clerk of the U.S. House of Representatives, was declared the winner. This was his entry:

"I believe in the United States of America as a government of the people, by the people, and for the people; whose just powers are derived from the consent of the governed; a democracy in a republic; a sovereign nation of many sovereign states; a perfect union, one and inseparable; established upon these principles of freedom, equality, justice and humanity for which American patriots sacrificed their lives.

"I therefore believe it is my duty to my country to love it; to support its constitution; to obey its laws; to respect its flag and to defend it against all enemies."

At the 1916 National Encampment in Chicago, Albert Rabing accepted the promotion to Commander-in-Chief of the VFW. As Commander, he continued the recruiting and goodwill trips he had begun as Senior Vice Commander, and rapidly became known as the "traveling commander." During his term in office, Rabing made a 1900–mile, twenty-two-stop tour of the nation to bring the VFW closer together. Because most of the previous Commanders-in-Chief had been from the east, many western members had never seen a Commander-in-Chief in the flesh. Rabing vowed to remedy that. In addition to instituting new posts, he made an effort to stop at as many of the older posts as was possible.

While Rabing was traveling around the country, a controversy that had long concerned the VFW and its predecessors was finally settled. After a twenty-six-year fight by the Medal of Honor Legion (a group of Medal of Honor recipients dedicated to upholding the honor of this prestigious medal), Congress finally took steps to examine the alleged abuses in the awarding of the Congressional Medal of Honor. At the instigation of New York Representative Isaac R.

A mother kissing her son good-bye before he departs for camp with the 7th Regiment. The declaration of war on Germany meant this scene would be repeated many times.

The Act also empowered a distinguished panel of five General Officers to convene and determine which of the Medals of Honor previously awarded should stand. After a three-month investigation, the panel concluded its examination and summarized its findings. On February 5, 1917, the panel announced that of the 2,625 Medals of Honor that had been awarded up to that time, 910 would be stricken from the rolls—including the one awarded William F. "Buffalo Bill" Cody, American frontier hero and showman. The United States Navy was the only branch in which no cancellations were recommended.

Less than two months after the Medal of Honor panel had announced its rulings, the United States presented its servicemen with a fresh opportunity to demonstrate their valor and patriotism. On April 6, 1917, at President Wilson's urging, Congress declared war on Germany.

Over the next eighteen months, the VFW would prove many times over that it had meant what it said when it promised President Wilson "the united support of the members of this organization, in any crisis that may arise." It would do so under the leadership of three Commanders-in-Chief: Albert Rabing and William E. Ralston, both attorneys, and F. Warner Karling, owner of a Kansas City, Missouri, furniture manufacturing company who had served two terms as Commander-in-Chief of the Army of the Philippines.

WARTIME

America's declaration of war galvanized the VFW into action. Over 60 percent of its members decided to

Sherwood, a Civil War general who had been complimented in special orders for gallantry in action six times, an act redefining the qualifications for the Medal of Honor was passed. Under the original act that created the Medal of Honor, the qualifications had been: "Gallantry in Action and other Soldier Like Qualities." The new act of April 27, 1916, stated the medal could be presented only to those who met the definition of "Valor Above and Beyond the Call of Duty."*

---

* In 1918, the Congress went even a step further when it amended the act so that the Medal of Honor could be awarded "...only to each person who, while as officer or enlisted man of the Army, shall hereinafter, in action involving actual conflict with an enemy, distinguish himself conspicuously by gallantry and intrepidity at risk of his life above and beyond the call of duty."

make the supreme contribution to their country's war efforts by going back into uniform. Those still at home channeled their efforts into four main areas: helping to win the war, fighting for entitlements for the veterans-to-be, advocating for the needs of servicemen's families, and recruiting new members.

Perhaps the VFW's most valuable assistance toward winning the war was in recruiting. In many of the larger cities, VFW posts held daily patriotic parades and mass meetings to aid the military in recruiting and public support of the war. On June 5th, National Draft Registration Day, posts all around the country threw open their doors and assisted in the effort to recruit manpower. D.R. Sullivan, of Post No. 92 in Kensington, Pennsylvania, turned his real estate office into a recruiting station and was instrumental in signing up 200 prospective recruits for the armed forces. In all, over 9.5 million men registered that day. Of these, 1,374,000 were drafted and 687,000 were retained for service.

Besides helping to register men for the draft, VFW posts helped with recruitment in other ways. Putting into action an idea first proposed at the 1915

National Encampment, the posts in Allegheny County, Pennsylvania, organized a Veteran Reserve Corps to take over when the National Guard of that state was ordered overseas. And Post No. 27 in Manila, P.I., General Pershing's home post, wired Commander-in-Chief Rabing an offer to raise an entire company for war service. Rabing forwarded the offer to the Secretary of War. The offer was acknowledged but refused.

To keep up the morale of the servicemen they had helped to recruit, many posts inaugurated a special "Vets to Vets" letter program. Through this program, posts tried to target men from their hometown who didn't receive mail from home. In the following letter excerpt dated December 30, 1917, a soldier in France expressed his feelings about the program to D.R. Sullivan, Commander of the R.P. Arnold Post No. 92. The writer, W.C. George, was the first man in France to be enrolled in the VFW during World War I.

". . . I received your letter a few days ago and cannot express in words how proud I was to learn I had been accepted in the Veterans of Foreign Wars, especially the first member of the present war. I felt

U.S. recruits en route to the front
(National Archives)

mighty proud the day I put on my uniform and am still proud of that uniform. But since I have become a member of the Foreign Veterans, my chest has a tendency to stick out a few inches further than heretofore. Believe me, it is a grand and glorious feeling. In your letter you asked for the addresses of two men who had no one to write to them. I will submit these names and I'm sure their spirits will raise wonderfully if they receive some little token."

In addition to keeping up the spirits of the troops, the VFW also tried to influence public sentiment about the war. VFW posts in some of the country's larger cities held daily parades prior to Registration Day. Other posts held meetings at the Post Home to foster patriotism and encourage young men to enlist.

Within the VFW, feelings of patriotism ran high. The ex-veterans of the VFW brooked no halfway measures and tolerated no subversive feelings. One post went so far as to court-martial their Congressman for voting against the declaration of war on Germany. The hapless Congressman was Ernest Lundeen of Minnesota, who had circulated a letter around his district claiming that the people of Minnesota had voted against declaring war. Enraged at his action, Patterson Post No. 7 sent Lundeen a letter requesting his resignation from the VFW. When he ignored the request, they proceeded with his court-martial. According to the Minneapolis *Tribune,* other organizations that protested Lundeen's action were: Herman Lodge No. 18, Knights of Pythias; the Lake Harriet Commercial Club; Flower City Lodge of Odd Fellows; and the Oden Club. The court-martial process took about a year, but eventually the national organization approved the court-martial and ousted Lundeen from the ranks in dishonor.

One last "direct support" service the VFW offered the armed forces during the war was to help the military overcome its shortcomings in equipment. Despite the VFW's continuous pleading with the federal government in past years for the maintenance of an up-to-date and well-equipped military organization, its advice had mostly fallen on deaf ears. As a result, the armed forces were thrust into another war

almost as ill equipped as they had been during the Spanish American War. For example, so behind were U.S. munitions factories that the only American-made cannon the First Army fired during the entire war were four fourteen-inch naval guns. Of the forty-five American Air Corps Squadrons at the front at war's end, only twelve were flying American-made planes. And American manufacturers could not begin to produce tanks in sufficient quantity until the Armistice.

About the only area of supply in which the armed forces had made significant progress since the Spanish American War was in feeding the troops. No longer were "embalmed beef" and rotten vegetables the major concern they had been in 1898. The public indignation that followed that war had forced the federal Judicial Branch to bring several army suppliers into court for fraudulently supplying the Army with unusable food. In addition, the military now employed experts in nutrition and quality control, operated sixteen Cooks and Bakers Schools, and made use of reliable refrigeration and dehydrated vegetables.

In 1917, the entire VFW National Encampment got into the act of raising money for much-needed equipment. The delegates and others attending the meetings sold pencils on the streets of New York City—the host city—in one of the nation's earliest street-sales fund-raisers. With the proceeds, the VFW purchased two ambulances for donation to the U.S. Army. Subsequently, Commander-in-Chief Ralston encouraged the entire organization to make a similar effort. Within a short time the VFW supplied the government with several more ambulances.

At the same time the members of the VFW were throwing themselves into the war effort, they were also looking ahead to the day when the troops now fighting the "War to End War" would be veterans. The veterans of 1898 knew from personal experience of the "war's over" apathy of the public; they knew they could not wait until the boys came home to secure for them the entitlements they had earned. Armed with this knowledge they constantly reminded the government and politicians of their promises.

*U.S. tanks in France, September 1918. Although manned by U.S. soldiers, these tanks—
much to the VFW's displeasure—were not made in the U.S.A.* (National Archives)

Pressure toward attainment of entitlements was applied at all levels of government. In Rhode Island, for instance, Connell Post No. 45 appealed to its legislature to amend existing laws because they were inadequate to cover the needs of World War I veterans. This objection was in keeping with the long-time VFW position that for the purpose of entitlements, veterans of all wars should be equal in the eyes of the government. So many veterans attended that legislature's hearing, held in February 1918, that it had to be moved to larger quarters. In the face of this support, opposition to the measure folded.

On a national level, the VFW worked to secure some form of insurance against disability or loss of life for service members. On September 2, 1914, Congress had approved an act which covered losses or damage suffered by our Merchant Marine or commercial companies due to actions of warring European nations. This War Risk Insurance Act, however, did not extend to members of the armed forces or to naval ships and their cargo. Finally, after years of prodding from the VFW, the government expanded the act's coverage. Shortly after war was declared, Congress approved the new War Insurance Act, and in October 1917, an addition to it in the form of medical insurance for servicemen. This new system was pronounced by its originators to be "modern, scientific, complete and free from all the deficiencies of the old Pension System."

Under this magnificent new arrangement, the Treasury Department administrated and dispensed the insurance, allotments, and disability and death compensation. Unfortunately, the act's provisions were not handled expediently or efficiently. As a result, the act was amended eight times, then finally repealed in 1924. The World War Disability Allowance that eventually replaced it is discussed later in this chapter.

If the War Insurance Act was ultimately disappointing, another entitlement the VFW succeeded in winning was not. The enactment of Public Law 178 in

1918 marked the achievement of a major VFW objective. With this act, the federal government finally conceded the need for vocational training for disabled veterans who required special training for complete rehabilitation. Before this time, the returning disabled veteran had been discharged and made to fend for himself. Even if his previous employment had been as a stevedore or steeplejack, as far as the government was concerned, the loss of one or both legs was not a problem. Under Public Law 178, he would be trained at special centers to qualify for employment where his loss would present less of a handicap. He would be re-educated to cope in a different environment and receive financial assistance for himself and his dependents.

While the VFW was pleading for entitlements for the men fighting overseas, it did not forget about the families these servicemen had left at home. Most importantly, the VFW continued to push for passage of the Widows and Orphans Pension Bill first introduced by Congressman Thomas Crago in 1912. Although the original version of the bill had died in the Senate in 1913, it was reintroduced in the House in 1918 under the joint sponsorship of Congressmen Wyatt Alken, Richard Austin, Leonidas Dyer, and John Langley. The bill, which gave widows of veterans of the Spanish American War and the Philippine Insurrection $12 a month plus an additional $2 for each child, was approved by the House on July 16, 1918. Two years later, in June 1920, the Senate, too, finally approved Crago's Pension Bill. (By this time, Crago's term had expired and he was the VFW's National Judge Advocate.)

While the VFW was working on behalf of veterans' families, many of these families were themselves taking an active role in veterans' affairs. At its organizational meeting in 1914, the VFW had approved the formation of a national Ladies Auxiliary. In July 1918, the Lt. Lansdale VFW Post No. 67 of Sacramento, California, and its Ladies Auxiliary launched two new auxiliaries in an attempt to make the VFW something for the enjoyment of the whole family. The new auxiliaries—the Sons of the VFW and a Junior Girls unit—made their first public appearance when they marched in the Memorial Day parade. Official authorization for these units, however, did not come until 1934. Because the VFW's auxiliaries became such an integral part of the organization, Chapter 9 provides an in-depth discussion of their history and activities.

Soldiers such as these men fighting with the 36th Division were prime targets of VFW recruitment efforts. (Department of War photo)

From the start of World War I, the VFW left no doubt that it seriously intended to become an organization for veterans of *all* wars, not just veterans of the Spanish American War. It worked to secure entitlements for *all* veterans, to obtain pensions for *all* veterans' families, and—most important to its future survival—to recruit veterans from *all* wars as members.

During World War I, the VFW continued to add members from earlier wars. For example, Colonel Teddy Roosevelt of Cuban Rough Rider fame officially became a member in 1917 when he handed his application to National Aide W.S. Voorsanger. The organization also targeted men fighting overseas in the current war. In fact, in its October 1917 issue of *Foreign Service*—the VFW's official magazine—the organization extended the "doughboys" overseas a special invitation:

"You are now somewhere over there in America's vanguard of democracy and we most heartily and cordially extend to you the right hand of comradeship and urge you to join the veteran organization that does things. This you can do by filling in and signing the application blank that appears elsewhere in these columns and be carried on our membership roll absolutely free of charge until you muster out of the United States Service at the close of the present war."

After the war, the VFW was able to recruit thousands of members face to face from among the occupation troops. Much of this recruiting was accomplished by Captain Robert Woodside, the former Adjutant General of the VFW who had resigned his post to enter the service.

Captain Woodside had been sent to France and assigned as a line officer in the 38th Infantry Regiment. He was wounded on October 9, 1918, and was in the hospital when the Armistice was signed November 11th. After his discharge from the hospital, Woodside set out to rejoin the 38th, which had been assigned to occupation duty in Germany. While waiting for a train in Metz, France, Woodside chanced to meet a lieutenant who was wearing a Philippine Campaign Bar. The Lieutenant belonged to the Jakie Smith VFW Post No. 83 of San Francisco. The two spent the day together closeted with several other army officers in a compartment on the train. "We talked mostly of the VFW," Woodside later confided. "All the officers in the compartment were interested and my faith in the VFW was restored." This experience, coupled

Armistice Day, 1918 (National Archives)

with the realization that the officers and men of the American Expeditionary Forces had the same desire for recognition of their services as had the Spanish American War veterans, led to Woodside's campaign to recruit new members.

When he reported to the 38th Infantry, Woodside found that Colonel Adams had assigned him to his staff. With Adams's permission, Woodside started recruiting for the VFW in earnest. Once National Commander-in-Chief Karling learned of Woodside's efforts, he appointed him Deputy Commander-in-Chief for Europe with the authority to appoint a full staff and to proceed as he saw fit.

With a schedule that permitted him to give a fifteen-minute recruiting speech to each of the fifteen companies in the 38th Infantry Regiment, Woodside set about organizing a post. Later it would be known as Rock of the Marne VFW Post No. 138 because of the Regiment's firm stand at the Marne River in the face of large German counterattacks during July 1918. Each company selected one officer and two enlisted men as its organizing committee. As the recruiting was completed, Woodside went from company to company giving the oath of obligation to new members. Upon arriving in Neuwied, Germany, for this purpose, the company commander informed him, "Bob, every man dog in Company A belongs to the Rock of the Marne Post, but seven. If they are too good to belong to the post, they are too good to eat with the rest of the company. I have them segregated."

With the help of his assistants, Woodside recruited approximately 80 percent of the 38th Regiment. The application for a post charter contained names of 1700 new members. The membership fee of six francs (about $1.16) included a VFW button and badge and the year's dues.

In the spring of 1919, the Rock of the Marne Post held a Memorial Service with General U.G. Mc-Alexander, the Regimental Commander on the Marne, as the speaker. For the ceremony, they had a floral Cross of Malta made with a receptacle in each arm of the cross. The roll was called by company, and as each company name was called, the First Sergeant of that company stepped to the cross, saluted, and deposited in the cross a card imprinted in gold letters with the name of each man from that company who had made the supreme sacrifice.

Shortly after this Memorial Service, the 38th was ordered to prepare for its return home. The men of the 38th were more than ready to return to "God's Country." They were part of the next to last overseas division to be disbanded, and were tired of being gouged by European shopkeepers. This song, most popular with the occupation troops, expressed their sentiments.

> "We drove the Boche across the Rhine,
> The Kaiser from his throne.
> Oh, Lafayette, we've paid our debt,
> For Christ's sake, send us home."

HOMECOMING

Even before the transports had begun moving our first military units to the war zones at the start of World War I, the VFW had known what problems would face veterans at the end of the war. They were the same problems that veterans of all wars face: the need for compensation, pensions, hospitalization, jobs, care of dependents, and adjustment to civilian life and the public's attitudes toward servicemen.

The Spanish American War veterans had never forgotten the trials and agonies they had undergone on their return home. At the beginning of World War I, they had vowed that the mistakes of 1898 and 1899 must not be repeated. Well aware of the public's postwar tendencies of "forget and neglect," they had built a fire under the federal government and their elected officials to make sure these veterans and their widows and orphans received the assistance they needed. As a result, by the time the first of the 2 million soldiers who were overseas at the start of the Armistice began to return, a start had been made at solving many of their problems. In response to VFW pleading, a federal veteran's welfare agency to be known as the U.S. Veterans Bureau was in the planning stages. It was shortly expected to handle all of the ex-serviceman's needs for hospitalization, compensation, pensions, and training. In addition, Public Law 178 now provided that disabled veterans would receive compensation and vocational training.

The VFW was not content to rest with these victories, however. They knew that without their intervention, the veterans' problems would increase, not decrease, with time. They knew that veterans' problems could be measured by an old formula: the more time that had elapsed since the end of the war, the greater the public apathy—the more apathy, the dimmer the chance of getting federal assistance.

To help veterans with their inevitable problems in getting entitlements, the VFW established three committees at the 1919 National Encampment in Providence, Rhode Island. The first committee, formed to stay abreast of legislative issues, was headed by Bertram E. Snodgrass. As part of this committee, Edward H. Hale, a disabled World War I veteran, was appointed to lobby on behalf of veteran's legislation on a day-to-day basis. A second committee was formed to investigate the actions of the War Risk Insurance Bureau and the Federal Vocational Education Board—the section of the federal government's rehabilitation program that retrained disabled veterans to give them marketable job skills. Named to this committee were three attorneys and National Judge Advocate General Royal C. Johnson, a Congressman from South Dakota. A third committee was established to handle claims against the War Risk Insurance Act and Vocational Training Bureau. This committee, to be based in Washington, D.C., was headed by National Senior Vice Commander-in-Chief Jack Singer. Within a year, Singer's committee would evolve into a permanent Washington office known as the National Service Bureau. With the establishment of this bureau, the VFW became the first veteran's organization to maintain a permanent office in the nation's capital.

Besides working to safeguard existing entitlements, the VFW also began work at the 1919 Encampment to secure new ones. Many members felt that World War I veterans should be entitled to a cash bonus to equalize the wartime difference between their wages of a dollar a day and the inflated wages civilian factory workers had earned. Another proposal, which was shortly abandoned, was financial assistance for veterans who wanted to purchase homes and farms. And finally, now that passage of Crago's Widows and Orphans Pension Bill was almost assured, the VFW decided it was time to try to liberalize pension benefits for the veterans

Thanks to the VFW and other veteran's organizations, World War veterans like these troops parading in New York on February 26, 1919, returned home to a warmer reception than veterans of the Spanish American War had. (National Archives)

themselves. Under existing pension laws, veterans who had served ninety days or more and were prevented from earning a living by a disability were entitled to compensation at these monthly rates: $12 for a disability of 25 percent; $18 for 50 percent; and $40 for total disability. But due to the military's sloppy and inadequate record keeping, many veterans could not verify their eligibility for a service-connected claim. Consequently, the VFW contended that pensions should be paid to veterans who had either service- *or* non-service-connected disabilities. All three of these entitlement issues were referred to the legislative committee.

While it was plotting its strategy for the next year, the VFW missed what Robert Woodside called "an outstanding opportunity for nationwide publicity." It failed to send a representative to New York to greet the 38th Division—Woodside's unit—on its return from France. Since fully 3,000 of the VFW's current 15,000 members belonged to the 38th's Rock of the Marne Post, this was a tactical blunder. Woodside's comment about the incident later was "Naturally, I was very sore." Sore or not, Woodside subsequently accepted an appointment as the VFW's National Chief of Staff.

By the end of the 1919 Encampment, the VFW's course for the next decade or so had been set. The VFW would continue its aggressive pursuit of entitlements for veterans while remaining true to its promise to remember fallen comrades and their families. The VFW would also continue to advocate for military preparedness, even though the events of the "War to End War" were swiftly fading from the nation's memory. And like the progressive organization it was, the VFW would continue to make internal changes that would help it become a more effective veteran's organization.

ORGANIZATIONAL CHANGES AND GROWTH

"How ya gona keep 'em on the farm,
After they've seen 'Paree'?"

This question, posed by a popular song of the era, was a quandary not only for the families of World War I veterans, but also for the VFW. Thousands of servicemen returned from overseas with a restlessness that home could not cure. Uncertain just where they wanted to find their place in peacetime society, many of them wandered around the country. To gather them into existing VFW posts or to form new ones with them as members was an unending task. And no doubt, veterans who did not settle down and establish a permanent residence robbed the VFW of some of the power it would otherwise have had at the polls. Still, in the years immediately following the war, membership in the VFW soared.

At the 1920 Annual Encampment in Washington, D.C., it was announced that membership had risen to over 20,000 members in five hundred posts, five times that of five years before. A year later, membership swelled to 60,000, and the VFW could claim posts in Andernach and Coblenz, Germany, thanks to the members of the U.S. 5th Infantry who established them. Growth slowed somewhat over the next few years, peaking at 67,749 in 1925, then inexplicably dropping to 62,840 in 1926. In 1927, the VFW scored a coup when the Greater Atlanta Post No. 300 presented a VFW Honorary Membership Medal to Charles Lindbergh upon his return from his historic solo flight across the Atlantic. The presentation, in front of 5,000 guests at the National Press Club, was the first honorary medal presented to Lindbergh by any veteran's organization. During the 1927 to 1928 term of Commander-in-Chief Frank Strayer, membership bounced back. Nine thousand members were added that year, bringing the total to 69,976 members in 924 posts.

Although these members of the Harlem Hellfighters, 369th Regiment, as well as other black World War I veterans, were eligible for the VFW, they could join only all-black posts. (National Archives)

As membership grew, the VFW found it necessary to expand its leadership proportionately. Three times over the course of four years, it restructured its interim governing body, the National Council of Administration. Until 1920, the National Council had consisted of three members—one from each of the districts into which the country was divided—plus the Commander-in-Chief and the adjutant general as ex-officio members. At the 1920 Encampment, the delegates raised the number of the council's members-at-large to five. The following year, the delegates to the Annual Encampment voted to add five more members to the Council: the Senior and Junior Vice Commanders-in-Chief, Quartermaster General, Judge Advocate General, and the Inspector General. And in 1924, the National Council of Administration again underwent some changes. Its members were now to be allotted according to a district plan and membership was expanded to fourteen members plus the national officers.

As another result of its tremendous growth in membership, the VFW found it necessary to establish a level of leadership and authority midway between the national and local levels. At the 1920 Encampment in Washington, D.C., the delegates adopted a new set of by-laws that provided that all posts within each state be organized into a *department*. This department would be headed by a state commander elected by delegates from those posts. The new arrangement would improve communication between the posts in each state and enable posts within a state to use their clout jointly when necessary.

Once departments were authorized, the VFW wasted no time in organizing them. Departments were established in all states in which membership requirements had been met, and provisional departments were established in the other states. Robert Woodside, Commander-in-Chief for the 1920 to 1921 year, and Chief of Staff Charles A. Pemburn personally organized many of the departments. Woodside sent Pemburn down the eastern coast as far as Georgia. "I followed along behind him, completing the organizing of the new posts he had started, until I caught up with him. He then returned to National Headquarters while I proceeded across the continent via the southern route organizing Departments and Provisional Departments as I went. I returned to the east coast by the northern route." It was the first coast-to-coast trip ever undertaken by a National Commander.

The first department established was the department of Washington, D.C. It was composed of five posts. Colonel George L. Tait, Postmaster of the District of Columbia, was the Department Commander and Edward H. Hale, Director of the VFW's Washington Office, was its Adjutant.

As membership continued to grow all across the country, it became apparent that the National Head-

quarters needed a more centralized location to effectively administer posts in the midwest and west. The need for faster mail service between the western states and headquarters staff was especially pressing.

During the early 1920s, some of the VFW leaders recommended that the National Headquarters be moved from 32 Union Square in New York City to the nation's capital. But the majority felt it should remain in New York, in a building owned by National Adjutant General Walter I. Joyce. In 1922, however, the National Council of Administration overrode those feelings and approved a search for a midwestern city to which the National Headquarters could be moved.

On June 26, 1923, Adjutant General Reuel Elton advised the posts that a suitable city had been found. With only two of the twelve members of the Council of Administration in opposition, he directed a move to Kansas City, Kansas. *Foreign Service,* the VFW national magazine, was to move along with the headquarters and finally find a permanent residence. The magazine had originally been published in Pittsburgh, then moved its editorial offices to New York City in 1918. In 1920, it had been moved to Washington, D.C., as part of the failed attempt to move the National Headquarters there, and in 1921, it had returned to New York City.

An informational flyer distributed to all posts in 1923 showed that Kansas City had fourteen trunk and thirty-two subsidiary railroad lines on which four hundred trains ran through the city daily. Mail deliveries to and from the most distant parts of the country took under seventy-two hours. The city boasted that it had "every known facility for conducting large business enterprises." Equally enticing was the state of Kansas's offer of space in the Soldiers and Sailors Memorial Building, then under construction.

The third floor of the Soldiers and Sailors Memorial Building was still not finished in 1924, when the National Headquarters completed its move to Kansas City, Kansas. Consequently, the VFW set up temporary headquarters in a two-story brick structure near its future home. Furniture for the new offices

Facts You Should Know About Kansas City

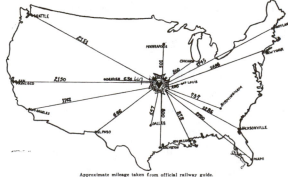

Approximate mileage taken from official railway guide.

There are 14 trunk and 32 subsidiary lines run 400 trains through Kansas City daily. Interurban lines radiate in all directions. Under 72 hour mail and express service with most distant parts of the United States, Kansas City contains every known facility for conducting large business enterprises.

At the Seattle encampment, the Council was authorized to move National Headquarters from New York to a more central location. Advices from the Adjutant General on June 26, 1923, state that only 2 of the 12 members of the Council are opposing the move to Kansas City.

The great majority of the Council favor putting National Headquarters, the "Heart of the V. F. W.", in Kansas City, the "Heart of the U. S. A."

Do you stand back of your Council or against it?

NATIONAL V. F. W. HEADQUARTERS IN THE NEW MEMORIAL BUILDING, KANSAS CITY, KANSAS

The entire second floor front, 10,000 square feet, donated to V. F. W., with a large club room on first floor front, and 20,000 square feet in basement.

In the heart of the business district.

1500 feet from City Hall, Court House, and Post Office; 5 blocks from three depots; in the new Civic Center, and close to all street car lines. No cost whatever to the V. F. W.

MEMORIAL BUILDING, KANSAS CITY, KANS.

was donated by Past Commander-in-Chief Karling, who was a furniture manufacturer in Kansas City.

During the first year the National Headquarters was in Kansas City, all went well and thirty new posts were instituted in Kansas and the neighboring states. Then a board of trustees assumed administrative control of the headquarters premises. The trustees first demanded the VFW contribute toward the building's maintenance. Next they demanded the VFW emblem be removed from the top of the flagpole in front of the building. It made no difference to the trustees that the flagpole had been erected by a local VFW post. The disagreement over the VFW emblem continued until the VFW moved its headquarters across the state line to Kansas City, Missouri, on January 1, 1930. There the VFW took up residence in a twelve-story building at Broadway and 34th Street, which it still occupies and has owned since 1946.

One final organizational change instituted during this period was the inauguration of the Military Order of the Cootie of the United States, an auxiliary whose primary purpose was fun and levity. The founders of this auxiliary began recruiting members at the 1920 Encampment, then during the year worked out a constitution and by-laws. At the 1921 Encampment, delegates and officers of the Executive Committee voted to allow the Cooties to become an auxiliary of the VFW on two conditions: 1) a member had to be in good standing in the VFW before he could be eligible for membership in the Cooties; 2) the Cootie organization had to agree to procure a suitable badge and divest itself of the junk jewelry with which many members decorated their uniforms. Fred Madden was elected the first National Commander of the Military Order of the Cootie. (For more information about the Military Order of the Cootie, see Chapter 9.)

This building at the corner of Broadway and 34th Street in Kansas City, Missouri, has served as VFW National Headquarters since January 1, 1930.

ENTITLEMENTS

From its inception, the VFW had taken it for granted that veterans should, by law, be entitled to certain benefits. But the federal government did not officially acknowledge this self-evident truth until the 1920s. In that decade, the government took several actions that signaled it was finally ready to take veterans' entitlements seriously. First, on August 9, 1921, the government transferred administration of veterans' entitlements from the Treasury Department to a separate Veterans Bureau.* This move, made after several years of pleading from the VFW, meant that for the first time there were government officials whose job was to focus full time on veterans' problems. Later, the VFW helped convince Congress to approve the establishment of approximately one hundred regional offices of the Veterans Bureau throughout the country. This was accomplished through passage of the World War Veterans Act of 1924.

The second way the federal government officially recognized the needs of veterans was by forming Veterans Affairs Committees in both the House of Representatives and the Senate. At the request of VFW Commander-in-Chief Lloyd M. Brett, in 1924 President Calvin Coolidge recommended to Congress that these committees be established. Subsequently, two VFW members—Congressmen Royal C. Johnson and Lamar Jeffers—helped obtain final enactment of a House Committee on World War Veterans Affairs. Congressman Johnson was named the first chairman of the new committee. The VFW also led the campaign to set up a Senate Veterans Affairs Committee. At the urging of Legislative Chairman Edwin S. Bettelheim, Senator Morris Sheppard of Texas agreed to sponsor a bill to this effect. The measure passed early in 1925 and the Senate Veterans Committee was formed as a sub-committee of the Senate Finance Committee.

Although the formation of the Veterans Bureau and Veterans Affairs Committees now provided the VFW with regular forums to air its grievances, gaining new entitlements was still far from automatic. Of the many battles the VFW fought for entitlements during this period, none was more controversial or hotly contested than the struggle for some kind of bonus or "adjusted compensation" to offset the economic hardship many World War I veterans suffered as a result of serving their country. An article in the November 1921 *Foreign Service* magazine summarized the VFW's rationale in pressing for this measure:

"The word Bonus is badly chosen. Recognizing this, efforts are being made to circumvent those effects by titling it "Adjusted Compensation." The VFW's fight is based on the young men who were drafted and were selected for two groups. One to fight for 'War Wages' of a dollar a day and the others to work in occupations that assisted the war effort and were paid as much as $15 a day. These decisions as to who went and who stayed were established by committees appointed by the government for this explicit purpose. If married, a private had $15 a month deducted for an allotment to his dependents and up to $6.60 for life insurance. This left him a grand total of $8.40 with which to purchase his personal toilet articles, cigarettes and anything else he desired. That this country did not deal equitably between the two groups is all there is to it. No discussion can change this basic fact. The time has come, not to stop treating the wounded and physically disabled, but to insist that something be done for the economically injured too. The need is just as great. . . . They have suffered and now are suffering from the consequences of economic dislocation due to war and the unequal economic treatment given to those two classes mentioned. Economic readjustment for these men is not charity, but justice."

To secure passage of this "adjusted compensation" bill, the VFW worked tirelessly to drum up grassroots support and backed two hundred attempts to introduce the bill into Congress. During the administrations of both Warren G. Harding and Calvin Coolidge, the VFW came tantalizingly close to victory, only to have the bill vetoed at the last minute by the president.

During Harding's administration, Commander-in-Chief Robert Woodside and other VFW members helped publicize the need for a bonus by joining with 75,000 veterans in a parade through New York City.

---

* The Veterans Bureau was replaced by the Veterans Administration on July 3, 1930.

This October 1921 parade was later dubbed the "Petition in Boots" by the press. The VFW's National Legislative Committee also did its part. After being reorganized and made a separate division from the National Service Bureau in May 1921, the legislative committee appointed Legislative Liaison Deputies for each state and legislative district and empowered the deputies to work directly through their own Congressmen. This meant that the officials who passed laws affecting veterans now had to work closely with men they depended on for re-election. Working with their Congressmen, in 1921 the committee members helped draft the "First Sweet Bill" (better known as the Bonus Bill). The committee members also personally contacted fellow veterans to ask them to encourage their Congressmen to support the measure.

When the Sweet Bill failed to pass the Congress, the VFW and its National Legislative Committee tried new tactics. The legislative committee organized VFW members into a "Committee of 10,000" whose sole purpose was to solicit public support of the "Bonus Drive." Again in 1922, the legislative committee spearheaded the VFW Bonus Drive and asked VFW members and other veterans to join a mass campaign to gain public support. During the drive, hundreds of applications to become members of the Committee of 10,000 swamped the office of Legislative Committee Chairman Edwin Bettelheim, prompting him to remark, "Instead of the Committee of 10,000, it should be called the Committee of 100,000." Many of the applications, at least from VFW members, came on an application form clipped from an issue of the *Foreign Service* magazine that carried this article:

"CAN YOU BEAT IT?"

"The British Government owes the Government of the United States some billions of dollars borrowed from us during the war. None of the principal has ever been paid and only a pittance of the interest due has ever been collected. The United States owed England $35,000,000 for the transporting of

American Soldiers to France in British ships. The British presented a bill the other day and the government in Washington promptly paid it. In the meantime thousands of our disabled soldiers are neglected and in want. CAN YOU BEAT IT?"

To help the VFW with its letter-writing campaign, many businesses, civic organizations, boards of trade, and Chambers of Commerce gave part of their clerical force to local VFW posts. Chambers of Commerce, from coast to coast, pushed other chambers within their organization to support the Bonus Bill by writing letters to their Congressmen and working to swing public sentiment to favor this bill. Some Disabled American Veterans Chapters requested forms so they too could be a part of the Committee of 10,000. Many others, both individuals and organizations, telegraphed the VFW wishing them success in this venture.

Despite this tremendous groundswell of support, President Harding remained firmly opposed to the bonus. According to his reasoning, "It [the bonus] established the very dangerous precedent of creating a treasury covenant which puts a burden, variously estimated between four and five million dollars, upon the American people, not to discharge an obligation—which the government must always pay—but to bestow a bonus which the soldiers themselves, while serving in the World War, did not expect." Thus, on the single occasion during Harding's term when a bonus bill managed to pass both houses of Congress, the president vetoed the bill. The House then overrode the veto, but the Senate sustained it.

Harding's successor, Calvin Coolidge, was equally opposed to adjusted compensation. When the bill again passed Congress in 1924, Coolidge vetoed it, objecting that "We owe no bonus to able bodied veterans of the World War. The first duty of every citizen is to the nation. The veteran of the World War performed this first duty. To confer upon them a cash consideration, or its equivalent for performing this first duty is unjustified. It is not justified when considered in the interest of the whole people; it is not justified when considered alone on its own merits. . . . Patriotism which is paid for is not patriotism."

By this time, however, Congress had changed its collective mind about the merits of the Bonus Bill. Immediately after receiving official word of the President's veto, the House voted in favor of passage by 317 to 78. On May 18, 1924, the Senate also overrode the bill by a vote of 59 to 26. In both cases the margin was well above the two-thirds majority needed to override. The bill, the Veterans Adjusted Compensation Act, awarded each veteran an endowment of $1.25 a day for overseas service and $1.00 a day for stateside duty. The endowment carried a 4 percent compound interest and was payable in twenty years.

For the VFW, these terms spelled only partial victory. Many World War I veterans needed immediate funds, not a piece of paper redeemable in twenty years. Because some veterans doubted they would live to receive their endowment, the bonus was quickly nicknamed the "Tombstone Bonus."

For the rest of the decade and well into the next, the VFW fought for at least a partial cash disbursement for those in dire financial straits. Chapter 4 details this fight and its outcome.

Closely related to the VFW's struggle for passage of the Bonus Bill was its drive to make war unprofitable for business and industry. The VFW strongly believed that those who made millions off the men who faced the enemy's guns, wire, and gas for a dollar a day should be stopped. Their targets were the manufacturers, bankers, and other suppliers of war materials to the government. A champion for the VFW's cause emerged in the person of Congressman Royal Johnson of South Dakota, who was also active in the Bonus Bill fight.

Johnson had been a member of Congress when war was declared and had, in fact, voted against its declaration. Once the declaration had passed, however, he resigned from Congress and enlisted in the Army as a private. He returned wearing the Distinguished Service Cross for valor. After Johnson's discharge, he was again elected to the House. There he led the crusade to outlaw war. One of his strategies

aimed at making war less attractive to business and industry was to propose a universal draft that would conscript labor and capital as well as manpower. Although Johnson's bill did not pass, by supporting it, the VFW served notice to one and all that it favored a universal draft. From Johnson's proposal also came the VFW's stance to "Tax the Profit out of War," a position that the VFW has maintained ever since.

Yet another way the VFW attempted to reduce the economic inequities associated with war was to continue its campaign to strengthen veteran's job preference. The VFW's contention that veterans *should* have this preference had many precedents. After the Revolutionary War, George Washington, General of the Armies and the country's first president, used patronage to ensure that the men who had served under him found jobs. He appointed them to federal posts. Following the Civil War, the Grand Army of the Republic exerted political pressure to secure veteran's preference through executive orders, directives, and appointments.

In 1865, the first legislation regarding veteran's preference was passed. The act ruled that "Persons honorably discharged from the military or naval service by reason of disability resulting from wounds or sickness incurred in the line of duty, shall be preferred for appointments to civil offices, provided they are found to possess the business capacity necessary for the proper discharge of the duties of such offices." The Pendleton Civil Service Act of 1883 went one step further by establishing the U.S. Civil Service Commission and Merit System in Federal Employment. The Pendleton Act also included provisions relating to retention of veterans in federal employment.

When thousands of veterans were unable to find work after World War I, it was clear to the VFW that these acts were inadequate. At the 1921 Encampment in Detroit, the delegates adopted a resolution that urged "That veterans be placed on the Civil Service List ahead of all others and no other persons be appointed until no veteran remains on the list." It went on to say that a veteran should be promoted ahead of all others in the same grade.

On March 3, 1923, President Harding issued an Executive Order calling for veteran's preference. Basically, it went a step further than previous Acts by stipulating in stronger wording that government agencies would adhere to a stricter policy of veteran's preference in hiring and job retention. Despite this measure, by 1928 there was still widespread unemployment among veterans, particularly among those over forty. In fact, the situation was worsening for many veterans as federal agencies across the nation reduced their staffs in the wake of increasing mechanization and economic reversals. In violation of the 1923 Executive Order, veterans were often *not* retained, and nepotism and political favoritism most always worked to the disadvantage of the veteran.

In the wake of all these difficulties, all the major veteran's groups sent delegations to President Coolidge to protest that the Civil Service Commission was negligent in carrying out the 1923 Executive Order. As a result of a conference held shortly after, Congressman Hamilton Fish, Jr., a member of the VFW, introduced a measure that would make the provisions of that order law.

On March 6, 1928, Edwin S. Bettelheim, Jr., the VFW Legislative Committee chairman, testified in favor of the bill before a Congressional committee hearing. After both houses passed the bill, the chairman accompanied Congressman Fish to the White House to urge Coolidge to sign the bill. But because the president felt the bill was flawed, he decided instead to create a committee to study it further.

That same day, the VFW legislative representative appeared before the president's commission with the VFW's recommendations about veteran's preference. The VFW asked that five points be automatically added to the Civil Service score of any veteran, and an additional five to that of a disabled veteran. It also recommended that wounded and disabled veterans be placed on a separate roster from which positions of guard, watchman, guide, or information booth employee would be filled. Each of these jobs, unless it involved the protection of government funds or required the presence of Army Guards,

should be offered to a veteran before it was offered to any other applicant. Further, no examinations except of character, habits, and evidence of military service should be required. Included in the VFW proposal was a recommendation that no non-veteran could be appointed while a veteran-preferred eligible remained on the list. These same preferences should apply to the wife and widowed mother of a veteran who was too disabled to work himself. The VFW proposal also contained strong wording as to how the veteran would be promoted, disciplined, or retained. It even suggested court action against supervisors who violated any of these veterans' rights.

After the study commission had digested all of the VFW's suggestions, it reported favorably to the president. Coolidge then issued a new Executive Order on March 2, 1929, which contained all of the VFW guidelines. Unfortunately, however, Congress would not pass a true Veteran Preference Act until 1944.

At the same time the VFW was backing legislation that chipped away at the returning veterans' economic handicaps, it also devoted its attention to the problems of veterans with physical handicaps and other medical problems. For example, the organization threw its support behind the Spanish American War Pension Bill that had been introduced by Montana Congressman Scott Leavitt and Colorado Senator Rice W. Means, a former VFW Commander-in-Chief. This bill liberalized existing Spanish American War veterans' benefits and increased hospital benefits for all veterans. It became Public Law 166 on May 1, 1926. The organization also strongly advocated for the New Johnson Act, a bill sponsored by Congressman Royal Johnson, Chairman of the House Committee on World War Veterans Affairs. When the Act passed on July 2, 1926, it liberalized and increased existing benefits. It also called for the construction of more hospital facilities.

Much of the work the VFW accomplished on behalf of veterans with medical problems was handled by the National Service Bureau in Washington, D.C. This was the office the VFW had opened in 1919 for the sole purpose of assisting veterans with claims against the War Insurance Act, which had covered them against injury or disability during the war. In 1924, when the World War Disability Allowance replaced the War Insurance Act, the Service Bureau continued to press for claims under the new rules. Under this new Allowance, disabled servicemen were entitled either to rehabilitative services to help them find a useful place in society, or to pensions if they were not employable.

During this period, a veteran had three courses of action if he wanted to make a claim. He could hire an attorney to handle it for him, he could ask the Red Cross to attempt to secure a settlement, or he could use the free services of the National Service Bureau.

For most veterans, hiring an attorney was out of the question. Historically, many claim lawyers had demanded exorbitant fees, which had to be paid out of the claimant's settlement. In 1924, the World War Veterans Act put an end to this practice by establishing a fee of ten dollars for legal handling of claims. But once most of the profit had been taken out of claims cases, many attorneys shied away from taking them. Consequently, the VFW's Service Bureau and other private organizations that charged no fees for their services were swamped with requests.

In the early years of the Service Bureau's existence, it had only three employees to handle the hundreds of claims that flooded in: a director, a claims examiner, and a stenographer. This small group was highly effective. During the two years that Edward Hale, the Bureau's first director, headed the office, over $300,000 in claims was recovered for veterans.

Hale's successor, Robert S. Handy, was especially adept at getting claims settled quickly. Handy would personally take a veteran's claim to the U.S. Veterans Bureau and follow it through to its settlement. This personal handling cut through the government red tape that otherwise literally slowed down the settlement. (The expression "red tape" originated from the Veterans Bureau practice of rolling up submitted claim forms, securing them with red tape, and stacking them in the basement for processing at a later date.

During a typical period between March and August 1921, the Veterans Bureau received 1,225 claims and settled only 616.)

Beginning in 1928, veterans of the Navy and Marines had their own VFW representative. That year, Commander-in-Chief Frank Strayer appointed Charles E. Weickhardt, a twenty-eight-year Navy veteran, to handle the problems of these ex-servicemen.

Because the Service Bureau worked so closely with the U.S. Veterans Bureau throughout the claims process, it was natural that the Service Bureau should become involved with other aspects of the federal agency's work. For example, the VFW Service Bureau sent "Field Veteran Welfare Squads" to check on the medical care needy veterans were receiving. These squads often worked with other veteran's organizations and the Red Cross, but many times the entire squad was composed of VFW members. After Congress passed the Relief Act of 1924, which entitled veterans of any war to receive medical treatment at designated government treatment centers and reimbursement of travel expenses incurred in getting to the treatment center, these squads primarily double checked that care was being given as promised.

The Service Bureau also worked hard to hold the Veterans Bureau to promises it made about veterans' entitlements. In 1921, the Veterans Bureau announced it was ready to work for a pension for any man who had a ten percent or greater handicap, and to see that hospital treatment or rehabilitation training was given to any man who had a combat-related disability. Subsequently, the VFW claims representatives processed veterans claims and filed for those who needed to establish their disabilities. They also submitted applications for veterans who required or desired vocational training. At best, the program was only minimally successful.

Throughout the decade, the VFW amply demonstrated that it was committed not only to securing entitlements for its own members, but for all American veterans—including those who were ineligible for VFW membership because they could not meet the "honorable service" requirement. The VFW believed that every veteran was entitled at a minimum to justice and humane treatment. Consequently, when complaints surfaced about harsh and unjust treatment of Courts-Martial prisoners at Leavenworth, Kansas, the VFW got involved. In 1924, Adjutant General Reuel Elton, Department of Missouri Commander Herb Snodgrass, and Mrs. H.H. McCleur of War Mothers of America conducted an investigation. They found some glaring abuses of justice and of normal humane treatment. The VFW and the War Mothers Organization asked the War Department for a review of these cases. To back up their request, they submitted a petition bearing 2.5 million signatures which called for a review. Secretary of War John W. Weeks ordered an investigation of men being held under unduly severe sentences. Many of these cases were then reviewed and the sentences lessened.

PATRIOTISM AND PREPAREDNESS

For the VFW, patriotism and preparedness have always gone hand-in-hand. To reduce the relationship to the simplest of terms: True patriots should keep the best interests of their country at heart, and it is obviously in a country's best interest to be ever ready to defend its citizens and principles when threatened. Consequently, any patriotic organization *should* advocate for preparedness.

After the war, the United States took several steps aimed at preventing war which incidentally weakened the nation's preparedness. In 1922, for example, the United States and Japan signed a naval agreement limiting the number of ships each would produce. Then in 1924, Great Britain, Japan, France, Italy, and the United States signed an agreement which set quotas for the number of warships each nation was allowed.

While urging Congress to adhere to these limitations, the VFW also strongly cautioned against disarmament. At the 1921 Encampment, the delegates opposed any disarmament that was not consistent with "the permanent integrity of the United States." They instructed their Adjutant General to see that a copy of the resolution was forwarded to President Harding. In 1923, the organization encouraged support for a citizen army composed of a strengthened Citizens Military Training Corps, Reserve Officers Training Corps, and National Guard Units. And at its National Encampment that year, the VFW passed a resolution calling for a standing army of not less than 125,000 men.

As the decade wore on, the VFW adjusted upward its estimate of how strong the armed forces needed to be in order to be adequately prepared. In 1925, the delegates at the annual encampment passed a motion that stated that the VFW was against any move to lower the strength of the armed forces, National Guard, ROTC, Citizen's Military Training Corps, or the Reserve Corps. By 1926, the encampment delegates were calling for more air power, and resolved "to support the increasing of the efficiency of the Air Corps. . . including the procurement of additional aircraft, the improvement of facilities and the providing for sufficient personnel." The 1927 Encampment went on record as supporting a Navy "Second to None," and two years later the delegates returned to the subject of air power. At the 1929 Encampment in St. Paul, Minnesota, delegates endorsed the program of the American Society for the Promotion of Aviation. Its goal was to organize aviation clubs throughout America for the purpose of training thousands of young men who would form the nucleus of the "nation's strongest arm of defense in event of war."

Besides recommending ways for the United States to increase the strength of her armed forces, the VFW also pointed out ways her strength was weakened. Chief among these was the lack of a universal draft. The VFW had no sympathy with men who had evaded military service, and excoriated them in the pages of *Foreign Service* magazine. To the VFW, it was bad enough that many of these men had earned exorbitant wages while veterans in the trenches lived on a dollar a day. But to add insult to injury, after the war, many draft dodgers claimed military service and disability as they panhandled money from the unsuspecting. At the 1925 Encampment, the VFW also condemned the attitude that gave rise to a saying, popular with several peace societies of that era, commonly referred to as the "Slackers' Oath": "Go to war if you want to, but know this: We have pledged ourselves not to give you our children, not to encourage nor nurse your soldiers, not to knit a sock or roll a bandage nor drive a truck nor make a war speech nor buy a bond."

Beginning in 1917 and throughout the decade, every VFW National Encampment called for some form of universal military training. The resolution submitted by Post 111 of Kansas City, Kansas, in 1928 was typical. In it, the post described the benefits universal service would provide both the nation and its youth:

1. Physical and mental development.
2. Discipline, very much needed in this day and generation, to instill a respect for law and order in minds of youth.
3. Inculcation of patriotism and love for the flag and the nation it represents.
4. The Americanism of the different elements which compose American life.
5. Democratization of our youth, making rich and poor alike learn, shoulder to shoulder, to perform our country's service when needed.
6. Vocational training, fitting the man to do the thing for which he is best fitted.
7. Teaching the laws of hygiene and sanitation, so that when he is called into service or in peaceful pursuit, he knows how to protect himself against the ravages of disease.
8. Training will purify the blood of the youth of our land and make them splendid

citizens and proud to live in the United States.

Unfortunately, the VFW's warnings about the need for military preparedness once again went unheeded. By the time World War II arrived, our national defense posture was in shambles. It was in such disarray that humorist Will Rogers commented that you can always tell when the next war will be by the lack of preparedness of our military.

While the VFW fought its losing battle to change the government's attitude toward preparedness, it was also working to change the average American's attitude toward his country. In 1921, the organization instituted its Americanism Program, which was aimed at revitalizing patriotism and love of the American way of life. The program's first public action was to establish a holiday that the VFW hoped would counter the Communists' annual May Day rallies. This new holiday, called "Americanization Day," was to be held on the 27th of April each year. A World War I captain named Walter I. Joyce was appointed to chair the first Americanization Day program. To draw attention to the program, Joyce and his assistants staged a flag parade at the 1921 National Encampment in Detroit. It was, according to contemporary onlookers, the largest such parade in the history of the country. Each person in the entire line of march carried a flag. The following year, the VFW again held a huge Americanization Day parade, this time at the 1922 National Encampment in Seattle, and with Vice President Calvin Coolidge in attendance.

In addition to founding Americanization Day, the Americanism Program also played a significant role in the campaign to have the "Star-Spangled Banner" adopted as the official national anthem. By the 1929 Encampment in St. Paul, Walter I. "Daddy" Joyce could report that 4 million of the targeted 14 million signatures had been gathered on petitions. By the time these petitions were presented to the House Judiciary Committee in 1930, another million signatures had been added. In addition, the VFW was able to present evidence that at least 15 million other Americans supported the measure. Bowing to this overwhelming sentiment, in 1931 Congress would declare the "Star-Spangled Banner" our national anthem.

Closely related to the VFW's Americanism Program was its nationwide campaign based on Teddy Roosevelt's old idea of "Taking the Hyphen out of America"—or converting those who regarded themselves as only part American into 100 percent Americans. In early 1921, the organization launched its drive under the slogan "One Flag, One Country and One Language." To reach this goal, the VFW advocated that immigrants be naturalized, only English be spoken, and foreign language newspapers be ousted. Eventually, the organization collected over 150,000 signatures on petitions urging the government to adopt this program to "Americanize America."

The Department of Michigan's Naturalization Program, which assisted immigrants in gaining their citizenship, received especially high marks for its effectiveness. In recognition of its achievement, in 1925 the Michigan State Council on Immigrant Education invited the department to membership. In 1927, the VFW's position on naturalization was in the national spotlight when Americanism Director Victor Devereaux was invited to speak to a Congressional hearing about the need to register aliens. Because of his testimony on this and other occasions, Devereaux and the VFW are credited with the enactment of a measure under which more than 5 million non-citizens were registered.

LOOKING AFTER ITS OWN

In the 1920s, the VFW extended a helping hand many times to those in need, not only to veterans and their families, but also to their fellow Americans. For example, in 1927 the VFW presented a check for

$10,000 to President Coolidge to aid in the relief of Mississippi Valley Flood victims. During this same period, the VFW established a nationwide program to help disabled and needy veterans (the Buddy Poppy program) and founded a home for veterans' widows and orphans. And on two major occasions, it helped ensure that fallen comrades would not be forgotten.

The Buddy Poppy Program. The Buddy Poppy program, the program that ultimately provided jobs and financial assistance for disabled and disadvantaged veterans, had a convoluted beginning. It began as the brainchild of Madame E. Guerin, who first conceived the idea of selling artificial poppies to help orphans and the needy in war-torn France. In 1920, the fledgling American Legion agreed to handle sales of the poppy in the United States, but the follow-

An early Buddy Poppy sale

ing year voted to give up the poppy in favor of the daisy, an "American flower." The "Poppy Lady" (Guerin) then contacted VFW Adjutant General Reuel Elton, and the VFW took over the sale of the poppy in this country.

In 1922, the VFW conducted the first nationwide poppy sale in the United States. The poppies were purchased through Madame Guerin's organization and the proceeds used to help the citizens of France. Then in 1923, the VFW opened a factory in Pittsburgh and began paying disabled veterans to make the poppies. In 1924, the VFW held its first national sale with American-made poppies, and for the first time all profits remained in the U.S. to help rehabilitate disabled veterans. That year, Navy Captain Homer Carroll, VFW Service Officer and Rehabilitation Representative of the Admiral Peary Post in Washington, D.C., decorated President Coolidge with the first poppy ever made by a disabled American serviceman.

On April 25, 1926, the U.S. Patent Office granted the VFW the trade-mark of "Buddy Poppy," protecting this symbol of veterans' sacrifices from encroachment by profit-oriented enterprises. Chapter 12 continues the history of the Buddy Poppy program up to the present day.

The VFW National Home. During the 1920s, the "Poppy Lady" was not the only woman to play a significant behind-the-scenes role in VFW activities. The visionary behind the establishment of the VFW's National Home for widows and orphans was also a woman. Her name was Amy Ross and she was just 23 years old the day she walked into the Detroit office of Clarence L. Candler, M.D., to propose her plan. As Candler, the Commander of the Department of Michigan Veterans of Foreign Wars listened, Ross explained her belief that the construction of a National Home would provide jobs for the thousands of employment-hungry veterans walking the streets of Detroit.

After Ross made her proposal in February 1922, the Military Order of the Cooties lost no time in championing the idea. The VFW as a whole was also en-

thusiastic about building the home, but for lack of funds could not give the project their go-ahead. Then, in a fairy-tale turn of events, a millionaire cattleman named Corey Spencer offered the VFW a homesite of nearly 500 acres near Eaton Rapids, Michigan. The VFW's National Council of Administration accepted the offer in late 1924. Sadly, Amy Ross never saw the "Child City" she had envisioned. She died just fifteen days before the Council gave its approval.

In March 1924, the widow and six children of a retired Army sergeant became the National Home's first residents. By 1928, there were 45 children in the Home and six cottages on the grounds in various stages of completion. That year, the Home's trustees hired its first full-time director, a Missourian named Charles Adams. Under Adams's direction, the Home finished out the 1920s with 60 children in residence.

For much of the decade, the National Home's growth went on amidst bitter controversy about who actually owned the property it occupied. That controversy and the subsequent story of the VFW National Home are detailed in Chapter 8.

The Unknown Soldier. By the end of World War I, about 116,516 American servicemen had lost their lives. To the members of the VFW, each of those men was far more than a faceless statistic: he was a comrade-in-arms. By the principles set out by the VFW's founding fathers, the organization was bound to honor the memories of these fallen heroes and ensure that their deeds were not forgotten. Needless to say, in the years following the war, the VFW concurred with the rising public sentiment that something needed to be done to memorialize the soldiers who had not come home.

In 1921, the federal government decided that the most suitable way to remember its fallen heroes was to follow the example of our allies, Great Britain, France, and Italy. Congress adopted a resolution calling for the selection of one unidentified soldier from World War I to be buried with full honors in Arlington National Cemetery. President Wilson signed this resolution on March 4, 1921, the last day of his term in office. The long and involved process of choosing the Unknown Soldier is neatly summed up by James Edward Peters in his book, *Arlington National Cemetery: Shrine to America's Heroes:*

"The Unknown was to be symbolic of all persons who had given their lives during that war. Every American could pay homage to this fallen soldier, believing him to be the son, husband, brother or friend who did not come home. To achieve this general feeling, it was imperative that there be no means to discover the soldier's actual identity. Even the revelation of the name of the cemetery from which he was chosen for re-interment might compromise the secrecy surrounding the unknown soldier's selection. So one candidate-unknown was chosen from each of the four American cemeteries in France. On October 22, 1921 each of the four bodies were exhumed and transported under honor guard to the City Hall at Chalons-sur-Marne, France for final random selection. During that night the honor guard shifted the positions of the four identical caskets so that no one—not even the Graves Registration detail—could differentiate between them. As a last guarantor of secrecy, all burial records of these four servicemen were destroyed. On October 24, Army Sergeant Edward F. Younger of

Sergeant Edward F. Younger placing a wreath at the Tomb of the Unknown Soldier. Younger was a member of Columbia Post No. 833 of Washington, D.C.

Chicago, who had been wounded in combat and highly decorated for valor, was given the honor of selecting the Unknown Soldier of World War I by placing a spray of white roses on one of the caskets. That spray of white roses accompanied the Unknown to Arlington and these flowers are buried with him. . . . The three remaining unknown soldiers were reinterred in the Muese-Argonne Cemetery in France while the chosen Unknown began his journey home, symbolic of those who could not make that journey."*

The Unknown's body was transported home on the *Olympia,* Admiral Dewey's flagship during the Spanish American War. On November 9, 1921, the *Olympia* docked at Washington, D.C. There it was met by a guard of honor and General of the Armies John J. Pershing, the Unknown's former commander. Pershing led the procession to the rotunda of the Capitol where the body would lie in state until Armistice Day, November 11th. During that twenty-four hour period, nearly 100,000 mourners paid their respects. When the guards closed the doors at midnight, many more were still outside.

Following the burial services at Arlington National Cemetery, President Harding conferred upon the Unknown the Congressional Medal of Honor and the Distinguished Service Cross. Representatives of America's allies also conferred upon him their nation's highest honors: the Victoria Cross of Great Britain, the Croix de Guerre of France, the Order of Leopold of Belgium, the Gold Medal of Bravery of Italy, and the highest honors of Romania, Poland, Cuba, and Czechoslovakia.

Following behind President Harding and General Pershing to the tomb was VFW Commander-in-Chief Woodside. At the VFW's National Encampment several months before, Woodside's organization had already conferred the rank of posthumous, honorary

National Aide, Medal of Honor Section, upon the Unknown Soldier and had also bestowed "a national decoration medal and insignia with dual ceremony upon this representative of our departed comrades." Now, in behalf of the Unknown's comrades-in-arms, Woodside placed upon the tomb a wreath symbolic of their caring and recognition of the honor awarded him.

Five years after the Unknown's interment in Arlington National Cemetery, Congress finally authorized completion of the monument. The fifty-ton, white marble monument has on its east side (facing Washington) three figures depicting Peace, Valor, and Victory. Its west side bears the solemn inscription:

HERE RESTS IN
HONORED GLORY
AN AMERICAN
SOLDIER
KNOWN BUT TO GOD

Following the interment of America's Unknown Soldier, the United States participated in a reciprocal ceremony on Memorial Day 1922 to decorate the grave of the French Unknown Soldier. Included in the U.S. delegation were two VFW members—National Adjutant General Reuel Elton and Captain Robert S. Cain of the Pennsylvania National Guard—as well as Myron T. Herrick, American Ambassador to France, and General Weygand. The former Allied Commander Marshall Foch was also in attendance. Comrades Cain and Elton, as guests of the French Government, later took part in similar ceremonies at other cemeteries and battlefields.

The VFW Siberian Expedition. Although the VFW wholeheartedly participated in the tribute to the Unknown Soldier, its part in the events leading up to the interment was relatively minor. The same cannot be said for the role the VFW played in what has become known as the "Polar Bear Expedition," a little-known but dramatic operation undertaken on behalf of

---

*   James Edward Peters, *Arlington National Cemetery: Shrine to America's Heroes* (Rockville, Md.: Woodbine House, 1986), p. 280.

In November 1929, Edwin S. Bettelheim, Jr., VFW Legislative Committee Chairman (second from right),
placed a wreath on the tomb of France's Unknown Soldier in the name of the VFW.
He was escorted by the Colorguard of Benjamin Franklin Post No. 605.

more than a hundred fallen comrades who would otherwise have been forgotten. To understand why the Polar Bear Expedition was needed, it is necessary to backtrack to the closing months of World War I:

In the latter half of 1918, the British and French requested America's assistance in fighting the Bolsheviks ("Reds") in Russia. The Bolsheviks were then attempting to seize power from Czar Nicholas, and the Allies thought America could help by guarding the Czar's supplies from the Reds. Exactly what connection the revolt in Russia was then believed to have with the conflict in Europe has now been forgotten. Some historians reason that the Allies feared that the Japanese might, after defecting from the Allied cause, join the Central Powers. Having switched their allegiance, the reasoning continued, they might have

tried to ship troops to the European Front via the Trans-Siberian Railroad. Other historians speculate that the Allies hoped to get the Czar's armies back into the war against Germany by guarding the supplies they were furnishing him.

Whatever the Allies' motivation for requesting that American troops be sent to Russia, the United States complied. Five thousand, five hundred American soldiers, 75 percent of them from Michigan, were formed into the American Expeditionary Forces, Northern Russia (AEFNR). These troops were detached from the 85th Division, and included the 339th Infantry Regiment, the First Battalion of the 310th Engineers, and the 337th Ambulance and Hospital Companies.

Dispatched to Northern Russia in the fall of 1918, the AEFNR stayed until they were pulled out in May 1919. During that time, they fought longer and more continuously than any other American unit in World War I, but their expedition was an exercise in futility. Significantly, the heaviest fighting and most of their casualties occurred some six months *after* the Armistice was signed. In all, 226 members of the AEFNR lost their lives, but because the War Department declared their service to have been strictly defensive, no combat ribbon was ever awarded.

The experiences Private Rory P. Rasmussen of Company H, 339th Infantry, described in his diary were typical:

"On September 14 we left Archangel on the Mickalczie. At 4 PM September 15 we landed at Onega on Onega River. Our barracks was a school house. We slept on the floor and did our cooking outdoors.

"On September 25, the enemy met us at daybreak, but were repulsed after 3 hours of fighting. One of our buddies was wounded, but one Bola (Bolshevik) killed and one captured. Continued guard duty until October 1st. We started out with 175 rounds of ammo. We walked over very frozen ground for 3 hours expecting to see the enemy until 5 when they shot at us. We lay on the ground fighting until 4 PM when we returned thru the woods to Chekuno. We had lost 6 men and 4 wounded.

"January 1st, the other half of the company fought the Bolos, four days, wounding lots of men. So cold that men froze their faces. On the railroad a serious battle with 93 casualties on both sides. Many Polish soldiers here, very good men.

"On January 29th a combat patrol went up toward Permeda capturing 11 prisoners and wounding more. This was the first time to see artillery fire. We did guard duty till February 10th when we went on patrol to Polusk—chased 130 Bolos back. On February 27 we came back to Chekuva where the American Headquarters was stationed. A patrol of 4 men went out every day to Bolozarki. Going in 2 days and coming in 2 days.

"On March 17 our patrol was captured and at 3 a patrol of 32 was sent out to find them and open the road to Obozerska. On the 20th, Cpl. Redman was killed when the enemy made a cavalry charge. On the 21st, nothing had been heard of the patrol 2 or 300 reinforcements had been sent—our mail as far as we know was captured by Bolos along with a convoy of ammunition.

"On March 23 about 75 of Company H and two companies of Eng. went up to Bolokeazern & made an attack on Bolos. I was sent by Lt. Bellegram back to get reinforcements from English—I was in grave danger going and more coming back thru an open road—as there were swamps on both sides. Many killed and wounded. On the first of April we tried again, having nearly 250 Poles with us.

"May 27 Pvt. Negaki from Hart was buried at Onega Cemetery at 11 AM. I was one of the pallbearers. . . . Carried a wooden casket on our shoulders ½ mile and then had to cover the grave."*

It was because the AEFNR had to bury men such as Private Negaki in Russia that the Polar Bear Expedition would be necessary. When the soldiers returned from Russia in 1919, the Graves Registration Bureau of the War Department succeeded in recovering only 112 of the 226 Americans who had died there. The

---

* Excerpts drawn from the *Detroit Free Press* and *Detroit Herald.* Copies housed in Michigan's Own, a Frankenmuth, Michigan, museum devoted to Michigan military history.

search for the remaining bodies was halted abruptly after the Bolsheviks succeeded in overthrowing the Czar and the United States refused to recognize the new government.

For nearly a decade, the bodies of these American soldiers lay entombed in the alien tundra soil, forgotten by all but their comrades and loved ones. Finally, early in 1929, the VFW came to the assistance of the Polar Bear Association of Detroit (an association of men who had served in the North Russian Campaign). Together they petitioned the American Government for action on recovery of bodies still in Russia, but to no avail. Then, early in 1929, Commander-in-Chief Eugene Carver began negotiations with the Russians through the War Department. His attempts failed, however, because the Russians refused to negotiate with a country that did not recognize their government. Next Commander-in-Chief Carver tried dealing directly through the Russian Embassy in Washington, D.C. In this instance the VFW dealt with the Russian Government as a private corporation. With the assistance of Secretary of War Patrick Hurley, a former National Officer of the VFW, the Russians consented to allow the VFW to recover the bodies of Americans remaining in the Archangel area. All papers, contracts, and commissions were carried out in the name of the Veterans of Foreign Wars of the United States. On March 4, 1929, Congress approved an appropriation of $79,592 to help the VFW locate and remove the American dead. This was added to the $15,000 the state of Michigan had already allocated from state funds.

Commander-in-Chief Carver appointed a mission headed by Edward S. Bettelheim, Jr., chairman; Captain Stuart D. Campbell, Paris member of the Graves Registration Bureau, vice-chairman; Walter C. Dundon, John C. Evans, Michael Macalla, Roy Derham, and Gilbert T. Shilson, members; and four members of the Graves Registration Bureau. With the exception of the Graves Registration Bureau captain and the chairman, all were veterans of the AEFNR's ill-fated campaign.

The VFW expedition found travel in Russia slow. For much of their 13,000–mile trek, expedition members had to travel by horse-drawn droshkies or wood-burning river boats that needed numerous refueling stops. Their progress was further impeded by the multitudes of curious natives drawn by the sight of their boat flying the VFW flag from the mast.

Many of the American grave sites were overgrown by weeds, while others were in plots being farmed by Russian peasants. Identification was always difficult and at times almost impossible. In many cases the "dog tags" had disintegrated, so identification rested on the recovery of billfolds or insignia and cards. In the end, 86 of the remaining 112 graves were found and the bodies recovered.

On December 28, 1929, these, the last members of the AEFNR to leave Russia, arrived home. Their ship was met in New York by Commander-in-Chief H.N. Duff, Senior Vice Commander-in-Chief Paul Wolman, other national officers of the VFW and its Ladies Auxiliary, and New York state and city officials. The remains of the few soldiers who were not from Michigan were then transported to their homes or buried in Arlington National Cemetery, near Washington, D.C. One of those buried in Arlington was a native of Japan who had enlisted in the United States Army at the age of seventeen. At his interment, the Japanese flag was flown and the Japanese Ambassador to the United States said at his grave side, "Japan is honored to know one of her brave sons is laid to rest side by side with American Comrades alongside whom he fought and died."

The remains of the fifty-six soldiers identified as being from Michigan were placed on a special train for the trip to Detroit. This train was met at all hours of the day and night, often in freezing drizzle and sub-zero temperatures, by representatives of VFW Posts and others wanting to honor these dead. A large crowd met the train in Detroit and accompanied the procession to White Chapel Cemetery, the place of the Polar Bears' final interment.

At the service in White Chapel Cemetery, National Commander-in-Chief Duff told mourners, "Today,

The final resting place of the Polar Bears in Detroit's White Chapel Cemetery

Mr. Governor, the bodies of these heros are now before you. They now belong to the State of Michigan. The VFW is proud to have been permitted to participate in this labor of love. . . . The Polar Bears are now home."

The bodies were placed in a mausoleum until the following Memorial Day, when their monument was dedicated. Then they were finally laid to rest.

The last note of Taps, blown over these honored dead at their interment in White Chapel Cemetery, signaled the end of an era. The "War to End War" had reached its conclusion. All that remained was, in the words of President Abraham Lincoln, to "Care for Him Who Shall Have Borne the Battle, and for His Widow and for His Orphans."

CHAPTER FOUR

THE RETRENCHMENT YEARS
1930–1940

Unlike many countries, the United States has no "military class." Its armed forces are made up of civilians who choose—or are chosen—to join one of the services, and who can elect to serve for a short period of time or a lifetime career. Once a serviceman's membership in the armed forces ends, he automatically returns to his former status as a civilian. Unless he is rich, his life will be affected by the same economic winds that affect the lives of other citizens. Hard times will be equally hard for him, and may even be harder if he sustained injuries or health problems while in the military.

Toward the end of 1929, the economic winds that had previously swept veterans and non-veterans alike into an era of unparalleled prosperity shifted their direction cruelly. In late October 1929, the hurried unloading of 16.5 million shares of stock on Wall Street caused stockholders to lose $26 billion in a twenty-four-hour period. Many individual investors and corporations were wiped out immediately; within a year, almost every citizen in the country had felt the deadly effects of the depression precipitated by the crash of the stock market.

During the late months of 1930, the restricted economy began to make itself felt in earnest. Lack of capital and lack of confidence in the economy translated into less purchasing power. This in turn called

Despite the deepening depression, these convention-goers at the 1930 VFW National Encampment in Baltimore were able to strike a jaunty pose.

for production cutbacks and fewer jobs. It was a vicious circle.

Unemployment rose steadily until at its peak in 1932 and 1933, about 13 million Americans were out of work. This was approximately one out of every six Americans of working age. Many unemployed were in desperate need of food, adequate clothing, and shelter. To try to meet these needs, some sold apples on street corners; many were forced to go on relief—which, at the rate of four to seven cents a day per family, seldom provided much real relief.

In many areas, the unemployed and their families congregated in squalid shanty towns made of scrap lumber and metal (nicknamed "Hoovervilles" after the president many blamed for the depression's continuation). By 1932, the nationwide Hooverville population exceeded one million, and many cities and towns had major sanitation and pest control problems as a result.

Thousands of job seekers drifted from town to town and state to state. They trudged the nation's roads as hitchhikers. They traveled by "borrowed boxcars" or "Hoover Pullman" on the nation's railroads. Many just crawled beneath the railroad cars and "rode the rods."

By 1932, roughly 2 million Americans, including 200,000 children, were roaming the country. Having to feed these drifters in the name of charity pushed many large cities to the brink of bankruptcy. Some, unable to collect enough taxes to stay afloat, could no longer pay their schoolteachers' salaries. To make matters worse, bank loans were all but out of the question for both cities and private citizens. In the first three years of the depression, more than 4,000 banks closed their doors.

Neither were the farms spared. By the fall of 1931, farm income had dropped to 50 percent of what it had been in 1929. The market for farm commodities was so depressed that in several northwest Iowa counties, county courthouses were heated by burning corn because it was cheaper than coal. Severe droughts, starvation, and foreclosures forced many farmers to turn to sharecropping and subsistence farming.

Frustrated with conditions, in July 1931 the farmers began taking matters into their own hands. Unwilling to see their families starve, farmers all across the farm belt forced their way into stores and stole food from the shelves. To help those who had not already lost their farms through foreclosure sales, they either forcibly prevented the sale from taking place or saw to it that the bids were so low that the original owner could buy his own farm back. Often these machinations were carried out with the assistance, or at least the concurrence, of local law officials, thus lending a semblance of legality to the proceedings.

As conditions progressively worsened, President Herbert Hoover continued to maintain his position that the nation's economy would spontaneously recover. He steadfastly opposed federal aid to the unemployed, claiming that prosperity was "just around the corner." In 1931, Hoover went so far as to suggest a one-year moratorium on collection of war debts to help out the European nations that were also experiencing depressions. It was a charitable gesture, but with the American economy in desperate need of an infusion of outside cash, one that the public would not condone.

All too soon, the VFW would learn that Hoover's position on veterans' entitlements was equally ill-conceived. But the VFW would also learn that its unquenchable belief in the nation's veterans and their rights could help it overturn obstacles that other veteran's groups considered immovable. It would prove that a dedicated group is a force with which to be reckoned.

ONE STEP BACK, TWO STEPS FORWARD

In the early years of the depression, the VFW's overriding concern was to obtain some quick financial relief for the nation's veterans. The VFW fixed on payment of a cash bonus for wartime service as the surest means to this end. As discussed in Chapter 3, in 1924 the government had granted World War I veterans "bonus" certificates that would be redeemable for cash in twenty years. At the time, the VFW had argued that it was senseless to promise a starving man that he would get money for food two decades later. Now the VFW stepped up its efforts to persuade the government to redeem the certificates early.

Immediately after passage of the "Bonus Bill" (Economic Adjustment Act) in 1924, the VFW had formed a special committee to work on obtaining some kind of cash settlement. This committee worked closely with Congressman Isaak Bacharach of New Jersey to develop a proposal Congress would accept. Finally, with the assistance of Wright Patman of Texas and Hamilton Fish of New York in the House and Arthur Vandenberg of Michigan in the Senate, the VFW-sponsored Bacharach Amendment was passed in 1931, during the final week of the 71st Congressional session.

The Bacharach Amendment allowed veterans to borrow up to 50 percent of the maturity value of their certificates—but with one catch. Only certificates that were at least two years old could be redeemed. Because the VFW believed that *all* certificate holders should be eligible for the loan provision, Legislative Representative Lecil S. Ray immediately asked Congressman Bacharach to sponsor a new amendment in the House. Once Bacharach consented, Ray asked Senator Royal S. Copeland of Michigan to handle the

With Adjutant General Robert Handy, Jr., looking on, employees of the VFW National Headquarters check returns from a nationwide newspaper poll of sentiment on payment of the bonus.

Senate side of the bill. Next, Ray talked to the majority and minority leaders of both Houses and reached an agreement that if the House approved the amendment, the Senate would pass it by unanimous consent vote. The amendment passed just minutes before that Congressional session adjourned and was signed into law by President Hoover. On February 27, 1931, the Bacharach Amendment became Public Law 743. Under the law, all veterans were now allowed to borrow up to 50 percent of the maturity value of their certificate.

The VFW quickly went into action. First, the National Service Bureau telegrammed the National Headquarters in Kansas City of the bill's passage. At once, Headquarters began printing and distributing thousands of loan application blanks. Then, in a ground floor room of the Tower building in Washington, D.C., the VFW staff began personally handling loan applications from the thousands of veterans lined up outside the building. By prearrangement with the Veterans Administration, checks on the loans were made out immediately upon receipt of completed applications.

Coming at this time, the loan was a lifesaver for many veterans and their families. Thousands who applied for the loan had no funds at all. By 1935, 3 million veterans had borrowed against their certificates. The majority had borrowed the full 50 percent.

As timely as the loan provision was, the VFW realized from the start that it was only a stop-gap measure. Even before the law permitting veterans to borrow 50 percent of the value of their certificates went into effect, the VFW was already pushing for the release of all "bonus" monies owed to veterans.

From VFW Headquarters, "Battle Orders" were issued to every post, county council, and department. These "orders" consisted of an eight-page printed sheet with background information on the bonus campaign and a recommended plan of action. It explained how to obtain newspaper and radio coverage of the issue, told how to prepare petitions, urged writing letters to Congressmen, and suggested giving talks before clubs and groups. The "orders" were accom-

panied by a pamphlet entitled "Bonus Campaign Ammunition," which contained twelve speeches that could be given on the Bonus issue.

Everyone in the VFW, from the upper echelons of command to the rear ranks, worked on the bonus campaign. Offices of congressmen were flooded with letters, petitions, and telegrams from their veteran-constituents. For example, Senator Bennett Champ Clark of Missouri, a proponent of the legislation, received more than 11,000 telegrams urging the bill's passage. On January 21, 1931, Past Commander-in-Chief Paul Wolman presented to Congressman Wright Patman, author of the bonus legislation, a petition favoring its passage. The petition contained 3 million signatures.

Besides working on the bonus campaign itself, many VFW members also took part in fund-raising activities to finance the campaign. In 1931, $9,100 was collected from posts, auxiliaries, other organizations, and individuals through a special drive. Posts and Auxiliaries that were short on funds used the time-honored system of holding ice cream socials, dinners, raffles, and rummage sales to raise money for the cause. Others offered services in lieu of money. They made phone calls explaining the issue and soliciting funds and collected names for the petitions. The monies raised were used to hire writers, experts in finance and public relations, and others who could aid in promoting the veterans' cause.

In 1932, the VFW's bonus campaign suddenly took on a new urgency. Early that summer, Congress passed Public Law 212, a measure that would slash veterans' entitlements to the bone. It now appeared that unless payment of the cash bonus was authorized, most veterans would receive no government assistance whatsoever for the duration of the depression.

Public Law 212, better known as the Economy Act, was passed with President Hoover's full approval. The act targeted two major areas for cutbacks: government employees' salaries and veterans' entitlements. The salary cuts were limited to 15 percent. But veterans' entitlements were to be reduced by $350 million a year, by far the largest reduction in any of the government's programs. Exactly where entitlements were to be cut was to be determined by a joint House and Senate committee, before the act went into effect in March 1933. The committee was to investigate all veterans' benefits currently being paid, then recommend ways to reduce the cost of these entitlements to the Veterans Administration and the government.

The Economy Act stunned the veterans of this nation. Like every other segment of the population, the veterans wanted the government to economize. Many, if not most of them, supported politicians who campaigned that year on platforms of taking the country "out of the red." But the veterans wanted the burden of economizing to be shared, not just dumped on their shoulders. It seemed grossly unfair that by signing the Economy Act, President Hoover could destroy most of the gains in entitlements won by the VFW in the past thirty years.

Coming as it did in the midst of the VFW's bonus campaign, the passage of the Economy Act caught the organization by surprise and unprepared. While the organization worked on preparing counter measures, VFW Legislative Representative Lecil S. Ray was told to inform everyone with whom he discussed the matter that the VFW's opposition to this act was unshakeable. In the meantime, the VFW rejected all compromises, including one from General Frank Hines, Director of the Veterans Administration, which would have lessened somewhat the effects of the act.

In 1933, Legislative Chairman Ray argued before a conference of VA officials that the proposed cut of $350 million was preposterous. He claimed that to reach that level of savings, pensions to "some battle casualties, amputees and others with severe injuries would also have to be withdrawn if the required limit was to be attained."

While the VFW was still scrambling to organize its opposition to the Economy Act, a number of prominent citizens formed a group to help marshal public support for the act. Members of the group, who called themselves the National Economy League, included: Archie Roosevelt, a tycoon who had made a fortune in wartime government contracts on shipping;

Admiral Richard E. Byrd, Arctic explorer and chairman of the group; General John J. Pershing, Commander of the Army Expeditionary Forces in World War I; Major General James C. Harbord; and Admiral William E. Sims.

Conveniently forgetting that many of its members received substantial retirement benefits and pensions from the federal government, this group criticized veterans who received entitlements for "treasury raiding." To give themselves a broader base from which to launch their assaults, the National Economy League actually formed a front group called the American Veteran's Association. Having the word "veteran" in the group's title did what it was designed to do—mislead the unknowing. When this group was finally challenged to prove its validity as a real veteran's association, a sham meeting was called in Washington. Other than that, the American Veteran's Association was never active.

Once the National Economy League, a.k.a. the American Veteran's Association, began verbally attacking veterans and their entitlements, abuse of veterans spread. Even radio and newspaper journalists who had championed the veteran and his services a short time before, vigorously joined in their denunciation. It would be fair to say, however, that most of the support for this assault, both moral and financial, came from the wealthy.

With veterans' entitlements in jeopardy and anti-veteran sentiment growing, a group of World War I veterans decided it was time to press for an early passage of the cash bonus bill. The bill had already passed the House, and soon it would be before the Senate. Word spread across the nation and a "Bonus Expeditionary Force" (B.E.F.) was spontaneously organized to march on Washington, D.C., in support of the bonus.

In early summer of 1932, 20,000 marchers converged on the nation's capital and set up camps at Anacostia Flats and at Pennsylvania Avenue at Fourth Street in Washington, D.C. Many of the marchers in this non-violent group were migrants who carried their total belongings with them. Some even brought their families along.

Under the leadership of Walter M. Waters, each group of campers was assigned a camp site. Sentries were posted and order maintained according to military regulations. Commissaries were set up to provide for the needs of the B.E.F.

The VFW was not in favor of the B.E.F. or its march. They believed a bonus would only be achieved by going through legislative channels, and that the B.E.F. was a threat to the legislative machinery that was slowly being put into operation. Local units did, however, assist marchers by sending them clothing, food, and money. VFW state departments, at least those along the line of march, asked their posts to allow the marchers to sleep in Post Homes and offer any other form of assistance that might be needed.

In Washington, D.C., local post and district officers were on hand, not as participants, but primarily to establish a first aid tent for the B.E.F. And at the request of the marchers, VFW member and Superintendent of Washington Police, General P.D. Glassford, assumed control of the B.E.F.'s funds and disbursed them as needed for food and other necessities.

On June 17, 1932, the evening of the Senate vote on the bonus, 10,000 members of the Bonus Expeditionary Force gathered on the Capitol lawn to await the outcome of the vote. After learning the bill had not passed, the marchers peaceably returned to the camps. Most packed up their belongings and started home. Some migrants returned to their shacks and tar-paper shanties at the camps to wait until Congress passed the bonus bill. With no homes to go to, they had no reason to accept the government's offer to pay their way home.

Many Washingtonians sympathized with the marchers. Others—particularly government officials—were afraid of them or saw them as threats to law and order. President Hoover evidently agreed with the latter group. Claiming that the bonus marchers were occupying buildings slated to be demolished to make way for government construction, Hoover ordered that the remaining B.E.F. members be dispersed. To ac-

complish this order, Army Chief of Staff General Douglas MacArthur dispatched four troops of cavalry, four companies of infantry, a machine gun squadron, and six tanks. What followed is one of the most shameful incidents in American history.

Armed with bayonet-equipped rifles, sabers, tear gas, and flaming torches, the Army cleared out and burned the camps. In the process, two unarmed veterans were killed, scores of men, women, and children were injured, and an eleven-week-old baby died from the gassing.

Following the Army's assault, President Hoover is reputed to have said, "Thank God, we still have a government that can deal with a mob." MacArthur justified his action by claiming that he "felt revolution in the air." But his aide, Major Dwight D. Eisenhower, had a different perspective on the debacle. He called it "a pitiful scene" that should not have been allowed to happen.

Although the national VFW organization had not supported the B.E.F., it harshly condemned the government's forcible dispersion of the marchers. At the 33rd Annual Encampment in Milwaukee that fall, former Department Commander Joseph C. Thomson of New York presented this resolution, which passed unanimously:

"Whereas, as soon as Congress adjourned, the President of the United States summoned the United States Army to rout and maim a pitiful and inoffensive crowd of ragged and unarmed bonuseers [sic], and

"Whereas, the United States presented to the world, just recently, the amazing spectacle of a nation asking the entire world to forbid the use of gas in time of war, as barbarous and uncivilized; and then ordered gas used against women, children, veterans and men, unarmed, defenseless, ragged and starving, all citizens of the United States, and

"Whereas, the use of the Army, with charging cavalry, drawn sabers, fixed bayonets, with guns loaded and ready to shoot, with tanks (whose use, the U.S. would also abolish in time of war) against men with no arms, men loyal to the United States, men, women and children, weakened by hunger and unemployment, was unnecessary, criminally brutal and uncalled for and morally indefensible, and

"Whereas, William Hushka of Chicago and Eric Carlson of Oakland, California, veterans, were killed as the result of that order, and

"Whereas the men thus ejected from Washington were American citizens, veterans who fought for the American Flag in World War I and lobbying in Washington for a lawful purpose, and

"Whereas, high governmental officials without right or cause, responsible for their humiliating and degrading spectacle, by public statement, in an attempt to justify themselves have also attempted to use the power of government and the influence of the press, to create the impression that these unarmed veterans were desperate, dangerous men, with criminal records, and under Communistic dominance, and

"Whereas, the veteran's strongest weapon of defense is the Ballot,

"Be it resolved that the VFW makes solemn protest against the unnecessary use of the Army and in order that the American public may become dramatically aware of this organization's attitude that posts possessing club houses be urged to mount sand bags and post a military guard from now on until November so that the Washington evacuation begun in July may be fully completed in November, and a copy of this resolution as adopted be given immediately to the press...."

The resolution went on to single out the individuals the VFW held responsible for the B.E.F.'s mistreatment: President Hoover, Secretary of War Patrick J. Hurley, and General MacArthur. In conclusion, the VFW resolved to "go on record as serious-

ly censuring those Government officials who were at all and/or in any way responsible for the un-humanitarian and un-American manner that was used in clearing the camps occupied by the so-called marchers and their families."

Besides condemning the physical abuse of veterans at the hands of the U.S. Army, the 33rd Annual Encampment also condemned the economic abuse the Economic Act would legislate once it went into effect. The VFW denounced the act as an "instrument of subversive forces of greed," but could not yet suggest an alternative method of economizing on programs for veterans.

Of the two major issues the VFW discussed at the 33rd Encampment, one—the Economy Act—was resolved relatively quickly. The other—the cash bonus—continued to bedevil the organization for several years longer.

To solve the problem of the Economy Act, the VFW allied itself with other veteran's groups and mounted a frontal assault on the act and its backers. By working with Congressmen who understood and believed in the veterans' causes, the veteran's groups succeeded in nullifying most of the provisions of the Economy Act within twelve months. The balance of the entitlements lost were also restored, but years later.

While the VFW was fighting to have the Economy Act overturned, it continued to plug away at the bonus issue. It attacked the issue with every weapon at its command—petitions, letters, telegrams, face-to-face discussions with elected officials, press releases, and public speeches. And it did so under the leadership of the man who was perhaps better qualified for the job than any other: James E. "Jimmy" Van Zandt.

When Van Zandt was elected Commander-in-Chief at the 1933 Encampment, he had already spent three years working for the cash bonus as VFW Chief of Staff and Junior Vice Commander-in-Chief. From Maine to Oregon and California to Florida, Van Zandt had spoken about the issue. His platforms ranged from the front porches of residences to the rear platforms of trains, from breakfast, luncheon, and dinner

James E. Van Zandt, photographed with members of the Japan Reservists Association in 1936 (Acme)

clubs to a corral fence in New Mexico. Nor was the time of day a hinderance to his speeches. Van Zandt once spoke at 3:30 a.m. at St. Cloud, Minnesota, and he is said to have given sixteen speeches in a twenty-four hour period in Alabama. On one speaking tour in 1931, Congressman Wright Patman, the author of the cash bonus bill, accompanied Van Zandt. Together they traveled through the midwest, addressing service clubs, women's groups, luncheon clubs, schools, business groups, and radio audiences. If someone was there to listen, Jimmy spoke.

As Commander-in-Chief, Van Zandt continued to crisscross the United States, making speeches about the bonus. On one occasion, he was joined by General Smedley D. Butler of Marine Corps fame. Because of his popularity and spontaneous manner of speaking. Butler attracted crowds at his every appearance. In New York City's Madison Square Garden, 20,000 heard speeches from Van Zandt, General Butler, and Father Charles E. Coughlin, a Roman Catholic priest from Royal Oak, Michigan, who broadcast his views

over the radio each Sunday. It was the largest group that Jimmy ever spoke to about that issue.

During Commander Van Zandt's three-year tenure in office (1933–35), he covered one million miles, averaging four cities, ten speeches, and one radio broadcast each twenty-four hours. In his final year in office, Van Zandt visited 1500 cities, delivered about 4,000 speeches, and made close to 400 radio broadcasts. These totals, impressive as they are, would undoubtedly have been higher if Van Zandt had not periodically been involved in accidents. During the six-year period that Van Zandt stumped the country, he survived three plane crack-ups, two auto accidents, and a train wreck. But whatever catastrophe befell him, Van Zandt came back fighting and as determined as ever.

While Van Zandt and other VFW members were trying to drum up support for the cash bonus, others were trying equally hard to generate opposition. One of the VFW's most formidable opponents was the American Veteran's Association, the same group that had been in favor of eliminating veterans' entitlements via the Economy Act. The AVA was allied with big moneyed interests, and by 1935 had contributions of close to $100,000 with which to oppose the bonus. Most of this fund had been subscribed by fewer than 275 people.

Another group opposed to the bonus bill was made up of students from Princeton and several other colleges. They adopted the name of "Veterans of Future Wars" and attempted to forestall the legislation by making it look ridiculous. They formed chapters of "Veterans of Future Wars" and demanded payment of a bonus for their future wartime services. Ironically, many of these students found their participation in a future war a reality in World War II.

The most powerful group to oppose bonus bill legislation was, of course, the four presidents of the United States who held office during the seventeen years the VFW campaigned for the bonus. Chapter 3 discusses the opposition of Presidents Harding and Coolidge. Their successors shared their opinion that a veteran's service should not entitle him to any special treatment. When pressed on the issue, Hoover said, "These [the veterans], like the others, are being provided the basic necessities of life by the devoted committees in those parts affected by the depression or the drought. . . ." Franklin D. Roosevelt's view was similar: "I hold that the able-bodied citizen, because he wore a uniform and for no other reason, should not be accorded treatment different from that accorded to other citizens who did not wear a uniform during the World War. . . ."

Certainly another factor that complicated and prolonged the campaign for the cash bonus was the lack of cohesion among the three major veteran's organizations: the VFW, the American Legion, and the Disabled American Veterans (DAV). Whether because of disagreements as to which organization should lead the campaign or differences in opinion about what veterans were entitled to, the three groups found it nearly impossible to agree on a course of action.

Until 1935, the groups held widely differing positions on the bonus issue. Alone among the groups, the VFW was always solidly behind the cash bonus. After setting up the special committee to work for that goal in 1924, it never wavered from its course. The DAV, too, maintained its position fairly consistently. From 1924 to 1931, it refused to take a stand on the issue. In 1932, it briefly endorsed the "cash bonus" proposal, but then resumed its previous noncommittal position until 1935. The American Legion was consistent only in its inconsistency.

In the 1920s, the American Legion had reluctantly helped the VFW pressure the Senate to pass the original Adjusted Compensation bill. But once the issue of a cash bonus was raised, the American Legion waffled back and forth on the position it should take. At its convention in 1930, the Legion opposed the bonus. Short months later, the Executive Committee of the American Legion reversed this stand and supported cash payment. Then, President Hoover spoke before the American Legion Convention at Detroit in 1931 and asked the organization to oppose the cash bonus. The American Legion obliged. (That same year, working without the assistance of any other veteran's organization, the VFW obtained passage of the 50 percent loan provision for veterans holding "bonus" certificates.) In 1932, the Legion joined the VFW and DAV in supporting the cash bonus proposal, only to reverse its position the following year. In 1934, the Legion once again advocated for the bill, then, before the next session of Congress, rejected the version of the bill supported by the VFW in favor of a new one written by Congressman Fred Vinson.

Finally, in 1935, the DAV and the American Legion both joined the VFW in an all-out effort to push for the passage of Congressman Wright Patman's version of the bonus bill. This change in attitude undoubtedly reflected the changing public opinion. Over a twelve-month period, public approval for the cash bonus, as measured by pollster Dr. George Gallup, rose 24 points to a high of 55 percent. That year, the Patman Bill passed both houses of Congress, but was vetoed by President Roosevelt. Sub-

Looking over the Patman-Vinson-McCormack Bonus Bill just before its passage are: (seated, left to right) Senators Clark of Missouri; Byrnes of South Carolina; Steiwer of Oregon. Standing: Commanders Ray Murphy, American Legion; James E. Van Zandt, VFW; M.A. Harlan, Disabled American Veterans.

sequently, the Senate failed by nine votes to override the veto.

The following session, Congress was presented with a slightly different version of the bonus bill: the Patman-Vinson-McCormack Bill. This bill was the work of Texas Congressman Patman; Kentucky Congressman Fred Vinson, later Chief Justice of the United States Supreme Court; and John McCormack of Massachusetts, Democratic Whip and a member of the VFW. Together with Congressman William Connery of Massachusetts, these men helped secure the bill's passage in the House of Representatives. In the Senate, assistance was provided by Senators James Byrnes, former Secretary of State; Bennett Champ Clark of Missouri; Fred Steiwer of Oregon; Elmer Thomas of Oklahoma; and others.

On January 27, 1936, the Senate passed the Patman-Vinson-McCormack Bill over a presidential veto. Under the new law, nearly three and a half million veterans were eligible for almost two billion dollars worth of Adjusted Service Bonds. These bonds, which

were immediately redeemable, were available to World War I veterans who qualified by August 1936.

By 4:50 p.m., January 27th, only a few hours after passage of the measure, Commander-in-Chief Van Zandt had received from General Hines, Director of the Veterans Administration, the first application forms for the cash payment. By 5:40 p.m., copies of the forms had been dispatched, via air mail, to national officers, department commanders, county council commanders, and local posts all over the country. On January 28th and 29th, thousands of veterans were lined up outside VFW posts to obtain and fill out the applications. Delivery of most of the bonds was completed by August 1st that year.

OTHER DEPRESSION-ERA ISSUES

Although the cash bonus and the nullification of the Economy Act are remembered as two of the VFW's greatest victories, it fought other legislative battles during that same period—some of them on very old turf. For example, the VFW successfully sponsored the Disability Allowance of 1930 (World War I Service Pension). This allowance—which the VFW won without support from any other veteran's group—provided pensions for World War I veterans who had served a minimum of 90 days and had sustained a permanent disability of 25 percent or more. Veterans did not have to prove their disability was service connected in order to benefit. VFW members also continued to advocate for more and better medical care for veterans. In 1940, their efforts were rewarded when Congress passed Public Law 868, which granted $20 million for the construction of veterans' hospitals. Later, this construction was closely monitored by members of the VFW, including Dr. Joseph C. Menedez, a New Orleans physician elected National Commander-in-Chief for the 1940 to 1941 year. During his term, he conducted a number of inspection trips to Veterans Administration hospitals to look over the facilities and equipment.

One old issue on which the VFW failed to make much headway was employment of veterans. In 1934, the VFW appointed an Employment and Civil Service Commission to address the need for preferential treatment of veterans in hiring and retaining employees for civil service jobs. This committee met with other veteran's groups to try to develop a workable civil service program. Unfortunately, these joint meetings resulted in no broad program affecting the civil service. During the years from 1936 until America entered the second world war, approximately 500,000 veterans remained unemployed.

While these legislative battles were going on, several minor skirmishes between the VFW and Congress were also concluded. After several years of campaigning by its Americanism Program, in March 1931 the VFW saw Congress adopt the "Star-Spangled Banner" as our national anthem. The VFW and Congress also finally settled a dispute that had begun nearly forty years ago. On May 2, 1940, Congress passed the Philippine Travel Pay Bill—a measure initiated at the 1901 Encampment of the Army of the Philippines, one of the VFW's founding groups. The bill belatedly benefitted the 15,000 American troops who had remained in the Philippines to quell an insurrection after the war with Spain had ended. When the soldiers enlisted, the law had entitled them, upon discharge from the service, to one day's pay and a commutation of allowances for each twenty miles to their homes. But while they were in the Philippines, Congress had passed a new law limiting travel payment to four cents a mile. The Army of the Philippines (and later the VFW) had long contended that the troops should be entitled to payment based on the earlier law—and in 1940, Congress finally agreed.

Although the VFW's main priority during this period was, as always, to assist veterans and their families, the organization also threw itself into community service. Throughout the depression, posts all over the United States initiated programs to help the needy. VFW members collected and distributed food and served free meals at Post Homes. In some areas, post members planted vegetable gardens and donated the produce to hungry families in the community. To aid in flood relief, in 1938 the VFW gave the Red Cross $250,000. In late September 1938, the VFW again went to the assistance of victims of a hurricane that swept the seaboards of Rhode Island, Connecticut, and Massachusetts.

As part of its community service, the VFW also started several youth programs. In 1937, borrowing a concept developed by the Department of Minnesota, it introduced a nationwide program to teach bicycle safety. This program was operated with the cooperation of local and state police. About the same time, the organization also received the exclusive right, from the Amateur Softball Association of America, to sponsor Junior Softball Tournaments throughout the country. In addition, the VFW established two programs for the children of its members—the Sons of the VFW, authorized by the 1934 National Encampment, and the Daughters of the VFW, authorized the following year. Chapter 9 describes the history and activities of both of these auxiliaries.

Although past veteran's organizations had admitted veterans' sons to increase their organization's longevity, this was not the VFW's intention. Since the VFW's founding, its members had recognized that the only way to keep their organization "evergreen" was to continually recruit veterans like themselves as new members. This meant that in the 1930s, as in previous decades, recruitment was a major priority.

In September 1943, the VFW would establish a separate department headed by H.W. Irwin—the Department of Extension—to "extend" the organization through recruitment of membership. But in the meantime, recruitment was mainly the responsibility of the VFW membership, while the establishment of new posts fell into the domain of the VFW's Chief of Staff.

The tireless Jimmy Van Zandt got recruitment for the decade off to a good start. Through his efforts as Chief of Staff in 1930 to 1931, more new members were recruited and more new posts were added than ever before in the history of the organization. In this year of severe business depression and nationwide retrenchment, six new departments were organized.

While Van Zandt was busily adding new posts and departments, his Commander, Paul Wolman, was ensuring that administering these local VFW units would be somewhat easier for their officers. As Commander-in-Chief, Wolman oversaw the compilation of the first Post Service Officers Manual. The manual standardized the procedures and assisted the Service Officers in performing their duties properly.

On January 22, 1932, the VFW used a novel approach to sign up an additional 21,000 members from

Despite FDR's opposition to the Bonus Bill, in 1936 delegates of the VFW invited him to the 37th National Encampment in Denver. (International News Photos)

all across the nation. That day it aired its first "Hello America" radio program. Speaking from Washington, D.C., over a network of fifty stations Commander-in-Chief Darold D. DeCoe swore the recruits in.

The following year, recruitment ace Van Zandt became National Commander-in-Chief. A.D. Vander-voort, Van Zandt's Chief of Staff, immediately set out to prove that his Commander wasn't the only one who could recruit. During his term of office, Vandervoort and his recruiters set an all-time record, averaging a new post a day and a thousand new members a week. As part of his membership program, Vandervoort mapped out "Veterans Defense Rallies" and established department quotas. He also sponsored a contest for comrades to see who could organize the most new posts during the year. Six men organized more than twenty posts each. They were George Plume of New York, James A. Martin of Ohio, Myron Reese of Pennsylvania, Fred W. Emig of Missouri, Leonard C. Merchant of Michigan, and Walter Daniels of Washington. Membership reached a new high in the organization's history as it soared to 187,469.

In 1936, membership reached 199,199, more than triple the 62,480 mark of ten years before. Then, over the next three years, membership decreased somewhat. This decline was probably due in part to the lingering effects of the Economy Act on veterans' personal finances. In addition, the VFW attracted less public attention once it had secured the cash bonus and the disability service pension for World War I veterans.

By 1939, the year of the fortieth anniversary of the VFW's founding, membership stood at 183,585. This 15,000–plus decline from 1936 was perhaps disappointing for the VFW recruiters of those years, but total membership was still astounding, considering that in forty short years the nucleus of thirteen founding members had multiplied over 14,121 times. (Bert DuRant, one of the founders and first vice presidents, had in fact confessed at the 1937 National Encampment that his main feeling about the VFW was pride at having had a part in founding a group destined to become so large and influential.)

That 40th anniversary year, the VFW made a point of recognizing the debt it owed to its small band of founders. In September, 1939, the "New Chiefs" of the present-day VFW met with all of the surviving "Old Chiefs" of the American Veterans of Foreign Service except James C. Putnam and Simon Heiman, who were unable to attend. They gathered in Columbus, Ohio, site of the organization's first meeting, to discuss common problems and to reminisce. Although nearly half of the original thirteen had died, they were still present in memory, as Bert DuRant explained in the October 1938 issue of *Foreign Service* magazine:

"Some of the thirteen are gone, never to return. But, I saw them all. Perhaps you couldn't have seen them, but they are clear to me: Charlie Click, [Francis] DuBiel, Dave Brown, Johnnie Clark, Oscar Brooking, George Beckman (all now dead) as well as George Kelly, John Malloy, James Romanis,

James C. Putnam's 1933 application for a disability pension.

Walker Waddington, all of Columbus; Simon Heiman, of Akron, Ohio and 'Bill' [James C.] Putnam of West Plains, Mo."

During the anniversary ceremonies, a bronze plaque was unveiled and dedicated in the rotunda of the Ohio State House. The plaque reads: "In commemoration of the founding, on September 23, 1899, of the first unit of the American Veterans of Foreign Service—the nucleus of the V.F.W."*

The VFW members themselves were not alone in recognizing their organization's coming of age this decade. Congress, too, acknowledged both formally and informally that the VFW was here to stay. In 1931, at the urging of Edwin S. Bettelheim, Jr., the VFW Legislative Representative, Congress agreed to have the annual VFW Encampment Proceeding printed as a Congressional Document by the Government Printing Office. In addition to extending Congressional recognition to the organization, this measure also saved the VFW several thousands of dollars in annual printing costs. Then on May 28, 1936, Congress passed Public Law 630, granting a Congressional Charter of Incorporation to the Veterans of Foreign Wars of the United States. This law, which was sponsored by Congressman Francis E. Walter of Pennsylvania and Senator Matthew M. Neely of West Virginia, gave the organization Congressional recognition, protection against infringement of name and insignia, and in certain states, legal benefits which are granted only to organizations chartered by Congress.

KEEPING AMERICA OUT OF WAR

In the mid-1930s, the United States was still slowly digging itself out of the depression with the help of FDR's Works Project Administration, Civilian Conservation Corps, and other federal programs. Elsewhere in the world, several nations were again flexing their muscles in seeming preparation for another war. In Germany, the military had begun rearming under the leadership of Adolf Hitler and his Nazi Party. Before long, the German government had entered into alliances with Japan, which had been fighting in Manchuria since 1931, and with totalitarian Italy. In Spain there was civil war. In 1934, the Japanese renounced the Treaties of 1922 and 1930. Nazis assassinated Austrian Chancellor Engelbert Dollfuss and replaced him with pro-Nazi Kurt Von Schuschnigg. In 1935, the Nazis repudiated the Treaty of Versailles and reintroduced compulsory military training for German youths. They also formed the new German Air Force, the Luftwaffe. Meanwhile, Italian leader Benito Mussolini invaded Ethiopia.

To prevent America's involvement in a possible second world war, Congress passed a series of neutrality acts in 1935, 1936, and 1937. These acts prohibited the sale of munitions and the provision of loans or credit to belligerent nations. They also forbade Americans to travel on ships of warring nations. (Although ineffective in keeping the country out of

---

* The date on the plaque is incorrect; the founding meeting took place on Friday, September 29, 1899, at 7:00 p.m.

World War II, these acts did prevent the U.S. from assisting the sovereign government of Spain in its fight against Francisco Franco and his mercenaries and from helping the Ethiopians in their efforts to repel the invading Italians in 1935–36.)

By and large, the members of the VFW agreed with the federal government's position on neutrality. Like other Americans, many believed that the losses of life and property sustained during World War I had been unconscionable. Others did not want the United States to risk losing her status as a creditor nation, even though most of the monies owed the nation from World War I were uncollectible.

Like the federal government, the VFW espoused neutrality until the end of the decade, often via its Americanism Department. This department was charged with building unity and solidarity to face the threat of another war. (In 1934–35, the National Council of Administration had replaced the earlier Americanism *Program* with a permanent National *Department* of Americanism. Walter I. Joyce, National Patriotic Instructor and Director of the Americanization Committee, had continued as its director.) The VFW also adopted neutrality/peace programs at most of its National Encampments in the latter half of the decade.

In 1935, the VFW National Encampment petitioned President Franklin Roosevelt and the Congress to "do all in their power to keep the United States out of another war." They passed a resolution asking that the United States enact a permanent neutrality policy and also approved a VFW Neutrality Code which requested:

1. That immediately upon declaration of war between two foreign powers an embargo shall automatically be fixed upon all exports designed to reach either directly or indirectly any of the belligerents.
2. That immediately upon declaration of war between two powers the United States Government is automatically released of the responsibility of protecting the private financial interests of individual American citizens in those particular countries.
3. That the armed forces of the United States be immediately withdrawn from any country in which a state of war exists and in any waters where the presence of American ships might be construed or interpreted as a violation of neutrality.
4. That American citizens be notified that all travel aboard the ships of belligerent powers is at their own peril.
5. That no government or private financial loans shall be extended to any nation that is at war officially or unofficially with another nation."

In 1936, the VFW again went on record as backing peace for the United States. This time it proposed a four-point program that asked the government to: adopt a permanent neutrality, take federal control of the manufacture and sale of arms and ammunition, conscript wealth and industry as well as manpower in time of war, and maintain an adequate defense force.

To enlist public support for staying out of war, in 1937 the VFW unveiled its "Peace for America" program. Through posters, windshield decals, newspaper publicity, public forums, and radio speeches, all posts helped popularize the VFW's position. As part of the program, in late November the VFW launched a campaign to "Keep America Out of War." The immediate objective was to collect millions of signatures on petitions and newspaper ballots endorsing noninvolvement. All VFW units received the petition forms and circulars describing the campaign and its objectives. The same circular and a press release were sent to 2,000 daily and 10,000 weekly newspapers and magazines, as well as to all radio stations in the U.S. Two hundred of the nation's outstanding patriotic leaders also received letters explaining the campaign and requesting their endorsement.

The VFW's campaign to "Keep America Out of War" was brought to a close on the steps of the nation's capitol on April 27, 1938, the VFW

Americanization Day. On that day, Commander-in-Chief Scott P. Squyres and National Auxiliary President Laurie Schertle presented petitions bearing signatures of 3,640,890 citizens, clubs, and organizations to Senator Key Pittman of Nevada, Chairman of the Senate Committee on Foreign Relations, and Representative William B. Bankhead, Speaker of the House. Pittman and Bankhead were standing in for Vice President John N. Garner, presiding officer of the Senate. Garner had been invited to accept the petitions on behalf of Congress, but had refused when he heard there would be radio coverage of the event. He had vowed never to give a radio talk when he became vice president, and he kept his word.

On this same Americanization Day, a VFW-sponsored bill, popularly nicknamed "Draft the Wealth," was introduced by fifty-five senators. The bill was designed to "take the profit out of war by steeply graded income and other taxes." This proposal reflected a conviction the VFW had held since shortly after the first world war: that if business and industry no longer stood to gain millions when the U.S. entered a war, support for war would fall dramatically. A companion bill, also sponsored by the VFW, was introduced into the House by more than one hundred Congressmen. Both versions of the bill failed to pass.*

After the "Keep America Out of War" campaign ended, the VFW continued the rest of its "Peace for America" program. As it continued to advocate for peace, however, it also continued to advocate for an adequate defense to preserve that peace. Individual members, as well as the national organization, were always on the look-out for chinks in America's defense. In New Jersey, for example, members of the General Joseph Wheeler Post No. 62 of Jersey City asked officials to investigate a Nordland German-American Bund camp near Andover, which displayed a Swastika flag and used the Nazi salute. VFW members photographed license plates of cars parked near the

WELCOME HOME — TO PRISON

THE plight of Grover Cleveland Bergdoll, notorious draft dodger and now practically a man without a country, should be an object lesson to the youth of this country. There is no telling what the future holds for him should he remain in Nazi Germany and prison doors are open wide awaiting his return to this country. As the old saying goes, he's "between the devil and the deep blue sea."

Yet Bergdoll deserves no sympathy from anyone, not even the sloppiest sentimentalist. He has himself alone to blame for the predicament he's in. A native-born American, he refused to serve when his country called him for military duty in time of need. He was physically fit and had no dependents, so there was absolutely no excuse for his ignominious action except physical fear.

(The Stars and Stripes/National Tribune)

camp. From these pictures, names of Bund members were obtained. When it developed that many members of the Bund were also members of the New Jersey

---

* In 1948, this same bill was reintroduced as H.R. 6258 by Congressman James E. Van Zandt, and again it failed to pass. To this day, many members of the VFW hope that legislation to tax the profit out of war will eventually be enacted.

State Guard, these guardsmen were drummed out of the state military forces.

Just as it had after World War I, the VFW also condemned draft dodgers and others whose actions they felt weakened the country's defense. In one notorious case in summer 1939, the VFW joined many Americans in censuring Grover Cleveland Bergdoll, a citizen who had been imprisoned for draft evasion during the first world war, but had escaped to Germany. Nineteen years later, he attempted to return to the U.S. under the alias of Herr Bennett Nash, but was apprehended by U.S. Army officers. When questioned by the press, Bergdoll said that he had "returned to pay a debt." He hoped to serve his sentence and then remain in America with his wife and son. The Department of Labor, however, felt that Bergdoll had given up his citizenship some time ago and said it was very likely Bergdoll would be required to serve out the balance of his previous sentence plus some additional time for escape, and then be deported as an undesirable alien. As the accompanying cut from the *Stars and Stripes* shows, the veterans strongly indicated their preference as to the treatment Bergdoll should receive.

Several months after the Bergdoll incident, the VFW's 1939 National Encampment met in Boston and proposed one last neutrality-peace program. It included the following recommendations:

1. Adequate, mechanized, motorized material and trained men.
2. Renounce war as an instrument of international policy.
3. Recognize the existence of war regardless of its formal declaration.
4. Advocate compliance with provisions of the Kellog-Briand Pact. [A treaty outlawing war, signed by sixty-five nations in Paris in 1928.]
5. Proclamation by the United States that it will not engage in any war of aggression.
6. Proclamation by the United States that it will support and defend the Monroe Doctrine.
7. Withdraw armed protection to American citizens, after a period of warning.
8. Prohibit the extension of credit or loans by the United States or any of its citizens, to any country, or its citizens, which is engaged in war.
9. Permit sales of supplies to any nation at war only if paid for, and only if ownership thereof is transferred at our shore lines, without any protection or responsibility whatsoever by the United States Government.
10. Prohibit any American merchant vessels from becoming armed.
11. Disclaim responsibility for the protection of any American merchant vessels which carry any merchandise to any country at war or into any danger zone, but permit clearance of American vessels only if adequate private insurance is carried on such vessels and members of their crews, which travel into any danger zones.
12. Take the profit out of any possible future war by steeply graduated personal and corporation income taxes.
13. Conduct an educational program on the costs of war.
14. Encourage peaceful international negotiations to adjust most irritating deficiencies, differences and inequities among nations.

Even as the VFW deliberated as to how to preserve peace in America, events that would make neutrality untenable were rapidly unfolding in Europe. On September 1, 1939, Adolf Hitler unleashed his armies and air forces on Poland. Two days later, Great Britain and France declared war on Germany. Shortly afterwards, Russia entered the fray on Hitler's side, helping to crush Poland from the east. By mid-summer 1940, most of Scandinavia, Holland, Belgium, and France had succumbed to Hitler's "blitzkrieg" (combined air/tank/infantry) tactics.

With Great Britain standing alone against the rampaging Germans, the U.S. quickly softened its stand

*In 1940, volunteers signed up for emergency duty with Virginia's
Home Defense Unit in case the National Guard was called to active duty.*

on neutrality. Congress voted vast sums for rearmament, and nearly a million men were drafted into military service. Both candidates for president—two-term incumbent F.D.R. and Republican challenger Wendell Wilkie—forcefully advocated helping the British any way possible. And when the VFW's National Council of Administration met in Chicago in September 1940, they too strongly endorsed an "Aid to Britain" policy.

CHAPTER FIVE

WAR AND CONFLICT
1941–1954

In 1941, Americans could look either east or west and find a shooting war in progress. In Europe, German forces had taken Kiev, Smolensk, and Odessa, and were advancing on Moscow. In the Orient, the Japanese Armies were working their way down the Asian mainland toward Singapore and making deeper inroads into China. Meanwhile, the Japanese Air Force used carrier aircraft to send two British capital ships to the bottom of the ocean, proving General Billy Mitchell's theory that airplanes could sink battleships. These wars were being fought on the land and over, on the seas and under and over. Men were perishing and ships were sinking in battles in which ships of one fleet never saw ships of the other. Civilians in countries involved in these struggles were dying without even seeing the flash of an enemy saber or hearing the roar of his cannon. In many corners of the world, home front and battle front were becoming indistinguishable.

In the United States, the average citizen was still content to root for Great Britain, France, and the other Allies from the sidelines. Although isolationists were now a distinct minority, few Americans were as yet advocating military aid to Europe or China. Congress, too, concentrated on economic rather than military assistance by approving the lend-lease bill—an act that authorized the U.S. to lend or lease weapons, raw materials, facilities, food, or other goods to nations whose defense was deemed vital to that of the U.S.

Then, on December 7, 1941, a day that President Franklin Roosevelt predicted would "live in infamy," planes from a Japanese task force struck the U.S. military installations in Hawaii. Caught unaware, the naval base at Pearl Harbor received the brunt of the assault. While sacrificing twenty-eight aircraft and three midget submarines of their own, the Japanese inflicted losses on American forces of nineteen ships, 3000 lives, and uncounted airplanes and vehicles. Among the ships destroyed were the battleships *Arizona, Oklahoma,* and *California.* At the same time Japanese forces were crippling the U.S. Pacific Fleet, they also launched surprise attacks on American military installations at Guam, Wake Island, and the Philippines.

The following day, the U.S. Congress swiftly declared that a state of war existed between the United States and the Empire of Japan. The lone dissenting vote on the declaration of war was cast by Jeanette Rankin, the U.S. Representative from Montana who had also voted against our entry into World War I. Two days later, when Japan's allies, Germany and Italy, declared war upon the United States, Con-

Just one week after the attack on Pearl Harbor, these members of Post No. 189 of New London, Connecticut, formed an auxiliary police force. Eventually, they took over many duties of the policemen serving in the armed forces.

gress adopted a resolution declaring that a state of war also existed with these two nations.

The VFW reacted just as quickly to the news of the bombing of Pearl Harbor. National Commander-in-Chief Max Singer was in Denver, Colorado, delivering a radio address when word of the attack reached him. Thirty minutes later he was airborne on his way to Washington, D.C. He, like the rest of the nation, was stunned by the Japanese attack. On December 8th, Singer ordered that the VFW's previously planned wartime program be put into effect. At that point, the VFW's War Service Commission, the board that would oversee the organization's wartime program, took over. The commission was headed by General Bernard W. Kearney, and also included four committee chairmen and directors of programs, the Adjutant General, National Legislative Representative, National Liaison Officer, and the National Patriotic Instructor.

Although many members of the VFW would see action on the various battle fronts, the VFW's major contributions to the war effort took place on the home front. The VFW was by now a highly adaptable and versatile organization, and its War Service Commission made sure the organization funneled its efforts wherever they were needed most. As a result, during the early years of World War II, the VFW's programs were mainly directed toward winning the war. Priority was given to recruiting and training manpower, boosting morale, defending the U.S. against enemy attack or sabotage, and other direct support activities. From 1943 on, however, programs became increasingly concerned with obtaining benefits for returning veterans. During the war and afterwards, the VFW continued to prove that it was truly an all-wars, all-services organization.

WARTIME PROGRAMS

Following the attack on Pearl Harbor, the VFW's first official act was to dispatch Legislative Representative Omar B. Ketchum with a request that Congress provide immediate life insurance coverage to all men in the service. Because the War Risk Insurance Act of World War I had long since expired, many men, both inside the country and overseas, were not covered. Together with fellow VFW member Casey Jones, Ketchum wrote a bill that would award a $5000 life insurance policy to every serviceman and cover his dependents as well. Congressman John McCormick of Massachusetts introduced the bill into Congress, and on the day after Pearl Harbor, Congress approved it. This bill remained in effect until April 19, 1942, when the National Service Life Insurance Act went into force.

Even as Ketchum was persuading Congress to enact the insurance legislation, the VFW national organization was offering its services to the U.S. Government and the Civilian Defense Director, Dean James Landis. After a series of talks, Landis assigned the VFW the job of enrolling auxiliary police and firemen. These auxiliary units replaced men who had answered their country's call to the colors, and performed normal police, fire, and emergency duties. In some areas, units also provided border patrols whose primary mission was to prevent invasion by enemy saboteurs. Members from all over the country carried on a recruiting drive and many Post Homes were turned into training centers for auxiliary volunteers.

In January 1942, the government gave the VFW and the American Legion the additional task of promoting a national physical fitness campaign. The VFW Representative on the Fitness Committee was Robert A. Higgins of Post 321, football coach at Pennsylvania State University. Under his guidance, fit-

ness programs for young people were initiated all across the country. Many men who took part in this program would have been declared unfit for military service without it.

In addition to recruiting and training others for wartime duties, many members served as volunteer firemen or took on other civil defense responsibilities themselves. Even in the smallest towns, far removed from any conceivable enemy attack, VFW members were trained in the basics of first aid. Some also volunteered to become spotters, and were taught to identify various types of aircraft. As air raid wardens, others made sure no light was visible during practice air raid drills, and held classes to teach civilians first aid, how to put out incendiary bombs, and how to stock and build an air raid shelter. Along the East and West Coasts, members patrolled beaches to prevent enemy submarines from landing their agents on our shores. Others manned communication centers to free

One of uncounted hundreds of VFW crews manning aircraft spotting stations during World War II

Members of Collinwood Post No. 2926 of Cleveland learning how to build a sandbag barricade as part of their Air Raid Warden course

The load of bombs carried by a Japanese balloon. The "chandelier" above the bombs was an automatic mechanism designed to release its load of destruction via a time device.

military personnel to guard defense facilities and potential targets along our coasts. Along the Texas-Mexico border, groups resembling posses of old also watched for enemy intrusions.

These protective measures were not as preposterous as they might seem. The Japanese were the first to discover the jet stream—the high altitude air current which moves rapidly from west to east. During the war, they released hundreds of hydrogen-filled balloons carrying clusters of small, high-explosive bombs. These balloons were propelled toward the U.S. by the jet stream. Because the bombs could not be guided after launch, they were more of a harassment than a war-ending threat. There were no reported injuries or damages. Most dropped harmoniously into the Pacific Ocean, although several did explode as far inland as the midwest. One landed in a field in western Iowa, less than five hundred miles from Chicago. The cornfield in Iowa where it went off was promptly cordoned off and discussion of it forbidden by wartime restrictions.

Another aspect of civil defense in which the VFW took a leading role was protecting the nation from

A "guerilla band" sponsored by Rio Post No. 2369 of McAllen, Texas. The veterans and patriotic citizens in this band stood ready for any emergency involving home defense, sabotage, or subversive activities.

enemy agents or saboteurs within the U.S. The responsibility for these activities naturally fell to the VFW's Department of Americanism. Under Americanism Director Victor E. Devereaux, an anti-rumor campaign was organized in 1942 and 1943 to prevent information leaks that could be damaging to the country's security. As part of this campaign, members helped popularize slogans such as "A slip of the lip can sink a ship." Posters bearing a lurid likeness to German Chancellor Adolph Hitler and to Japanese Prime Minister Hideki Tojo also gave Americans pause to think before saying anything about the war effort. More than one hundred clubs, mostly along the nation's coasts, took part in this campaign.

Closely allied to the Americanism Department's rumor-swatting campaign were its counter-espionage activities. Throughout the war, members were asked to report to the Director of Americanism any suspicious activities or acts of sabotage, especially in high-security areas such as the areas surrounding naval shipyards and the aircraft plants of California. The director then forwarded tips to the F.B.I. or other federal security agencies. For their protection, members were not individually credited for their tips. Their reports became a secret part of the official law enforcement investigation and were treated as confidential. Consequently, it is difficult to judge the effectiveness of their efforts in retrospect.

In some regions, VFW members organized counter-espionage activities over and above those prescribed by the Department of Americanism. For example, the Department of Michigan and the Michigan State Police jointly organized the 47 posts which made up the Wayne County Council into a group to investigate acts of subversion in the industrial center of Detroit. The Wayne County Council then sent questionnaires to all VFW members in the area listing types of security work they could volunteer to perform. Those accepted for volunteer assignments were trained under State Police supervision and reported to that authority any acts of sabotage or other Fifth Column activity.

Besides working to protect the U.S. from subversive activities, the Americanism Department also carried out its everyday job of promoting Americanism and democracy through education. One of its major educational efforts during the war was to assist the U.S. Office of Education in a tutoring program for functional illiterates. Included in the program were more than a million men who had been rejected by the armed services because they could not read or write. The Americanism Department also attempted to educate the general public about the principles of democracy by gathering and printing prominent citizens' views on what constituted a democracy, then forwarding them to leading news services and public speakers. These views were widely quoted. In addition, many magazines and over 2,000 daily and weekly newspapers published a series of "Flag Etiquette Lessons" and "Fifth Column Facts" taken from booklets written by Victor Devereaux and published by the VFW. Through its "Speak Up for America" radio programs, the Americanism Department informed its wartime listeners about patriotism and the rights and responsibilities of those living in a democracy. The program, first aired in 1940, was broadcast over 485 radio stations by 1948. A final contribution of the Americanism Department was toward the education of America's youth. During World War II, it furnished supervision for over 200,000 of the nation's young people in bicycle clubs, musical corps, Sons and Daughters of the VFW groups, rifle clubs, model aviation clubs, and Scout Troops.

Another educational program—this one carried out by the organization as a whole—was probably the VFW's most direct contribution to the war effort. The program had its roots in the Army's desperate need to expand its Air Corps. In 1942, the Army needed fliers badly. It needed a multitude of technicians of all kinds to fill its rapidly expanding air arm. Unfortunately, thousands of recruits were being turned away because they could not pass the required exams. To salvage these would-be airmen, Lieutenant General Henry H. "Hap" Arnold, commanding general of the Army Air Corps, asked for the VFW's assistance.

The VFW had already shown its support for the Air Corps by collecting $150,000 for the purchase of fifteen training planes. Now the department commanders from twelve midwestern states met in Chicago with ranking Army Air Corps officers and War Department officials to discuss ways to increase enlistments. The upshot of their meeting was the establishment of the Aviation Cadet program—a training program to test and drill young men eighteen to twenty-six years of age so they could qualify for the Air Corps. VFW member Mark Kinsey, a Des Moines, Iowa, newspaperman and radio writer, was selected to head the program.

Kinsey and his staff quickly worked up a program to help prospective aviation recruits pass the entrance examination. They prepared pamphlets, and supplied tests, aptitude screening material, application blanks, and study manuals to over 1400 Aviation Cadet Committees in forty-six states. Posts then supplied, free of charge, special classes in mathematics, physics, English, geography, history, or any other subject in which a recruit was weak. All tests were continually updated to stay abreast of Air Corps requirements.

During its seven months of operation, the Aviation Cadet program was extremely effective. In one subject area alone, 83 percent of those who had failed the examination on their first try passed after being tutored by VFW members. In all, the VFW successfully recruited 75,000 men for the Air Corps and 45,000 for other branches of the service. The VFW received hundreds of letters from young fliers thanking the organization for enabling them to "make the grade."

Both the Army Air Corps and the Department of War hastened to express its official appreciation for the VFW's assistance. From Major General J.A. Ulio of the War Department came the following message: "The War Department has long appreciated the generous and patriotic assistance given by the VFW in recruiting aviation cadets. Your collaboration has been an important factor in the enlargement of our Air Forces." And writing to Commander-in-Chief Robert T. Merrill on December 4, 1942, General H.H. Arnold said, "I have been following with close attention the successful campaign by the Veterans of Foreign Wars in the recruiting of Aviation Cadets. I congratulate you on the fine organization which you, yourself, and which your organization, has exhibited in the Army Air Forces."

Although the Aviation Cadet program, the Americanism Department programs, and other VFW programs conducted at the national level received the most publicity, many worthwhile projects also went on in the trenches (on the local level). Throughout the war, for example, local posts selflessly pitched in to alleviate shortages of materials essential to wartime industry. They could do little about the rationing of consumer goods such as meat, sugar, coffee, canned goods, and cheese which made feeding their members' families difficult, but posts organized and led thousands of scrap drives to feed the demands of industry. Together with other groups and individuals, they helped collect 43,919 tons of fat, 255,513 tons of tin cans, 6 million tons of waste paper, and 26 million tons of scrap iron and steel.

Some VFW posts organized Red Cross first aid classes, War Bond sales, and Home Defense Corps. Members of "Home Defense Corps" performed a multitude of duties, ranging from firefighting to conducting coastal and border security patrols. When deemed necessary, men on some patrols carried sidearms—often personally owned pieces. Other posts worked with the USO or performed hospital work. One post (No. 1010 of Emeryville, California) had 10,000 automobile bumper stickers printed with the message "Remember Pearl Harbor." Several posts and departments held fund-raising drives to buy ambulances for the Army, and the Cook County Council of the Department of Illinois raised enough funds to furnish cigarettes to the seventeen veterans' hospitals. Several hundred posts formed blood donor clubs to supply sick and wounded servicemen with blood and blood plasma—lifesaving commodities that could not be purchased.

The waste paper salvage committee of Post No. 2085, Ontario, California, collected 147,178 pounds of waste paper.

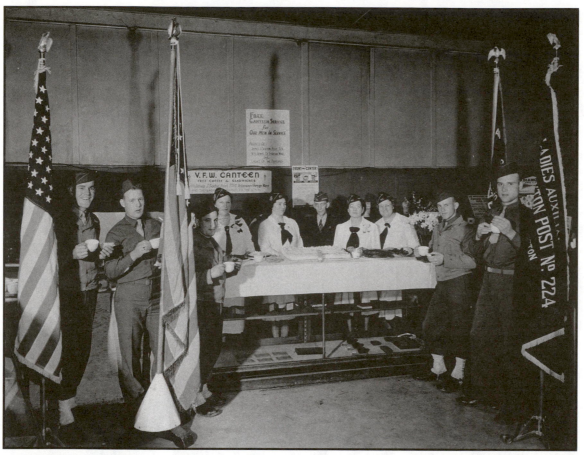

This canteen, operated by Post No. 224 of Aberdeen, Washington, and its Auxiliary, served members of all branches of the service.

Local Ladies Auxiliaries also devoted themselves to the war effort. Besides assisting posts with local and national programs, Auxiliary members tried to ensure that each serviceman, no matter where he was stationed, received mail from home. Auxiliaries sent Christmas boxes filled with home-baked treats, canned goods, and knitted items. They also mailed hundreds of letters via the Post Office's newly introduced V-Mail—a weight-saving measure that transferred letters to microfilm, then reprinted them on paper upon arrival overseas. In addition, Auxiliaries visited servicemen in veterans' hospitals and sent them homemade baked goods, books, and cigarettes.

In recognition of the VFW's vital role in the war effort, Commanders-in-Chief were kept informed about the progress of the war and how activities on the home front were contributing to the war effort. Several of the Commanders-in-Chief were sent by our government on secret overseas military tours.

Commanders-in-Chief Robert T. Merrill (1942–43), Carl Schoeninger (1943–44), and Jean Brunner (1944–45) all personally visited overseas battlefields during their terms in office. Together with Navy Captain James E. Van Zandt, who had resigned from the House of Representatives to take a commission, Commander-in-Chief Joseph Stack (1945–46) inspected hospitals and installations throughout the Pacific on a trip that covered over 200,000 miles. With the knowledge gained from these trips, the VFW leaders were able to boost morale back home by assuring families that their sons were receiving, if needed, the finest medical treatment available and that the extra effort those on the home front were putting into the war was making a difference.

Thanks to their first-hand knowledge about the way the war was progressing, the VFW's leaders easily recognized when the time was ripe to change from a wartime program to one aimed at handling the

Members of VFW Post No. 1300 of St. Louis, Missouri, were among the donors in the "Barrel of Blood" campaign sponsored by Post No. 127, Jewish War Veterans of the United States.

Officers of Post No. 657 of Dayton, Ohio, and its Auxiliary preparing Christmas packages to send to servicemen from their hometown

American soldiers wait in readiness aboard a U.S. Coast Guard manned vessel during crossing of the English Channel in the D-Day invasion of Normandy.
(Official U.S. Coast Guard Photo)

for new veterans now, before "the war's over" apathy made their attainment more difficult.

Aware that many millions now in their country's military service would have an increased need for rehabilitation, the VFW gave high priority to expanding and overhauling its Rehabilitation Service. In 1931, this Service had taken over several duties from the National Service Bureau, including the responsibilities for handling claims submitted to the government's War Risk Insurance Bureau, Bureau of Pensions, and Bureau of Vocational Training and Rehabilitation.

In 1943, Commander-in-Chief Carl Schoeninger ordered a survey to determine the number of veterans who would need rehabilitative services and the degree to which they would need them. Then, in order to provide the most efficient service possible, the Rehabilitation Service was removed from VFW politics. In the past, rehabilitation officers had been selected by the national organization and had processed claims from an office in Washington, D.C. Now, department commanders and their Councils of Administration recruited them from the ranks of veterans disabled in World War II and assigned them to work for their sponsoring department. This move brought understanding, eligible young men into careers as Service Officers (sometimes referred to as Rehabilitation Officers). Salaries for these future Service Officers were jointly paid by the national organization and the department that the Service Officer would be representing.

To train the new officers, Fred Beard, a Regional Rehabilitation Officer, conducted an intensive, six-week course. The course covered everything the officers needed to know about handling claims, adjudication work, organization of the Veterans Administration, report writing, and re-employment opportunities for veterans.

As a result of these improvements—and others instituted after Colonel George E. Ijams was appointed Director of the National Rehabilitation Service in 1945—the VFW Rehabilitation Service grew into what many veterans and government employees con-

postwar problems its veterans would encounter. That turning point came in 1943, when Allied forces went on the offensive in both the European Theater of Operations (ETO) and the Pacific Theater of Operations (PTO) and reclaimed areas such as Stalingrad, Rostov, and Kharkov in Russia; Tunis and Bizerte in North Africa; the Aleutian Islands; and Guadalcanal in the Pacific. Only in isolated spots such as China and parts of Russia were the Allies still content to just hold on or to continue their policy of strategic withdrawal. Confident that the war would reach a speedy conclusion, the VFW began shifting its emphasis away from winning the war and towards securing benefits

By VE Day, May 8, 1945, the VFW was well on its way to securing many of the benefits needed by the flood of new veterans. (U.S. Army Photo)

A class of disabled World War II veterans studying to become VFW service officers

sidered the "best in the world." At times, in fact, the VFW handled as many veterans' claims as all other agencies combined. And it did so without federal aid. Changes in the Rehabilitation Service were financed in part by funds from the national organization and from a nationwide Welfare Fund Drive.

Revamping the Rehabilitation Service was not the VFW's only accomplishment during Schoeninger's year in office. Working with Congress, the VFW also laid the groundwork for passage of several major bills that related to the veteran's welfare. The VFW set the stage at its 1943 Encampment by adopting VFW Resolution 374. With this resolution, the VFW became the first veteran's group to go on record favoring federal aid in the education of veterans. Over the next months, the VFW collaborated with the American Legion in developing a bill that would provide far-reaching educational benefits for veterans. Then in June 1944, Congress passed Public Law 346, the Service Man's Readjustment Act.

The Service Man's Readjustment Act, more commonly called the G.I. Bill of Rights, provided veterans of World War II with funds to continue education that was interrupted by the war, or to obtain training or formal education that would improve their ability to

Major Richard I. Bong, World War II flying ace. Members of Bong's Post No. 847 of Superior, Wisconsin, voted to make a special donation of $10 to the VFW Welfare Fund Drive for each of the 27 Japanese planes Bong had shot down.

secure gainful employment. It offered tuition and living expense monies, government-backed loans for educational purposes, and some provisions for unemployment compensation. In short, as Vice Presidential Candidate Harry S. Truman told the 1944 National Encampment, the act was "intended to give returning soldiers an opportunity to get into the civilian setup of the country on a basis where they will not face apple-selling and things of that sort as we did after the First World War."

Today the G.I. Bill is perhaps the best-known piece of veterans' legislation ever passed, but it came within a hair's breadth of dying in committee. In fact, this landmark bill might never have reached the floor of Congress if it weren't for former VFW Commander-in-Chief (now Congressman) Bernard W. Kearney. When the bill was deadlocked in the Senate and House conferee group it had to clear before coming up for a vote, Kearney managed to produce the tie-breaking vote. Together with World War I Ace Eddie Rickenbacker, he had Congressman John S. Gibson of Georgia escorted across half a continent in time to cast the deciding vote. Kearney persuaded the police to give Gibson a high-speed ride to the airfield in Georgia where a plane arranged for by Rickenbacker waited. Gibson was then flown to Washington, D.C., and rushed by a second set of policemen to the Capitol.

With the VFW's support, several other important veterans' bills were passed in 1944. Among these was the Mustering Out Pay Act, passed February 3, 1944. This act was intended to reduce some of the economic hardships veterans of other wars had experienced immediately upon returning home. Provisions included payment for unused leave time and transportation to the returnee's home of record, as well as a VFW-backed provision of differential payment for men with foreign service.

Among the beneficiaries of VFW-supported veterans' legislation were these soldiers who served in the China-Burma-India Campaign. Here they are shown leaving the Far East bound for home in 1944. (Signal Corps Photo)

To lessen the financial hardships of troops still on active duty, the VFW also sponsored an act to provide hazardous duty pay to combat infantry soldiers. Although this proposal was opposed by the War and Navy Departments, it passed on June 30, 1944.

Another major VFW objective was achieved when Congress passed Public Law 313. This bill increased Spanish American War pensions from $60 to $75 a month, and compensation for non-service-connected permanent disability from $40 to $50 a month,

A silent testimonial to the reason behind hazardous duty pay: at one of the distribution points where remains of the dead of World War II were assembled before being escorted to their homes for burial, National Officers of the VFW listen as the National Chaplain offers a memorial prayer.

and boosted compensation for veterans over 65 to $60 a month.

The final act beneficial to servicemen was the Veteran Preference Law of 1944. Thanks to this law, job preference for veterans no longer had to be granted on a war-by-war basis by regulation, directive, or presidential proclamation; it was now a matter of statute law. In addition, the new federal law allowed returnees—as a step to ease the transition back into civilian life—fifty-two weeks of unemployment compensation at $20 a week. During the four years covered by this statute, over 8 million veterans subscribed in full or in part to this "52–20 club." For veterans who wanted to go into business, the government guaranteed half of a $2000 loan bearing a maximum interest charge of 4 percent. In addition, the government helped job-seeking veterans find employment.

Although the provisions of the Veteran Preference Law reduced some of the employment problems that returning veterans typically faced, the VFW recognized that still more needed to be done to ease veterans back into the civilian work force. The organization wanted the nation's leading labor unions, as well as the federal government, to give job-seeking veterans favorable treatment. To this end, Commander-in-Chief Schoeninger appointed a Labor Relations Committee headed by former Commander-in-Chief Paul Wolman. In 1944, this committee met in Washington, D.C., with representatives of the American Federation of Labor (AFL) and the Congress of Industrial Organizations (CIO).

By the end of the meeting, the union leaders and the VFW labor committee had worked out an agreement in which the unions recognized many rights and needs of returning veterans. This agreement was based on the premise that veterans who had served honorably constituted "a citizenry to whom the Nation owes consideration by reason of such service."

Included in the agreement were provisions that: unions would grant membership to all veterans who acquired appropriate job skills while in the military; service in the military would count toward seniority in the unions; and veterans who were unable to perform their previous job due to a service-connected disability should be given another job. In return, the VFW and its members acknowledged the right of the unions to organize and bargain collectively in behalf of its members. Although the VFW and union representatives did not hold any additional meetings or monitor the agreement to make sure it was carried out, many veteran members of labor organizations owe their employment to the seniority provisions of this agreement.

After reaching its agreement with the unions, the VFW successfully fought for one more Congressional measure to better the veterans' employment situation. In July 1945, Congress passed a VFW-sponsored law which benefitted veteran-entrepreneurs by giving them second priority after the federal government in buying war surplus materials. The bill, Public Law 375, prevented the veteran from being "brushed off" by government bureaucrats who had previously sold the surplus goods primarily to speculators.

The VFW's many efforts on behalf of veterans—on the home front, in the legislative arena, in union circles—did not go unremarked. During the war, overseas veterans joined the VFW by the thousands. Between 1940 and 1945, membership increased by over 350 percent, growing from 201,170 to 741,310. By 1946, a year after Allied victory had been declared first in Germany, then in Japan, membership had climbed to 1,544,444—the highest level it would reach until 1970. And by 1949, the VFW's 10,000 posts stretched from coast to coast and from Tokyo and Yokohama to Paris and Bremen. For the VFW, looking after the needs of all these new members in peacetime posed a challenge equal to any it had faced in wartime.

Marines on a South Pacific island being sworn into the VFW by Sergeant Hal Wirtz, Past Commander of Post No. 904 of Los Angeles

PEACETIME INTERLUDE

On April 12, 1945, President Franklin Roosevelt died of a cerebral hemorrhage, four months into his fourth term. He was succeeded by Harry S. Truman, the first VFW member ever to become president of the United States. A former captain of the "Dizzy" D Battery, 129th Field Artillery, 35th Division of the United States Army in World War I, Truman had had a long and active association with the Veterans of Foreign Wars. He had been a National Legislative Liaison Deputy, Commander of Post 35 in Kansas City, Missouri, and Chairman of the 1931 Kansas City Encampment Committee. In fact, Truman's role in the 1931 Encampment may have been what boosted him into national politics. At any rate, it brought him to the attention of Missouri Democratic

Party leaders who had been looking for an A.E.F. man to nominate for U.S. Senator. In 1934, and again in 1940, Truman was elected a U.S. Senator from Missouri, and in 1944, he appeared before the VFW National Encampment as the Democratic vice-presidential candidate.

Even with a fellow VFW member in the White House, the organization still had its work cut out for it. The VFW did not expect Truman to automatically champion all its causes, nor did he. And even though the VFW had made major legislative strides in the last years of World War II, there were still many arenas in which the organization needed to use its political muscle. Among major postwar concerns facing the VFW were rehabilitation, medical care, pensions, employment, and housing for the 16 million veterans who served in World War II. The need to maintain an adequate defense—another longstanding concern—was also a high priority.

To Commanders-in-Chief Joseph M. Stack and Louis E. Starr fell the duties of getting the organization back on a peace-time track. Stack, chief of the detective bureau for Allegheny County, Pennsylvania, assumed office after the 1945 National Encampment in Chicago. Starr, an Oregon attorney, took over following the 1946 Encampment in Boston—a convention chaired incidently by John F. Kennedy, the twenty-nine-year-old commander of the Brockton, Massachusetts, Joseph P. Kennedy, Jr., Post 5880.

During their terms in office, both Stack and Starr grappled with the same overwhelming entitlement problem: where were the millions of veteran returnees to live? Many who had lived with their parents before

entering the service had since married and needed homes of their own. Others had suffered service-connected disabilities and now had special housing needs. Under the auspices of the Service Man's Readjustment Act, over a million GI's had flooded the nation's colleges and universities, causing severe housing shortages in many college towns. To compound problems, there was a dearth of construction materials, and materials that were available were primarily being used for industrial building, not new home construction.

President Harry S. Truman receiving a formal invitation to attend the 47th National Encampment of the VFW. Pictured, left to right: John Breen, encampment housing coordinator; John F. Kennedy, general chairman of Encampment Committee; Representaive John McCormack (Mass.); Truman; Senator Leverett Saltonstall (Mass.); VFW Commander-in-Chief Joseph Stack; Past Commander-in-Chief Eugene Carver; J.J. Spurrier, aide to the Commander-in-Chief (Press Association, Inc.)

For troops returning from Europe after World War II, there was little elbow room afloat or ashore; hence the VFW's emphasis on veterans' housing programs.
(N.Y. Press Assn. Photo)

In the fall of 1945, the VFW Council of Administration met and endorsed a long-range housing program. They sent a telegram to President Truman urging him to make veterans' housing a priority. Within ten days, President Truman appointed Wilson Wyatt as his housing expeditor and asked Congress to institute housing controls so that industry would no longer be able to compete with private citizens for scarce lumber and building materials. In May 1946, Congress obliged by passing the Veteran Emergency Housing Act of 1946 (Public Law 388). Even after the law's passage, however, many veterans still had difficulties getting housing. Sometimes unscrupulous contractors charged more than the price stipulated in their contracts or attempted to force the buyer to

finance through a lending agency specified by the builder. At the VFW's insistence, many of these cases were investigated by government representatives of the National Housing Expeditor's Office. Charges of fraud were then brought, where warranted, against the builder.

About the same time the VFW was helping veterans settle into new homes, the organization coincidentally found a permanent home for its own national headquarters. In 1946, the organization was given the opportunity to purchase the Porter Building, the building in Kansas City, Missouri, it had leased since 1940. At $550,000, the price was steep, but because the building had more space than the VFW needed, the organization was able to lease out parts of the building to help meet the mortgage payments. Today the headquarters building houses offices for the Adjutant General, Quartermaster General, Program Directors, Public Relations and Editorial staff of the *VFW Magazine,* and National Supply Department. With the inflationary trend of the last several decades, the property is worth many times the amount paid for it.

After wrestling with housing issues in the early postwar period, the VFW turned its attention to a different entitlement problem: adequate medical care for veterans. The VFW's major battle in this area occurred in 1949, following a Presidential Order curtailing VA hospital construction. The order, which would have prevented the addition of some 16,000 desperately needed beds, came from VA Administrator Carl Gray. Ironically, Gray had previously testified that there was a need for every bed.

In 1949, members of the VFW's National Rehabilitation Committee spent three weeks testifying against this move before a Senate committee, headed by Senator Claude Pepper of Florida. The VFW pointed out to the Senate committee that the waiting lists for hospital care submitted by the VA did not give a true picture of the number of veterans who needed treatment. Many veterans had been discouraged from applying by the long waiting lists; these veterans were not even considered in the VA report. Furthermore, Gray's new orders—which allowed hospitals to be built only near a medical school or in areas with high concentrations of veterans—posed a hardship for veterans in many areas. Not providing beds for veterans with tuberculosis or neurological problems endangered not only their lives, but those of their families and others. According to the VFW committee, many veterans who needed neurosurgical help were locked in jails because no hospital beds were available. The VFW also noted that the drastic shortage of doctors in VA hospitals could be alleviated if doctors were relieved of their record-keeping duties. Finally, the VFW spoke out against the VA's treatment of patients who had both service-connected and non-service-connected conditions. The hospitals provided care only for a veteran's service-connected conditions and forced veterans to finance care of non-service-connected conditions themselves or to seek treatment in the charity wards of other hospitals. Both the VFW and the Disabled American Veterans organization presented a twelve-point position paper condemning this practice and suggesting the reforms needed in VA hospitals.

While the VFW was trying to wrest better medical care for veterans from the government, it was also pursuing another perennial entitlement issue—increased pensions for disabled veterans. The VFW argued that an increase was needed because of inflation and the higher cost of living. Opponents in Congress, however, maintained that the hike should not be granted unless veterans were required to pass an unemployability test to qualify for pensions. Pennsylvania Representative and former VFW Commander-in-Chief James Van Zandt vehemently attacked this argument, and in the end, his view prevailed. On June 1, 1949, Congress approved an across-the-board increase of 5 percent.

As vital as the VFW's campaigns for veterans' entitlements such as pensions, medical care, and housing were, they were not the only issues that concerned the organization during this period. The organization also lent its support to broader causes—most importantly, to world peace.

As Chapter 3 discusses, the VFW had embraced the idea of global peace and international cooperation immediately after World War I. Now, after the second "War to End Wars," the rest of the nation—and the world—also finally professed themselves ready to lay down their arms. What was needed to maintain international peace and security, the world leaders felt, was an alliance similar to the failed League of Nations. What was needed was an international forum in which countries' differences could be resolved through discussion, not bloodshed.

From April 25 to June 26, 1945, representatives of about fifty nations gathered in San Francisco to draw up a charter for the proposed peace organization. The VFW sent a consulting delegation to this United Nations World Conference on International Organization. The delegation was headed by Jr. Vice Commander-in-Chief Louis Starr, and also included L.G. Taggart, National Patriotic Instructor, and Frederic M. Miller, Chief Justice of the Iowa Supreme Court. (Judge Miller was a member of the jurists' panel that had formed the World Court Statute, the act creating and giving scope to the World Court Organization.)

At about the same time the United Nations charter was being ratified (October 24, 1945), the VFW held its own version of the United Nations by hosting a United Nations Veterans Victory Conference. At the VFW's invitation, veterans' representatives of twenty-two nations convened to present plans for outlawing future wars. During the convention, those who had fought the war were given a chance to air their views on how peace could prevail through unity of purpose between nations. Their ideas and recommendations were forwarded to the United Nations in hopes of giving that organization added foresight and understanding.

Through the efforts of Colonel George E. Arneman, former advisor to F.D.R. on Russian affairs, the VFW also kept abreast of U.N. activities abroad. Stack had hired Arneman as consultant to the Commander-in-Chief, registered him with the State Department, and sent him overseas to represent the VFW in

One of many reasons the VFW favored world peace: Suresnes American Cemetery at Suresnes, France, which contains the bodies of 1541 Americans killed during World War II

an official capacity at all meetings concerning U.S. policy, United Nations sessions, and conferences. Arneman also scrutinized international events of importance to the VFW and sent coded messages about his observations back to national headquarters.

Although its support of the United Nations and its aims were unwavering, the VFW did not relax its stance on military preparedness. As it had since its founding, the organization continued to insist that the best guarantee of peace was a defense force strong enough to enforce that stand. Because of this conviction, in 1946 the VFW established the National Security Committee. The group met regularly with

Army and Navy officials on matters of defense and security. Charter members of the committee appointed by Commander-in-Chief Stack included: Paul C. Wolman, Past Commander-in-Chief of the VFW; James E. Van Zandt, Past Commander-in-Chief of the VFW and present member of the House Committee on Armed Forces; Brigadier General Ralph K. Robertson of New York City; Charles Sawyer, Secretary of Commerce; L.P. Cookingham, city manager of Kansas City; Teller Ammons, former Governor of Colorado; and others. Today this committee and its director are responsible for keeping the organization updated on the international scene, our defense posture, and any subversive activities that might weaken the nation.

Hardly had the ink dried on the U.N. charter when America's former ally, the Soviet Union, began to take actions that justified the VFW's position on defense. By blockading Berlin, seizing power in Czechoslovakia, and tightening their control on all of the small countries in their sphere of influence, the Soviets made it clear that they understood no policy that was not backed by military strength equal to or greater than their own. Under Commander-in-Chief Lyall T. Beggs (1948–49), the VFW took a firm stand against what it termed "additional Russian aggression." In 1947, it applauded Congress's passage of the Marshall Plan, a strong foreign aid bill designed to prevent further Russian inroads in countries unable to finance their own reconstruction. To back this hard-line stance with some military muscle, on June 24, 1948, Congress passed a new Selective Service Act that covered all eligible males from eighteen to twenty-five years of age. In contrast to the wartime draft, this new draft could be invoked for a specified period of time, rather than just for the period of conflict plus six months. It also permitted draftees to receive R.O.T.C. training, serve with the National Guard or Organized Reserves, and serve a shortened period in the Regulars with a follow-up in the Guard or Reserves.

Throughout the postwar era, all VFW positions and activities were widely publicized, thanks to the groundwork laid by Commander-in-Chief Stack. Stack knew the value of good public relations and took a number of steps to increase the VFW's profile. In 1945, he hired General Bonner Fellers, General Douglas MacArthur's former military secretary, as the VFW's director of public relations. In addition, Stack began the practice of appointing a personal secretary and public relations man who traveled with the Commander-in-Chief and handled press releases, publicity hand-outs, and radio appearances. Also during Stack's administration, a press relations section was set up in Washington, D.C., under the direction of public relations specialist Neil Kimball, and the *National News,* a monthly magazine in newspaper format, began publi-

cation. Finally, the VFW began broadcasting two new radio programs, "Calling All Veterans," and "Our Land Be Bright."

The new radio programs were especially effective in furthering public awareness of the VFW—at a minimum of cost. The "Calling All Veterans" program, which first aired in 1946, received donated air time estimated at $2 million for the $25,000 cost of producing the show. This success was mainly due to its use of *platters*—canned shows that were aired at different times over 450 stations across the country.

The "Our Land Be Bright" program, which began in 1947, received an estimated $4 million in free air time. So popular was this program that it was carried over 900 of the nation's 1500 stations. Listeners to the program heard such nationally known talent as Margaret O'Brien, Jack Carson, Jane Wyman, Ronald Reagan, Jack Benny, Herbert Marshall, Abbott and Costello, Henry Fonda, Dana Andrews, Glenn Ford, and Dennis Morgan. Other speakers included Senator Warren R. Austin of the United Nations, General George C. Kenny, Major Alexander Seversky, Bob Considine, and Lowell Thomas. These speakers covered topics such as housing, air power, education, national security, rehabilitation, veterans' benefits, youth activities, Communism, and voting.

By the end of the decade, the VFW's public relations machinery was well oiled and primed for the organization's biggest celebration to date. 1949 marked the organization's Golden Jubilee Year, and the VFW proudly invited the whole nation to take part in a number of anniversary festivities. April third through the ninth was named "Golden Jubilee Week." The highlight of this public celebration was a special, hour-long NBC radio show which focused on the accomplishments of the VFW during its 50 years of existence. The show featured comedian Bob Hope as host, as well as Commander-in-Chief Lyall Beggs, singer Dinah Shore, actors Jack Carson and Dennis Morgan, and Janis Paige, the 1949 National Buddy Poppy Girl.

Another Golden Jubilee project enlisted 637 radio stations and 850 newspapers in the distribution of more than 300,000 free booklets outlining the benefits to which all veterans and their dependents were entitled. Also in conjunction with its 50th anniversary, the VFW and its Ladies Auxiliary sponsored a "Poetic Verse Contest" with the theme, "Why I Love America." The contest was designed to increase and instill patriotism in the citizens of the nation. The first place prize of $20,000 was won by a Utah veteran, "Pop" Warner.

At the VFW's Golden Jubilee Encampment in Miami, Florida, three eminent members of the organization were featured speakers. The first was none other than President Harry S. Truman, by now a twenty-two-year member. As part of his address, President Truman told the assembled delegates, "I am proud to be a member of the nation's oldest active veterans organization."

The next man to pay tribute to the VFW was James C. Putnam, co-founder of the American Veterans of Foreign Service, and thus of the VFW. Three years ago at the 1947 Encampment in Boston, the seventy-year-old Putnam had refused to be chauf-

feured along the two-mile parade route, declaring, "I'm walking with the boys, that's all there is to it." Now the spry Spanish American War veteran strode to the podium to praise long-time comrade and co-founder, James Romanis, for the enormous contributions he had given the organization. Speaking about his own feelings he said, "It is given to few men, I think, to have a dream so richly realized as has been my early dream of a veterans' organization that would not die with its generation." (Even as Putnam spoke of his dreams of forming an "evergreen" organization, another formerly powerful veteran's organization had all but faded into oblivion. The Grand Army of the Republic had held its 83rd and last encampment that August 1st in Indianapolis, Indiana. Only six of the surviving sixteen members were able to attend.)

To cap off the Golden Jubilee Celebration, past Commander-in-Chief James Romanis spoke in homage of the men who had inspired the formation of the VFW a half century ago: the American veterans. Romanis said, "To my mind the war veteran is an outstanding citizen. He typifies the real American. In

President Harry S. Truman addressing the 50th VFW National Convention.
Commander-in-Chief Charles Ralls is second from left.

When North Korea invaded South Korea, President Truman immediately ordered the U.S. Army and Navy to the defense of her ally. Here F4U's (Corsairs) returning from a combat mission over North Korea circle the USS Boxer. (National Archives)

spirit he is a rambling, gambling, adventuring explorer, always seeking betterment of conditions for himself and his people. Undaunted by adverse circumstances he pushes ever onward to his goal. Regardless of to what parts of the world his quest may carry him he is always willing to take a chance, ignoring the odds that may be against him."

THE WAR ON COMMUNISM

In 1950, the "Russian aggression" that the VFW and much of the free world had been condemning abruptly escalated. At issue was the way in which the tiny Far Eastern nation of Korea had been divided at the end of World War II. The United States had been

granted control of the populous, agricultural region south of the 38th parallel, while the Soviet Union had received the sparsely settled, industrial region to the north. With the help of the United Nations, the South Koreans had held elections and drawn up a democratic constitution, but the Northern Koreans remained under the Communists' heel. The Soviets adamantly resisted all attempts by the United States and the United Nations to reunite the sundered nation.

Then, on June 25, 1950, the North Korean Army made its move. Backed by Russian tanks and planes, the Communists surged across the 38th parallel and invaded the newly formed democracy to the south.

American reaction was swift. Within twenty-four hours, President Truman announced he would send the Army and Navy to the aid of South Korea. Other democracies quickly followed suit. With U.N. approval, Great Britain, Australia, New Zealand, Canada, the Netherlands, France, Turkey, Thailand, the Philippines, and Brazil all sent troops in early July. When the U.N. Security Council asked the U.S. to take command of this world army, Truman appointed General Douglas MacArthur to the job.

At first, the VFW stood solidly behind all of Truman's actions. In August, Commander-in-Chief Clyde A. Lewis called the president's response to the invasion "courageous and to the point." Lewis further advised that "no resource, including manpower, should be spared in implementing our vowed intention to halt the spread of Communist aggression in Korea as well as to protect Formosa which stands as a symbol of democratic integrity."

In conclusion, Lewis declared, "There are times when patience is no longer a virtue and certainly time has come for the free people of the world to, by show of force, serve notice that they will no longer tolerate the pushing around they have been receiving at the hands of Soviet Russia and its stooges. Whether our move will bring a back down by Soviet Russia remains to be seen, but whether it does or not it is high time we took a stand against Communist aggression anywhere in the world."

As the war progressed, the VFW began to find some fault with the Truman administration's handling of the Korean situation. The 13,000 delegates of the August 27 through September 1, 1950 encampment were especially critical of White House policies. In no uncertain terms they made it clear that they were fed up with the policy of appeasement and apathy they felt had been displayed by the Secretaries of State and Defense. They called upon the President to seek out new leadership of the "Highest Integrity and Non-Political Favor" to develop new policies concerning foreign policy and national defense.

On national defense issues, the delegates passed resolutions asking Congress for: the mobilization of the National Guard; expansion of the Selective Service draft for all males between the ages of eighteen and thirty-five who had no previous military service; establishment of an adequate radar network, supported by an effective Air Force; conversion of necessary manufacturing facilities to furnish the armed forces with needed, up-to-date equipment, and expansion on a global scale of America's intelligence operations. Concerning America's foreign policy, they proposed legislation that would prohibit the surrender of any of the U.S.'s sovereign power to any world federation or league of nations; severance of trade relations with the Soviets and their satellite nations;

A U.S. soldier comforts a friend who has just lost a buddy in battle, August 1950. (U.S. Army Photo)

At the 1950 National Convention, delegates spoke out sharply against perceived lapses in the national defense posture.

withdrawal of the Marshall Plan from any nation that furnished any material to the Soviets or aided their military effort; and continued aid to the United Nations to enable them to better deal with any outbreak of aggression. If the VFW had its way, it would signal the Communist world that the U.S. would no longer tolerate their aggressive tendencies, even if armed force was the only means of halting them.

While no names were mentioned, discussions that these resolutions sparked gave the press sufficient reason to report that the VFW demanded the resignation of both Secretary of State Dean Acheson and Secretary of Defense Louis A. Johnson. Later, resolutions critical of the Johnson's handling of the Department of Defense were brought across the encampment floor. Shortly afterwards, Johnson tendered his resignation and was replaced by General George C. Marshall, U.S. Army Retired.

The most bitter disagreement to arise between the VFW and the Truman administration was over the government's treatment of General Douglas MacArthur. Friction first developed between MacArthur and the administration when Commander-in-Chief Clyde Lewis invited MacArthur, as commander of the

forces fighting Communism in Korea, to send a message or greeting to the 51st Encampment. Not only was the general a member of the VFW, but his father, General Arthur MacArthur, had been a Commander-in-Chief of the Army of the Philippines, which had merged with the American Veterans of Foreign Service to found the VFW.

MacArthur obligingly sent a message to national headquarters praising the actions Truman had taken in Korea and setting forth his views on the need for defending Formosa from the Communists. These views, which were not shared by the Truman administration, included a recommendation that Formosa's air force and army be used to attack selected points on the Chinese mainland. This MacArthur believed would ease the pressure being applied against our forces by Chinese forces now in Korea. Then, several days before the encampment convened, Secretary of Defense Louis Johnson abruptly ordered MacArthur to withdraw his message.

As ordered, MacArthur withdrew his message. The VFW, too, never disclosed its contents. But the wire services had already released the message to the press, and over 400,000 copies of *U.S. News and*

World Report carrying the general's words had been printed and shipped out.

For several days after MacArthur's message was leaked, front-page editorials kept the controversy reverberating around the world. MacArthur's detractors argued that generals fight wars, while politicians make statements and determine policy. His defenders claimed that MacArthur, with his long service in the Far East, knew more about how the situation should be handled than did the White House. The VFW made no secret of whose side it was on. Commander-in-Chief Lewis cabled MacArthur, "Regret any embarrassment this may have caused you. Be assured the VFW is with you to a man." And the 51st Encampment unanimously passed a resolution presenting General Douglas MacArthur with the organization's highest award, the VFW Gold Medal Citizenship Award. The editors of many newspapers viewed this as a direct rebuke to those who had directed MacArthur to withdraw the message.

In April 1951, there was a new controversy over Truman's treatment of MacArthur, and again the VFW took the general's side. By now, the Communist Chinese were actively aiding North Korea. The U.N. forces had twice been driven south of the 38th parallel, but had regrouped and fought back to a position somewhat north of their original line. Truman was ready to call for a truce; MacArthur was not. Mac-

General of the Army Douglas MacArthur in happier days watching representatives of Allied nations sign the document of Japanese surrender aboard the USS Missouri. *(Signal Corps Photo)*

*Members of the 1st Marine Division engaging
enemy forces in December, 1950*
(Defense Dept. Photo [Marine Corps])

Arthur wanted to seize the opportunity to eradicate Communism in the Far East by blockading the Chinese coast, bombing the mainland, and invading southern China with the help of Chiang Kai-shek's army. Truman feared that this move would lead to World War III, since Russia was bound by treaty to assist China. When MacArthur refused to agree to a cease fire, Truman relieved him of command.

Just days after MacArthur's ouster, the VFW showed its support for him by inviting him to open the organization's New York City Loyalty Day Parade. Here Commander-in-Chief Charles C. Ralls presented MacArthur with the VFW Gold Citizenship Medal and its accompanying citation. Then General MacArthur launched the parade with words that, under the circumstances, certainly did him credit: "Today, the word is loyalty."

Despite the VFW's occasional differences of opinion with the Truman administration, the organization's contributions to the war effort were as unstinting as usual. Some of the VFW's earliest work was aimed at building public support of the fight against Communism by heightening appreciation of the American way of life. In 1950, for example, the organization started an American Sovereignty Campaign to combat the United World Federalist Movement. This movement was one of the many idealistic move-

ments to arise from college and university campuses. The crux of the movement was to unite all the countries in the world under one government and thus eliminate war. To accomplish this goal, each country would have to give up its sovereignty and all of its laws. With World War II just past and another going on in Korea, the idea found fertile ground in many wishful minds. Twenty-one states passed resolutions favoring world unity. Not surprisingly, members of the VFW, who had recently returned from rescuing nations whose sovereignty had been taken from them, rejected the idea. National and state VFW Headquarters appointed committees to alert the American public to this menace, and national and state legislative representatives worked against any legislation that favored the movement. Congressmen and state legislators were bombarded with letters and phone calls opposing the World Federalist Movement. The VFW Auxiliary formed active committees called "Minute Women" and joined with the men in exposing this movement for what it really was, wishful thinking. The campaign succeeded in persuading all but three of the twenty-one state legislatures to rescind legislation that was favorable to the Federalist Movement.

The "Loyalty Day" campaign was another strategy the organization used to stir up the nation's patriotism. During this campaign, the VFW urged the American people to ask their elected representatives for a national holiday that would glorify America's principles just as the Communists' May Day celebrations glorified theirs. This idea was not new. A few VFW posts had held forms of "Loyalty Day" celebrations as far back as the early 1920s. These posts were primarily from large cities where Communist organizations were active. Their celebrations consisted mostly of small parades, dinners, featured speakers, and prominent displays of the Stars and Stripes.

Many eminent Americans supported the Loyalty Day campaign. In 1950, J. Edgar Hoover, Director of the F.B.I., wrote to the VFW, "I wish you all success concerning Loyalty Day. I can think of nothing more suitable for the occasion than those inspiring words of

Infantrymen on an M-4 tank move to attack during an assault of the 17th Regiment, 7th U.S. Infantry Division against Chinese Communists, June 13, 1951. (National Archives)

Theodore Roosevelt, 'We will have room in our country for but one flag, the stars and stripes, and we should tolerate no allegiance to other flags whether a foreign flag, or the red flag, or the black flag. We have room for but one loyalty, loyalty to the United States.'

"I'm sure that the ceremonies you will enjoy on Loyalty Day will stress the precious privileges you enjoy as Americans, however, those privileges bear attendant responsibilities. First, discharge well the duties of citizenship. Uphold the law and justice and make the community a better place in which to live. Second, learn all you can about those who practice anti-Americanism and subversive activities and promptly report all information to the Federal Bureau of Investigation."

In response to a bill introduced in 1955 by Pennsylvania Congressman James Van Zandt, Congress officially named May 1, 1955, as Loyalty Day,

but it was only for that year. Undaunted, Van Zandt introduced another measure to have May 1 declared as Loyalty Day each year. This measure was finally

While fighting in Korea continued unabated, the U.S. government tried to slash veterans' entitlements. Here Marines in Korea advance toward their objective, the hill in the background. (Defense Dept. Photo [Marine Corps])

passed in 1958, when Congress declared it Public Law 529.

While the VFW was supporting the war effort, it was, of course, also looking out for the rights of the servicemen fighting in Korea. In fact, several times during the Korean conflict, the organization had to mobilize to prevent cuts in existing benefits.

In 1951, the government attempted to weaken the Veterans Administration by slashing its budget and reassigning the oversight for certain veterans' entitlements to other federal agencies. (This was a management similar to that used by the Hoover Administration.) In May, the VFW adopted this resolution about the proposed move: "The VFW strenuously opposes any plan that would take from the immediate control and jurisdiction of the Administrator of Veterans Affairs any of the functions of the government that would have to do with the care and treatment of veterans." A copy of the resolution was presented to President Truman, the Administrator of Veterans Affairs, senators, congressmen, and interested governmental committees. The VFW's pressure did its job. The control of veterans' affairs remained in the province of the Administrator of Veterans Affairs.

Also during this period, Truman administration leaders tried again to make large cuts in the VA budget in the area of veterans' medical care. For three weeks in April, VFW personnel testified to the need for more hospital beds. Thanks to their testimony the cuts were not made; still, the battle was not won overnight. Both Commander-in-Chief Frank C. Hilton and his successor, James W. Cothran, found much of their time in office occupied with long and difficult struggles to prevent these cuts.

DOMESTIC ISSUES

Although many VFW activities during the early 1950s were somehow related to the conflict in Korea, the organization also busied itself with other issues. On the organizational side, Commander-in-Chief Frank Hilton ordered that the VFW national organization be streamlined to allow faster and more efficient service to members. In 1951, the responsibilities of Quartermaster General and Adjutant General—which had been fulfilled by one man—were divided up between two men. Robert B. Handy, Jr., the man who had been performing both jobs, gave up his Adjutant duties to Julian Dickenson, while continuing in his Quartermaster duties. Under Handy's direction, additional staff was hired in the Washington, D.C., office to help the organization gain services for the Korean veterans.

As it had throughout its history, the VFW also threw a great deal of energy into community improvement. In 1950, the VFW and its Ladies Auxiliary inaugurated the most intensive nationwide community service program ever undertaken by an organization. To encourage all posts, districts, and departments to get more involved in their communities, a contest with cash prizes totaling $35,000 was announced. The prize for the post with the best community service program was $10,000; first prize for the best Auxiliary program was $2,500. Before the contest period ended on May 31, 1951, 503,000 separate community service projects were accredited. One hundred twenty-three posts in forty-three departments received national awards for their projects assisting schools, churches, organizations, and citizens within their community.

World War II veteran Donald Dunn, winner of the farm in the Columbia River Basin

Statements received from post commanders following the contest attested to its success. For example, Post 615 of Wilmington, Delaware, noted that "Through community services, the name of the Veterans of Foreign Wars has gained new meaning among citizens"; Post 4421, of Monroe Georgia, that "Our community services have won the respect and admiration of everyone"; and Post 3819 of the District of Columbia, that "Our services have given us a better understanding of our neighbors."

Because the VFW accomplished so much good for individual communities during the contest period, the contest itself won an award from the Freedoms Foundation: the second place Gold Medal and a cash award of $300. This award is given to organizations whose speeches, publications, or other activities have the most positive effect on the public.

In one other nationwide contest conducted during the war, the VFW had the honor of selecting the winner of a truly unique prize. The contest itself was sponsored not by the VFW, but by Washington State's Columbia Basin Celebrations Committee. This committee was looking for an original way to cap off the completion of the Columbia Basin Federal Reclamation Project—a project that was connected with the construction of the Grand Coulee Dam and which involved the irrigation of a million acres of semi-arid, but very fertile land.

To commemorate the opening of the project, the Celebrations Committee decided to give an eighty-acre farm in the Columbia Basin to a deserving war veteran. This prize, valued at $50,000, included an attractively furnished home, livestock, farm buildings, planted crops, machinery, and other equipment and supplies. Because of the VFW's work on behalf of war veterans, the committee asked the VFW to select the winner.

The VFW put together a rule booklet and sent a copy to each post and department. The rules and regulations were then supplied to media in the areas where the posts would conduct their searches. With the help of prominent citizens, each post selected the "most worthy" candidate in its community, then forwarded the candidate's name to the state- or department-level judges. The winners from each of the forty-eight states, Alaska, Hawaii, and the Canal Zone were in turn referred to the National Judging Committee. In the end, Donald Dunn, a World War II veteran from Kansas, was declared the winner and given the farm in the Columbia River Basin near Moses Lake, Washington. During the previous year, Dunn's farm and crops had been wiped out by a flood.

More important than its part in selecting one veteran to be honored in the Columbia Basin Celebration was the work the VFW did to secure legislation honoring *all* American veterans. With the help of its endorsement, in 1953 Congress passed a bill stipulating that November 11th would henceforth be celebrated as Veteran's Day, not Armistice Day. Now, rather than commemorating the end of World War I, the nation would pause on that day to reflect on the contributions of veterans of every war.

TRUCE

On June 27, 1953, a truce between North and South Korea was finally signed. The fighting had lasted three years to the day. During that period, 5,720,000 Americans had served in Korea, and the United States had sustained 157,530 casualties. Many who survived had crippling injuries and were in need of serious rehabilitation and other assistance. Others—some 500,000 by 1954—enrolled in the nation's colleges and universities under the GI Bill. They, too, had special employment, housing, and financial needs. Fortunately, many of the programs and much of the

Ground forces, especially infantrymen like these members of the 3rd Infantry Division battling Communist Chinese troops, suffered the heaviest losses during the Korean War. (U.S. Army Photo/Courtesy 3rd Infantry Division Marne Museum)

machinery required to meet these needs was still in place from the "popular" war, World War II.

While the VFW worked to help the new veterans readjust to civilian life, it also continued its war on Communism. Its major objection to the Communist party, then as now, was that Communists advocate the overthrow, violent or otherwise, of other governments. This Communist philosophy is incompatible with the purpose of the VFW as stated in Article I of its constitution: . . .*to maintain true allegiance to the Government of the United States of America, and fidelity to its constitution and laws; to foster true patriotism; to maintain and extend the institution of American freedom; and to preserve and defend the United States from all her enemies, whomsoever."* As it had for over a quarter of a century, the VFW pressed Congress to outlaw the Communist party. Finally, in 1954, Congress passed a law making the Communist party illegal in the U.S.

At the 1954 Encampment in New York City, the VFW made a public statement about its opposition to Communism in Korea by inviting President Syngman Rhee of the Republic of South Korea to speak. Together with the other distinguished guest, His Eminence Francis Cardinal Spellman, Rhee addressed the Encampment Memorial Service. That year the Memorial Service was dedicated to past Commanders-in-Chief and past National Auxiliary Presidents.

Later in 1954, Merton Tice, the South Dakota lawyer elected Commander-in-Chief at the 1954 Encampment, publicized the VFW's position on Communism in Eastern Europe. In an address over the airwaves of Radio Free Europe, Commander Tice assured the 70 million enslaved peoples of Eastern Europe that the United States supported their struggle for freedom.

The Korean War was over, but the Cold War had just begun.

CHAPTER SIX

RECYCLING THE BATTLE 1955–1973

Today the cost of the Korean War is commonly measured in American lives lost. And it is undeniable that the toll was horrendous. The percentage of Americans involved in the struggle who were killed in combat was higher than in any previous war. But, at least from the veterans' point of view, there were also other serious costs to consider.

Not negating the sacrifices of the men and women who died in Korea, it would be fair to say that one of the most severe casualties of all was the attitude of the American public. This was, after all, the first war in which the United States did not come away with a clear-cut victory. Although the war was not lost on the field of battle, but at home, it was the returnees who suffered the backlash of public opinion. As a consequence, the VFW and other veteran's organizations met considerable resistance in securing new entitlements for veterans—as well as in holding on to those already won. Resistance became even harder to overcome as the United States was gradually drawn into the most unpopular war ever: the Vietnam War. As in the First World War battle of Isonzo, the VFW would have to fight for the same territory again, and again, and again. . . .

CLAIMING NEW GROUND, DEFENDING OLD

Given the nation's anti-veteran climate, it was vital that the VFW have leaders who were willing to fight for what they believed in. Fortunately, the VFW had never lacked for fighters. From the end of the Korean War to our withdrawal from the Vietnam War, a succession of leaders with an unshakable commitment to the veteran's well-being stepped forward.

Timothy J. Murphy, the Navy veteran chosen as Commander-in-Chief at the 56th National Encampment in Boston, was to be the last Commander elected by the assembled delegates. In following years, the members of each of the four conferences (Eastern, Western, Southern, and Big 10) would take turns selecting the Commander from their own ranks. This method ensured that members of the smaller conferences could be elected to the VFW's top office with the same regularity (every four years) as members of larger conferences.

Another organizational change made under Murphy's direction was the formation of a corporation to run the National Encampments. Previously, the National Encampments had been run by the County Councils. Often debts, claims, and lawsuits had plagued the national organization long after the encampment was closed out. Murphy's plan called for a corporation composed of nine members—the Commander-in-Chief, Senior Vice Commander-in-Chief, Junior Vice Commander-in-Chief, Adjutant General, and Quartermaster General, plus four members of the department in which the encampment was being held. This allowed for both local and national input.

While the VFW was putting its own house in order, it was also keeping a close eye on several new threats to veterans' welfare. A major threat came from the Hoover Commission. This commission, headed by former President Herbert Hoover, had been established to look into possible reforms within the executive branch of the federal government. Among the reforms recommended in the commission's report was that the government cancel all plans to construct additional VA hospitals. It also proposed selling or otherwise disposing of any VA hospital that could no longer be operated economically or effectively. Worse, the report recommended denying treatment for veterans with non-service-connected disabilities who had not demonstrated the need for treatment within three years after discharge. In no cases were veterans with non-service-connected disabilities to be given treatment unless they could prove that they could not afford to pay for it. The veteran's statement of his inability to pay would then be subject to verification by the Veterans Administration. If the statement could not be substantiated, the VA would be authorized to collect for the cost of his care. The report further suggested that veteran's pensions and disability allowances should be examined, reduced, and in some incidences, stopped. This report was to be given further weight next year when the American Medical Association (AMA) attacked the VA hospital system on the grounds that 85 percent of veterans receiving care had non-service-connected disabilities, and, moreover

that most of them could afford to pay for their own treatment.

Needless to say, the VFW strongly opposed the Hoover Commission's findings. Over the next several years, the organization made sure all members of Congress were aware of some of the untruths and misleading information that it claimed the Hoover Commission's report contained. While fighting bitterly against the report's proposal to close and sell VA hospitals that were not being run economically, the VFW went along with the suggestion of cancelling any contracts for new hospitals that were not already completed or under construction. By paying frequent visits to the White House and working through the Veterans Affairs Committee of the House, the VFW leadership eventually managed to soften most of the proposed changes. Meanwhile, to counter the AMA report, the VFW conducted its own inspections of VA hospitals. Finally, in 1958, the VFW's investigations prompted Congress to direct a twelve-year plan to update VA hospital facilities.

Another threat to veterans' entitlements that reared its head during Murphy's year was the appointment of the Bradley Commission, which was charged with scrutinizing other veteran's programs and pensions. According to Congressman and former three-time VFW Commander-in-Chief James E. Van Zandt, this commission "Took up where the Hoover Commission left off."

Before the Bradley Commission could release its report, the VFW's 57th National Encampment was upon it. This encampment was slated to be held in Dallas, Texas, a region in which racial discrimination was still rampant. Because Murphy did not want black VFW members to be treated differently than white members, he went to Dallas and held discussions with hotel managers, newspaper reporters, restaurant owners, and other potential trouble makers. He was assured that no discrimination would be permitted. In the meantime, two Past Commanders-in-Chief sought to skirt the issue completely. They brought action in federal court to prevent the encampment from being held in Dallas. After lengthy and costly hearings in

Commander-in-Chief Timothy Murphy's surprise entrance astride a horse was a highlight of the 57th National Encampment in Dallas.

Washington, D.C., the action was dismissed. The court, however, lauded the VFW for its commitment to making sure no members' rights were infringed upon, and stated that the VFW's actions would do much to discourage discrimination in public places. In any case, not a single delicate incident was reported at the encampment in Dallas.

Senior Vice Commander-in-Chief Cooper T. Holt of Tennessee accepted the reins of the organization's top office at the 57th National Encampment on August 17, 1956 in Dallas, Texas. At age thirty-two, he was the youngest man in the history of the organization to be honored with its national commandership.

Under Holt's direction, the VFW teamed up with President Eisenhower and VA Director Harvey V. Higley to improve the plight of the nation's veterans. Together they attacked the Bradley Report and its conclusion that veteran's service was just another responsibility of a citizen and their service "nothing special." In fact, President Eisenhower became the report's biggest antagonist. He wrote Commander-in-Chief Holt

that he believed that "war duty was extraordinary service." The trio also railed against a Senate that had squelched sixteen veteran's bills already passed by the House while authorizing more spending than any other peacetime Congress in history. This spending included a 50 percent pay raise for themselves and large raises for other top government job holders. Feeling the pressure brought to bear by the VFW, President Eisenhower shelved the Bradley Report and its recommendations were disregarded.

Accompanied by every Department Commander, Commander-in-Chief Holt delivered a no-nonsense message to Congress on February 5th, 1957. The VFW insisted on a stronger military, expanded care and services in VA Hospitals, and a militant opposition toward Communism. They also demanded that all U.S. prisoners of war in Communist North Korea and China be freed. National Legislative Service Director Omar B. Ketchum appealed for a letter-writing campaign to Congress to protest its indifference toward the welfare of veterans.

At the 1957 Encampment in Miami Beach, Florida, Commander-in-Chief Holt again took a shot at Communism. In one of his last official acts, he charged that the Russian Embassy was directing espionage and propaganda activities inside the U.S. Holt called upon the convention delegates to ask President Eisenhower to sever relations with the Soviet Union.

Also at this convention, the official term "encampment" was dropped. With the approval of a national by-law, all references were changed from "National Encampment" to "National Convention."

Finally, a former U.S. Army staff sergeant, Richard L. Roudebush, was elected Commander-in-Chief for the ensuing year.

Roudebush took office at the start of a temporary thaw in Congress's attitude toward veterans. In September 1957, H.R. 52 granted a 24 percent increase in pension payments to all totally disabled veterans and a 10 percent increase to those with disabilities amounting to 50 percent or more. Shortly afterwards, a new veteran housing bill came up for a vote. While this bill would raise the mortgage rate from 4½ to 4¾ percent on G.I. housing loans, it would also provide an additional $300 million for direct loans in small towns and rural areas. With lenders, home builders, home buyers, and the VFW all advocating passage, the bill cleared the House, but ran into difficulty in the Senate. After debating the interest rate for two days, the voting resulted in a 47 to 47 tie. Vice President Richard Nixon cast the deciding favorable vote. With his advisors equally divided on the issue, President Eisenhower almost gave the nation's builders nervous breakdowns as he waited until the final day before signing the bill.

Into the summer of 1958, Congress continued to be more receptive to veterans' needs than usual. In July, Congress passed a precedent-shattering bill increasing pension payments to Indian Wars, Mexican War, Civil War, and Spanish American War veterans and their widows. Then in August, an eight-year-old campaign of the VFW bore fruit when President Eisenhower signed Public Law 529, making May 1st Loyal-

ty Day. (Loyalty Day is discussed in more detail in Chapter 12.) Also during Roudebush's term, the so-called "new" pension law was amended, liberalizing benefits to veterans and their widows. This law raised disabled veterans' pension payments by 25 percent if the disability was due to combat action.

Outside of the legislative arena, Commander-in-Chief Roudebush was invited to view the selection of the Unknown Soldier from World War II. This Unknown Soldier, and the Unknown Soldier from the Korean War, were to be interred in Arlington National Cemetery beside the Unknown Soldier of World War I on Memorial Day, 1958. The selection of the World War II unknown took place beneath the missiles on the deck of the USS *Canberra,* a guided missile

President Dwight Eisenhower believed "war duty was extraordinary service" and was influential in helping the VFW reach several long-time goals.

cruiser. The Commander-in-Chief described the scene in this manner:

"As I looked down on the three flag-draped caskets, under that protective umbrella of America's newest weapons, I could not help but think that this was a tribute to these men, no matter who they were, what they had been, regardless of their race, color or creed.

". . . Three special caskets were brought aboard this cruiser from a sister ship, the USS *Boston*. First were the coffins of the Pacific Theater Unknown of World War II, and his contemporary, the unknown from Europe, and then the coffin containing the Korean conflict representative, [who had been selected earlier].

"A bugle sounded a single note and the sailors along the wet deck snapped to attention and saluted the fallen heroes.

"The young Korean War Medal of Honor holder [HM1/C William R. Charette of Ludington, Michigan], hesitated only slightly before he selected the casket containing the body of the hero who will ever pay homage to the dead of World War II. The body was then taken, along with its Korean War counterpart, via the U.S. Navy Destroyer *Blandy* to their native soil. The other body, the one not chosen by . . . Charette, was then prepared for burial at sea.

"Chaplains of four faiths gave prayers before the body slipped from beneath the American Flag and vanished beneath the spray of the sea."

When asked about his choice of caskets, HM1/C Ludington said, "Until I stood up there, I didn't know which one I would select. It was as if someone was telling me which one." He had paused only briefly before placing the red-and-white wreath of carnations atop the casket on the right, saluted, and returned to his previous station.

Relating his own feelings about the ceremony, Commander Roudebush said, "Except for bits of conversation, the entire ship was quiet. Looking at the faces of the assembled sailors and marines and noting their reactions, I prayed to God, "Never let us experience another ceremony such as this today."

After the bodies of the Unknown Soldiers from World War II and Korea had lain in state in the Capitol rotunda, a color guard composed of members of the District of Columbia escorted a large delegation of VFW members in the four-mile procession to Arlington National Cemetery. Approximately 4,000 members of patriotic and veterans groups took part in this parade, which was witnessed by a crowd of over 100,000.

At Arlington National Cemetery, the two Unknown Soldiers were entombed beside the Unknown Soldier from World War I. Commander-in-Chief Roudebush took part in the ceremony. He was accompanied by Senior Vice Commander-in-Chief John W. Mahan, Junior Vice Commander-in-Chief Louis G. Feldmann, and Past Commander-in-Chief Robert G. Woodside. Woodside had participated in the ceremony interring the World War I Unknown.

On June 1, 1958, Roudebush took part in a ceremony of a different sort. He turned the first spadeful of dirt at the start of construction of a long-time VFW dream. The VFW had long believed that having a permanent office in the nation's capital would help it more effectively influence federal legislation for veterans. That shovel full of dirt testified to a $2 million commitment to that belief.

Roudebush's successor as Commander-in-Chief, John W. Mahan, a thirty-five-year-old attorney from Montana, quickly demonstrated just how valuable it was to have an office in Washington, D.C. Because the 59th National Convention had voted for an extensive legislative program, Commander-in-Chief Mahan moved his family to Washington for the duration of his term. What resulted has been variously described as "The Year of the Big Change" or the year "Mr. VFW Goes to Washington."

Almost every day, from January 1958 to June 1959, Mahan could be seen making his way through the Halls of Congress. Pictures taken of these visits show him with Senators John F. Kennedy of Massachusetts, Robert S. Kerr of Oklahoma, Harry F. Byrd of Virginia, Eugene McCarthy of Minnesota, Russell B. Long of Louisiana, Stuart Symington of Missouri, and others. Here, in the Commander-in-Chief's own words, are the results of that legislative year:

1. We supported a Veterans Committee in the Senate and the VFW continued that fight for many years until we were successful.
2. We supported a Cabinet Post for the VA Administration and the VFW continued that fight for many years until we succeeded.
3. We supported and won approval for nuclear powered submarines and aircraft carriers.
4. We supported and won approval for a monument to be erected above the Battleship *Arizona* in Hawaii.*
5. We supported a strong national Defense, and never missed an opportunity to warn of the then danger of Communism.
6. We were involved with Mr. Dulles of the State Department and the then Mayor of Berlin in bringing to the attention of the world the Berlin crisis. We made West Berlin a symbol of liberty.
7. We spoke with President Eisenhower and his staff, as well as many members of Congress, to increase the veteran pension and compensation programs. Then a 100 percent disabled veteran only received $225 a month.
8. We worked with Summer Whittier, VA Administrator, as well as the White House on a building remodeling and replacement program for VA facilities and were successful in bringing about a long-range program.
9. We asked Congress to consider and pass a law for extra-hazardous duty performed by our servicemen. Today you note those in Saudi Arabia receive it.
10. We asked Congress to open up hospital beds for veterans in Army, Air Force, and Naval Hospitals in the areas of the country where the veterans were moving in, such as Florida, California, and etc.
11. I told the veterans Congressional Committee in February of 1959 that the VFW's position was that an overseas combat veteran should be automatically admitted to a VA Hospital without the need to sign a *PAUPER'S OATH*, and today I still feel that way. . . .
12. We all worked to strengthen and broaden the G.I. Bill of Rights, especially as to home loans in the rural areas and to extend the direct loan provision of the law."

The VFW's many legislative coups were not the only notable accomplishments during Mahan's year. In 1958, the VFW also became a co-sponsor of the Voice of Democracy program—an annual high school speech competition on patriotic themes. The first Voice of Democracy program co-sponsored by the VFW was won by a young man from Georgia, James W. Rachels. Rachels received an award of a $1500 scholarship to the college of his choice and an offer of a $500 scholarship to the School of Journalism at the University of Missouri. (In 1961, the other co-sponsor, the National Broadcaster's Association, dropped the program and the VFW became the sole sponsor. See Chapter 12 for more details.)

In contrast to Mahan's year, veteran's legislation moved at a snail's pace during the term of Louis G. Feldmann. From 1959 to 1960, the Senate remained

---

* The Congressional law the VFW supported allowed the memorial to be placed directly over the sunken battleship in Pearl Harbor.

bogged down with a protracted debate on civil rights issues. Stymied by Congress's lack of time for veteran's issues, Feldmann embarked on several new programs of his own.

Feldmann's first program was not directly connected with the VFW. The program, aimed at establishing channels of communication between American veterans of World War II and their Soviet counterparts, had been begun by President Eisenhower and Eddy Rickenbacker. The program was financed in part by millionaire Averill Harriman, former Chairman of the Board of the Union Pacific Railroad, Ambassador to England and later the Soviet Union.

Feldmann's second major program was instituted in response to what the Commander-in-Chief said were "great criticisms I heard from people with great experience." According to Feldmann, ambassadors, generals, members of Congress, and Vice President Richard Nixon had all voiced the same criticism of the VFW: "That while we called ourselves Veterans of Foreign Wars because we fought overseas, we had never sent a Commander-in-Chief overseas to observe on behalf of the organization, as President Eisenhower put it, 'Those countries which had a radical change in government during or since World War II.'"

With the sponsorship of the U.S. Information Agency, Commander-in-Chief Feldmann planned a trip to Japan, Korea, the Philippines, Vietnam, Thailand, Burma, India, Pakistan, Iran, Jordan, Israel, Egypt, Italy, Tunisia, Morocco, Turkey, and Saudi Arabia. He and his wife were accompanied by Admiral Lovette, who was a former Navy diplomat and Chief of Navy Public Relations and currently VFW Director of Public Relations.

Feldmann's tour was filled with interesting moments. In Thailand, two monkeys, one hanging from a tree by his tail and holding the second one by his tail, stole the banana the Commander-in-Chief was eating. In Calcutta, a water buffalo attacked their taxi with its horns, severely denting one side of the car. En route, Feldmann hobnobbed with the likes of Nehru Gandhi's daughter, the Crown Prince of Thailand, Crown Prince Faisal of Saudi Arabia, and the King of Morocco. His flight home nearly ended in disaster when three out of four engines quit running, but the fourth engine managed to keep going until just as the plane was landing. In his report of his travels, Feldmann indicated that he believed he had accomplished what those with "great experience" felt the leader of the VFW should accomplish—that is, he had learned how the U.S. military presence had contributed to changes around the world.

The day following his return, Feldmann met with General Douglas MacArthur. When the press photographers asked to take a picture, General MacArthur put his arm around Commander-in-Chief Feldmann's shoulders. "I want to do this," MacArthur said, "to show the American public that I appreciate the Veterans of Foreign Wars and I think it is the greatest organization in the world. I am proud of my father for many things, but I am proudest of the fact that he was one of the organizers of this great organization."*

The following month, President Eisenhower, too, paid tribute to the VFW. The occasion was the dedication of the new Washington Office Building. At first, there was some question as to whether Eisenhower would take part in the ceremony. Feldmann had earlier angered the President by criticizing him for depriving some veterans' widows of their justified pensions. But after some "politicking" by the VFW and members of Congress, the dedication went on as planned on February 8, 1960.

As Eisenhower's term in office drew to a close, two new presidential hopefuls appeared eager to jump on the VFW bandwagon. During the 1960 National Convention, both Richard M. Nixon, the Republican candidate, and John F. Kennedy, the Democratic candidate, addressed the attendees. (Several months later, the VFW helped to get out the nation's votes by spon-

---

* General MacArthur's father, General Arthur MacArthur, was National Commander of the Army of the Philippines, 1906–1907.

John F. Kennedy greeting sons of VFW delegates from Massachusetts at the 1960 National Convention.

soring a radio show called "Torchlight parade." The program urged the public to "Light their porch lights on the evening of November seventh and light out for the polls November eighth.") The convention delegates were also given the chance to ask questions of the Chiefs of Staff from all branches of the armed forces, as well as the Director of the CIA, Chief of Information, U.S. Army, and Chief of the Joint War Plans Division. When the convention ended, a Texas businessman named Ted C. Connell had been elected the new Commander-in-Chief.

Commander-in-Chief Connell stepped into a hornet's nest of accusations against, and challenges to, veterans. The attack began with the September 1960 issue of *Changing Times* magazine, which accused the government of "squandering tax funds on able-bodied

and well-to-do veterans." The magazine placed the blame on organized veteran's groups. Omar B. Ketchum, executive director of the VFW Washington office, wrote a scathing reply. Next, *Look* reporter Fletcher Knebel charged that the Veterans Administration was "a haven for evaders and chiselers." VA administrator J. S. Gleason, Jr., responded that "Inferences of this nature are a serious and totally unwarranted reflection on honest and dedicated VA employees, and the disabled and deceased veterans in whose behalf they are privileged to serve."

Open season on veterans continued as a group of civilian employees in Ohio challenged the Veteran Preference Law of 1944. After being laid off during a civilian work force reduction at the Wright-Paterson Air Force Complex near Dayton, Ohio, they brought suit charging that the preference law was unfair. The court ruled in favor of the preference law, and both the Ohio Federal District Court and the U.S. Court of Appeals upheld the decision.

The next attack that had the VFW up in arms was directed at World War I hero and Medal of Honor holder Alvin York.* His trouble went back to 1941, when he had allowed his military experiences to be written about and made into a film—on the condition that the money be donated to his community's high school. In turning over his earnings of approximately $160,000, he ran afoul of the Internal Revenue Service. The IRS assessed him $25,000. Unable to pay, York brought the matter to court. After years of litiga-

On behalf of the VFW Alvin York laid a wreath of Buddy Poppies at the Tomb of the Unknown Soldier on Memorial Day, 1941. (Acme)

tion failed, Senator Joe L. Evins and Speaker of the House Sam Rayburn established a fund to pay the assessment. Commander-in-Chief Connell spoke on York's behalf on the "Ed Sullivan Show," and presented Representative Rayburn with a check for $1000 on behalf of the VFW. Rank-and-file members worked tirelessly in additional fund-raising efforts to further build the Sgt. York Fund.

Countering some of the unfavorable publicity that veterans had been getting, Chief Connell used National VFW Week (April 30th to May 6th) to promote the following: Sunday, Religious Freedoms Day; Monday, Loyalty Day; Tuesday, Community Service Day, Stand Up and Be Counted as Loyal Citizens Day; Wednesday, Jobs for Disabled Vets Day; Thursday, National VFW Home Day; Friday, VFW Youth Welfare Day; Saturday, VFW Open House Day, (a day on which all posts invited the community, especially all veterans, to visit).

At the end of his turbulent year, Connell handed the leadership over to a man with connections in very high places. Commander-in-Chief Robert E. Hansen of Minnesota had a friendship with President Kennedy going back several years. As the Junior Vice Commander-in-Chief at the 1960 convention, Hansen had been assigned to escort presidential candidate John F. Kennedy to the meeting for his speech to the delegates. At that time, Kennedy had confided to Hansen that he never understood how one was elected Commander-in-Chief of the VFW. "I'm glad," he said, "that I'm only running for the Presidency of the United States."

Over the course of his term, Hansen had several more meetings with Kennedy. The first occurred after Hansen had traveled to Paris to present the Bernard M. Baruch Gold Medal Award to General Lauris Norstad, Supreme Allied Commander, Europe. Because of the Berlin Crisis, Norstad had been unable to return to the U.S. to accept the award at the VFW's

---

* On October 8, 1918, York, then a corporal, had captured a German machine gun battalion, killing 25 of the enemy and taking 132 prisoners.

Parade at the 1961 VFW Convention in Miami

62nd National Convention. President Kennedy was eager to learn what the response to the presentation had been. When Hansen's flight home following the presentation was delayed, President Kennedy postponed another scheduled meeting to hear Hansen's report.

Hansen remembers that meeting vividly. "I was accompanied to that meeting with the President by an old friend, Senator Hubert Humphrey. As we were ushered into the Oval Office, President Kennedy opened the meeting from where he was rocking in his rocking chair by saying, 'Now, Commander, you realize that I am an old VFW Post Commander. So don't try to give me any guff today.'" To this Hansen replied, "I'm well aware of that Mr. President."

Later, Hansen again met with Kennedy to discuss that year's VFW goals. These included two long-time objectives: increases in veteran's pensions and the formation of a Senate Veterans Affairs Committee. (The first goal would be attained in 1962, but the second, not until 1971.)

If the VFW's legislative goals were not immediately attainable, there were other goals that were. First, the VFW stepped up its Americanism program. To alert the American public to the dangers of world Communism, posts made radio spots and pre-written speeches available and distributed pamphlets to schools and other organizations. The Community Activities Program, too, was active, upgrading the Sons of the VFW organization to full program status and adding several new youth programs. In addition, the VFW Insurance Department was established to run the first insurance programs sponsored by the VFW. These included the post insurance and accidental death programs. Following the death of Barney Yanofsky, 62, editor of the *VFW Magazine,* the Public Relations and Publications departments were also revamped and combined into one department.

The same year the VFW lost the services of Yanofsky, it also lost the services of another widely known member. In February 1962, Robert B. "Captain Bob" Handy, Jr., otherwise known as "Mr. VFW," retired after forty-one years. Over the years, he had served as Director of the VFW National Service Bureau, Inspector General, Quartermaster General, Adjutant General, Business Manager of the *VFW Magazine,* and Chairman of the National Buddy Poppy Committee. During lean times in the 1920s, Handy had even secured a personal loan of $3000 to pay the VFW's bills. About Handy, national Senior Vice Commander-in-Chief Byron Gentry was to say, "No man has made a greater contribution to a greater organization." (Handy died on April 12, 1971.)

After Quartermaster General Handy's retirement, James A. "Al" Cheatham was elected to replace him as the chief financial officer of the VFW. Al Cheatham had worked in the financial area of the National Organization since 1946.

Before stepping out of the limelight himself, Commander Hansen rounded out his year by making trips both to Europe and the Pacific. His status as Commander-in-Chief and a Naval Reserve Officer gave him top clearance and allowed him to fly as "extra crew" on military aircraft. With Publications Director John Smith, Commander Hansen entered East Berlin via Checkpoint Charley and later flew in a Navy anti-submarine plane over the Taiwan Straits. He also represented the VFW at the dedication of seven U.S. cemeteries located in Europe, Africa, the Philippines, and the USS *Arizona* Memorial at Pearl Harbor, Hawaii.

At the 63rd National Convention in Minneapolis, there was much heated rhetoric about the threat of Communism. Cuba's increasingly friendly relations with the Soviet Union had recently given the Cold War much more realistic dimensions, and the seemingly never ceasing advance of Communism was on all many Americans' minds. Amidst this discussion, Byron B. Gentry was elected Commander-in-Chief. A Californian, Gentry had been a professional football player, lawyer, lecturer, poet, a Deputy City Attorney for Los Angeles, and Pasadena City Prosecutor.

During Gentry's year, a record ten bills affecting veterans' welfare were enacted with the strong support of the VFW. Among other provisions, these bills expanded hospital care, increased veterans' disability compensations, and boosted dependents' pension checks. One of the most important bills, H.R. 1927, gave the VFW a pension victory favoring ageing veterans. The main terms of the new law had been formulated in Resolution 244, adopted by the 63rd National Convention. These terms were:

1. Increase income limitation with respect to the lowest and middle income groups under the present law.
2. Increase monthly rates of pension for those whose annual income is in the lower income groups.
3. Eliminate disability requirement for veterans 65 or older.
4. In determining income, exclude any amount paid for the burial expenses of a spouse or children.
5. Exclude earned income of spouse in determining annual income.
6. In determining income limitations, any profits from the dispositions of real property, not in the course of trade or business, shall not be counted.

Besides pushing through a record number of bills that year, the VFW also racked up more Community Activity projects than ever before—720,000 of them were verified between April 1, 1962, and March 31, 1963.

The year 1963 also saw the inauguration of a new tradition. At the suggestion of Ed Maccari of the Junker-Ball Post 1865 of Kenosha, Wisconsin, the post decided to have a special day each year on which they would honor that year's National Chaplain, those who gave their lives for America, and the loved ones who had passed away during the preceding twelve months. This program has changed little over the years. Every year, the Chaplain speaks at a banquet held in his honor, and holds church services and then a memorial service at the Junker-Ball Post.

At the tail end of Gentry's term, during the National Convention, the VFW decided to expand its fiscal management by the appointment of an Assistant

Quartermaster General. A new by-law specified how this post was to be filled. Following the annual election of the Quartermaster General, he was to recommend his choice for Assistant Quartermaster General. After the Commander-in-Chief approved the Quartermaster's nominee, it was up to the National Council of Administration to give final approval. After his nomination by Quartermaster Al Cheatham, Herbert W. Irwin, a certified public accountant, became the organization's first Assistant Quartermaster General.

CONFLICT AT HOME AND ABROAD

Starting in 1963, the VFW increasingly began to turn its attention to the threat of Communism posed in Southeast Asia and elsewhere around the globe. Many members of the organization subscribed to the popular theory that if one country in a particular region fell to Communism, its fall would also knock down the countries around it like so many dominoes. So as rumors spread that the U.S. was sponsoring acts of sabotage and terrorism aimed at holding Communism in South Vietnam at bay, tensions understandably mounted. In late 1963, these tensions were heightened as U.S. pilots began strafing Communist targets, helicopter crews started flying combat support missions, and more and more of the American "military advisors" sent to train South Vietnamese troops had to fire back at Communist troops in self-defense.

When Joseph J. Lombardo became Commander-in-Chief at the 1963 convention, one of his first acts was to survey firsthand the situation in Vietnam, as well as in the Chinese islands of Quemoy, Matsu, and Formosa (Taiwan). He spoke out against what he perceived as lapses in our defense posture. Quoting Thomas Jefferson, he said, "Eternal vigilance is the price of liberty." He also decried the situation in Cuba, commenting "I'd rather be dead than Red" when he viewed the "Cactus Curtain," the fence line separating the U.S. naval base at Guantanamo, Cuba, from Communist Cuba.

On November 22, 1963, a sniper's bullet momentarily stilled all VFW activities, including its war on Communism. When Lee Harvey Oswald brutally assassinated President John F. Kennedy as he rode through the streets of Dallas, the VFW—like the rest of the nation—was paralyzed by grief. Without conscious direction, the rank and file of the organization responded emotionally. Meetings were cancelled, Post Charters were draped in memory of a fallen comrade, and hundreds of thousands of VFW members stayed glued to their television sets watching the ceremonies at Arlington National Cemetery. To memorialize the slain president, Post 5880 in Brockton, Massachusetts, was renamed the Joseph P. and John F. Kennedy Post.

When a Cambodian radio broadcast expressed pleasure at the assassination, the VFW naturally took a strong stand supporting the U.S. government's protest. "Our country has been giving approximately $30,000,000 in aid to Cambodia each year and yet the Cambodian Border has been a Communist highway for moving men and arms into South Vietnam," Chief Lombardo charged in the February issue of the *VFW Magazine*.

With the threat of increased U.S. military action in Southeast Asia growing every day, Commander-in-Chief Lombardo took time to remember the price already paid in pursuit of liberty. During a European trip, he participated with Queen Elizabeth in a ceremony honoring British veterans, and with Charles de Gaulle laid a wreath at the Arc de Triomphe. He also visited the Supreme Commander of NATO, General Lyman Lemnitzer, and the Berlin Wall. The VFW Rehabilitation Program did its part to improve veterans' lives by successfully representing 150,000 claimants for annual benefits totalling $168 million.

Other noteworthy events during Lombardo's term included the selection of a replacement for Washington Office Director Omar B. Ketchum, who had died. For this assignment, Lombardo chose Past Commander-in-Chief Cooper T. Holt. Also that year, the *VFW Magazine* bought its first computers so that the magazine would no longer need to be hand-addressed. When the changeover to computers proved too much for the Adjutant General's Department—then responsible for overseeing the VFW's publications—the problem and responsibility for the publication were reassigned to the Quartermaster General's Department and Herbert Irwin. By 1964, Irwin had not only solved the computer problems but expanded the system.

By the time John A. Jenkins took over as Commander-in-Chief at the 65th National Convention in Cleveland, the VFW's efforts in support of service members fighting in Vietnam were beginning to attract notice. In a letter to the organization, Vietnam

Arizona Senator Barry Goldwater addressed the delegates at the 65th National Convention.

veteran Peter Forgues summarized what the VFW had meant to him personally:

> "When we returned to civilian life we learned about the crackpots, the ignorant and the misguided. Very few seemed to know or care what we had been doing in Vietnam. I was told I had been involved in a dirty war in Vietnam. Bitterness was in me. It seemed all our efforts and the lives of our fallen comrades were unappreciated by our own people. Then true Americans stepped forward to aid the fighting men and veterans of Vietnam and their families. Right out in front the VFW was spearheading the fight against erroneous stories and supporting the true facts about Vietnam. The VFW did not just 'coast out' this black period and wait until the war became more popular, but the men of the VFW went out seeking us veterans, clasping our hands and welcoming us back. They made known their personal feelings of the job we had done and invited us to join them. . . ."

In fact, not only did Forgues accept the invitation, but he also helped form a VFW post in Windsor, Vermont.

While the VFW's support for the Vietnam War was strong, there was another "war" that was distinctly unpopular with the organization's members. This was President Lyndon Johnson's "War on Poverty." At least at first, it seemed as if this war was to be waged to the detriment of veterans' programs. Their worst fears were realized when President Johnson called for the closing of thirty-two VA hospitals. "Evidently," Chief Jenkins said, "The Great Society is not for veterans."

To save the VA facilities from the ax, Jenkins immediately ordered the formation of a "VFW Truth Squad" made up of VFW members knowledgeable about veterans' health needs. Its purpose was to conduct its own investigation of the thirty-two hospitals and counter any mistaken conclusions that might be

Air Force F–102s were sent to Southeast Asia in August of 1964 following the Gulf of Tonkin crisis. Here U.S. Air Force pilots race for their supersonic "Delta Daggers" at an Air Base in Vietnam. (Official USAF Photo)

reached by the presidential panel appointed to study the closings.

Following several months of investigation, in March 1965 Jenkins sent a telegram to the White House summarizing the VFW's findings. The telegram said, in part: "After a complete examination of the testimony of hundreds of witnesses from all over the United States, I am more convinced than ever that the statistics and reason that originally formed the basis for your decision are incorrect and completely untenable. The bureau of budget and/or the individuals advising you on the subject were ill advised or they purposely transmitted erroneous information to you. . . ."

Commander-in-Chief Jenkins also appeared before the House Veterans Affairs Committee to denounce the proposed VA closings. He asked the committee members if the nation's veterans were to be the "First Casualties in the War on Poverty." When VA Administrator William J. Driver and his top aides attempted to defend the closings, the VFW spokesmen accused them of double talk. As South Dakota State

Commander Raymond Gallagher pointed out, "There is something wrong with our democracy if the President can execute with the stroke of a pen and Congress, made up of our elected representatives, is powerless to stop it."

Finally, thanks in part to VFW pressure, Congress urged President Johnson to reconsider the closings. Johnson ordered a postponement of his order until May 1, 1965.

If the attempted closing of VA facilities had an up side, it was that it forced the VFW and other veteran's organizations to examine their abilities to influence legislation for veterans. As a result, Chief Jenkins wrote a blistering letter to the *VFW Magazine,* charging that the Administration was phasing out veteran's programs. Not surprisingly, Johnson soon issued a Presidential Order countermanding fifteen of the thirty-two ordered hospital closings.

Johnson's order opened the floodgates to a host of programs beneficial to veterans. The Vietnam G.I. Bill, which had previously been a poor stepsister to the Korean War G.I. Bill, was expanded so that more funds were allotted for students' maintenance and sustenance, pension and compensation checks, mortgage entitlements, and other benefits. Over a quarter million dollars was added to the pension checks of veterans and their widows. And the G.I. Housing Bill increased the amount of mortgage money that a veteran could borrow from the government from $7,500 to $12,500.

Despite notable progress on veteran's issues during Jenkins's term, criticism of the nation's veterans persisted. Much of this criticism could be traced to our stepped-up military involvement in Vietnam following Congress's vote in summer 1964 to allow the use of "armed force." As the first U.S. Marine combat units arrived in Vietnam in early 1965, anti-war and anti-veteran sentiment swelled.

Paratroopers of the 173rd Airborne Brigade returning after a morning-long Search and Destroy Mission in late 1965. (U.S. Army Photo)

This criticism was so troublesome that Andy Borg felt compelled to speak out against it when he became the VFW's new Commander-in-Chief at the 66th National Convention in Chicago. "A veteran is something special," Borg proclaimed. "He became something special the moment he slipped into his uniform. The fact that he was selected put him in a class by himself. The fact that he was committed to fight to the death for freedom around the world made him something special."

Taking their cue from Borg, the convention delegates passed resolutions dictating a strong show of support for the Vietnam War and ensuring more home-front support for the war. Local units were asked to make special efforts to welcome these veterans home and to assure them that their sacrifices were appreciated by all except the "vocal minority." The organization's policy was total support for the troops regardless of whether or not members supported the government's policy of conducting the war.

Other resolutions proposed opposing the admission of "Red" China to the United Nations, maintaining U.S. control of the Panama Canal, and sending materials to help modernize the Armed Forces of the free Chinese on Taiwan. (Even today, the VFW stands firm in its conviction that the Panama Canal Treaty should be rescinded and control of the canal returned to the United States. It is also still dedicated to helping the Republic of China maintain its sovereignty and freedom from the Communistic regime of the People's Republic of China.)

Just as previous Commanders had, Borg paid a visit to Vietnam to observe the war. After conferring with General William C. Westmoreland, Commander of all U.S. forces in Vietnam, Borg decided to send a message from himself and the VFW to the Viet Cong. "To the Viet Cong, from the VFW, via the U.S. Army," he wrote on the business end of a 105mm howitzer shell, then left it to the Army to deliver his message.

With VFW support, several important bills made it to the floor of Congress during Borg's year in office. First, after a ten-year fight to provide all "Cold

On April 27, 1966, Vice President Hubert H. Humphrey accepted scrolls bearing the signatures of 30,000 New Hampshire residents who supported U.S. defense of Vietnam. Humphrey pronounced the scrolls "deeply gratifying." Left to right: Raymond W. Colby, Jr., of the American Legion; William G. McDonough, of the Disabled American Veterans; Senator Thomas McIntyre of New Hampshire; Humphrey; Raymond F. Lewis of the Disabled American Veterans; Norman Gauthier, VFW, who originated the idea of gathering the signatures.

War" veterans with educational and loan privileges, a permanent G.I. Bill was passed. No longer would these benefits be established on a conflict-by-conflict basis. Instead, this bill assured each returnee that he would receive entitlements of equal or greater worth than had veterans of previous eras. Because of all the VFW efforts in winning Congressional approval of the measure, President Johnson invited Commander-in-Chief Borg to witness its signing.

The second important bill was introduced into Congress by Representative Richard L. Roudebush, past Commander-in-Chief. The bill prohibited desecration of the U.S. flag and had the whole-hearted support of the VFW and other veteran's organizations. The bill stipulated that anyone who knowingly cast

contempt upon any flag of the United States by publicly mutilating, defacing, defiling, or trampling upon it could be subjected to a fine of up to $1000 or up to one year in jail. "The bill," Past Commander-in-Chief Roudebush says, "was introduced by me out of a veteran's love for his Flag. All around the country, malcontents and others who had given nothing to what it symbolizes were burning and desecrating it as a sign of their self-indulgent ideology."

In a statement to the *VFW Magazine,* Roudebush said, "While an individual may have the right to dissent, he also has the responsibility not to infringe on the rights of others in doing so. By burning or mutilating an American Flag an individual is destroying property that belongs to millions of other Americans and thus is violating the rights of those millions."

This federal law against flag desecration was eventually passed in 1968. It would remain on the books until June 11, 1990, when a five-to-four vote by the Supreme Court declared that it violated the First Amendment principle of free speech and was therefore unconstitutional.

The sentiments behind the flag bill were sorely tried at the 1966 National Convention in New York. Throughout the convention, anti-war protestors demonstrated outside the convention hall, while residents of Fifth Avenue complained about the Annual Military Parade, claiming that the martial music disturbed them.

Leslie M. Fry, the man who emerged from this troubled convention as Commander-in-Chief, had little time to prepare for the issues confronting him. In March 1966, Fry—then an attorney in Reno, Nevada—had been elected Senior Vice Commander-in-Chief by the National Council of Administration.

The election was held to replace D. Summers of Riria, Idaho, who had resigned on the advice of his doctors.

Despite having to play catch-up, Fry quickly began acting on both national and veteran's issues. Of paramount importance to the VFW was, of course, the progress of the war in Vietnam. To keep a close eye on the action, Commander Fry made several trips to Vietnam. He became close friends with General William C. Westmoreland, who always asked him to report on what he had observed and what course he recommended.

Fry's comments and observations about the war were published in newspapers throughout the United States and in several foreign countries. Here he summed up the reasons he thought the U.S. was losing the war:

"It was my impression of the Vietnam situation that it was run by the Pentagon and the heads of government in Washington, D.C., not realizing fully the extent of the conflict in Vietnam, not understanding the people

A U.S. Navy river patrol boat making a fast run down one of the many rivers of the Mekong Delta. (U.S. Navy Photo)

of Vietnam and not understanding the whole situation that was confronting our military in the field.

"I think a typical example of this was one night when I was on a carrier in the bay off of Hanoi. I spent several hours during the middle of the night in the fire control center where they were making up sorties for the next day. Target after target that had been identified as an active target was a 'No-No' by reason of the fact that either the President of the United States or the Pentagon had said that that particular target would not be bombed. This was all contrary to the belief and observations made by the combat officers who had flown over the area, recognized the targets and took photos. The photos proved the activity in the areas selected for bombing, but were denied by the people in Washington. This happened on many occasions, in fact throughout the entire war. In my humble estimation it was the reason for the result obtained in Vietnam. I took it as being a living example of what not to do in the event of a conflict.

"Another such incident happened at the time I was visiting Lt. General Larson on the East coast of Vietnam. He made a release stating the number of [enemy] divisions in Cambodia just across the border, their capabilities and armament. The next day Secretary of Defense Robert S. McNamara appeared on the scene and gave the general orders to withdraw his statement, saying it was not true.

"When I arrived at the general's headquarters the following day, he gave me a two and one-half hour briefing on what was across the border in Cambodia and the fact that due to orders from Washington, he could do nothing about it. The enemy troops in Cambodia would come across the line, strike and pull back. Our troops could do nothing about it.

"I have always been on the side of the military man who served in any capacity in Vietnam and highly recognize those men as doing a magnificent job. They were prevented from winning the war by reason of control of the war in Washington, D.C., and the failure to inform the people of the United States of the facts." If the message Fry brought back from Vietnam did not win him popularity points with the U.S. government, he made up for it during an audience with General Francisco Franco, the chief of state of Spain. During their conversation, Franco told Fry that he liked having U.S. military bases in his country. This was important information that the U.S. government had been unable to extract from him. And as it turned out, Fry's privileged information allowed the United States to renegotiate its continued presence in Spain without having to offer special considerations to that government.

At home, the VFW focused on the routine activities that help an organization flourish. Commander-in-Chief Fry devoted considerable attention to making sure the organization continued to grow in members. For recruitment purposes, he visited as many departments and posts as possible. Then in 1967, the VFW inaugurated a special recruiting incentive: Department Commanders who had achieved exemplary status by meeting or exceeding their required membership quotas were rewarded with a trip. (In 1967 and for many years thereafter, the destination was Hawaii.) By the end of Fry's year, membership would reach 1,367,160.

To keep the VFW on firm financial ground, Fry found it necessary to take the Ladies Auxiliary to task. Over the past years, the Auxiliary had contributed substantial amounts to the national organization, but in the 1966 to 1967 year their donation amounted to just $20,000. Working with Senior Vice Commander-in-Chief Joseph A. Scerra, Fry tried to impress upon the women that they were a part of the overall organization and should therefore consider their contribution to the overall program with a great deal more concern.

In 1967, Department Commander Max Masow obligated 90 crew members of the destroyer USS Charles S. Sperry *as members of Post 529, Somerville, Massachusetts.*

Since that time, the Ladies Auxiliary has made significant contributions each year.

In addition to being on the receiving end of donations, the VFW was, of course, often asked to contribute to worthwhile causes. One request for donations, although denied, yielded an unexpected bonus. In late 1966, Dr. Kenneth D. Wells, president of the Freedoms Foundation at Valley Forge, requested a $30,000 donation to the foundation. A tie vote by the National Council of Administration left it up to Fry to make the decision. After a lengthy discussion with Dr. Wells, Fry turned down the request.* The two men parted as friends. Then, shortly thereafter, Dr. Wells sent Fry a description of the VFW and its goals, which has since been used many times by the organization:

The VFW is not really an organization, it is a concept—an idea—an endless devotion—a rallying point—a center of patriotic concerns and love of fellow man such as the world has never seen. . . .

It was August 1967 when Joseph A. Scerra (Sheer-ah) accepted the reins of leadership from Leslie M. Fry at the convention in New Orleans. At the time, the nation's streets were a hotbed of unrest. Not only were war protestors becoming ever more vocal, but race riots were erupting in many of the country's larger cities. Meanwhile, gangs whose primary interest was *not* civil rights were using the race issue as cover for looting and other crimes. Poorly trained National Guardsmen were patrolling the streets on foot and in armored vehicles and often shot at anything

---

* The VFW makes an annual donation of $2500 to the Freedoms Foundation Library at Valley Forge. The organization sometimes also makes one-time contributions for specific projects.

that moved. Innocent people were being killed by both sides.

Not surprisingly, Scerra's acceptance speech focused on these problems. "The number one priority of our organization," he told convention delegates, "has always been national security. And the greatest danger to our form of government must invariably come from within. I refer to the campaigns of violence and sedition which are being waged by certain lawless elements throughout the land. We, who have fought the nation's wars, we, who have demonstrated our love for it as law-abiding people, will no longer stand mute while its enemies pillage our cities and towns. Nor will we refrain from publicly denouncing the maudlin hypocrites who excuse the pillagers. Positive Americanism . . . that's what I am calling for."

In response to Scerra's call for Positive Americanism, the VFW attempted to better communities by carrying out community activity projects, furnishing speakers for community gatherings, supplying scripts and thirty- and sixty-second spots for radio announcers, and increasing their youth activity programs to help keep kids off the streets.

During Operation "Task Force Oregon" in 1967, members of the 1st Calvary Division escorted Vietnamese women to a refugee collecting point. (U.S. Army Photo)

To bolster the U.S. government's efforts in Vietnam, the posts stepped up their efforts to send relief goods such as food, clothing, medicine, and agricultural and building tools overseas. These goods were earmarked for troops who were helping the South Vietnamese rebuild their ravished country. Commander-in-Chief Scerra also played a role in helping to rebuild the South Vietnamese political system. As part of a committee appointed by the president, he observed the South Vietnamese elections and reported on their honesty.

The VFW also paid particular attention to the needs of all Vietnam veterans: both those who had already returned and those who would never return. The members pressed Congress for more grave sites in National Cemeteries and advocated for Veterans Assistance Centers to help veterans readjust to civilian life. Later, the VA would establish a series of "storefront" counseling centers for Vietnam veterans. The VFW also fought long and hard with the Office of Management and Budget, which was determined to cut staffing in VA hospitals.

One other bone of contention during Scerra's term was the attempt by French president Charles de Gaulle to weaken the U.S. by demanding gold instead of American currency. Scerra condemned de Gaulle, reminding VFW members that many service members, including himself, had never heard of de Gaulle until he was a "refugee in England," run out of his country by the Germans. "The 'Old Mouse,'" as Scerra referred to de Gaulle, "was returned to France by something we can never reclaim, the lives of several hundred thousand of our comrades. We can reclaim, however, the $7,000,000,000 they still owe us from World War I and the $10,000,000,000 they owe us from World War II. It certainly would make our treasury stronger."

At the 69th National Convention, the term of Commander-in-Chief Richard Homan was ushered in on a high note. During the Distinguished Guests Banquet, President Johnson signed H.R. 16027. This bill increased pensions for veterans with total service-con-

U.S. Coast Guard Patrol Cutter Point Banks *heading out of the Coastal Surveillance Center for patrol duty aimed at detecting Viet Cong activity* (U.S. Coast Guard Photo)

nected disabilities by $100 a month, and pensions for those with less extensive disabilities by 8 percent.

Another important legislative victory followed when the 90th Congress passed H.R. 16025, the "Widow's Education Bill." This bill, which became Public Law 90–631 in 1969, offered educational benefits to over 250,000 widows of veterans who had died of service-connected disabilities, as well as to the wives of permanently and totally disabled veterans. The passage of this law had long been a priority of the VFW and other veteran's organizations.

Commander-in-Chief Homan's year was also notable for the start the VFW made at forging a good working relationship with President Richard M. Nixon. Shortly after taking office, Nixon sent the following letter to Homan:

THE WHITE HOUSE
Washington

February 3, 1969

Dear Commander Homan:

Although my membership in the Veterans of Foreign Wars has always been a source of pride to me, its meaning has taken on new substance during the brief period since my inauguration as President. Letters and telegrams of support and congratulation have come to the White House from fellow members throughout America. These messages have expressed abiding faith in our country and its institutions and have offered prayers of hope for this nation and for me.

Over the years you have heard me say at VFW conventions and meetings that America's veterans constitute the finest element of our population, and that I know their deep devotion to their country. Their welcome expressions of confidence in America's future have given me strength and encouragement as I begin to exercise the sobering responsibility of providing new leadership for our country, and I greatly appreciate each one.

Nothing would please me more than to stand at the head of a receiving line stretched across the nation so that I might shake the hand of each of these men and thank him personally. Because this is not possible, I hope that you will express my deep gratitude to all the officers and members of the VFW and its Auxiliary for their welcome support and their generous prayers.

With every good wish,

Sincerely,

Richard Nixon

Later, Homan would write Nixon to assure him of the full support of the VFW for the Anti-Ballistic Missile (ABM) program. "This deterrent should be acknowledged by both China and Russia that we are willing to negotiate or fight. The choice is theirs," Homan said. (At this time, the ABM program was under fire from Congress because of its development cost and unknown protection capabilities. Eventually, the program was scrapped in favor of relying on the ability of the U.S. military to deter enemies by launching a retaliatory strike.)

The 70th National Convention found the nation in turmoil. It was a time of political charges and counter-charges, marches and moratoriums, returnees and draft dodgers, POWs and MIAs. Many Americans had just recently gotten their first real look at the anguish and agony of war. For the first time, the nation now had the nightly option of watching each day's horrors and carnage via television satellite while seated at the dinner table. Often VFW national and department of-

Marines of Company B, 1st Battalion, 5th Marine Regiment, north of An Hoa, Vietnam (U.S. Marine Corps Photo)

ficers were called upon to help the public make sense of these troubling images. Many of them were invited to speak to civic groups, church meetings, and students on campus. They were interviewed on television and radio, and asked to contribute to newspapers and magazines.

Into this arena stepped newly elected Commander-in-Chief Ray Gallagher. Gallagher's logo and theme for the year was "CAM." CAM stood for "Communicate and Motivate." But as anyone knowledgeable about mechanics knows, a cam is also an integral part of an internal combustion engine. Without a cam, the engine will not run. Commander Gallagher's cam and engine ran well, propelling the VFW through another successful year.

As Commander-in-Chief, Gallagher was at the White House on eleven occasions. The first meeting revolved around a discussion of world problems. As Gallagher recalled, "I asked him [President Nixon] about the situation in Laos and suggested it was time he came out to the public and told them about the war going on in Laos. The President responded by saying the enemy would use it as propaganda. I replied that the enemy needed no propaganda sources in the United States as they had McGovern and Fulbright leading the way in talking about the secret war in Laos. . . . " Within a month, Gallagher was invited to the White House and given a copy of a speech that Nixon was to deliver in half an hour. In the speech, Nixon took Gallagher's advice and told the country about the war in Laos.

During another conference with the president, Gallagher laid the groundwork for expanded VA funding. On this occasion, Nixon put his arm around VA administrator Donald Johnson and told the Commander that Johnson was the VFW's friend in Washington. This Gallagher hotly disputed. He pointed out that many returning Vietnam veterans desperately needed dental care and that VA hospitals cried out for renovations, but Johnson would not press the President for the funds. Within a few weeks of this discussion, president Nixon released $15.9 million for dental care, and a substantial amount for renovation projects. This money had been held up by the veterans' arch enemy, the Office of Management and Budget. Shortly after the money was released, Congressman "Tiger" Teague of Texas called Gallagher and thanked him for his work. Gallagher told Tiger that "it was a team effort, we were all trying to get the money." Teague's response was, "But it took somebody to get it to the horse's _."

This tiff with Johnson was not the end of the VFW's problems with the VA. In July 1970, Commander-in-Chief Gallagher had another run-in with Johnson during a segment of NBC's "Ed Newman Show," a popular talk show. It was the 40th anniversary of the Veterans Administration, and most of the guests invited to the program—including Johnson and the National Commanders of the American Legion and AMVETS—meant to pay tribute to it.

After Johnson had made an opening statement extolling the VA, both the American Legion commander and the AMVETS commander verified his testimony. The American Legion commander, in fact, claimed that his organization was the "Watchdog of the Veterans Administration" and therefore knew that the VA was in wonderful shape.

When Commander Gallagher stepped to the podium, he told viewers he was sorry to have to disagree with his friends, but that VA facilities were in terrible condition. They were rat-infested, short of staff, and critically underfunded. After the show, the volume of mail at national headquarters increased markedly. Many of the letters were from American Legion members asking why their commander had not told them about these conditions.*

---

*   Donald Johnson was a national commander of the American Legion before becoming the administrator of the Veterans Administration.

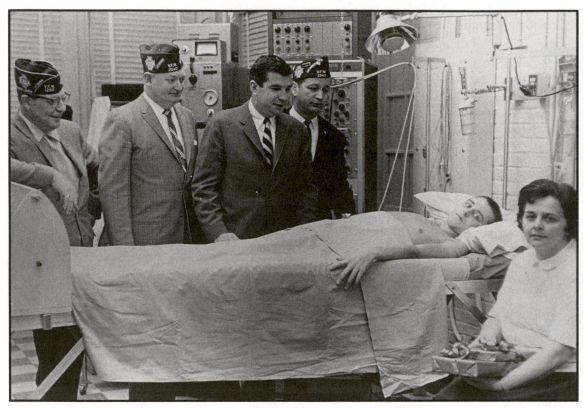

Fred B. Rooney (hatless) and three fellow Pennsylvanians visiting Vietnam casualty SP4 Barry Schaffer of Kunkletown, Pa., at Walter Reed Hospital in Washington, D.C. Others (left to right): VFW National Council member John Piparato, Past District Commanders Robert Hachtman and George Strake, and Mrs. Harold Schaffer, Barry's mother.

While the nation was still stirred up about conditions in VA facilities, the VFW launched "Operation Alert." As part of this investigation, state commanders and service officers were asked to inspect their local VA hospitals and prepare a news report citing the wrongs in the system. These news reports were widely published and further helped the VFW win support for its campaign. Thanks to the VFW's insistence that VA problems be corrected, at the Washington Conference that February, Johnson announced that the VA had proposed a budget of $8.635 billion—its highest ever.

Important as it was to resolve the problems with the VA, the VFW also devoted attention to other issues in 1969 and 1970. Chief among these was, of course, the Vietnam War. As in previous years, much of their efforts were aimed at countering unrest and activities mounted by small but vocal groups of war protesters. In the fall of 1969, for example, the organization received a request from President Nixon to help draw attention away from a moratorium march slated for November 15th. In the month before the march, State Commanders helped out by issuing news

releases opposing the march. Then on November 15th, the VFW released to the media a print of a man with a "washed out" mouth titled "The Silent Majority." (In photographer's parlance, "washed out" means no features are visible.) The VFW's point—that the majority of citizens disagreed with the "Vocal Minority" who opposed the war—was well received. In a speech in early November, President Nixon called on the "Silent Majority" to oppose the "Vocal Minority," and once again the volume of mail at national headquarters increased dramatically.

Another important action in support of the war came after the TET offensive of January 1968. During this offensive, the North Vietnamese had attacked American forces with a suicidal intensity reminiscent of the banzai attacks of the Japanese in World War II. It was one of the bloodiest and most destructive battles of the Vietnam War, and although North Vietnamese casualties outnumbered American casualties ten to one, it fueled the American public's desire to "get our troops out of there." In response to a plea by General William C. Westmoreland, the VFW started

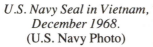

U.S. Navy Seal in Vietnam, December 1968. (U.S. Navy Photo)

the "Tet Relief Fund" to help aid the suffering in Vietnam. In a short time, the VFW had collected over $85,000 toward this humanitarian project.

The VFW also focused on the plight of American POW/MIAs. Together with Junior Vice Commander-in-Chief Joseph L. Vicities, Commander-in-Chief Gallagher made a twenty-two-day trip around the world to ask assistance in getting the names and dispositions of these all-but-forgotten servicemen. Upon their return, they wrote the ministers of the countries they had visited, requesting that they ask for the release of information about POW/MIAs in their country.

When Commander-in-Chief Herbert R. Rainwater took office in August 1970, he took up the campaign for the release of POW/MIAs. With Ladies Auxiliary President Mary Cottone, Rainwater traveled to Paris. There they attempted to deliver a petition bearing over two million signatures which demanded humane treatment and the release of American prisoners held by the Communist North Vietnamese forces.

Rainwater and Cottone tried unsuccessfully for three days to make an appointment with North

Vietnam's Chief Delegate Mai Van Bo. Then they appeared at the North Vietnamese Residence. After accepting the cards of Rainwater and Cottone, underlings kept flashing the victory sign and shouting "NO, NO, NO." Much discord was heard from inside the residence and the French Security Police asked Rainwater and Cottone to leave.

"My crusade has just begun," Rainwater announced following the refusal of the petition. He promptly ordered the VFW to begin a letter-writing campaign. The letters would be delivered to the Vietnamese Embassy in Paris. In the meantime, "Chief" Rainwater traveled to India, where he delivered the petition and discussed the POW/MIA cause with a different high-ranking North Vietnamese official. Later, returned POWs would tell Rainwater that pressure from the VFW contributed toward their better treatment.

Pressure from the VFW also led to two legislative victories during Rainwater's term. First, the passage of Public Law 91–500 did away with the "pauper's oath"—the statement that veterans over 65 had to sign before receiving VA medical treatment for non-service-connected disabilities. President Nixon acknowledged that this change was accomplished only by years of hard work on the part of the VFW. Second, after a twenty-five-year struggle by the VFW, a Senate Veterans Affairs Committee was established. This committee held its first session on March 9, 1971. Because of the VFW's role in its establishment, Commander-in-Chief Rainwater was invited to attend. Over five hundred VFW members accompanied him to the new Senate office building to witness this historic occasion.

In May 1971, the VFW's pride in its legislative accomplishments gave way to anger and dismay over the treatment of Lt. William C. Calley. Convicted of premeditated murder in the death of twenty-two civilians during action at Mai Lai in March 1968, he was sentenced to life imprisonment. At the time, the only other possible penalty for this verdict was death. (Today the sentence in a military trial may be lessened if mitigating or extenuating circumstances are proven.)

Rallying to Calley's cause, the VFW offered to post an appeal bond for Calley, only to learn that under military law there were no provisions for appeal bonds. Commander-in-Chief Rainwater condemned this state of affairs, pointing out that "Our military courts haven't changed much since the Civil War. What kind of justice can be expected when the military appoints the judge, the jury and the prosecutor? Every member of our organization knows full well there have been Mai Lai's in every war. What kind of justice is it to try a soldier for doing his duty? If this is to be the case we should court martial every airman who dropped a bomb or strafed, every sailor firing on remote targets and every soldier who ever carried a rifle on foreign soil."

In response to VFW urging, Representative John P. Saylor of Pennsylvania introduced two bills into the House. The first would require the military to adopt a bail bond system and the second stipulated that the government be responsible for the legal fees of men accused in the Mai Lai incident.

Commander Rainwater's next step was to demand the resignation of Secretary of the Army Stanley R. Resor. "The resignation of Stanley Resor is the first step in the mitigation of the circumstances in which Lt. Calley stands convicted," wrote Rainwater in an article for the *VFW Magazine.* "It would allow the President to appoint a more competent Secretary of the Army. Resor was the civilian head of the Army during the Mai Lai events and must assume responsibility for the consequences which he should have dealt with personally. Calley's conviction and sentence have indicated gross dereliction of duty by Resor. As a top government official, Resor has deserted Calley, the Army and his nation during their time of need. The name Stanley R. Resor has become a blight on the history of courageous and honorable leadership so evident in the history of our nation. . . ." In June of 1971, Secretary of the Army Stanley R. Resor resigned.

Following his sentencing, Calley was taken to the Fort Benning stockade to await his transfer to the Federal Prison at Ft. Leavenworth, Kansas. Four days after the sentencing, President Nixon intervened and ordered Calley to be removed from the stockade at Ft. Benning and confined under "house arrest" in his Bachelor Officers' Quarters at that post. Shortly thereafter, President Nixon commuted the sentence to the time already served. Because Nixon did not pardon Calley, however, the conviction still stands. And as of 1991, a bail bond system has yet to be adopted by the military.

Upon his election as Commander-in-Chief of the Veterans of Foreign Wars at its 1971 National Convention, Joseph L. Vicites found his work already cut out for him. The Office of Management and Budget's long-standing reluctance to adequately fund the VA and veterans' entitlements in general was again becoming an irritant. The crusade to free the POWs in Southeast Asia also was still going strong. The draft dodger issue, however, had moved to the front burner and was gathering a full head of steam. A good deal of the clamor for amnesty for draft dodgers came from the parents of those who had fled rather than serve their country. With the war winding down, these same

Monroe County (N.Y.) VFW Auxiliary Ladies Drill Team members marching during the 1972 convention parade (Photo courtesy of the Ladies Auxiliary to the Veterans of Foreign Wars)

parents were now begging their Congressmen for legislation that would enable their sons to return home without paying a penalty for breaking the law.

In the face of softening sentiment toward draft evaders, Senator Robert Taft of Ohio introduced a bill calling for amnesty for those who had fled abroad to avoid military service. Commander-in-Chief Vicities sent Taft a telegram that left the Senator with no doubts as to how the VFW viewed the issue. "If they, the draft dodgers, want to return, they should be prepared to suffer the consequences and face judgement by their peers, which should include family members of young Americans who died in Vietnam." President Nixon concurred with the VFW stance on draft dodgers and stood firm in that conviction in the face of the first wave of public disagreement. (Just how much President Nixon valued VFW support was revealed in a meeting with Commander-in-Chief Vicities. "If you want to get something done, give it

to the VFW and they will get it done," the President told him.)

With more public sympathy lavished on the plight of the exiled draft dodgers than on returning Vietnam veterans, the VFW faced some difficult challenges during the term of Patrick E. Carr (1972–1973). First, there were the usual tussles with the VA over its facilities. After continual warnings from the VFW brought no changes from the VA, the VFW joined with Congressional veteran's committees in working out these stipulations: Congress would order the VA to maintain an average daily patient load of no less than 85,000 and to maintain not less than 97,500 beds in its 165 VA hospitals. President Nixon immediately signed the bill and Congress made it clear that there was to be no cut in VA Hospital care. Almost immediately, however, the VA announced that it planned to reduce its daily patient census to 80,000 by the 1974 fiscal year. The VA and OMB also proposed slashing pensions for disabled veterans by almost 50 percent, straight across the board.

After the announcement of the proposed pension reductions, the VFW once again began working with its Congressional veteran's advocates on counter measures to maintain and strengthen the current programs. Commenting on the VFW's actions, the *Washington Post* quoted an unnamed Congressional source as saying, "The VFW came on strong against the cuts. Again the VFW takes the lead, some follow, others do nothing." Another *Post* article noted, "No one caught the trend until the VFW called it to the attention of Congressional and White House leaders."

The final act in this drama of discrimination against the veterans came on February 14, 1973, when President Nixon ordered the VA to withdraw its proposed rating schedule, thus leaving the current pensions intact. It was a clear-cut victory for the VFW.

The VFW's victory was made even sweeter when retiring Secretary of Defense Melvin Laird thanked the VFW for its support of national defense issues. "It made," he said, "the job of maintaining an adequate defense force much easier to accomplish."

Commander Carr's year wound down on a positive note as the VFW successfully negotiated a 25 percent increase in the Vietnam G.I. Education Bill, and a federal court agreed with the VFW's contention that veteran's preference should be upheld in state as well as federal jobs. These and other advances gained since the Korean War would be increasingly important in the months and years ahead. There were, after all, six million veterans of the Vietnam War—many of them seriously scarred, both physically and emotionally. As they swelled the ranks of the nation's veterans, they would undoubtedly tax the services already in place and arouse a need for more and better services and benefits. More than ever before, America's veterans would need a strong and experienced veteran's advocate like the Veterans of Foreign Wars to plead their cause.

CHAPTER SEVEN

EVERGREEN
1973–1992

By mid–1973, there were approximately 29 million veterans in the United States. Together with their families, these one-time members of the Army, Navy, Marines, Air Force, and Coast Guard accounted for about one hundred million citizens, or one-half the population of the United States. These veterans, of course, were not all members of the Veterans of Foreign Wars, or even veterans of foreign wars themselves. But that made little difference to the 1.7 million veterans who *did* belong to the VFW. As charged by its Congressional Charter, for nearly three-quarters of a century the VFW had fought for the rights of all veterans, whether they were members or not. It had no intention of changing its policy now.

As in years past, the VFW would conduct its battles on two fronts. Following the mandate of its far-sighted founders, it would continue to fight first of all for our nation's veterans. The struggle for increases in pensions, job rights, educational benefits, and improved medical care for veterans would continue unabated. The VFW would also wage war in service to our nation. Once again, it would turn its attention to community projects, Americanism, and youth programs, as well as to Communism and other threats to the country's defense.

Fighting for these gains was an awesome responsibility. But it was also something that hundreds of thousands of veterans could testify that the VFW did exceptionally well. VFW members had long ago learned that just because the shooting had stopped, it did not mean the war was over. More importantly, however, they had also learned that no matter how hard-won their victories, the fight was well worth the effort. This alone would have been enough to sustain them through the struggles facing them in the remaining decades of the twentieth century. And, by all indications, it should be enough to fuel the VFW's efforts for as long as they are necessary.

PEACE FOR THE COMBAT SOLDIER, NOT THE VETERAN

When Ray R. Soden took office as Commander-in-Chief at the 74th National Convention, it was the first time in a decade that American servicemen somewhere in the world were not being killed by an

One of the first assignments for Commander-in-Chief Ray Soden was to present President Nixon with a set of the resolutions passed at the 1974 Convention.

enemy. But the VFW still had plenty of foes to battle. Two of the oldest enemies were the Office of Management and Budget and the Veterans Administration. Neither was prepared to step up its assistance to veterans and their families without a fight.

The OMB took the first shot at veterans' benefits. Its proposed 1974 budget recommended that one billion dollars be cut from the veterans' care budget. It called for an end to the $250 burial allowance Congress had granted each veteran, and tried to count money earned by the veteran's spouse when computing the veteran's pension. Both of these attempts were stymied, but the OMB would try again and again to discontinue the burial allowance. In addition, the OMB announced it would only allow an 8 percent in-

crease in pensions, even though Congress had approved a 13 percent increase.

The VA, too, aroused the VFW's ire. The VFW had long protested that its administrator, Donald Johnson, was unresponsive to their needs and failed to adequately represent their interests. On March 29, 1974, the organization's cause was joined by thousands of Vietnam veterans marching in the U.S. capital. These veterans agitated for a leadership change in the VA. Yet two days later, President Nixon reaffirmed his support and confidence in Johnson. He asked Johnson to make a study of VA hospitals and clinics, and also asked the OMB to restudy veterans' services.

Reaction to Nixon's move was swift. "Like putting a fox in charge of the henhouse," was how Tennessee Congressman Olin E. "Tiger" Teague characterized the action. He went on to say, "The VA's problems have brought morale to its lowest point in twenty-five years." Senator Alan Cranston joined the fray by remarking that putting Johnson and the OMB in charge of this study was like "putting Dracula in charge of the blood bank." This time, the Disabled American Veterans Paralyzed Association and the World War I Veterans joined the VFW in calling for Johnson's ouster. Senator Cranston announced that an investigation would be made into complaints his office received about the VA. Finally, in June 1974, Donald Johnson resigned. He was replaced by former VFW Commander-in-Chief and Congressman from Indiana, Richard Roudebush.

The American veteran also scored a partial victory over the Office of Management and Budget during Soden's term. Rather than receiving the 8 percent increase recommended by the OMB, veterans with total service-connected disabilities, widows, and orphans received a 17 percent pension increase. Veterans with less than total disabilities were awarded a 15 percent increase.

Financial issues were not the only areas of disagreement with the federal government during Soden's term. The VFW also vigorously opposed the ever-more-frequent calls for leniency for draft dodgers, deserters, and conscientious objectors. When Secretary of Defense Melvin R. Laird and Secretary of the Army Robert F. Froehlike spoke in favor of amnesty, Commander-in-Chief Soden immediately wrote a letter of protest to President Nixon. "I find," Soden wrote, "the actions of Mr. Laird and Mr. Froehlike an unconscionable breach of faith with you and with the men and women who suffered and in 57,000 cases died." Shortly afterwards, the VFW was vindicated on a related issue when the U.S. Supreme Court ruled that service by conscientious objectors in hospitals did not constitute military service, and therefore did not qualify them for G.I. Bill benefits. This was what the VFW had long contended.

Amnesty was still a major VFW concern when John Stang took over as Commander-in-Chief at the National Convention in August, 1974. Senator Ted Kennedy of Massachusetts addressed the group of delegates. He criticized the VFW for its resolution 401, which expressed the organization's opposition to amnesty. Before he could even outline his terms for

the draft dodgers' return, he was greeted with a chorus of "NO, NO, NO." Angrily, the delegates rejected Kennedy's suggestion that they reconsider their position on the issue.

The VFW's last hope of blocking amnesty was stilled on August 9, 1974. On that day, President Nixon resigned from the Presidency to avoid possible impeachment for his role in bugging Democratic headquarters at the Watergate Hotel in Washington, D.C. Nixon's successor, former Vice President and Speaker of the House Gerald R. Ford, had a completely different outlook on draft dodgers. Ford felt that a policy of amnesty was needed to reunite the country, which had been all but torn apart by the war in Vietnam.

In September of 1974, Ford issued a Presidential Clemency Order allowing all Vietnam-era draft dodgers who had gone to Canada to freely return to the United States. They would initially be given an undesirable discharge. But upon completion of a period of alternative service in VA hospitals, this discharge

Some VFW posts took the problem of veterans' unemployment into their own hands. Here Mayor Bruce R. Graves, of Portsmouth, N.H., cuts a ribbon to open a Veterans Job Fair sponsored by Post 168 in March, 1974.

could be upgraded to a clemency discharge. They would not be eligible for the G.I. Bill or other veterans' entitlements. Still, the VFW was adamantly opposed to both the Clemency Order and the alternate service in VA hospitals. Commander-in-Chief Stang wrote to VA Administrator Roudebush complaining that it was ridiculous to give these draft dodgers and deserters jobs in VA facilities when thousands of Vietnam veterans were unemployed. In the end, few, if any, draft dodgers performed alternate service in VA hospitals, according to Roudebush and Stang.

Although the VFW opposed staffing VA hospitals with draft dodgers, one of its main complaints against the VA *was* about the inadequacies in both materials and staffing. These shortcomings were made public in December 1974 when President Ford released the findings of a VA study compiled at Nixon's request by Dr. John Chase. The study had been completed in July 1974, but held back by the White House until Stang prodded Ford to reveal its conclusions. When released, the study bore out the VFW contention that many veterans were receiving "second class care." Ridiculously, this second class care was being administered in what was touted as the "Best Hospital System in the World." To add insult to injury, for years the VFW staff of four investigators had reported these very conditions to the VA via the VFW Washington office. To begin reversing these conditions, Congress allotted the VA an additional $86 million, but this money was barely enough to correct the hospitals' most acute deficiencies.

Incredibly, despite the findings of the Chase study, more attacks on the VA hospitals were in the offing. Early in 1975, yet another government survey of veterans' entitlements—the Twentieth Century Fund—was made. This study recommended eliminating VA hospital care for all but service-connected disabilities, and eliminating veterans' pensions as soon as Social Security reached an "adequate level." Fortunately, this study carried little weight. In fact, in 1976, President Ford asked Congress for money to design eight new VA hospitals, and construction of two of them was begun.

Although there were disappointments in Stang's year, there were also significant victories. In January of 1975, for example, Stang announced that Vietnam veterans attending college under the G.I. Bill would receive an additional 23 percent in allowances. This, the Commander said, "was because we were strong enough to make our voices heard." (Pursuit of this goal had been a mandate of the 1974 Convention.) Shortly, the cost of these educational benefits would be assessed against the Department of Defense rather than the Veterans Administration. In part because of VFW support, Congress would also agree to continue the G.I. Bill educational benefits (as well as the Home Loan provisions) as a recruiting tool to help ensure that high-caliber individuals enlisted in the all-volunteer armed forces.

Another high-priority goal was achieved in September of 1975, when President Ford signed H.R. 7767. This bill provided for a $105 increase in disability pensions for those with a 50 percent or more disability, and a 12 percent increase for other disabled veterans.

As a backdrop to all the other activities of Stang's term were the projects sponsored by posts, districts, and departments across the country in honor of the nation's upcoming 200th birthday. These projects varied widely from post to post—and there were over 10,000 posts—but each had an underlying patriotic theme. Many posts made costumes for children to wear in parades or distributed posters and coloring books to help them learn about America's heritage. Adults, too, entered costumed marching units and patriotic floats in parades. Other popular projects included writing articles or sponsoring radio and TV spots with a patriotic theme.

If President Ford was not over-anxious to win over the VFW, there were other politicians who were. Two of these—presidential-hopefuls George Wallace of Alabama and Ronald Reagan of California—spoke at the 1975 National Convention in Los Angeles. Although the delegates certainly did not agree on which candidate should be the next president of the United

States, they did agree on a new Commander-in-Chief: Thomas C. "Pistol Pete" Walker.

For the first half of Walker's term, the major impediment to progress on veterans' issues could be found in the White House. Ford got off to a good enough start by signing into law a VFW-supported bill that stipulated that Veterans Day would no longer be celebrated on the fourth Monday in October, but on its traditional November 11th date. But then, for some reason, Ford did not respond to the VFW's request for an audience to discuss the veterans' issues and legislative mandates raised in the 1975 convention. This made Ford the first president in forty years who had not met on a one-to-one basis with the newly elected VFW Commander-in-Chief. He was also the first president to fail to invite the Buddy Poppy Child to the White House. Consequently, when a VFW representative was later given two days' advance notice to meet with Ford and representatives from sixteen other veteran's organizations, the VFW declined.

A thaw in the VFW's relationship with Ford came in the spring of 1976. This increased receptiveness may have been linked, in part, to testimony by Commander-in-Chief Walker before both the House and Senate Committees on Veterans Affairs. Walker testified that the organization was very displeased with the VA budget for the year. Shortly afterward, as mentioned above, Ford announced he would ask Congress for funds to design and build new VA hospitals. He also approved a measure extending the length of time a veteran had to use educational benefits from eight to ten years. The defense budget, too, was increased for the first time in years.

Amidst all the Bicentennial festivities, the VFW paused to give serious concern to world events that could threaten America's two centuries of freedom. The spread of Communism in South America, in particular, became an important issue. To get a firsthand look at the situation to the south, Commander-in-Chief Walker embarked on a tour. In Chile, he discussed his concerns about Communism with General

President Gerald R. Ford neglected to invite the Buddy Poppy child to the White House during his first year in office, but later made up for his oversight. Buddy Poppy girl Marla Maraquin, accompanied by Commander Thomas C. Walker and National Auxiliary President Glenn Grossman, gave Ford the honor of buying the first Buddy Poppy for 1976.

Augusto Pinochet, Chile's ruler. Pinochet assured him of his strong opposition to Communism. Later, the American Ambassador to Chile would complain, "It takes me two or three months to set up a fifteen minute meeting with the General and the VFW gets in to see him for two hours within twenty-four hours after they arrive in town." (General Pinochet had taken over as Chile's leader after a military junta overthrew the government of Marxist President Salvador Allende in September 1973. Pinochet promised elections by 1985. On March 11, 1981, he was inaugurated for an eight-year-term as president.)

At the 77th National Convention in New York City, neither President Ford nor Democratic presidential candidate Jimmy Carter appeared. Ford was busy wrestling the Republican nomination away from hard-charging challenger Ronald Reagan and refused to appear. Carter's excuse was that he had agreed to "attend a barbecue sponsored by Capricorn Records." The VFW viewed Carter's refusal, in particular, as a tactical error. Commander-in-Chief Walker explained why in a final telegrammed invitation to Carter: "The VFW is aware of your controversial stand on pardoning those who ran from their obligations during the Vietnam War. [He recommended full pardons.] We are totally unaware of your stand on veteran's programs as you have issued no public utterance after being invited to address the VFW's 77th National Convention with its 1.8 million veterans and 750,000 Ladies Auxiliary."

If the VFW was in the dark about the views of the man who was soon to become President of the United States, they knew exactly where newly elected Commander-in-Chief R. D. "Bulldog" Smith of Georgia stood. The previous year, as Senior Vice Commander-in-Chief, Smith had made it clear that one of his main concerns was the way the federal government had been handling "Cold War" issues. He was especially critical of promises the U.S. Government had made to the U.S.S.R. to reduce components of its national defense and allow Soviet inspections of those reductions without receiving similar inspection rights in return. In a statement to the VFW's *Washington Reporter,* Commander-in-Chief Smith said, "We [the VFW] say, and we're going to keep on saying, that the uncritical acceptance of detente by millions of our hood-winked fellow citizens started with a massive massage job on the common sense and resolution of the American people. We ask, 'where is the prudent Soviet behavior that so-called detente was supposed to usher in?'"

As Commander-in-Chief, Smith fired his second salvo at the Senate committee formed to pare down the number of standing committees in the Senate by 50 percent. This committee, chaired by Illinois Senator Adlai Stevenson, had targeted the Veterans Affairs Committee for dismantling. This was a committee that the VFW had labored for years to get and was not about to relinquish without a fight.

Fortunately, some senators were opposed to dismantling the Veterans Affairs Committee. Strom Thurmond of South Carolina, for instance, stated that the committee was authorized as a separate committee, and advised a hands-off policy. The VFW moved quickly to consolidate and build upon this support. While other veteran's organizations paid little if any attention to the proposed dissolution, VFW Past Commanders-in-Chief, Council Members, and just plain members traveled to Washington to urge senators to retain the committee. In addition, VFW and Ladies Auxiliary members made thousands of phone calls to senators' offices, and Commander Smith brought the Commander or Quartermaster from each state to lobby their senators personally. (This was the first time the VFW had ever brought its members to Washington, D.C., to lobby.) Thanks to these efforts, the number of senators in favor of keeping the committee doubled.

About the campaign to save the Veterans Affairs Committee, Commander-in-Chief Smith told the *VFW Magazine,* "Never have I been so proud of the VFW. In the first blizzard of the year they came. From Alaska, Hawaii and everywhere else they came. Wearing VFW hats, 3000 of them trudged up and down Capitol Hill, across the Capitol grounds from the House to the Senate carrying to their representatives their message.

It was the small man speaking out, and every representative knew it." It was an example of grass-roots politics at its best. The campaign was a total victory for the VFW, its members, and the senators who supported veterans' rights.

Other gains recorded in Smith's year included a 6 percent increase in veterans' pensions and compensation and an increase in the VA budget. A new veterans' employment program was also begun. Called "HIRE" (Help through Industry Retraining and Employment), this program trained or secured employment for over 100,000 veterans. In addition, the Director of the Veteran's Employment Service received a new title and loftier position: Special Assistant to the Secretary of Labor. (This position is now called Assistant Secretary of Labor for Veterans Employment and Training Services.)

Despite the VFW's many victories during Smith's year, it failed completely to block an unprecedented move by newly elected President Carter. On the first day of his administration, President Carter issued a "blanket" pardon to everyone who had refused to serve in the Vietnam War. In March 1976, "Bulldog" expressed his—and the VFW's—outrage at Carter's pardon. "It is an insult to every man who has ever fought and died for his country and to all the men who have served honorably in our nation's Armed Forces." He went on to explain that the reason the VFW opposed any hasty, mass up-grading of less-than-honorable discharges was because "the speeding up of this process prevents close scrutiny or study of each case with the final result being the upgrading of all less-than-honorable discharges." The VFW's objections fell on deaf ears.

Disagreements with White House policy showed no signs of abating as Commander-in-Chief John Wasylik, Jr., took over from R. D. Smith at the 78th National Convention in Minneapolis. At the convention, the delegates railed against the proposed Panama Canal Treaty. The treaty would require that this canal—built with U.S. funds by American workers who had risked infection by deadly tropical diseases—be turned over to the Panamanians. Attendees and delegates were especially galled by the provision that would require the U.S. to pay Panama $833 million to use the canal during the period between ratification of the treaty and the U.S.'s relinquishment of the canal in the year 2000.

Shortly after the convention ended, Commander Wasylik went public with the VFW's position on the canal treaty, appearing on ABC's national "Issues and Answers" program. Then, with heavy support from the Americanism Department, the VFW launched its "Save the Canal" campaign. This campaign culminated on March 7, 1978, when 3,000 VFW members demonstrated on the Capitol steps. Despite their efforts, the Senate ratified the treaty by a vote of 68 to 32. A second treaty with Panama was also ratified over the objections of the VFW and the majority of the American people.

Another foreign policy issue that found the VFW at odds with the U.S. Government was the issue of Taiwan, the Republic of China. The VFW decried the administration's move to make friends with mainland China with an eye toward improved trade relations. It feared that this could only be accomplished at the expense of our long-time allies on Taiwan. The organization was convinced that turning our backs on the free Chinese in favor of Communist China was not in the best interests of the U.S. or the rest of the free world. In a statement to the *VFW Magazine* early in his term, Wasylik warned that this move "would condemn 16,000,000 free Chinese to a long night of communist barbarianism" and "stain America's honor for a long time." He promised to let Secretary of State Cyrus Vance know where the VFW stood on the issue: "For freedom, human dignity, and against all modern forms of slavery called communism, it is that simple." Despite VFW protests, the U.S. Government persisted in trying to "normalize" relations with the People's Republic of China. It did, however, continue to allow Taiwan to upgrade its defensive posture by purchasing American weapons.

Although the VFW had little success influencing U.S. foreign policy during Wasylik's term, it made good progress on domestic issues affecting veterans.

First, with strong VFW support, President Carter signed into law a bill (Public Law 95–126) which denied veterans' benefits to service personnel whose discharges had been upgraded under his special review program and former President Ford's clemency program. Second, with the help of VFW pressure, Congress defeated an attempt by Carter's administration to do away with the Veteran's Preference Law. Third, at VFW instigation, Arkansas Representative Paul Hammerschmidt introduced a bill (H.R. 1349) to provide medical services for survivors of those who died on active duty.

Also during Wasylik's year, the VFW gained strong allies in both the Veterans Administration and the House of Representatives. When Max Clelland, a veteran and triple amputee, took over as VA administrator, he promptly let the VFW know he valued their input. At the VFW Annual Washington Conference in 1978, he told the National Legislative Committee, "I know I'm taking over the third largest government agency and it will be very difficult. I know that the voices of the VFW are behind me and that is very reassuring." That year, too, David L. Cornwall, Congressman from Indiana, became the first Vietnam veteran to serve on the House Veterans Affairs Committee. Congressman Cornwall was a member of VFW Post 8302 of Paoli, Indiana.

Perhaps the most notable achievement of Wasylik's term involved not U.S. policy, but VFW policy. At the 1977 National Convention, the delegates had voted down a bylaw change that would have admitted women on the same restricted eligibility status allowed men who had been awarded a campaign badge for honorable overseas service. Over the course of his year, Commander Wasylik, who supported the measure, directed the VFW leaders to work in their home areas to overcome resistance to the admission of women. He continued his efforts until the 1978 National Convention in Dallas, when the issue was again brought up for a vote.

At the convention, Wasylik told the assembled delegates, "It is only right that everyone with a campaign ribbon be eligible for membership. We are not endorsing the Equal Rights Amendment or women in front line combat. Let's keep the question right where it belongs. Is it fair to let in women with campaign ribbons?"

The debate raged for two hours. Then, by a two-thirds majority (9,745 to 4,011), the convention delegates repealed the seventy-nine-year-old rule against allowing women to join the Veterans of Foreign Wars.

Besides deciding the issue of women members, the delegates to the 79th Convention also considered a number of defense-related matters. Among other things, the delegates advocated: restoration and enhancement of discipline, morale, esprit de corps, and professionalism in the armed forces; no further reductions or constraints on U.S. strategic forces not fully compensated by verifiable Soviet reductions; a viable and effective Selective Service System and restoration of the president's authority to induct civilians; a U.S. Navy second to none; reversal by Congress of President Carter's decision to stop production of the B–1 Bomber; repeal of Vietnam induced restrictions on the President's ability to act forcefully as Commander-in-Chief; and continued VFW opposition to detente and the like.

At the end of the convention, Eric Sandstrom, a self-proclaimed "blue collar worker" from Washington state, emerged as the new Commander-in-Chief. He chose as the theme for his year "Because We Care," then immediately began working to demonstrate why this was an apt motto for the VFW. In particular, the VFW made it clear that they cared about Vietnam veterans, who were largely spurned by the American people. Besides welcoming home these veterans, the VFW invited them to join the organization and offered them a place to hold rap sessions and meetings for their Vietnam Veterans Associations. In an article in the *VFW Magazine,* Sandstrom summed up why these veterans were so important to the VFW:

"Over 96 percent of the Vietnam veterans served honorably and received honorable discharges. That figure matches the figure given veterans of other wars. Let's get the record straight. Most Vietnam veterans

The VFW actively recruited Vietnam veterans as members.

pine Islands, Iwo Jima, and Guam (where he had been wounded in World War II while part of the invading Marine contingent). In the Mid-East, he toured Egypt, Israel, Lebanon, and Cyprus. While on this tour, Sandstrom discussed the Middle East situation with both Anwar Sadat of Egypt and Menachem Begin of Israel. Later in the year, he visited Chile, Argentina, Peru, Venezuela, Costa Rica, Panama, Mexico, and the U.S. Naval Base at Guantanamo Bay, Cuba. Here he got a first-hand look at the area the VFW had considered for some time the Western Hemisphere's "hot spot."

About his travels, Sandstrom recalled, "I was disappointed by the attitude of President Marcos of the Philippines and could see problems of unrest growing among his people. The same was true of the attitudes among the peoples of Lebanon and Panama. The really big disappointment was my having to talk to the people of China on Taiwan about the possibility that President Carter would withdraw United States recognition of them and instead recognize Red China."

What Sandstrom called the "really big issue" of his year came at the 1979 National Convention in New Orleans. Here the delegates debated the formation of a Political Action Committee (PAC), which would enable the VFW as an organization to support pro-veteran politicians (or, as Howard Vander Clute, Jr., the next Commander-in-Chief, put it, "to take an active part in this nation's political process by putting their money where their mouth is"). Television, radio, and newspaper reporters brought the debate to the people all over the nation. In the end, the delegates agreed to the formation. Cooper T. Holt, Assistant Adjutant General and Director of the VFW Washington Office, was appointed the first director of the Veterans of Foreign Wars/Political Action Committee (VFW/PAC). (The VFW/PAC is discussed in more detail in Chapter 12.)

are fine, upstanding and readjusted. The VFW is proud to claim more than 500,000 of them as members and comrades. We will continue to help those who still need help with their problems, 'Because We Care.'"

By the start of Sandstrom's term, the influx of Vietnam veterans had brought the national membership to about 1.8 million. To help reach the 2–million-member mark, Sandstrom visited every state and department over the course of the year. During these visits, he participated in numerous membership roundups.

In addition to his domestic travels, Sandstrom also made several overseas tours. On a European trip, he helped to institute the Department of Germany. In the Far East, he visited Taiwan, Korea, Japan, Philip-

Past Commander-in-Chief Cooper T. Holt, the first director of VFW/PAC, shown here with Jamie Weaver, 1975 National Poster Child for the March of Dimes.
(March of Dimes)

CLASHES WITH CARTER

From the VFW's point of view, the Political Action Committee was formed none too soon. Facing them in the White House was Jimmy Carter, the most anti-veteran president ever, in the VFW's opinion. In his acceptance speech at the National Convention, new Commander-in-Chief Howard Vander Clute, Jr., left no doubts that he planned to fight Carter Ad-

ministration policies tooth and nail. "Today we see the Administration laughing at the Congress and doing as it pleases," he said. "We see the Administration tightening the screws on the veteran's health care system. The Director of the VA [Max Clelland], who should be the champion of veterans' programs, applauding each cut and backing each piece of negative legislation instead of fighting for adequate care for the veteran and veterans' programs. . . . The attitude of Congress has become one of 'Why pass measures funding veterans' programs when the administration won't spend it?'" The only solution to these problems, Vander Clute said, was "to take positive action."

One of the first positive actions Vander Clute took was to ask the Chairmen of the House and Senate Veterans Affairs Committees to hear testimony from VA hospital directors and chiefs of staff about the effects of new budget cuts imposed by the Office of Management and Budget and the Carter Administration. Vander Clute suggested that these VA personnel be required to testify under oath, and that the first question asked of them should be, "Did you receive any orders by any means which require you to testify in any particular manner?"

Although the Veterans Affairs Committees agreed to these hearings, testimony did not begin right away. In the interim, President Carter issued a statement which the VFW viewed as "double talk." He said that he "strongly backed the congressional mandate that care for the nation's veterans should be second to none." At the same time, he announced that the VA Medical System would have to meet the stricter requirements of a "straight line budget." Early in 1979, the Carter Administration further angered the VFW when a VA spokesman issued a press release announcing that the VA had started hiring personnel again and had added 2000 new employees. This release glossed over the fact that the VA lost an average of 2,200 employees per month, and that they would have had to hire 4,400 new employees just to return to the previous level of staffing.

In February of 1979, the Senate and House Veterans Affairs Committees finally held a joint hearing on VA issues. Not only were VA Director Max Clelland, hospital directors, chiefs of staff, and directors of nursing services called to testify, but Commander-in-Chief Vander Clute and the heads of other veteran's organizations were called as well. At these hearings, Director Max Clelland, who had previously refused Congressional orders to restore 3,100 hospital beds he had removed from service, changed his tune somewhat. He agreed that the VA was hampered by lack of funding and admitted that 8,000 full-time medical staffers were needed. (According to House Veterans Affairs Chairman Ray Roberts, this 8,000 figure was about the same reduction as the Carter Administration had planned for the 1979–80 fiscal year.)

For his part, Commander Vander Clute informed the committees that the Vietnam War "produced the most crippling disabilities, both physical and mental, of any conflict to date. During the 17 years between 1962 and 1979, the veterans population has increased by 8,000,000 while hospital beds have been reduced by 34,800. With the restrictions under Carter mandates, daily hospital census has fallen by 40,918 veterans. We have submitted six cases of veterans who have died or almost died after being refused treatment by VA Hospitals. . . ."

Senator Alan Cranston congratulated the VFW for bringing the deplorable conditions in VA hospitals to Congressional attention, but President Carter was apparently unswayed. Each year since he had been in the White House, the VA's portion of the federal budget had grown smaller. His proposed cut for the 1980 fiscal year would bring it to 3.4 percent.

Despite Carter's unresponsiveness, the VFW continued to fight for increased VA funding. During "Operation Alarm," VFW Department Commanders visited one or more VA hospitals in every state. The deteriorating conditions were then documented in a report submitted to the VA, President Carter, and the Congressional leadership.

This report reached at least one receptive audience: Congress. In early 1980, President Carter vetoed H.R. 7102, the Veterans Administration Health Care Personnel Act. This act would require

that the beds and staff members cut from the program be replaced. Both the House and the Senate promptly overrode his veto by votes of 401 to 5 and 85 to zero, respectively. It was the worst defeat of a presidential veto in the history of Congress.

Besides warring with President Carter over veterans' issues, the VFW also attacked his handling of national security issues. On November 4, 1979, when a mob of frenzied Iranian students took ninety American Diplomatic and Embassy personnel hostage in Tehran, the VFW laid the blame at Carter's feet. "It was," Vander Clute claimed, "Carter's national defense policies that brought about this situation." These policies, according to Vander Clute, consisted of "mumble, fumble, duck, and dodge." The VFW also excoriated Carter for his support of the Selective Service System. It made no sense to VFW members that the President should first pardon all Vietnam-era draft dodgers, and then tell the nation's youth that they must sign up for the draft. Although the draft lotteries had ceased in 1973, the law requiring draft registration was still in effect.

To add to the problems that beset Vander Clute's year, in December 1979 the VFW first became aware that the VFW National Home was being criminally mismanaged. This imbroglio and its aftermath are described in Chapter 8.

In one of his last official acts as Commander-in-Chief, Vander Clute made a posthumous presentation to the wives of the servicemen who had died trying to rescue the American hostages in Iran. The wives of Major Lynn D. McIntosh (Mrs. Ann McIntosh), Major Richard L. Bakke (Mrs. Kassandra Bakke), and Staff Sergeant Dewey L. Johnson (Dianne Johnson) accepted the VFW Americanism Award on behalf of their husbands.

If President Carter hoped for a respite from VFW criticism at the end of Howard Vander Clute's term, his hopes were dashed with the election of Commander-in-Chief T. C. Selman. Like Vander Clute, Selman had a poor opinion of Carter's policies, and termed them "Flutter, Stutter, Fumble, and Stumble." To make it harder in the future for similar anti-veteran politicians to reach the White House, Selman promised the convention delegates that any presidential candidate who asked for VFW endorsement would henceforth be required to pledge support for the VA System, all veterans' programs, and our national defense policies.

Sadly, Commander Selman's term ended almost as soon as it began. On September 6, 1980, he suffered a stroke at his Homecoming Celebration at Houston's Shamrock Hilton. On October 21, he died, stunning the organization. Burial services were conducted at the First Baptist Church in his hometown of Freeport, Texas.

Following Selman's death, Senior Vice Commander Art Fellwock of Evansville, Indiana, ascended to the organization's top position. At the same time, Junior Vice Commander-in-Chief James R. "Bob" Currieo moved up to Senior Vice Commander-in-Chief. The Eastern States Conference was asked to select a member to fill the Junior Vice Commander-in-Chief slot. They selected Clifford G. Olson, a Korean War veteran from Massachussetts. He was then elected by the National Council of Administration, the governing body between national conventions, and sworn in by Commander-in-Chief Arthur Fellwock.

As Commander Fellwock scrambled to take over programs already set in motion by Selman, he came face to face with many of the same problems that had bedeviled his predecessors. First, the VFW pleaded unsuccessfully with Congress to open enough National Cemeteries to allow each state to have one. According to the VFW, this was the only way to ensure that veterans would be interred reasonably close to their survivors. As usual, the VFW also found itself caught in the middle of the struggle for better VA funding. This time around, the major problem was that the Carter Administration released only enough funds to buy two of the nine CAT scanners approved for purchase by Congress.

Although the VFW could do little to make President Carter release funds for the VA hospitals, many VFW members were personally able to make a difference in the quality of life at these facilities. From

October 1, 1980 to September 30, 1981, 11,885 VFW and Ladies Auxiliary members donated over 1.4 million hours performing services for hospitalized veterans. Their help was estimated to be worth $3,722,372. Added to that was another $3 million in transportation costs and donations to VA facilities and VA patients.

On April 20, 1981, the VFW was saddened by the death of another long-time organizational leader. Julian Dickenson, VFW Adjutant General since 1950, died within months of his announcement that he intended to retire after the 1981 National Convention. Past Commander-in-Chief Howard Vander Clute was appointed to fill the vacancy.

THE REAGAN YEARS

Vice President George Bush was the featured speaker at the 82nd National Convention held in Philadelphia from August 14th to August 20th, 1981. A long-time member of Post 4344 of Houston, Texas, Bush had received his life membership cap from Commander Fellwock the previous year.

Because Commander Fellwock had followed the course set by T.C. Selman for the previous year, he was re-elected Commander-in-Chief for the 1981–82 term so that he could have a chance to inaugurate his own programs. As before, however, Fellwock ended up spending a significant amount of time leading the fight to prevent cuts in veterans' programs.

The threat to veterans' programs began in late summer of 1981, when Congressional Budget Office proposals recommended cutting the federal budget by $6.5 billion. This reduction would be attained by slashing benefits for wartime veterans and their families, pension benefits for veterans with non-wartime disabilities, and compensation for veterans with less than

40 percent non-wartime disabilities. If this budget were adopted, thirty VA hospitals would have to close. Later, the Office of Management and Budget proposed closing all VA Regional Offices in the states. Instead, three massive consolidated processing centers would handle all claims. This would strip applicants of some of their recourse to due process.

The VFW immediately went on the offensive. Commander-in-Chief Fellwock took VA Administrator Chester Nimmo to task for comments he had made about certain portions of the care given veterans by the Veterans Administration. On March 30, 1982, Commander Fellwock informed both the House and Senate Veterans Affairs Committees' Chairmen, "If the veterans in need are denied medical care or overtures are made to mainstream veterans' health care, we will fight it here in the halls of Congress, we will fight it at the White House and we will fight it in every county and parish throughout the nation. This I promise you."

By mid-summer, the VFW had clinched its victory against the would-be budget slashers. Commander Fellwock informed the members that "our standing tall and endorsing a high percentage of the winners in the Congressional races . . . allowed our nation's veterans to receive their fair share of the annual budget. There will be no closing of VA Medical Centers or VA Regional Offices." Moreover, the number of Vietnam "Store Front" centers was to be increased. Instead of the 91 Vietnam Vet Centers originally planned, there would be 143. These centers, furnished and funded by the Veterans Administration, provided returnees with counseling services and a place to share concerns and experiences with one another.

Other significant achievements of Fellwock's second year included the presentation of $180,000 raised by the VFW and Ladies Auxiliary to Jan Scruggs, president of the Vietnam Veterans Memorial Fund. In all, the VFW would raise $300,000 to help fund the Vietnam Memorial Project. Also during Fellwock's term, the VFW won the first case ever allowed for veteran's disability based on Post

Traumatic Stress Disorder (PTSD). The veteran had first applied for disability compensation in July of 1979. After several rejections, an appeal by the VFW convinced the Bureau of Veterans Affairs (BVA) to remand the case back to the regional office. This allowed for an Agent Orange examination, which led to a favorable ruling from the BVA in March 1981.

Although domestic issues occupied much of Fellwock's time, he was also attentive to national security issues. In particular, he wrote a series of articles and speeches to bring the problems developing in Central America to the attention of Congress and the organization. Small groups of rebels with Communist leanings and Cuban backing were attempting to take over America's southern neighbors, Guatemala, Nicaragua, and El Salvador. "If we continue to neglect these happenings," he said, "it could result in the domino effect. We will wake up some morning and find them in Miami."

The VFW's 83rd National Convention in Los Angeles was a star-studded occasion. Comedian Red Skelton entertained the members at the Distinguished Guests Banquet. Also in attendance was famous pilot, World War II hero, and former comrade-in-arms General James H. Doolittle. He was introduced to the guests by Adjutant General Howard Vander Clute. At the end of the convention, James R. "Bob" Currieo stepped into the organization's number one position.

When Currieo took over, the VFW was still rankled by remarks VA Administrator Nimmo had made criticizing veterans' benefits and casting slurs upon the veterans themselves. Although the remarks had been made earlier that year, the rank and file members were still upset about them. New Commander-in-Chief Currieo called on Nimmo to ask him to publicly justify or retract his remarks. In his reply, Nimmo placed the blame for his "so-called" remarks on liberals in the news media who, he claimed, wanted "to erode confidence in public officials."

Whether or not as a direct result of pressure from the VFW and other veteran's groups, Nimmo resigned. When Harry P. Walters was nominated to replace him as VA Administrator, the VFW once again called for this position to be elevated to cabinet rank. Washington Office Director Cooper T. Holt delivered this request to the Senate Veterans Affairs Committee, pointing out that the VA was "larger than five other agencies combined, whose directors are of cabinet rank." (The first Secretary of Veterans Affairs, Edward J. Derwinski, would be appointed March 15, 1989.)

Even with a new administrator at the helm of the Veterans Administration, the VFW still found plenty to quarrel about with the VA. The organization's biggest problem was with the VA system's failure to begin studying the effects of Agent Orange and other herbicides on the health of servicemen who had served in Vietnam. In November 1982, VFW personnel testified before the House Veterans Affairs Committee about the VA's failings in this area.

Unwilling to let the Agent Orange issue be swept under the rug, the VFW adopted as its battle cry "Compensate Viet Vets for Agent Orange Now." At the Washington Conference in early 1983, Commander Currieo announced that the VFW intended to do everything in its power to help Vietnam veterans exposed to Agent Orange get assistance. On one of his six visits to the White House, Currieo spoke with President Ronald Reagan about this subject. The VFW also joined with four other veteran's organizations— The Amvets, the American Legion, the Vietnam Veterans of America, and the Veterans of the Vietnam War—in supporting a bill introduced by South Dakota Representative Thomas Daschle. This bill would shift the burden of proof from the veteran applying for compensation to the government. When Commander-in-Chief Currieo held a joint press conference with Representative Daschle about Agent Orange, the *Washington Post* gave it front page coverage. Still, the bill evoked heated debate in the House and much testimony was given on both sides of the issue. One opponent, who chose to remain nameless, swore that "this will never see the light of day." Even though that Congressman would be proven wrong, it was a long, drawn-out fight. The first skirmish in the battle would

not be won until passage of the Vietnam Vets Dioxin, Radiation Exposure Act of 1984.

Besides working to help Vietnam veterans who had been exposed to Agent Orange, the VFW also continued to support the construction of a Vietnam Veterans Memorial. In November 1982, Junior Vice Commander-in-Chief Billy Ray Cameron and Assistant Adjutant General Cooper T. Holt took part in the dedication of the monument. During the dedication, the VFW hosted a social gathering at the VFW Memorial Building where its Washington offices are located. Over 10,000 Vietnam veterans and family members who had lost loved ones in that conflict attended.

In 1983, following a resolution passed by the 83rd National Convention, the VFW concluded a new agreement of cooperation with the American Red Cross. This statement of understanding replaced a Cooperative Disaster Plan adopted by the 1950 National Convention in Chicago. The statement allows the Red Cross to use VFW facilities for feeding and shelter during times of disaster and offers the voluntary assistance of VFW and Ladies Auxiliary members.

The year 1983 also saw the end of a year-long challenge to the VFW's tax-exempt status. The Internal Revenue Service (IRS) had questioned whether an organization that engaged in lobbying could maintain its tax-exempt status. On May 23, the U.S. Supreme Court ruled that an organization may lobby Congress without losing its tax-exempt status.

One final accomplishment of Currieo's year was the tour he and former National Judge Advocate Larry Rivers took of Honduras, Guatemala, and El Salvador. This tour was undertaken to help the VFW leadership learn about the problems facing America's neighbors in the Southern Hemisphere, and about the assistance they were receiving from the United States.

While in East Honduras, Commander-in-Chief Currieo visited a military base where Honduran and Salvadoran troops were being trained. As a retired U.S. Army sergeant major and instructor in combat surveillance, Commander Currieo wanted first-hand knowledge of what was happening and being taught in this training camp. Before leaving the country, he secured an interview with Alfonso Rebella, who at that time was the leader of the Contras. The Contras were battling the Sandinistas, the ruling party in Nicaragua. As Currieo recalled, he met with Rebella in an apartment building whose location, he said, was "unknown to me. It would have been better described as an armed camp rather than a group of residences. For an hour we discussed their movement and its associated problems. A major problem was always the lack of supplies. The vaunted CIA help was slow in coming and most often non-existent."

After his inspection tour, Commander Currieo issued a plea to our government for continued support of those who were fighting for freedom in both Nicaragua and El Salvador. "Without interference," Currieo said, "the communists in both countries will continue to spread disruption and strife throughout South and Central America."

Currieo's successor, Commander-in-Chief Clifford G. Olson, Jr., took office at the 84th VFW Na-

tional Convention. He began his term on a high note, when President Reagan signed a bill on the convention floor authorizing $75 million for job training of Vietnam and Korean era veterans. Then he went on to announce several major goals for the organization, two of which were realized during his term. First, he announced his intention of reaching the 2 million member goal that the organization had been climbing toward for the past several years. Although the organization's total membership stood at 1,960,000 by the end of 1983, to reach this goal the VFW would have to add far more than the 40,000 members it appeared to need to bring the total to 2 million. This is because the VFW annually loses about 7 percent of its members. Consequently, the organization needed to add approximately 180,000 new or reinstated members to its rolls. The goal was reached on July 31, 1984, the final day of the 1983–84 membership campaign. VFW membership now totalled 2,000,149. Telegrams of congratulations were received from President Reagan, the VA Administrator, and chair-

President Ronald Reagan presented his pen to Commander James Currieo after signing the Emergency Veterans Job Training Act of 1983.

men and minority leaders of both the Senate and House Veterans Affairs Committees.

The second major goal reached during Olson's term was the passage of a bill legislating care and compensation for Vietnam veterans suffering from the effects of herbicide exposure. Thanks in part to a VFW "grassroots" write-in campaign, in June 1984, the Vietnam Veterans Dioxin, Radiation Exposure Compensation Standards Act passed the Senate (it had already passed the House) with a roll call vote of 95 to zero. For the first time, the government acknowledged that many of the physical problems that plagued returnees from Vietnam were probably linked to the Agent Orange defoliant. But it had still not earmarked funding to compensate veterans for injuries caused by exposure to this chemical. The VFW's role in securing the passage of this legislation was attested to in a letter that J. Thomas Burch, Jr., National Coordinator of the Vietnam Veterans Coalition, sent to Washington Office Director Cooper T. Holt. In it, Burch said, "While aware that many organizations contributed to the effort, we are aware that your organization was the first to endorse Agent Orange Compensation legislation and was by far the most supportive of such legislation. Your organization and its strong lobbying did indeed do much to bring this legislation into reality."

Another victory for Vietnam veterans was scored on Memorial Day, 1984. On that day, the body of an unknown Vietnam veteran was interred in the Tomb of the Unknown Soldier in Arlington National Cemetery. This ceremony had been a VFW priority since June of 1983, when then Commander-in-Chief Currieo urged both Secretary of Defense Caspar Weinberger and President Reagan to honor the unknown heroes of Vietnam by selecting one for burial beside the unknowns from previous conflicts.

On May 28, 1984, the VFW took part in another solemn memorial service. Adjutant General Howard Vander Clute, Jr., represented Commander-in-Chief Olson at the fortieth anniversary of the D Day landings on the coast of Normandy. During the ceremonies, the French government ceded to the United States a burial ground containing the bodies of 10,000 Americans who had participated in the landings and campaigns which freed France from the German invaders.

The first steps toward memorializing the VFW's achievements were also taken during Olson's term of office. After years of discussion, the initial funding needed to begin work on a VFW museum was set aside. Today the museum is housed on the first floor of VFW headquarters in Kansas City. Here members can view photographs, artifacts, and other memorabilia related to the history of the VFW and the wars and expeditions in which its members have served.

To cap off Olson's year, on July 21, 1984, the VA Medical Center in Altoona, Pennsylvania was officially renamed in honor of a well-known VFW member: Pennsylvania Congressman James E. Van Zandt. It was an honor that few men achieve during their lifetime, but an honor that Van Zandt deserved. A veteran of World War I, World War II, and Korea, Van Zandt had also found time to serve two terms as the Department of Pennsylvania's State Commander, and three terms as National Commander-in-Chief of the VFW. The VA Medical Center in Dublin, Georgia, was also renamed on May 28, 1984. Its name was changed to the Carl Vinson VA Medical Center, after long-time veterans' advocate and U.S. Representative Carl Vinson (D) of Georgia.

At the National Convention in Chicago during August of 1984, the VFW stood squarely behind its own. The delegates passed Resolution 206 encouraging members and posts to contribute to the legal fund to assist General William C. Westmoreland. Westmoreland was suing Columbia Broadcasting System (CBS) over alleged slanderous statements made about him and his conduct of the Vietnam War by CBS newscaster Mike Wallace. Although the national organization has a long-standing policy against involving the entire organization in personal disputes and public suits, it does not discourage individual members or even posts from such involvement. In this case, the resolution pointed out that Westmoreland's long record of dedication and service closely parallelled the objectives of the VFW as set forth in its constitution. (The suit was later dropped without any clear-cut judgement against either side.)

During the convention, a man who had served in the U.S. armed forces during Westmoreland's tour as Commander-in-Chief of all allied forces in Vietnam was elected Commander-in-Chief. Billy Ray Cameron was, in fact, the first Vietnam veteran to hold this office. At forty, he was also one of the youngest. (He would be reminded of his age many times over the course of his term. On one occasion, for example, Cameron was to be the featured speaker at a banquet. When he became separated from his official escort, Cameron attempted to explain his way into the hall without a ticket. "I'm the Commander-in-Chief and I need to get into the banquet as I'm tonight's speaker," he told the door guard. "There's no way you're the Commander-in-Chief," was the reply. "You're too young.")

Throughout his year, Commander Cameron was able to focus primarily on veterans' and domestic issues. Because President Reagan's administration was committed to a strong national defense, the organization could—for once—turn its full attention to other matters. Still, to gather firsthand information for the VFW, Cameron visited thirteen foreign countries during his term. In Taiwan, he was the guest speaker at a gathering of representatives of forty-eight free nations of the world. In Korea, he viewed a tunnel dug under the Demilitarized Zone (DMZ) which separates North and South Korea. It was evident to Cameron that the tunnel had been constructed so that North Korea could once again conduct some form of military activities inside the borders of South Korea. On his trip to Germany, Commander-in-Chief Cameron paid for his son and daughter to accompany him so that they could experience the difference between a free society such as ours, and a Communist-dominated society such as East Germany.

Back at home, Cameron and the VFW found their time increasingly occupied in fighting cuts in veterans' funding. As usual, part of this battle was directed against federal budget cutters who wanted to slash VA funding. On several occasions, Cameron spoke out against these proposed reductions before Congressional committees, but to no avail. Also during Cameron's year, the VFW struggled to prevent the adoption of a "means test" to determine whether veterans could afford to pay the government for their medical care at VA hospitals. This measure, aimed at veterans under 65 who did not have service-connected disabilities, was implemented early in 1985.

The VFW also rallied against what they saw as the cause of these attempted cuts: David Stockman, the director of the Office of Management and Budget. Although the VFW had long disagreed with Stockman's policies, things were brought to a head in March of 1985 when Stockman issued a public statement that members of the United States military were more interested in their retirement payments than they were in defending the country. Immediately, Commander Cameron wired a telegram to President Reagan expressing the VFW's displeasure. "The Veterans of Foreign Wars will not be satisfied, Mr. President, until Stockman has been fired and you have repudiated his lies," Cameron told him. "We also demand that Stockman apologize to this nation's veterans and its Armed Forces." Chairman of the House Veterans Affairs Committee, Representative G. V. "Sonny" Montgomery added to the hue and cry. He objected to Stockman's use of the term "Sacred Cow" when describing certain veterans' benefits on television, and pointed out that funding for veterans entitlements had already slipped from 5.1 percent of the budget in 1975 to 2.7 percent in the proposed budget for 1986.

As the quarrel with Stockman continued, Cameron wrote an article for the *VFW Magazine* suggesting that President Reagan fire David Stockman, who had taken several fresh verbal swings at military retirees. The arguments that ensued between Stockman and the VFW following publication of this article made headlines all around the nation. Finally, Stockman resigned—whether because of VFW resistance to his brand of budget and treatment of veterans is not known.

For Commander-in-Chief Billy Ray Cameron, welcoming Vietnam veterans into the VFW was a personal crusade. Here members of the 7th Marine Regiment cross an enemy-made footbridge 17 miles southwest of Da Nang, Vietnam. (Official USMC Photo by Cpl. G. W. Wright)

Another significant event in April, 1985 was the retirement of Al Cheatham after twenty-three years as Quartermaster General and thirty-nine years of total service to the VFW. Herb Irwin, the Assistant Quartermaster General, was elected to take his place. Jim Bowden was appointed Assistant Quartermaster General.

When not occupied defending veterans and their rights, Commander-in-Chief Cameron devoted a great deal of time to recruiting. Because he was the first Vietnam veteran to lead the national organization, he thought it prudent to welcome other Vietnam veterans into the VFW as well as show those "Doubting Thomases" from past conflicts that the new veterans

had the same consideration for the organization and its objectives as older veterans did.

To extend the VFW's invitation to as many Vietnam veterans as possible, Cameron visited as many posts and members as his time permitted. As a result of his efforts and those of the membership program, the organization easily achieved its membership goal for the year and went on to reach 2,020,495. Thousands of Vietnam veterans joined the VFW—an occurrence that Cameron considered the highlight of his year. The organization had now shown a gain in membership for over thirty years in a row.

In addition to speaking with Vietnam veterans about the VFW and its goals, Cameron discussed their concerns about their 2,400 comrades who had not returned from Southeast Asia. Cameron also became aware that 8,000 U.S. servicemen were still missing from the Korean conflict, and over 100,000 were unaccounted for from World War II. Cameron became so involved in this issue that as of 1991, he was still chairman of the VFW's National POW/MIA Committee. Partly because of Cameron's efforts, the POW/MIA issue became a rallying point for the entire organization. The VFW began taking a leading role in trying to force an accounting of these Americans by keeping pressure upon government leaders and encouraging its members to write to their congressmen, the president, and the North Vietnamese Ambassador to the United States.

On a more upbeat note, Director of Americanism Raymond Price was named VFW liaison to the Commission on the Bicentennial of the Constitution of the United States. The VFW agreed to give book covers with a Bicentennial theme to school children, and to make Bicentennial flags and other commemorative items available through the National Supply Department. For the five years of the official federal celebration—1987 to 1991—the Americanism program also assigned a theme dealing with the Bicentennial of the Constitution or the Bill of Rights for each Loyalty Day celebration.

As a measure of the success of his year, Billy Ray Cameron was named one of ten outstanding Vietnam veterans in the United States. His award was presented by comedian Bob Hope and General William C. Westmoreland at a banquet in Washington, D.C.

When John Staum replaced Cameron as Commander-in-Chief at the 86th National Convention in Dallas, he already had a good idea of the direction his year would take. As he told the delegates, the veterans would have to put forth a concerted effort just to hold their own during the coming year. Progress would be difficult, he predicted, because the Republican-controlled Senate Veterans Affairs Committee had been inactive during the previous year.

Despite the obstacles, the VFW chalked up some significant gains during Staum's term. According to Past Commander-in-Chief Staum, one of the most important of these was in membership. Although recruitment got off to a slow start, Staum quickly helped get it back on track with membership roundups and calls to each District Commander and Commanders of Posts of over 1,000 members. By the end his year, 5,000 new members and 240 new posts had been added, making this the 31st consecutive year of membership gain.

Another significant gain of the 1985–86 year was the passage of the Montgomery-Hammerschmidt Bill. This bill made VA health care an entitlement. Under the new law, the VA is *required* to provide care for several categories of veterans. By making veterans' health care an entitlement, this bill almost totally nullified the "means test."

Yet another notable achievement was the dedication of a $150,000 beautification project undertaken on National Headquarters property in Kansas City, Missouri. The project, dedicated the week of April 18, 1986, consists of a sweeping concrete wall bearing the words "VETERANS OF FOREIGN WARS OF THE U.S." At the left end of the wall is the VFW emblem; on the opposite end, the Ladies Auxiliary's emblem. Flagpoles, flying flags of the United States, VFW, and Ladies Auxiliary, are mounted atop the wall. Contained in the wall is soil from battlefields all over the world where Americans fought.

As in every year, there were also areas in which the VFW lost ground. In Staum's opinion, the biggest loss of the year resulted from the adoption of the Gramm-Hollings-Rudman bill, a bill intended to gradually reduce the federal deficit. This bill allowed President Reagan, with one swipe of the pen, to eliminate the cost of living allowances (COLA) increases for retired military personnel and to reduce the budget for some VA health care programs. Only rapid, forceful action by the VFW prevented like cuts in service-connected and dependency indemnity compensation.

Besides the successes and failures of the year, there was also one important issue that was, in Staum's words, "left hanging." Although the VFW repeatedly brought the problem to the attention of Congress and President Reagan, the POW/MIA issue remained unresolved. Had it been settled, Staum knew that "it would have made the lives of many less worrisome and others able to live with less unfulfilled hope and anticipation."

By the time Staum left office, he had formulated some very definite ideas about the realities of the office of Commander-in-Chief. One of his more decided opinions was that the Commander and his two subordinates should make overseas trips only if they have a definite purpose for going and report the results of the trips to the membership via the *VFW Magazine*. He felt that many overseas trips taken by Commanders were not justified. The sole overseas trip he made during his year (to Taiwan, Korea, Japan, and Hawaii) was mostly financed by the Taiwanese.

During Staum's term as Commander, the VFW had relatively few skirmishes with the Veterans Administration. This may have had something to do with the fact that VA Administrator Harry Walters—at least in Staum's opinion—was the best man ever to occupy that position. Unfortunately, the man elected to replace Staum would not have the luxury of working with an Administrator so responsive to VFW concerns. When Norman Staab, a veteran of forty months of service in the Army of Occupation in Germany, took office at the 87th National Convention, the VA had a new Administrator—Thomas K. Turnage.

The Office of Management and Budget greeted the VA's new leadership by recommending a one-billion-dollar cut in its funding. Bypassing the usual routes, Commander-in-Chief Staab complained directly to President Reagan that a cut of that size would devastate the Veterans Administration. Other veteran's organizations also voiced their concerns. As a consequence, the budget passed by Congress not only restored the billion dollars, but also increased VA funding by $472 million.

Still, the VA was wracked with problems. VA hospitals were suffering from a shortage of nurses, and inadequate support services meant that nurses could not concentrate on the patients' needs. Because VA nurses did not receive tuition reimbursement, few of them were able to upgrade their skills. Even though the VFW and other veteran's organizations worked to bring these shortcomings to light, the "quick fix" legislation passed by Congress was not—and is not—enough to solve staffing and training problems in VA hospitals.

The VFW also took a long, hard look at the care veterans were receiving in non-VA facilities. Commander-in-Chief Staab ordered the establishment of a National Hospital Committee. Through this committee, the VFW would provide relief to veterans in community hospitals, nursing homes, soldiers and sailors homes, state veterans' homes, domiciliaries, and other facilities.

In addition to wrestling with medical care issues, Commander-in-Chief Staab devoted quite a bit of time to increasing the number of life members in the VFW. Already, the number had grown from 86 members in 1951—the year Commander-in-Chief Ray Brannaman instituted the Life Membership Program—to 500,002 by the end of 1985. Still, Staab felt the number should be higher. As he noted in the February 1987 issue of *VFW Magazine,* "Life membership benefits the individual member, the post, the department and the national organization. Few, if any other programs, of any organization, offer benefits to all of the involved as

does this program." To make it easier to sign up new members, the membership form was changed so that it could be used either for annual or life membership. The bylaws were also changed to allow new and reinstated members to sign up as life members, rather than extending this privilege only to those who were already annual members. In addition, Life Membership Director Robert Greene proposed that life memberships be made available for purchase with a credit card. These changes brought life membership to a new high of 542,496. Meanwhile, the Post Extension Department, under Director Joseph Ross, installed a record 297 posts during the 1986 to 1987 year.

A traveling Commander—like many before him—Staab visited every department in the organization, some as many as three or four times. During the three years he spent as Junior and Senior Vice Commander-in-Chief and Commander-in-Chief, he also made fact-finding trips to Panama, Costa Rica, Honduras, El Salvador, Mexico, France, Egypt, Israel, Italy, England, Belgium, Germany, Taiwan, Korea, Thailand, and Hong Kong. And on October 28, 1986, Staab was the speaker at the Statue of Liberty's 100th anniversary celebration, having been invited by Ladies Auxiliary President Rosemary Mazer.

In the course of his travels, Staab experienced what he considered one of the highlights of his year. As he explained in his August 1987 "Command Post" column in the *VFW Magazine,* this was "the audience in the Vatican with Pope John Paul II, that holy man whose beatific smile radiates sanctity and charity for all humanity. Being in his presence was awesome and inspiring. Like ourselves, he is an old soldier, a fighter for his native Poland in the Polish underground, who continued his battle for his country as a "Prince of the Church" contending with Poland's Communist regime."

The 1987 National Convention was held in New Orleans, Louisiana. Its delegates elected a former Army staff sergeant, a veteran of four combat jumps and an amphibious landing, to lead the organization during the coming year. His name was Earl L. Stock and he was from New York.

Shortly after his election, Commander Stock and Washington Office Director Cooper T. Holt visited President Reagan in the Oval Office. Here Reagan announced that he would support raising the Administrator of Veterans Affairs position to Cabinet level. This announcement brought the VFW one step closer to reaching a goal set several years before. Now veterans' advocates had only to overcome resistance in Congress.

Offsetting the VFW's progress towards elevating the VA to cabinet level was its utter failure to carry out Resolution Number 725. This resolution, adopted by the 88th National Convention, opposed giving veterans' status to those who did not serve on active duty in the military, naval, or air services, and who did not take an oath to bear arms. The VFW hoped to block action under Public Law 95–202, which would give Armed Forces discharge certificates to Merchant seamen and Civil Service crew members who had served in active oceangoing service during World War II. The VFW opposed granting veterans' status to these seamen on two grounds. First, a large influx of wartime "civilians" would further tax the already overburdened and underfunded VA system. Second, it seemed unfair that men who had received the highly inflated pay rates of home front civilians and had had the option of quitting after any voyage should now receive part of the meager entitlement given service people by a grateful Congress.

Despite the VFW's protests, on January 19, 1988, the Secretary of the Air Force declared that certain Merchant seamen's services did indeed qualify them for VA benefits. Merchant seaman who had served in active oceangoing positions from December 7, 1941, to August 15, 1945, would now be considered veterans and be eligible to receive discharge certificates issued by the Armed Forces. Civil Service crew members aboard U.S. Army Transport Service vessels in oceangoing service were also declared eligible for benefits. In general, these new veterans and their survivors would qualify for all benefits provided World War II veterans, including compensation for service-connected disability, pensions, and medical care. Although the VFW had opposed this move, it was now obliged, by its Congressional Charter, to provide service assistance for this group.

Also over the VFW's protests, the Commission of Fine Arts rejected the placement of a statue of a woman Vietnam veteran at the Vietnam Veterans Memorial in Washington, D.C. Thanks in part to the efforts of Diane Carlson Evans, a VFW member from Wisconsin and co-founder of the Vietnam Women's Memorial Project, the VFW had voted to support this statue at the 1985 National Convention. The project had also been endorsed by all the other major veteran's organizations, Secretary of the Interior Donald Hodel, the Vietnam Veterans Memorial Fund, and many others. Two senators and a representative have since introduced legislation specifically authorizing the placement of this statue at the Vietnam Veterans Memorial. Senator Dale Bumpers (D) Arkansas has scheduled hearings in his committee on Public Lands, National Parks and Forests to consider this legislation.

The VFW was quite a bit more successful in its attempts to obtain a monument for Korean War veterans. In October 1987, President Reagan signed H.R. 2205, which authorized the American Battle Monuments Commission to establish a Korean War Memorial. The law provided for one million dollars in federal funding and allowed the project to accept private donations. Since the VFW had long been a strong advocate of this project, raising funds for the Memorial quickly became a high priority. The VFW was the second largest donor (first among the veteran's organizations), giving in excess of $500,000. The Ladies Auxiliary to the Veterans of Foreign Wars was also in the top ten donors, contributing over $90,000.

Throughout Commander Stock's year, an ongoing concern was the spread of Communism in Central America. To educate VFW members and the American public about the danger of a Communist takeover, Kenneth Steadman, Director of VFW National Security and Foreign Affairs, published an article in the July 1988 issue of the VFW *Washington*

Action Reporter. In his article, he pointed out what he believed to be U.S. Government blunders in this area. He felt, for instance, that the U.S. indictment of Panamanian military dictator General Manuel Noriega only increased his anti-U.S. public posture in Panama. He also believed that, by cutting off aid to the anti-Sandinista Freedom Fighters in Nicaragua, Congress was turning Nicaragua over to the Communists. He warned that it was only a matter of time before similar anti-U.S. sentiments arose in Honduras, Guatemala, and El Salvador.

While the VFW's concerns about Communism in Central America were growing, the organization was able to relax its vigilance somewhat in Europe. On November 1, 1987, the Memorandum of Understanding regarding the intermediate-range nuclear forces treaty between the U.S. and the U.S.S.R. was signed. At the urging of Commander Stock and others, the Senate approved the treaty. The VFW supported this treaty because it contained provisions for verifying compliance as called for by VFW resolutions.

In summing up the accomplishments of his year at the 89th National Convention in Chicago, Commander Stock singled out one perpetual problem area still unresolved: the plight of the POW/MIAs in Southeast Asia. He pointed out that much work still needed to be done, "even though in dribs and drabs the Vietnamese are returning home sets of remains of American servicemen killed there during the war. You may be certain that every influential personage in Washington has been thoroughly advised on our position on the POW/MIA issue, and, of course, I am certain that my successor also will continue the campaign for a resolution of this most heart-rending problem."

"WE REMEMBER"

Stock's certainty about his successor's dedication to the POW/MIA campaign was an "odds-on" conclusion. The man preordained to succeed Stock was a Vietnam veteran named Larry Rivers. Upon his election, Rivers told the 1988 convention, "Our theme for this, our 90th year, is a simple one: 'We Remember.' So beautiful in its simplicity, yet so powerful in the message it conveys. As we celebrate ninety years of faithful service to America and her veterans, we do indeed remember. We remember the many challenges we have faced, the many obstacles we have overcome, and the impressive list of accomplishments that we, together, have compiled." And it went without saying that the VFW remembered the POW/MIAs.

To keep the POW/MIA issue in the forefront of everyone's consciousness, the VFW worked to carry out a number of resolutions previously passed by the organization. Resolution 401 of this 89th National Convention demanded that the issue remain one of the government's highest priorities; No. 402, that the government vigorously pursue negotiations with Laos to allow us to investigate aircraft crash sites for remains and to follow up on reported sightings of live POWs; No. 421, that Congressional appropriations to international lending agencies be contingent on those countries' cooperation in the search for U.S. POW/MIAs of past wars; No. 438, that Congress pass a law requiring the POW/MIA flag to be flown on every government installation in the world; Nos. 444 and 445, that the president appoint a permanent POW/MIA affairs advisor on the embassy staff in Vientiane, and that maximum economic and diplomatic pressure be brought on the North Korean government to account for the 8,000 U.S. servicemen still missing from that war.

While the battle over the fate of POW/MIAs continued, the VFW won several clear-cut victories. Perhaps most notably, it finally succeeded in having the position of Administrator of the Veterans Administration elevated to Cabinet level. On October 25, 1988, the VA Cabinet Bill sponsored by Senator Strom Thurmond was approved by Congress and signed by President Reagan. In the January 1989 *Washington Action Reporter,* Washington Office Director Cooper T. Holt called this move "a bold and innovative step toward better serving veterans and the nation." But, he also warned that, "in order for the newly created Department to even begin to realize its full potential, it is absolutely essential that the first Secretary of Veterans Affairs be a skilled and dedicated leader as well as a veterans advocate." He expressed his regret that an eminently suitable candidate—G. V. "Sonny" Montgomery, Chairman of the House Veterans Affairs Committee, had asked that his name be taken out of the running for this position.

On March 15, 1989, Edward J. Derwinski, a well-known Illinois legislator from a Chicago district, was appointed as the first Secretary of Veterans Affairs. A life member of VFW Post 2791 in Tinley Park, Illinois, Derwinski was serving as an Undersecretary of State at the time of his appointment. Soon after his appointment, Derwinski wrote a letter to Commander-in-Chief Rivers paying tribute to the VFW for its part in attaining department status for the Veterans Administration. He went on to say, "I am fully prepared to be your advocate in the Cabinet. I further commit to you that we will take the opportunity to rejuvenate veterans programs and take the steps necessary to better deliver on America's promises to her veterans."

DEMOCRATS

G.V. (SONNY) MONTGOMERY, MISSISSIPPI
DON EDWARDS, CALIFORNIA
DOUGLAS APPLEGATE, OHIO
DAN MICA, FLORIDA
WAYNE DOWDY, MISSISSIPPI
LANE EVANS, ILLINOIS
MARCY KAPTUR, OHIO
TIMOTHY J. PENNY, MINNESOTA
HARLEY O. STAGGERS, JR., WEST VIRGINIA
J. ROY ROWLAND, GEORGIA
JOHN BRYANT, TEXAS
JAMES J. FLORIO, NEW JERSEY
KENNETH J. GRAY, ILLINOIS
PAUL E. KANJORSKI, PENNSYLVANIA
TOMMY F. ROBINSON, ARKANSAS
CHARLES W. STENHOLM, TEXAS
CLAUDE HARRIS, ALABAMA
JOSEPH P. KENNEDY II, MASSACHUSETTS
ELIZABETH J. PATTERSON, SOUTH CAROLINA
TIM JOHNSON, SOUTH DAKOTA
JIM JONTZ, INDIANA

MACK FLEMING
CHIEF COUNSEL AND STAFF DIRECTOR

REPUBLICANS

GERALD B.H. SOLOMON, NEW YORK
JOHN PAUL HAMMERSCHMIDT, ARKANSAS
CHALMERS P. WYLIE, OHIO
BOB STUMP, ARIZONA
BOB McEWEN, OHIO
CHRISTOPHER H. SMITH, NEW JERSEY
DAN BURTON, INDIANA
MICHAEL BILIRAKIS, FLORIDA
THOMAS J. RIDGE, PENNSYLVANIA
JOHN G. ROWLAND, CONNECTICUT
ROBERT K. DORNAN, CALIFORNIA
ROBERT C. SMITH, NEW HAMPSHIRE
JACK DAVIS, ILLINOIS

ONE HUNDREDTH CONGRESS
———
G.V. (SONNY) MONTGOMERY
CHAIRMAN

U.S. House of Representatives
COMMITTEE ON VETERANS' AFFAIRS
335 CANNON HOUSE OFFICE BUILDING
Washington, DC 20515

Dear Comrades:

I want to take this means to thank the Veterans of Foreign Wars for your initiative, input, support, and encouragement, which have enabled the Congress to protect and further strengthen our veterans' programs. Our success has been directly related to the deep concern and involvement of the VFW on behalf of not only your members, but for all veterans.

The Committee and the Congress have long looked to the VFW for insight and guidance as to the proper development of veterans' benefits and services. Key to this process is the VFW's ability to listen to its membership and to clearly convey those views and concerns to the Congress. That characteristic, in my opinion, is the very essence of a viable service organization.

The VFW should take great pride in its instrumental role in the formation and passage of legislation that has refined probably every program administered by the Veterans Administration during my eight years as Chairman. Testimony presented by your Washington office before our Committee has always been forceful, sound and dependable. Your record on behalf of veterans of all wars is impressive. Veterans are fortunate to have the VFW looking out for their best interests.

I am proud to be a life member of the VFW and I look forward to many more years of seeing those VFW caps up and down the halls of Congress.

Sincerely,

G. V. (SONNY) MONTGOMERY
Chairman

Cooper T. Holt, director of the VFW's Washington office, endorsing George Bush for president of the United States

Derwinski was as good as his word. He started out by asking for and getting an additional $340 million for veterans' health care and $844 million for veterans' programs.

A second landmark victory during Rivers's term occurred on November 18, 1988, when President Reagan signed into law the Veterans Judicial Review Act. For the VFW, this was the culmination of years of intensive effort to expand due process for veteran claimants, their dependents, and survivors. The law provides that if a veteran seeks and is denied a benefit, the claim will be reviewed by the U.S. Court of Veterans Appeals after the claimant executes a "Notice of Disagreement." In some cases, the appeals may reach as high as the Supreme Court.

The VFW scored other important legislative victories in Rivers's year. First, the organization helped persuade President Reagan to sign into law the Veterans Benefits and Improvement Act of 1988. This bill, which became law on November 18, 1988, was the brainchild of House Veterans Affairs Chairman "Sonny" Montgomery. It brought a realistic update to the current G.I. Bill, increasing some of the allowances given for educational purposes and allowing members of the National Guard and Reserves to benefit for the first time from a G.I. Bill.

Another major VFW coup was the defeat of a House resolution that would have required the president to give Congress a report within forty-eight hours of any covert actions undertaken. In protesting the move, Commander-in-Chief Rivers wrote a letter to each House member, warning that the provision "would prevent the president from taking decisive action in emergencies and limit allied cooperation and assistance in covert operations. . . . We believe that instead of placing restraints on the president, Congress should strive to build better cooperation and trust between and among the branches of the government." In the end, the forty-eight-hour resolution was deleted from H.R. 2833, the Intelligence Oversight Act of 1988.

The VFW chalked up a political victory after VFW/PAC officially endorsed Vice President George Bush for president of the United States. Bush, a combat-decorated veteran and life member of Post 4344 of Houston, Texas, easily defeated Massachusetts Governor Michael Dukakis in the November 1988 election.

As usual, the VFW skirmished with the Office of Management of Budget on several occasions. First, an OMB proposal to charge military retirees and dependents of active-duty military personnel for medical services at military facilities was withdrawn after Commander-in-Chief Rivers denounced it as a "betrayal of trust with service people." Rivers also decried a proposed cut of 8,957 full-time VA medical personnel as another example of the OMB's disregard for veterans. Fortunately, the Commander-in-Chief's early warning helped veterans' backers in Congress to derail most of these intended cuts.

The VFW also tried to work around disagreements with the VA itself. In 1987, then Commander Norman Staab had called on the VA Administrator to lead the way in developing, coordinating, and implementing programs for homeless veterans. When no action was taken on this issue, the VFW called on the VA, the Department of Health and Human Services, the Department of Labor, and other federal, state, and local agencies to provide services and employment training for these veterans. Through its Resolution No. 618, it urged governors and state legislatures to provide domiciliary and medical care for homeless veterans. And particularly in urban areas, individual members of the VFW began learning how they could help other veterans on a one-on-one basis.

The major disappointments of Rivers's year revolved around Americanism issues. First, the VFW began a frustrating struggle to have English declared the official language of the United States. Following Resolution No. 105, the organization sought legislation to "1) limit bilingual education to short-term transitional programs only; 2) initiate a speedy return to voting ballots in English only; 3) make opportunities available to immigrants for learning English; 4) maintain the English language as a condition for naturaliza-

The VFW vigorously opposes desecration of the U.S. flag for any reason. VFW and Auxiliary members such as these members of Post 8217 of St. Paul, Minnesota, routinely teach proper flag etiquette to members of their

tion; and 5) enact legal protection for the English language, at state and national levels, through the designation of English as our official language." Although the VFW joined forces with an organization called English, USA, little headway was made toward achieving any of these goals. And according to the current Director of Americanism, Ray Price, it could be many years before any steps recommended by Resolution 105 are taken.

Even as the VFW was struggling to get this new legislation passed, the Supreme Court dismayed and angered the VFW by overturning another law the organization had wholeheartedly supported. On June 11, 1989, the Flag Act of 1968—which prescribed penalties for desecrating or burning an American flag—was declared unconstitutional by a vote of 5 to 4.

Commander-in-Chief Rivers minced no words in summing up the VFW's opposition to this action. In his "Command Post" column in the August 1989 issue of the *VFW Magazine* he declared:

> "As Americans and veterans, we find it offensive, knowing that in our nation's 200 year history Americans have fought, died and were carried to their graves under that Flag. It is incomprehensible to us that there are those who would choose to desecrate that symbol which protects and guarantees their freedom of speech—their freedom of expression. To choose to desecrate the Flag as a political statement is shocking and offensive to the VFW.

> "The VFW is extremely disappointed with the Supreme Court decision, which, obviously, was a controversial one as evidenced by its 5–4 vote. The VFW will continue, as it has throughout its 90 year history, to engender honor and respect for the Flag through its nationwide educational and patriotic programs."

As the flag controversy gathered steam, the VFW paused to pay tribute to a man who had helped to steer the organization through many such conflicts during his years of service as Executive Director of the Washington Office. In August 1989, Cooper T. Holt announced that he would retire in September. Among the many prominent Americans to express regret at his retirement was Senator Alan Simpson of Wyoming, who described Holt as "an extraordinary person . . . very tough . . . very firm, fair, honest . . . and highly opinionated." Harry Walters, former VA Administrator, also lauded Holt: "He's like a stingray sometimes . . . tough and effective. And it's all directed toward advocacy for veterans. He's a legend in terms of the way he has influenced things in Washington." Even President Bush would claim, "I don't know what it's going to be like without him around here. . . . Among members of the VFW, others who stand for a strong defense . . . Cooper has earned the gratitude of veterans everywhere for making the VFW his lifelong cause. But, also for the way he has conducted himself in Washington and elsewhere in this high office."*

Not surprisingly, the flag issue topped the agenda at the 90th National Convention in Las Vegas, Nevada. Twenty-seven separate resolutions aimed at protecting the United States flag were introduced. In the end, the delegates adopted only one: a resolution that the VFW push for a constitutional amendment prohibiting the desecration of the flag.

Walter G. Hogan, the VFW's new Commander-in-Chief, testified before the Senate Judiciary Committee in favor of the amendment. Other veteran's organizations and private citizens also called for an amendment prohibiting flag desecration. Although little progress has been made to date, the VFW has resolved not to let the issue rest until the flag receives the protection it deserves.

While the struggle to protect the flag was just beginning, several old battles also occupied the

---

* In September 1989, Past Commander-in-Chief Larry Rivers succeeded Holt as Executive Director of the Washington Office.

VFW's time. First, the organization continued to press the U.S. Government to demand that the North Korean and North Vietnamese governments account for our POW/MIAs. Out of respect for their former comrades-in-arms and compassion for the POW/MIAs' families, they kept up their demands that bodies of all American servicemen be returned. Their efforts were given a boost in 1987 when General John A. Vessey, Jr., was appointed Special Presidential Emissary to Vietnam. Now, for the first time, the U.S. had a voice speaking with the authority of the president to the North Vietnamese about normalization of relations. General Vessey impressed upon the North Vietnamese government that no normalization would be possible until progress was made in resolving the POW/MIA issue. Vessey's efforts also raised hopes among the American people that the government was finally doing something to bring home the POW/MIAs.

CHIEF OF NAVAL OPERATIONS

A SALUTE TO NINETY YEARS OF THE
VETERANS OF FOREIGN WARS

The Veterans of Foreign Wars of the United States has contributed greatly to the defense of the nation and the welfare of its veterans. Even when the lesser-hearted have turned their back on these important causes, the VFW has remained a true and persistent guardian.

Reflection on the VFW's ninety years reveals a characteristic which permeates its history: <u>Service to America</u>. From their first day in uniform, VFW members have devoted themselves to keeping our great nation free and ensuring our military people are properly rewarded for the great sacrifices they make.

The state of the Navy and the entire U.S. military is superb. Recent events in the Persian Gulf have shown the country and the world that America's military can indeed effectively fight the forces of despotism and terrorism. A measure of credit must go to the VFW for its unflagging support.

The VFW has been an important player over the years in conveying our message to Congress and the American people. Today, VFW's strong support of the Navy will help us maintain the readiness edge we have accrued in the past several years.

On behalf of all Navy men and women, I express enormous gratitude for the efforts of the VFW over the past ninety years. You continue to serve your country well. Best wishes.

C. A. H. Trost
C. A. H. TROST
Admiral, U.S. Navy

Trying to win increased funding for the Department of Veterans Affairs was another familiar fight for the VFW. This fight took on increased urgency when the VA estimated that one quarter of the nation's veterans were over 65 years old in 1990, and that this fraction would increase to over one-third by the year 2000. To date, the VA had continually been trying just to catch up and to meet its deficiencies in care. Obviously, it was not prepared to meet the needs of this tremendous wave of ageing veterans.

Commander Hogan spoke of the VA's crying need for funding in his required annual report to the House and Senate Veterans Affairs Committees during the VFW's Annual Washington Conference in March. He urged Congress to "provide the Department of Veterans Affairs with a fiscal year 1991 budget that would honestly meet the needs of our veteran population." An "honest" budget, by VFW definition, is one that would provide enough money to operate a first-class VA medical care system, a first-class entitlement and benefit program, and a responsive Veterans Administration. To show Congress

CHIEF OF STAFF
UNITED STATES AIR FORCE
WASHINGTON   22 JUL 1988

TO THE MEMBERS AND FAMILIES
OF THE VETERANS OF FOREIGN WARS

I commend the VFW's continued, unwaivering
support of our Nation's defense. Since 1899, your
organization's support for proper recognition,
fair treatment and deserved benefits for our
combat veterans has contributed to the
preservation of our liberties. At the same time,
the VFW's peacetime participation in education and
community programs has significantly enhanced the
way of life each of you fought to protect and
improve.

One of the cornerstones of our Republic is
the tradition of the citizen-warrior -- that
ultimately the security of the United States rests
with our people. On behalf of the men and women
of the United States Air Force, I salute the VFW
for its commitment to preeminent American ideals.

LARRY D. WELCH, General, USAF
Chief of Staff

exactly what such a budget would look like, for the fourth consecutive year the VFW co-authored (with three other veteran's organizations) an independent budget for the VA. This budget was prepared by veterans for veterans and based solely on need. Unlike other budgets given to the Congress, it was not based on monetary constraints formulated by some management and budgetary agency of the government. Although there is no proof that such independent budgets result in increased funding, many veterans' advocates believe these budgets are invaluable in convincing Congress of need.

Yet another on-going struggle waged during Hogan's year was to obtain compensation for veterans who had been exposed to toxic herbicides while serving in Vietnam. The VFW strongly supported H.R. 3004, a compensation bill introduced by Representative Lane Evans of Illinois. In urging passage of this bill before the House Veterans Affairs Committee, James N. McGill, Director of VFW National Legislative Service, said:

"We believe that one day scientists will affirm what many veterans already know—herbicides are quite capable and quite likely to produce a range of serious disabilities and even death. Unfortunately, many veterans do not have the luxury of being able to wait for scientific affirmation—they, their families and dependents are in immediate need of help. The time to act is now."

Although H.R. 3004 did not pass, it resulted in legislation that moved Vietnam veterans one step closer to getting assistance for herbicide exposure. Just before Christmas of 1989, President Bush signed Senate Bill 892 into law. This bill ended the VFW's ten-year struggle for recognition of, and compensation for, death or injury resulting from use of Agent Orange. It allowed the Administrator of the Veterans Administration—on his own authority—to compensate veterans who were proven to have contracted non-Hodgkin's lymphoma, soft skin carcinoma, or chloracne from exposure to Agent Orange. (Unfortunately, because this compensation was not guaranteed by law, it could be denied at the whim of any VA Administrator or new Administration.) The law also referred the defoliant issue

In late 1990, U.S. troops began pouring into Saudi Arabia to launch Operation Desert Shield, and the VFW promptly joined with the American Legion in launching Operation Hometown. Here members of Post 1151 (Creighton, Nebraska) and its Auxiliary pitch in to assemble packages that will give troops stationed in the Persian Gulf a taste of home.

to the National Institutes of Health for further research.*

A class action suit filed by a group of Vietnam veterans suffering from these diseases led to further progress for victims of defoliant exposure. The suit resulted in a verdict forcing the suppliers of the defoliants to give a lump sum payment to those injured by their product. Amounts up to $3000 could be awarded each individual. Federal laws subsequently mandated that these payments could not be counted as income when determining any form of pension, VA or otherwise.

Important as these advances were, they were upstaged by events in Central America going on at about the same time. On December 15, 1989, Panama's notorious drug-dealing dictator, Manuel

Noriega, declared that a state of war existed between Panama and the United States. Then, in an unprovoked attack the next day, U.S. Marine Lieutenant Robert Paz was gunned down at a roadblock in Panama City. On December 20, 1989, the U.S. military launched Operation Just Cause. From the land, sea, and air, 27,000 U.S. soldiers, marines, and aircrewmen struck Panama. Their goal was to capture Manuel Noriega.

Noriega evaded the assaulting forces and hid in a Vatican papal nunciature (embassy). After two weeks, however, he turned himself over to U.S. authorities to face trial on drug trafficking charges. The VFW, which had staunchly opposed returning the Panama Canal to Noriega and paying him over $800 million to accept it, was vindicated. (At the time of this writing, Noriega is still being held in the United States pending trial on trafficking in drugs.)

Shortly after Operation Just Cause ended, it was announced that all armed forces personnel who had participated in the invasion would be awarded the Armed Forces Expeditionary Medal. This medal would, of course, entitle these service men and women to join the VFW. And once again, the wisdom of the founders' "evergreen" policy was proven.

As the organization entered its 91st year, it could claim more active posts (10,399) than ever before in its history. This included fifty-five posts located in a dozen countries: Germany, France, Great Britain, Korea, Taiwan, the Philippines, Guam, Kwajalein (a U.S. territory), Panama, and Japan, including Okinawa. There were also posts in the Virgin Islands and Puerto Rico, as well as four posts in Mexico under the jurisdiction of the Department of Texas. And for the thirty-fifth consecutive year, total membership of the Veterans of Foreign Wars grew. This was as it should be, according to Commander-in-Chief Hogan: "Influence, for better or worse, is tied directly to membership figures."

* Making a definitive judgement as to whether other medical problems are the result of exposure to Agent Orange and other defoliants used in Vietnam is now the responsibility of the National Academy of Sciences.

At the 91st VFW National Convention in Baltimore, Maryland, newly elected Commander-in-Chief James L. Kimery took over the reins of the organization which had become, without a doubt, the most influential veteran's organization in modern times. The theme he announced for his term was, appropriately enough, the "Vanguard of Excellence."

DEPARTMENT OF THE NAVY
HEADQUARTERS UNITED STATES MARINE CORPS
WASHINGTON, D.C. 20380-0001

IN REPLY REFER TO
5720
PAM
20 JUN 1988

My perception is that the VFW and the Marine Corps share several common goals, including a strong defense establishment to ensure national security.

I fully support the VFW's objective to promote Americanism through education in patriotism and constructive service to the communities in which we live. This closely resembles the Marine Corps' objective of fostering good relations with local communities. Like the VFW, the Corps also seeks to inspire patriotism and gain the support and cooperation of the American people.

Marines and former Marines have traditionally been supportive of the VFW, and I expect this to continue as the VFW celebrates the 90th anniversary of its founding. Happy anniversary, and Semper Fidelis.

Sincerely,

A. M. GRAY
General, U.S. Marine Corps
Commandant of the Marine Corps

CHAPTER EIGHT

THE VFW NATIONAL HOME

"Dear God, let us so deliberate this day that the widows and orphans of our departed comrades will enjoy the manifold blessings and comforts which surround us. So guide us in our deliberations that we will not allow our passions, prejudices, or interests to betray us, and that we may be able to render to all orphans and widows their just due without distinction. Please, Dear God, fold your arms of love and protection around our National Home and look after the spirits of our departed comrades. Amen."

This prayer is used to open each meeting of the Board of Trustees of the VFW National Home. Its words—written in 1945 by former trustee Dr. D.F. Monaco—reflect the spirit of caring that led not only to the foundation of the Home, but to the formation of the Veterans of Foreign Wars itself.

James Romanis, Irving Hale, James Putnam, and the other Spanish American War veterans who founded the VFW's precursors were all motivated primarily by concern for their fellow veterans. From the start, that concern extended to the families of their comrades-in-arms, as well. Often, money collected at meetings for a sick or dying comrade was earmarked not only for medication for the veteran, but also for food for his wife and children. Not surprisingly, providing a haven for deceased veterans' widows and orphans quickly became a priority. But despite its members' good intentions, nearly a quarter century passed before the VFW took the first steps to establish a home for veterans' families.

The impetus for the founding of the VFW National Home came from Amy Ross, a twenty-three-year-old Michigan resident. A warm-hearted woman, Amy was concerned not only about the plight of the thousands of children orphaned during World War I, but also about the ragged armies of veterans roaming the streets in search of employment. To Amy, the best solution to both problems was to enlist the jobless veterans in constructing a home for their deceased comrades' children.

On a cold and windy day in February 1922, Amy walked into the Detroit office of Dr. Clarence L. Candler, M.D., the Commander of the Department of Michigan Veterans of Foreign Wars. Amy hoped Candler could help to make her dream a reality, and he did not disappoint her. Commander Candler and the Department of Michigan immediately started looking into the feasibility of Amy's project. When they realized that the project was beyond the capabilities of the Department of Michigan alone, they passed the idea on to the national organization.

The Military Order of the Cootie quickly rallied around Amy's cause. At its 1923 National Convention in Norfolk, Virginia, the Cooties authorized their supreme commander to select a site and investigate the cost of erecting and maintaining a home suitable for veterans' orphans. When the city of Norfolk learned of this move, it offered to donate a site for the facility.

Before any construction could begin, the National Council of Administration met in Kansas City, Kansas, in January 1924 to review the entire project. The Council considered the results of a survey conducted by Cootie Committee Chairman Frank Strickland as to the number of orphans who might need a home. This number turned out to be substantially larger than anticipated, and the VFW did not currently have the funds to carry out a program of such magnitude. Consequently, the project was postponed until more funds could be raised.

Amy's idea continued to simmer on the VFW's back burner until summer 1924. Then, a millionaire cattleman from Michigan presented Dr. Candler with an offer that sounded too good to be true. The cattleman, Corey J. Spencer, had heard about Amy's idea and wanted to give the VFW land on which to estab-

lish its national home. He offered the VFW a 472–acre farm near Eaton Rapids, Michigan, known locally as the Grand River Stock Farm. Dr. Candler advised Spencer that if his offer was firm, to submit it in writing. Shortly afterwards, Dr. Candler received Spencer's offer, which stated that the land was "an absolute gift in fee simple" with but two stipulations: 1) It would provide a home for his wife and himself if adversity should overcome them; 2) If the property should be sold, "the money [was] to be put in an educational fund for the use of worthy students."

It was probably the most costly "absolute gift" the VFW would ever receive.

On October 5, 1924, the National Council of Administration appointed a committee to investigate Spencer's offer and gave it "full power to accept the offer if it deemed fit." Committee members included: Past Commanders-in-Chief Tillinghast Huston, Al J. Rabing, and Robert G. Woodside; J.C. Thompson,

Old Grand River Stock Farm, beginning of the VFW National Home

Judge Advocate, Department of New York; Dr. C.L. Candler, Commander, Department of Michigan; and General H.N. Duff as an ex-officio member.

On November 21, 1929, while the committee was still deliberating, Amy Ross died. To the VFW fell the sad task of giving a military funeral to the twenty-five-year-old woman. In his eulogy of Amy, Dr. Candler said, "Amy Ross is dead. No, she has just commenced to live. . . . When that little city rises out of the ground near Eaton Rapids, called the VFW National Home, you will hear Amy singing a lullaby to some veteran's orphan." The go-ahead for Amy's "little city" finally came on December 6, 1924, when the National Council of Administration voted to accept Spencer's offer. Following the election of "Comrade Spencer" as a member of the Home's Board of Trustees—although he was never an active member of the VFW, nor qualified to be one—he and Dr. Candler prepared the articles of incorporation.

The articles bore the date of December 20, 1924, and were filed on January 7, 1925. Significant provisions were:

Name: "VFW National Home"

Purpose: "To establish a home, or homes, for the veterans of Foreign Wars, their widows, orphans and dependents."

Assets: "472 acres of farm land and buildings valued at $100,000. Complete farming equipment, live stock [sic], tools, grains, etc., valued at $25,000."

Means of Financing: "Life Membership (in the National Home) of $10.00 for each member, yearly membership of fifty cents for each member and donations."

Qualifications of Officers and Members: "Must be a member in good standing of the Veterans of Foreign Wars, OR HAVE PERFORMED SOME MERITORIOUS SERVICE WORTHY OF REWARD, OR HAVE SUBSCRIBED AND PAID FOR A LIFE MEMBERSHIP, OR IF NOT A VETERAN THEY MUST HAVE SUBSCRIBED AND PAID FOR A LIFE MEMBERSHIP."

First Officers:

Albert J. Rabing, President

C.L. Candler, Vice-President

Joseph C. Thomson, Secretary

Corey J. Spencer, Treasurer & Asst. Secretary

First Trustees: General John H. Dunn and

Past Commanders-in-Chief Tillinghast Huston and Robert Woodside.

All of the first officers listed above signed the articles.

The by-laws, which had been prepared for the approval of the National Council of Administration, added several other important provisions. The most noteworthy was that "only members in good standing in the VFW National Home and in good standing in the Veterans of Foreign Wars of the United States, or the Auxiliary thereto, shall be entitled to vote at any regular or special meeting of the corporation." In other words, there were to be two classes of members: voting (VFW and Auxiliary members) and non-voting (all others). But the articles of incorporation, which specified that anyone could belong to the Home simply by paying dues, recognized only one class of member. It is doubtful if this section of the by-laws could have stood up under any serious challenge. (In 1936, the by-laws and articles of confederation were revised, eliminating this discrepancy.)

The by-laws also provided for the selection of trustees. Corey J. Spencer was to be a trustee for life, as were the trustees of the Baseball Fund (see below). The VFW Commander-in-Chief, National President of the Ladies Auxiliary, and Department of Michigan Commander were all members for their terms of office, and the Governor of Michigan was named an honorary trustee. Five others were to be elected for staggered five-year terms. (In 1978, a by-law change increased the term of office to six years.)

According to both the articles of incorporation and the by-laws, the primary means of financing the National Home was to be through payment of dues.

Cory Spencer (seated, center) with men he sent at his own expense to make all posts aware of the benefits of the new VFW National Home. George Dobben (back row, left) was the only VFW member in this group.

But the VFW actually planned to use funds derived from an entirely different source to start up the National Home. How the organization came to have these funds is a story in itself:

In 1922, the New York Yankees won the American League title and the New York Giants won the National League title to advance to the World Series. So evenly matched were the two teams that the series was tied at three games apiece. Even the seventh game, which would decide the championship, was a cliffhanger. Then, late in the game, with the score tied at three, the game was called because of darkness.

Scores of baseball fans protested that the game was called not because the players were unable to see, but because the club owners wanted to make more profit by holding an eighth game the following day. In response to the many protests, Baseball Commissioner "Judge" Keneshaw Landis ruled that the money paid for admission to that seventh game would be given to charity.

That year, one of the owners of the Yankees franchise was Past Commander-in-Chief Tillinghast Huston. When the admission funds were divided up for charity, Huston managed to secure $20,000 for the VFW. This money was placed in escrow under the name "Baseball Trust Fund." It was this fund—along with its accrued interest—that was supposed to provide the initial operating capital for the VFW National Home. (Because of contributions by the VFW and its Auxiliaries, the National Home never had to dip into these funds for operating costs. Instead the funds were reserved for either some really special project or dire need.)

AN OPENING CLOUDED BY CONTROVERSY

Less than two months after the articles of incorporation were drawn, a mishap in Detroit gave the Home its first residents. While en route to pick up his retirement check, retired Army Sergeant Edward Pollett was struck and killed by a streetcar. Because his pension ceased with his death, his widow and six children were left destitute. Post No. 1146 of Halfway, Michigan, where the Pollett family resided, contacted State Commander Candler and arrangements to move them to the recently acquired farm began.

Donations for the Polletts started arriving almost immediately. Chapter No. 1 of the Disabled American Veterans of the World War contributed a check for $25 earmarked for the Amy Ross Bungalow Fund. Many donations came from pensioners, people with disabilities, and others scarcely able to meet their own needs. Aside from money, the first gift that could not be eaten was an Associa mahogany wall chime clock. It was donated by Charles Wright of New York in behalf of his long-time friend, Past Commander-in-Chief Albert Rabing.

Although Mrs. Pollett and her children arrived in Eaton Rapids on March 9, 1925, the family did not move into the farm's frame house until a week later. First, the deed to the farm, mortgages, notes, and agreement had to be executed and recorded. These formalities were taken care of on March 10, 1925.

The VFW got its first hint of trouble to come when Corey J. Spencer and his wife, Nettie Webb Spencer, signed the deed over to the "Veterans of Foreign Wars National Home," rather than to the "VFW National Home," the correct name. The deed also contained *five* conditions, three more than promised:

1. The premises shall be known as the "National Home of Veterans of Foreign Wars of the United States of America."
2. The premises shall be used and maintained perpetually—for aged or infirm Veterans of Foreign Wars of the United States, their wives, widows, children and dependents.
3. Corey J. Spencer, at his option, shall be a member of the governing body, having in charge the control and management of said home.
4. Educational facilities shall be provided on said premises or in the immediate vicinity thereof, with a curriculum sufficient in scope to enable the children residing at the Home to obtain proper schooling without cost.
5. Should grantors [the Spencers] or either of them become in need, they shall be entitled to the privileges and care in said Home to the same extent and like manner as members in good standing of the Veterans of Foreign Wars, the grantee corporation.

The deed further provided that "should it be necessary at any future date for 'the Home' to sell and dispose of said premises or any part thereof" and should the Spencers or their heirs "elect not to take advantage of the rights of reverter," then the Home "shall cause the proceeds of such sale or sales to be placed in a fund to be known as the Corey J. Spencer Trust Fund for education of worthy young people and persons no longer young wishing to further their education"—all "in nature of a loan to be repaid."

These additional, unexpected conditions were intolerable to the Home's founders. Even had the purists among them been able to justify Spencer's position as a member of the Home and an officer of its Board, they would never have stomached the fourth and fifth conditions. Clause four destroyed one of the founders' most cherished dreams—for the children to attend public schools and live the most normal lives possible rather than be subjected to an institutional atmosphere. Clause five imposed a heavy expense and obligation upon the Home. Furthermore, the deed's reference to the Spencers' "rights of reverter" meant that the Home did not truly own the land. The Home could never sell or exchange any minute part of the property. Nor, if Spencer elected to turn the money into a trust fund for worthy students, could any part of the money invested in the VFW's name be recovered.

This bollixed deed was subject to two mortgages. The first was for $15,000 to Prudential Insurance Company and the second for $13,000 to Margaret S. Langley (a clerk in the office of Webb Mortgage and Insurance Agency, founded by Mrs. Spencer's father). These mortgages covered property that had been assessed in 1924 at $28,550—$22,050 for the land and buildings and $6,500 for all personal property including tools, crops in hand, and equipment.

The VFW first formally protested Spencer's sleight-of-hand with the Home's deed at a trustee meeting in June 1925. National Judge Advocate Cook objected to the deed on the grounds that: 1) it referred to the Home by the wrong name; 2) it contained a reverter clause that would allow the Spencers to also assume all buildings and improvement to be constructed on the Home grounds; 3) children would be kept out of public schools. Cook later met with Spencer in Detroit to straighten out these difficulties. At Cook's request, Spencer agreed to clear the title and limit the reverter clause to only part of the sale money or property.

Despite Spencer's promise, he had not made the requested changes by the start of the VFW's National Encampment that August in Tulsa, Oklahoma. This inaction greatly irritated the delegates. A committee composed of Jesse Walcott, John Ballinger, and Charles Wagner, Chairman, spent approximately twelve hours a day for five days trying to persuade Spencer to make the requested changes. Just before the last day of the encampment, an agreement was reached that appeared satisfactory to both sides. The reversionary clause, the school clause, and the clause making Spencer a member of the Board of Trustees were all removed. Subsequently, a motion to accept

the revised deed and to approve the Home as a separate Michigan corporation passed with but one dissenting vote.

Incredibly, following the discussion and vote on the new deed, Spencer tried to take the floor to announce that he had changed his mind and would not revise the deed. Action by the Michigan delegation restrained him.

In September of that year, Charles Wagner was appointed Asst. Judge Advocate General, specifically to revise the deed. With Spencer adamant that he had withdrawn his agreement to revise the deed, the process was long and arduous. At one point, Spencer said that he approved the new draft, but that his wife did not. Later he insisted, "As long as I live, at my option, I am going to be a member of the governing body unless at any time you wish to pay me $35,000." With negotiations between the two men deadlocked, Spencer requested that former Commander-in-Chief Al Rabing step in.

To ease the situation, Rabing agreed to buy the $13,000 Langley Mortgage from Spencer. He also agreed to help purchase the farm equipment and other personal property that had come with the Home. (On August 8, 1925, the Home's directors had adopted a motion to purchase this property by issuing five demand notes for $1,000 bearing 6 percent interest. For reasons not recorded, Joseph C. Thomson, Secretary to the Board, signed six notes instead of five.) Now, Rabing paid off two of the notes and interest on three others, contending that there should only have been five notes, not six.

Thanks to Rabing's intercession (and the $15,721.50 he paid to the Spencers), a revised deed dated October 23, 1925 was finally approved. According to a history of the Home published by attorney Charles A. Wagner in 1958, the "revised Deed used the correct name of the corporation viz 'V.F.W. National Home'; it enlarged the purposes; left Spencer as a trustee (we submitted to that); granted the Spencers care at the Home if in need; freed the Home from conditions as to its use after December 31, 1934; and to take the place of the reverter to the Spencers the

Home could at any time, either before or after December 31, 1934 free itself of all these conditions by payment of $35,000.*

Although Corey Spencer had agreed to the revised deed, he was far from mollified. In April 1926, he tried a new mode of attack on the Home. To extract payment of $1,144 in auto insurance premiums the Home owed his mortgage and insurance agency (the W.B. Webb Co.), he brought suit in county court. The Webb Company also garnished the Home bank account. Ironically, Rabing had earlier directed Spencer, as the Secretary of the Home's Board of Trustees, to reduce the insurance coverage by 40 percent, but Spencer had not done so. Amid much controversy, the Home agreed to pay the entire amount plus 3 percent interest to Spencer.

Given Corey Spencer's apparent ill will toward the Home and everyone associated with it, it is surprising that the Board of Trustees should have elected him as Secretary to begin with. But even after Spencer brought suit against the Home, Spencer was again elected Secretary of the National Home Corporation at the November 1926 Board of Trustees meeting. In fact, throughout the VFW's long and bitter association with Spencer, the organization's leadership consistently refused to initiate any action that would discredit Spencer or halt his attacks against the VFW.

Taking the Home to court was Spencer's last major assault on the organization he professed to support. At the Trustees' meeting in May 1927, Spencer finally conceded that there should only have been five demand notes for $1,000, not six as he had claimed, proving the VFW's original contention. Again no action was taken by the Board against Spencer. By the November Board meeting, the second mortgage—originally termed the Langley Mortgage—was paid in full to Mrs. Rabing, Executrix of Al Rabing's estate.

The final dealings between the Spencers and the VFW National Home were almost amicable. In 1931,

pursuant to its agreement to provide a home for the Spencers if need be, the Home provided Mrs. Nettie Spencer with monetary help and fuel. The Home also supplied food, most of which was paid for by Comrade Duff himself. By 1934, the effects of the depression had reached even the proclaimed millionaire, Corey Spencer. On May 21 of that year, Spencer sold the Home a quit claim deed to the property for $250. On August 23, 1935, the Home paid off the Prudential Mortgage, and finally held clear title to the property.

THE FIRST FIVE YEARS

While ownership of the Home's property was still in question, the trustees had naturally hesitated to authorize any major improvements to the Home. But once the revised deed—without reverter clause—was approved in late 1925, the way was cleared for expansion.

The first priority was to provide new living quarters for the residents. Although the Home had started out with only seven residents (the Pollett family), by 1927 the population would grow to twenty-one children. In 1926, the Department of Michigan set a precedent by volunteering to foot the bill for construction of a cottage—thereby clearing the way for the Home to grow in population. The cornerstone for this cottage, to be known as the "Michigan Cottage," was laid on August 3, 1926. The following year, the second cottage, New York Cottage No. 1, was built. In 1928, the Home concluded that a cottage capable of housing ten occupants was the most feasible and economical to construct. With forty children already

---

*   Spencer did not lower the asking price for his "fee simple" offering even though Comrade Rabing had assumed the $13,000 Langley mortgage and its interest and two of the $1,000 notes and their interest.

General Smedley M. Butler with early residents of the Home

in residence and another eighteen on its waiting list, the Home promptly announced it would build four more cottages at a cost of $30,000.

When the population swelled to sixty children in 1929, the trustees devised a plan to take some of the financial burden off of departments that wanted to build cottages. The trustees ruled that when any department had raised 50 percent of the cost of a cottage, the Home would lend that department the other 50 percent so construction could begin.

Other than cottages, the only building constructed during the Home's first five years was the laundry, completed in 1928. By 1929, the Ladies Auxiliary had, however, raised over $25,000 towards the construction of a much-needed hospital. With a loan of an additional $10,000 from the Home, they had more than enough money to build a facility that would meet the standards of the Michigan Board of Health. The Home also took steps to improve its grounds. In 1927, a natural swimming pool was produced by damming a creek that flowed through the property. To provide both food and revenue, it planted two hundred apple trees, fifty peach trees, and several cherry trees and raspberry bushes. In 1928, the trustees also authorized the purchase of the Briggs Farm, a sixty-acre property one mile east of the Home. This property would be used to house a poultry operation and a piggery operated by farmers from nearby farms. (This purchase was not actually made until 1930.)

Thanks to the generosity of the departments, the Ladies Auxiliary, and individual contributors, the Home did not have to raise a great deal of money to finance its development during this period. But the Home did need to devise a variety of strategies to come up with operating funds, as well as to raise the approximately 60 cents per child per day* it needed to keep its residents fed and clothed.

One of the trustees' earliest fund-raising ideas was to levy a per capita tax on all VFW members, but a motion to that effect failed to pass at the 1926 En-

---

*   This was the 1927 estimate. The cost per child per day rose to about $4.42 in the early 1950s, and soared to $161.72 in 1985.

campment in El Paso. Instead, the encampment approved another means of funding. Beginning in 1927, one cent for every poppy sold in the Buddy Poppy Sales Campaign was to be allocated to the Home. In the first year alone, the campaign netted $35,000 for the Home. In 1928, the proceeds were sufficient to finance the construction of four new cottages. In fact, so closely did the Poppy Campaign become linked with the Home that the 1929 National Encampment adopted the Ladies Auxiliary's recommendation that a National Home child have the honor of presenting the first poppy to the President of the United States each year.*

Projects conducted in association with the Americanization (Americanism) program were another steady source of income for the Home. Typically, members of the Home, the VFW, or some contracted outside firm sold literature or films with an American theme, and the Home received a royalty from each sale. In 1927, the Home's royalties amounted to $667 a month.

Besides using these unique means of raising funds, the Home also relied on the traditional mainstay of all charitable organizations—donations. Throughout the year, a steady stream of cash donations and used clothing flowed into the Home; at Christmas time, the stream turned into a torrent. In 1929, for example, holiday donations included 300 pounds of candy, 160 pounds of nuts, three cases of oranges, ten bushels of apples, large quantities of toys, and $2000 in cash. Several years later, Christmas donations actually became so bountiful that the Home had to make a plea for benefactors to send money, rather than gifts. On one holiday, the director explained, "We received 350 stuffed dolls when we had only two girls of the age to appreciate this type of present. Fifty pounds of beads were received, enough for a regiment of tots. Enough small toys to allow

each child to receive 15 or 20 apiece. Candy, if evenly divided and given out, would have amounted to seven pounds for each child."

Charles F. Adams, first director of the VFW National Home, and Mary Pollett Whalen, one of the Home's first residents

---

* To this day the National Buddy Poppy Child is a boy or girl ages six through ten who is selected by the National VFW Poppy Committee. He or she presents the president of the U.S. with the first poppy of the campaign and represents the campaign in parades, at special events, and in news releases.

Occasionally, one-of-a-kind financial needs called for one-of-a-kind solutions. In 1929, for instance, the Home found itself committed to supporting the family of a veteran who had died of leprosy. Rather than risk infection by admitting the children to the Home, the trustees decided to send the widow twenty dollars a month for two years.

By the end of the Home's first five years, its operations had grown so complex and its population so large that the trustees realized that the Home needed a full-time, live-in director. In August, 1929, they hired Charles F. Adams of Booneville, Missouri, to serve in that capacity. Adams had years of experience in working with children and young people in adoption agencies, reform schools, welfare agencies, prisons, and mental institutions.

DEPRESSION YEARS

The depression of the 1930s spelled doom for many charitable institutions that depended on their supporters' generosity for survival. Yet even though the National Home was in desperate straits more than once, it somehow always managed to bail itself out. By mid-decade, it was actually on solid enough financial ground that it was no longer regarded as "just an experiment." And as its founders had intended, each boy and girl at the Home could look with complete trust to the VFW for the protection, care, and love that normally would have been given them by their fathers, but was denied them by the inhumanity of war.

After the stock market crashed in October 1929, the depression took its time getting to Eaton Rapids. For the first year, in fact, life went on pretty much as usual. The Eaton Rapids School System, in particular, felt prosperous enough to notify the Home in 1930 that it could handle up to 250 children from the Home. This assuaged many of the Home's worries. Since educating children at the Home had never been financially possible, residents had always been enrolled in the Eaton Rapids public schools. But because of Corey Spencer's original stipulation that a school be established at the Home, there was always the fear that the Eaton Rapids School System might someday decree that no more—or only a token number of—Home residents could attend the public schools.

As it was for the surrounding community, 1930 was also a good year for the National Home. Despite the drought, the farming operation managed by local farmers produced 3500 bushels of oats, 350 bushels of wheat, 175 tons of hay, and 450 tons of silage. This, it was estimated, would be more than ample to feed the Home's 235 sheep, 23 milk cows, 8 horses, 3 ponies, 8 hogs, 3 goats, 16 heifers, and 1 bull. The garden produced $2000 worth of vegetables, of which $225 worth was sold.

The Home's fund-raising picture was also rosy that year. Post No. 1578 contributed $1000 toward equipping a dental lab in part of the hospital. (The hospital was completed in 1931.) The Home also earned over $77,000 in royalties from the sale of literature distributed through the Americanization program. And, after the White House had endorsed the poppy campaign and June Allen had present the first poppy to President Hoover, the Home received more than $43,000 as its share from the poppy sales.

In 1931, the depression struck the Home with a vengeance. The Home's income dipped more than $25,000, and there were doubts that the Home could meet its expenses. To help rescue the Home, the National Encampment passed a resolution that one week of every year would be declared "National Home Week," and that each VFW post would be encouraged to hold fund-raising events for the Home that week. Another resolution called for a Memorial Orchard. Under this plan, apple trees would be planted at the Home and sold for ten dollars with an accompanying plaque listing the name of the post purchasing that particular tree.*

As the depression dragged on, the Home's income continued to plummet. Receipts from the Poppy Campaign and Americanization projects were down 43 percent from 1930, and the 1,600–tree Memorial Orchard that had been planted could not begin to make up the difference. The Home's situation grew grimmer still after President Franklin D. Roosevelt ordered all the nation's banks to close briefly in 1933 to give them time to change their banking policies and restore the nation's confidence in them. When Michigan's banks closed, they tied up much of the Home's operating funds. Only a loan from the national VFW and a $4,000 donation from the Ladies Auxiliary and the Allegheny Council kept the Home afloat. Because of the tenuous state of the Home's

finances, the director's salary was reduced from $3,600 to $3,000. The one bright spot amongst all this financial gloom was that the value of the Home had climbed steeply since its founding. In 1934, the worth of the property was assessed at $294,522. And since Spencer Corey had finally signed a quit claim deed earlier that year, all of these assets were the Home's.

After 1934, the depression loosened its hold on the economy in some areas of the country. In the midwest, however, it continued until the start of World War II. During this period, every day was a fight for survival. The beef herd had to be destroyed because of disease, and the constant struggle for funds became automatic. To stay solvent, the Home tried many fund-raising projects. It sold books and literature on American themes, Kiddie Christmas Charms, and trees in its Memorial Orchard. It encouraged VFW and Auxiliary members to purchase Life Memberships in the Home, then placed their membership fees in an endowment fund and used the interest to help finance the Home's operations. The legality of raising

The VFW Home Hospital was financed by the Ladies Auxiliary. Today, this building has been converted into a Health and Education building.

---

* This plan was implemented in 1932 and discontinued in 1949. Donors' names were then transferred to a bronze plaque displayed at the Home.

Picking up the Yuletide mail, 1934

funds via sweepstakes or lotteries was also investigated. Even with the chance that they might be illegal, the extreme need for money prompted the Home to participate in at least two of them. In addition, it enlisted the help of local posts and Auxiliaries in selling Christmas and Easter Seals, which pictured the Home or the Home's children. (These seals were not connected in any way with the National Easter Seals organization.)

In 1936, the Home was forced to ask each department that sponsored children at the Home to pay for part of their expenses. The trustees passed a motion that "Whereas there is not at present time sufficient income to provide for the maintenance of the children at the Home, in the future all applications be covered by an arrangement to share at least 50% of the maintenance of the cottage."

In 1939 and 1940, the trustees tried once again to get the VFW to support the National Home by taxing each member of the VFW and the Ladies Auxiliary. The trustees requested a fifty-cent tax for VFW members, and a twenty-five-cent tax for Auxiliary members. But when the request was brought up at the 1940 National Encampment, the delegates refused to even

Four young residents (Charlotte Biddle, Edith Johns, Wilmer Christian, Muriel Morgan) in front of the Home's bus, circa 1934

National Home boys in 1938

consider it until the Home had supplied all posts and departments with "an itemized and audited report covering all phases of operation and maintenance of the V.F.W. National Home, including a statement of all moneys received from every source whatsoever, and a detailed breakdown of expenditures." (To this day, no tax or per capita assessment has ever been imposed on the VFW or any of its Auxiliary's members.)

No doubt, expenses could have been sharply reduced during the depression if the Home had not continued expanding both its population and its physical facilities. But the Home was a very successful operation and attracted more residents each year. Although the Home did turn away some applicants, its population grew from 83 children and 7 mothers in 1930 to 170 children and 14 mothers in 1939—not to mention 26 more children and 2 mothers on the waiting list.

As the Home added residents, it naturally had to build new cottages to house them. But although construction of cottages was financed by departments, their maintenance was only partially covered. The Home's share of the cost of maintaining the eight new cottages built during these years was considerable. Other new construction only increased the sum the Home had to pay for utilities, paint, repairs, insurance, and general upkeep of its property. For example, in 1939, a new community center was dedicated at a ceremony that included Eleanor Roosevelt, wife of President Franklin Roosevelt, as principal speaker. When the building was completed the following year, the added maintenance cost to the Home was estimated at $7,000 to $12,000 a year. During this period, the Home also built a second-story addition to the storage and office building and an apple storage building. Despite the maintenance burden each new building placed on the Home, its administrators never suggested to its benefactors that funds contributed for construction might be better spent in maintaining existing facilities.

If financial management was not the administrators' strongest suit during the depression, they did manage to put the Home's articles of incorporation and by-laws in order. After revising these documents so that they complied with Michigan's laws, the administrators put the changes to a vote at a special stockholder's meeting on July 25, 1936. The revisions passed by a vote of 737 to 19. Major changes in the articles of incorporation included:

1. The name was set as "Veterans of Foreign Wars National Home"—the same name the organization had originally opposed.
2. The purposes were more clearly defined as "a Memorial. . . . charitable Home" primarily "for orphans, widows, members and other needy dependents of the Veterans of Foreign Wars of the U.S."
3. Members were classified as (and limited to) "Active" or "Associate," with provision for Honorary Membership by Board Action. Active members were required to be in good standing in the VFW or Auxiliary and have paid for a life membership. Active members were to have the sole right to vote for Trustees and on all other matters.
4. All officers (except honorary) were to be "active" members of the Home.

The depression years at the Home were noteworthy not only for the financial troubles they brought, but also for several "firsts." In 1930, the first and second deaths of residents of the Home occurred. Early in the year, Donald Rhodes died from scarlet fever and pneumonia at the age of eleven months. In November, Alice Dobson, age fourteen, succumbed to kidney infection. Homer Frazier became the first resident of the Home to obtain an appointment to West Point, only to be declared physically ineligible for admission after he contracted undulant fever. (Instead he went on to graduate from Albion College in Albion, Michigan, in 1940.) And, on June 16, 1940, Blanche Seafort was the first girl to be married while still living at the National Home. This wedding, held in the community center, reflected one of the Home's most important guiding principles: that it should provide the orphaned sons and daughters of America's overseas veterans with lives as normal as those of the average American boy or girl.

THE WAR AND POSTWAR YEARS

When the United States entered World War II, many graduates and residents of the National Home heeded Uncle Sam's summons. By 1945, 90 of the Home's boys and girls were in the nation's armed forces; by the following year, the number had climbed to 113. During the war, three of the Home's alumni made the supreme sacrifice: Laurence Sims, killed at Pearl Harbor, December 7, 1941; Maurice Chadwick, killed in France, November 6, 1944; and Tony Walter, killed on Luzon, the Philippines, February 4, 1945.

Besides bringing an opportunity for many of the Home's young people to follow in their fathers' footsteps, the war also brought relief from the depression. Throughout the war years (1941–1946), the Home's revenues far exceeded expenditures. Part of the reason may have been that government restrictions on building materials forced the Home to limit costly construction of new buildings. At the same time, many of the Home's fund-raising activities were more profitable than ever before. In 1941, for instance, the Seals program brought in $61,916, nearly $40,000 more than it had the previous year. In 1946, profits from the Seals Campaign mushroomed to well over $295,000. The income from poppies and other sources showed similar gains, while donations—such as the gift of a Civil Defense fire truck from the state of Michigan in 1945—poured it.

In the latter half of the decade, revenues continued to be high—at least on paper. In September 1947, the trustees received a check in the amount of $59,340.79—closing out the Baseball Trust Fund, which had been maintained intact through the depression years. Shortly afterwards, the Home became embroiled in what Home historian Charles Wagner called an "inglorious" dispute over monies owed it by the VFW. At issue was the Home's share of $171,000 from the 1947 poppy sale and an additional $23,931 from the Welfare Fund which the National Council of Administration had directed be distributed to the Home that year.

In 1947, the VFW was unable to pay this money to the Home because the national VFW bank account contained only about $149,000, all of which had already been obligated for other purposes. In 1948, the VFW was still unable to come up with the Home's money. The VFW asked the Home to forgive its debt or to take out space in the *Foreign Service* magazine at a fixed rate per page until the indebtedness had been satisfied. But the Home refused.

In 1949, the VFW finally paid $57,000 of the poppy money, and the Home's Board of Trustees forgave the national organization its Welfare Fund indebtedness. But the VFW still refused to pay interest on the remaining poppy monies owed the Home. At last, after much turmoil and bitterness, both sides agreed to a repayment plan of $15,000 a year, without interest.

Once the Home had gotten its financial legs back under itself following the depression, it began once again to expand. In 1943, it was predicted that the Home's capacity would have to be doubled in order to be able to care for the World War II orphans. As if to encourage construction, the trustees repealed their earlier ruling that a state had to establish a maintenance fund before building a cottage. But although a nursery was added in 1945, the Board did not actually issue orders for the start of five new cottages until 1949. Also completed in 1949 were an addition to the hospital and a combination guest lodge and chapel—the latter completely financed by the Ladies Auxiliary. The Chapel was dedicated in part by a Protestant Minister, a Catholic Priest, and the Department of Michigan Chaplain, Rabbi Herbert Eskin. The following year, the Home saw the addition of both the farm implement shed and the Cootie Swimming Pool.

*National Home
residents enjoying
the Cootie
Swimming Pool*

As in the previous decade, the Home had its share of "firsts" in the 1940s. In March 1942, for example, the first two National Home graduates—Tom and Woodrow Pollett—became the first two Home alumni to join the VFW. Hard on their heels, that June George Hendrickson was the first Home graduate to be signed by a professional baseball team (the St. Louis Cardinals).* In 1948, when George Seafort replaced J.W. Ralston as assistant director of the Home, it marked the first time a Home graduate was hired as a staff member. And, as usual, each year a resident of the Home presented the first Buddy Poppy to the president of the United States. In 1948, the honor of giving a poppy to Harry Truman fell to five-year-old Sandra Marie Smith. When she left the

president's office, Sandra clutched in her small fist a Benjamin Franklin half dollar, a memento from the president that she vowed to keep forever.

COMING OF AGE

★

The VFW National Home entered its second quarter century amidst the suggestion of scandal. In 1951, Past National Soloist Father Harold E. Whitted submitted a six-page complaint report about the Home to the trustees and demanded the immediate resigna-

---

* After George's death in 1966, his widow and children became the first second generation family to enter the Home.

Charles E. Henry, left, and Ed Plummer inspecting the Home's new switchboard.

tion of Home Director Charles Adams. The exact nature of Whitted's complaints have since been forgotten, but it is known that Adams circumvented the Board of Trustees several times in making decisions. He authorized construction of a new administration building without consulting the Board, and then, after construction had started, approved an increase in contractor's fees without asking the Board's permission. Whatever Adams's other transgressions, when added to his abuses of authority, they were enough to persuade the trustees to accept his resignation as of November 1, 1951.

To replace Adams, the board hired Stanley Walker at a salary of $8,400. Walker became the Home's director on January 1, 1952, but served only eleven months before his wife's ill health forced him to resign. Assistant Director George Seafort, a Home alumnus and ordained minister, served briefly as interim director until Charles E. Henry was appointed the new director.

Henry took office just in time to witness one of the most memorable Christmas celebrations ever held at the Home. The memories were provided courtesy of the airmen of the Non-Commissioned Officers Open Mess of the 6603 Air Base Group stationed at Goose Air Base, Labrador. These airmen had decided to make Christmas of 1952 a truly happy one for some group of deserving children. Upon learning of the Home through the Veterans Administration, the men knew there could be no more deserving group than the orphans of their deceased comrades in arms.

The 6603rd's NCO Open Mess voted to allot $5,000 to the children's Christmas. Colonel Joseph A. Thomas, their Commanding Officer, approved the appropriation and assigned staff sergeants Wilbur F. Lantz, Richard A. Lane, and Victor A. Scheuren to temporary duty at the Home.

While at the Home, the three sergeants read the children's letters to Santa to determine which present each wanted most, then set about making the orphans' dreams come true. By Christmas morning, they had amassed a mountain of watches, radios, toy vehicles of every size and make, radios, party dresses, ice skates, dolls that walked and talked, and enough other gifts to stock Macy's toy department. As the children gazed upon the largest Christmas tree they had ever seen, Staff Sergeant Lantz passed out the gifts. The first and largest present—a playpen and mattress—went to the youngest child, a five-month-old boy. Then each child in turn received the toy or item he had wished for most. By the time Christmas was over, the children, if they had had any way of influencing Air Force promotions, would have elevated the three staff sergeants to the rank of five-star generals—such was the joy and happiness they knew that holiday season, thanks to those three sergeants and the men of the Non-Commissioned Officers Mess.

Before they returned to Labrador, the three sergeants unveiled one final present for all the children at the Home. Thanks to the scrounging, dickering ability that is inbred in any successful sergeant, they had managed to raise $2,000 more than they needed to buy all the children's presents. With this money, they equipped a hobby shop for work in wood, metal, or plastic that would serve as a memorial to the men stationed in Goose Bay. For themselves, they took back hundreds of feet of film and other records as visible proof of the success of their project.

Other gifts received from the Home over the next few years helped it to become more self-supporting. In 1953, for example, the Cooties donated a new Seagrave fire truck to the Home. Soon afterwards, local fire fighters held seminars to teach some of the Home's older boys and girls the correct way to extinguish different types of fires, and the Home's fire department was born. Because a fire department run by teenagers was so unusual, many newspapers featured the Home's fire fighters in their Sunday supplements.* On one occasion, several bales of hay were set on fire so the fire fighters could be photographed in action. This scheme backfired when the fire fighters

arrived and put out the fire before the photographer could get set up. The action had to be run again, this time at a controlled pace, slower.

The "Old Girl"—the fire truck donated by the Cooties—served the Home faithfully for twenty-one years. Then in 1974, it was replaced with the "Hot Tomato," a newer model that could drive and pump at the same time and had aluminum ladders rather than wooden ones. It could also respond more rapidly to emergencies outside the Home. This new truck was purchased with over 8 million coupons from Betty Crocker products that were collected by posts and Auxiliaries all over the country.

Later gifts that helped increase the Home's self-sufficiency included $7,000 for the purchase of a new school bus, donated in 1961 by Post 9723 in Goekue, Okinawa, and a new dairy operation, contributed in 1956 by the Department of Montana and its Ladies

The National Home Fire Department

---

* In 1982, they were even featured on the ABC television program "That's Incredible."

Aerial view of the VFW National Home, circa 1950s.

Auxiliary. This new "Montana Farmstead" was complete with milking machines and self-feeders. It allowed the Home to double the size of its dairy herd and its subsequent output without increasing the size of its work force. It also provided hands-on training for Home residents interested in entering the dairy business. For years, this operation supplied all the milk and cream the Home's residents needed, but later state regulations mandated that all milk used at the Home be pasteurized. As a result, the Home's milk must now be processed by a commercial operator in a nearby town.

As in the first quarter century, during the second twenty-five years donations also helped to finance many new buildings and other additions to the Home. In 1954, for instance, the Departments of Indiana, North Carolina, Pennsylvania, and South Dakota all started construction of cottages. In 1956, the department of Ohio sponsored the creation of the James Romanis Memorial Lake to honor the Ohio native who helped to found the VFW. Then in 1957, the VFW National Home Administration Center, begun

under the direction (or misdirection) of Charles Adams, was finally dedicated. Among those present at the ceremony was Casey Stengel, manager of the New York Yankees. Stengel attended as a representative of organized baseball, which had supplied the money for construction through the Baseball Trust Fund.

In his remarks at the dedication, Stengel jokingly took credit for the building's construction. Stengel, who had played for the Giants in the 1922 World Series, claimed, "If it weren't for me, none of us would be standing here in the rain. If I hadn't played such a dumb game, we would of won four to three. I singled late in the game, but pulled a muscle going to first. While I was standing there wondering whether I should tell manager John McGraw about it, he called for a hit and run play. I just made it to second and would have made it to third except for my sore leg. McGraw took me out for a runner, but it was too late. He only got as far as third. If I had told McGraw about the pulled muscle, you wouldn't have had this building. But now I'm real glad I didn't."

Another important addition to the Home during this period was a 128–plot section of Rose Hill Cemetery in Eaton Rapids. The land was given to the National Home Alumni Association in 1959 by the city of Eaton Rapids. The Alumni Association, which had been formed in 1953 by former resident L.W. Carr "to simply do whatever we can to help the place that has done so much for us," then transferred the deed to the property to the National Home. Before doing so, however, the association arranged to have the remains of the six children who had died while living at the National Home reinterred in this new section of the cemetery. It also dedicated a stone monument bearing the VFW emblem, the words "VFW National Home," and a quotation from the Bible.

The final major addition made in the Home's second quarter century was a tri-level cottage erected on the site of the old farm house. Built by the Department of North Dakota in 1962, it offers visitors to that residence a bird's-eye view of the thirty-two cottages

The monument in the VFW National Home section of Rose Hill Cemetery, Eaton Rapids, Michigan.

and twenty other buildings that make up the National Home.

At the same time the face of the National Home was changing, there were, of course, many changes of faces within it. As in past years, residents of the Home continued to graduate and go on to become upstanding members of the adult community. In 1961, for example, Jack Koch became head coach of Eaton Rapids High School. That same year, Frank Bonta, who had come to the Home in 1933, was named Director of Admissions at Albion College in Albion, Michigan. And in 1966, for the first time since World War II, a Home resident again made the supreme sacrifice. PFC Elgie G. Hanna was killed by a sniper's bullet while on patrol near Quang Tri, Vietnam, just thirty-three days after arriving in the country. Following a burial service at the Home's Memory Chapel, Hanna was laid to rest at the Rose Hill Cemetery.

Changes in staff did not occur nearly so often as changes in residents. In January 1972, however, Charles Henry retired after nineteen years as the Home's director. To take over the job of Director and Secretary-Treasurer, Samuel E. Story of Ocala, Florida, resigned as Adjutant/Quartermaster of the Department of Florida and as an employee of the Atlantic Coastline Railroad. A past post, district, and department commander of the VFW, Story brought extensive knowledge of the VFW and business to his new position.

In spring 1974, another new employee joined Story on the supervisory staff. Abram L. Winters of Clearwater, Florida, was hired to fill the recently created position of Assistant Treasurer. As Assistant Treasurer, the one-time president of Winamac Electric took over the responsibilities for budget and fiscal operations, Life Membership programs, retirement program, Seals Program, and special projects.

With Story and Winters at its helm, in 1975 the Home celebrated its fiftieth anniversary. As part of the year-long celebration, a group of students from the Home toured the country putting on short plays and skits. The next year, the Home again pulled out all the stops to mark the Bicentennial of the United States.

Elgie Hanna's last rites at the VFW National Home Chapel.

Junior Vice Commander John Wasylik spoke at a special ceremony and the Bicentennial Administration Building—an addition to the Administration Center—was dedicated.

As one year flowed uneventfully into the next, it began to seem as if all the Home's major problems had been solved. . . .

TROUBLE IN EATON RAPIDS

In 1979, two events that shook the National Home to its foundations occurred. First, the Home ran afoul of the Michigan Department of Social Services (DSS) when that department instituted new regulations providing for increased monitoring by state agencies.

As the result of allegations made to the media about child abuse and sexual abuse at the Home, several investigations were launched. VA investigator Mr. F.L. Robinson quickly cleared the Home of all charges. The DSS's own investigation team also found that "no monumental problems" existed at the Home, so there was no need to suspend its license.

Secondly, and more importantly, two of the Home's administrators were accused of criminal misconduct.

The first rumors of corruption at the Home reached VFW National Commander-in-Chief Howard Vander Clute, Jr., in December of 1979. That month, he received a phone call from one of the Home's employees about odd happenings there. The caller told Vander Clute that building materials and new appliances were being stored at the Home, only to be hauled away later by truck. "In fact," the caller informed the Commander, "a load is leaving right now."

Vander Clute immediately started an investigation. At his direction, VFW Adjutant General Julian Dickenson appointed two members of the

Washington, D.C., staff to conduct a secret inquiry. But before the investigative committee could even arrive, both men who were under suspicion resigned. The resignation of Assistant Treasurer Abe Winters was effective December 18, 1979; that of Director Sam Story, the day after.

Effective the day of Story's resignation, the Board of Trustees appointed Dickenson as Acting Secretary and Treasurer of the National Home. Dickenson then named the men previously assigned to conduct the inquiry—Edward L. Burnham, Assistant Adjutant General, and Herbert Irwin, Assistant Quartermaster General—as his representatives in conducting "all financial and administrative matters and all other matters necessary for the proper operation of the VFW National Home." He also gave Burnham and Irwin sole custody and control of all the Home's assets, receipts, and funds.

When Burnham and Irwin arrived at the Home on December 24, they found that the FBI had already begun an investigation. Undeterred, they conducted their own inquiries, as detailed in their inter-office memorandum of January 2, 1980, to Adjutant General Dickenson:

". . . . Our initial meeting was with Sam Story. He turned over keys, safe combinations, his American Express and telephone credit cards, a letter of resignation from Winters and a court order to turn over the Home records to the FBI on December 26, 1979.

"Sam stated that he would cooperate in any way possible but he could not discuss the matters that led him to step aside. . . .

"A meeting of the House Parents and children was held at 11:00 a.m. at the Community Center. At this meeting we told those assembled that Sam Story had stepped aside from all duties at the Home and that we were there to insure the continued operation of the Home without interruption.

"Accompanied by Sam Story and [Home Attorney] George Cholack we drove to the bank in Eaton Rapids. . . . Control of all National Home accounts was transferred to our custody with either of us registered as the only persons authorized to sign checks on National Home accounts. At this time the Home safety deposit box was plugged and sealed with no access to anyone until such time as we could arrange to survey the contents. . . .

"It was apparent that employee morale was in a bad state. Secrecy, suspicion and fear were all pervasive. Our open door policy was a welcome relief to the staff. We sensed an almost immediate change in attitude, a willingness to talk without fear of recrimination, a realization that our reason for being there was in the best interest of the Home.

"The FBI agents met with us on December 27, 1979.

"We offered our complete cooperation with their investigation. They accepted our offer to make records available to them at the Home rather than to seize them as authorized by the court. The contents of the safe deposit box, at the bank in Eaton Rapids, were inventoried in their presence with Sam Story.

"During our meeting with the FBI agents, they informed us of a search of Sam's office which they had conducted with a search warrant on the Friday prior to our arrival. We consented to their request to search the computer room where they indicated they expected to find a bag of money and a relay switch box. Their search turned up the switch box and four paper bags containing $6404.00, in one dollar bills.

"The FBI agents were at the Home again on Friday December 28, 1979 conducting interviews with members of the staff. We passed on the information that had been reported to us concerning some building materials that were showing up without explanation on the Home property. . . .

"At this point, we have no certain knowledge of malfeasance or misfeasance on the part of anyone, but from our observations we are of the opinion that financial and administrative matters of the Home have been mismanaged."

While the jury was still out on the "malfeasance or misfeasance" of Story and Winters, the Home set about reassuring its staff, residents, and supporters that its finances were sound. Fidelity bonds in the amount of $200,000 each were secured for Herb Irwin, Ed Burnham, and Interim Director Jack Carney as a vote of confidence in their character and ability.

After his appointment as interim director on January 5, 1980, John Carney took further steps to re-establish the staff's confidence in the administration. Most importantly, he tore out walls of the room (approximately six feet by eight feet) that Sam Story had ordered constructed in the director's office. This "inner sanctum" supposedly was to allow the director a place to continue his work uninterrupted while visitors were touring the Home. But in fact, the room housed electronic gear that recorded conversations from all employee telephones at the National Home.* Carney also ordered the re-insulation of twenty-seven of the Home's cottages—not only to reduce power bills, but also to assure the employees that the Home's management was looking to the future and to the continued operation of the Home. This move was an excellent morale booster.

By July 16, 1980, when Commander-in-Chief Vander Clute testified before the Grand Jury, the Internal Revenue Service had joined in the investigation of Story and Winters. "This," Vander Clute predicted, "will mean an additional delay of at least one to two months. No indictment can be handed down by one agency when another federal agency is conducting its investigation."

In 1982, Sam Story and Abram Winters were indicted by a Federal Grand Jury and tried in Grand Rapids Federal Court. Both were convicted of income tax evasion and of transporting stolen goods—property purchased by Story in the name of the VFW National Home—across state lines, to land owned by the Storys in Arkansas. Although Story attempted to appeal, each man served three years in federal prison, then was placed on probation for an additional five years. Winters's wife, Sharon, was also convicted, but served her sentence in a county jail in Michigan.

Because of the criminal activities of Story and Winters, the VFW ordered a General Court-Martial convened for each of them. The Courts-Martial directed that both men have their membership in the VFW terminated by dishonorable discharge. Story's name was removed from the rolls of Major J.M. Tillman Post No. 2420, Lake Wells, Florida, and Winters's name was removed from the rolls of Sunshine City Post No. 6827, St. Petersburg, Florida.

At about the same time the investigation of Story and Winters was coming to a head, the Home was also smoothing out its relationship with the Michigan Department of Social Services. In April 1980, Dr. John Dempsey, director of DSS, and seven of his staff visited the Home to re-establish communication between the DSS and the Home, and to help the Home plan for its upcoming licensing evaluation. Subsequently, Tonia Holcomb, the supervisor of children's programs, and attorney George Cholack attended a court hearing aimed at naming guardians for the National Home children who had no guardian of record. Documents were submitted to the court for appointment of Ms. Holcomb as guardian of their persons and Attorney Cholack as guardian of their estates (conservator).

On June 23 to 26, DSS representatives again visited the Home to complete their licensing study. After considering the Ingram County Health Depart-

---

* As past president of an electronic parts manufacturing company, Abe Winters likely played a major role in installing and maintaining this equipment.

ment Inspection Report, the Department of Michigan Fire Safety Inspection, and their own findings, the DSS recommended that a regular license be granted for the care of up to ninety-eight children.

REBUILDING

The disastrous events of 1979 and 1980 had long-lasting effects on the National Home. They led the Home to drastically restructure its administration and to redistribute authority among its leaders. More significantly, they also caused groups that had previously given their unqualified support to the Home to openly criticize the Home and its operations. In effect, the VFW and its auxiliaries placed the Home on probation—a probation that continues to this day.

Following the departure of Story and Winters, both the DSS and the VFW investigative team instigated changes in the Home's administration. The

DSS required the Home to replace Story not with another director, but with an *executive* director—someone qualified not only to administer the physical and financial operations of the Home as Story had been, but also qualified to oversee the Home's child care programs. In September 1980, the Home's trustees hired a child care specialist, Dr. Theodore Wilson III, as the executive director.

After Wilson took office, the representatives of the VFW's Adjutant General (Burnham and Irwin) worked with him and the trustees to improve communication between the executive director and the staff. Burnham and Irwin also recommended that each supervisor be given the authority to make decisions in his or her area of responsibility.

The absolute control that had previously been vested in the Home's director was now divided among three areas. The Home's director would retain overall direction and responsibility, while the directors of child care and of maintenance and the physical plant would directly supervise employees working in their areas. Each area was assigned specific responsibilities and required to work with the others so that the operation of the Home as a whole would be smoother and

Summertime fun at the National Home

more efficient. Guiding this restructuring was the "total commitment to insure quality care for the children and the families at the Home." Without this commitment, the VFW and the Board of Trustees stated, "We need not continue the operation."

Even with the commitment of all concerned, questions about the advisability of keeping the Home open were soon raised. At the Annual Washington Conference in 1981, Commander-in-Chief Arthur Fellwock announced a plan to investigate the Home and evaluate its value and usefulness in today's society.

The Home responded to Fellwock's proposed investigation with a public relations effort designed to inform the VFW membership of the Home's ability to help those in need. The main ammunition for this campaign was the conclusion reached by a team of child care experts from the University of North Carolina who had been hired by the Home to evaluate its programs. This team had concluded that the Home had "endless potential" to carry out its mission.

To enlist further support for its continued operation, the Home sent each VFW post a brochure enumerating the advantages of keeping the Home open. Accompanying this brochure was a sample resolution extolling the National Home's contributions as "a living memorial to the deceased combat veteran and as a Home to provide love, care and education to the needy children and widows of deceased and disabled combat veterans eligible for membership in the Veterans of Foreign Wars." The resolution concluded with a recommendation that the "National Headquarters of the VFW and Ladies Auxiliary work closely with the Board of Trustees and the new professional staff of the VFW National Home, commencing immediately, to actively promote the services of the National Home among its membership and those eligible for membership and to encourage families of dead or totally disabled combat veterans, especially of the Korean and Vietnam War eras, to consider taking advantage of the services provided at the National Home."

Posts were asked to bring the resolution on the floor at a post meeting, then forward it with their approval to the district level. After receiving approval at district and department levels, the resolution was eventually to be sent to the national convention.

Despite the Home's efforts at self-promotion, the committee appointed by Commander-in-Chief Fellwock declared the Home a definite drag on the organization's finances and fund-raising efforts. Its recommendation was to close the Home and use the monies raised to expand the organization's service work for its veterans. Strangely enough, the Ladies Auxiliary was more willing to accept this recommendation than were its male counterparts. In a highly emotional and sentimental exchange on the convention floor, those against the Home's closing managed to pass a motion to table the issue, which for all practical purposes ended the movement.

To understand the delegates' reluctance to close the Home, it helps to understand the position the Home occupies in the minds of the members. Ever since the first family took residence there, the Home has been held out as a crutch and savior of a member's family in the event of his death. To many members, it is "Peace of Mind" insurance. At each and every meeting, at any organizational level, a prayer is included for the National Home and its occupants. The Home is and has been a source of organizational pride. This pride and sentiment have always successfully blocked any attempt to show that there may be a more efficient and economical way of looking after the welfare of the members' children.

Although the Home's future could be put on indefinite hold, its day-to-day activities could not. It continued to take an active role in the community, hosting, for example, a "Heritage Ball" in its community center as part of the Eaton Rapids Centennial Celebration in 1981.

More importantly, the Home established a new scholarship program, demonstrating its ongoing commitment to the future success of its residents. In the past, college-bound residents had been able to borrow money for their education from a student loan fund at the Home. Because the loan fund was relatively small, however, funds had been limited and students were often required to repay their loans almost immediately. In 1983, the Home began *giving* rather than lending its graduates financial assistance. The funds for this assistance came not only from the Home itself, but also from special donations from Ladies Auxiliary Departments, Districts, and individual units; Cootie Pup Tents, Grands (Departments), and Regions; VFW Posts, County Councils, Districts, and Departments. Individual bequests were another source of education funds. In 1983, for example, R. Robert Dale, an Illinois Air Force veteran, bequeathed the Home over $950,000 in money, stocks, and bonds to be used to further the education of Home graduates.

Under the new scholarship program, students could receive funding for a two- or four-year undergraduate program, and in some cases, for graduate studies as well. Although students were asked to help finance their educations by seeking "work study" funds from their educational institution, the program would furnish money for rent, books, tuition, medical expenses, clothing, and incidentals. Students were not (and are not) required to reimburse either the Home or the sponsors of the scholarship program.

Also in 1983, the Home held the first of what were to become annual "Adventure Challenges"— sightseeing trips that incorporated healthy doses of exercise. That year, bikers from the Home pedaled more than 200 miles up the state to the Makinac Bridge spanning Lake Michigan. In 1984, the bikers rode all the way to the VFW National Convention in Chicago, crossing Lake Michigan by ferry.

In 1985, Earl Deterding of Nebraska became the first boy chosen as the National Buddy Poppy Child. That year, the Home also observed its sixtieth anniversary. Festivities included an alumni reunion, dedication of the Alumni Museum, a barbecue, and a balloon launch.

The Home's year-long anniversary celebration was still going on when opponents of the National Home renewed their attack. Fueling their arguments against the Home was an article that appeared in the June 1985 issue of the *VFW Magazine*. Under the heading "VFW National Home Facts," this article reported that the proposed budget for the National Home in 1985 to 1986 was $4.25 million. According to the article, this meant that each of the Home's seventy-two residents cost it more than $59,000 per year. ($4,250,000 divided by 72 equals $59,027.78.) Even with cost-cutting measures already being implemented by the Home's Board of Trustees, this was still an enormous amount per child and great fuel for the fires of the anti-Home forces.

As is the case in most in-house controversies, no records were kept of the number of VFW and Auxiliary members pro or con the Home's closing. But as word of the cost per child spread, it began to affect the Home's fund-raising activities. In the 1985–

Shawn Norton, a member of the Home's Fire Department, in action.

86 year, fewer than 5 percent of the VFW and Auxiliary members contributed to the National Home Seals Program, which ordinarily covered the lion's share of day-to-day expenses.

Throughout the battle over the Home's fate, the support of the Ladies Auxiliary remained strong. During the term of National Auxiliary President Joan Katkus (1988–89), the Auxiliary donated $250,000 from its Health and Happiness fund to redecorate the interior and exterior of the Home's health and education building. In 1988, the Auxiliary's National Council of Administration voted to renovate the nursery and community center as its next Home project. (see letter above)

On October 1, 1988, the Home gained another strong ally when Maryjane Peck took over as the Home's executive director. Peck, who had worked for the Michigan Department of Social Services for seventeen years and is a specialist in the field of child care, immediately adopted a "move ahead" policy.

As if her letter were a blueprint of her intentions, Peck quickly set about bringing the Home up to the standards she thought were necessary. Topping her agenda was the renovation of many of the older cottages and their furnishings. She also embarked on an energetic speaking campaign to improve the Home's public image and to persuade the VFW's membership that the Home still had a great deal to offer.

Thanks in large part to Peck's enthusiasm, money for the cottage renovations continues to come in. In 1989, over 1,500 people journeyed to the Home on Michigan Day (July 16), the Home's annual celebration day. Over 230 post and Auxiliary flags were registered, making it the largest turnout since the old days when the celebrations included a carnival.

THE NATIONAL HOME TODAY

Today the campus of the VFW National Home sprawls across 640 acres. Its 36 cottages house approximately 104 residents, including about 75 boys and girls under the age of 18.

Cottages sponsored by the Department of Indiana (left) and the Department of Maryland.

States maintaining one or more cottages at the Home are:

California	New York
Colorado	Nevada
Connecticut	North Carolina
Florida	North Dakota
Illinois	Ohio
Indiana	Oklahoma
Iowa	Oregon
Kansas	Pennsylvania
Maryland	South Dakota
Massachusetts	Tennessee
Michigan	Virginia
Minnesota	Washington
Missouri	West Virginia
New Jersey	Wisconsin

Many states that do not sponsor a cottage make contributions by helping to perform other necessary operations around the Home. For example, the Department of Maine and its Ladies Auxiliary provide the Home's orthodontic program with its equipment and supplies. With the help of other states, the Department of Montana supports the "Montana Farmstead" and its herd of sixty-six healthy milkers.

For admission to the Home, the VFW National Home has set only one requirement: "that the child, children of that family must have a parent or grandparent who is a VFW or Ladies Auxiliary member. Admission to the VFW National Home is not contingent upon the ability of any agency, auxiliary, post or parent to provide financial support."

A child, sibling group, or family may be referred to the Home one of four ways: by a VFW or Auxiliary member; by public courts or welfare agencies; by child placement agencies; or by private referrals through church associations or other channels. Often VFW service officers and the National Home Chairmen from each Department work with local social services agencies to identify children and families who are eligible for, and could use, the National Home's help. Once it has been established that the responsible parent is a VFW or Auxiliary member, that parent and/or his or her children become eligible for the Home's services.

After a new resident enters the Home, priority is placed on helping him resume the most normal life possible, as quickly as possible. This is in keeping with the Home's philosophy that each child should be treated, in so far as possible, as if the circumstances surrounding his or her growing up were no different than that of a child in any family. Under the "Natural Parent Plan," children who arrive at the Home with their mother or father continue, if possible, under their care; children who arrive alone are absorbed into a "family." The family may consist of up to ten children living in the same housing unit under the care and supervision of a "House Mother" (child care worker). The House Mother—either the natural parent of children at the Home or someone hired for the position—sees that the children are fed, clean, properly clothed, and that their other needs are attended to. Although children are often assigned to the cottages sponsored by the state from which they have come, they may be assigned to a family unit in any cottage.

Many dedicated, caring staff members help the House Mothers maintain the Home's family atmosphere. Two of the most dedicated are Dora Chapman and Frances Rossman. Dora, a registered nurse, worked in the Home's thirty-five bed hospital until it closed in 1971, then was employed as one of the Home's telephone operators and receptionists. She is the daughter of Roy S. Williams, who ran the Home before its first director, Charles Adams, was appointed. With forty years of service to the Home, Frances Rossman has served its residents longer than any other employee. Currently she serves as executive secretary for the scholarship program.

To enhance the Home's family atmosphere, uniforms for the residents are not allowed. Residents are encouraged to maintain their individuality, and so are free to dress as they wish. Children are also enrolled in local public schools so that their association with area children automatically helps integrate them into the community.

Individuality is not the only value emphasized at the Home. Children are also encouraged to develop a sense of responsibility, just as they would be in a more traditional family setting. Each child, young or old, is asked to perform two hours of community service every week. These tasks are assigned according to the child's age and ability. As an incentive, hours worked by the children may apply toward the "purchase" of a skateboard, scooter, bicycle, or other desired item. No child is required to obtain an outside job. Allowances for teenagers, however, are deliberately kept low to encourage older children to

As this photo from the early 1940s attests, Home residents have always earned their keep. Pictured are Phillip Sherman of Pennsylvania and Danny Reynolds of Illinois.

take jobs to earn additional spending money and to learn good work habits.

Like the children, adult residents and staff also help out around the Home. They are asked to give twenty hours of community service a month. Parents may also be encouraged to arrange for paid employment on or off campus or to further their education at local institutions. This is especially true when it seems possible—and in the best interests of all concerned—for the parent to gain the skills necessary to leave the Home and to provide a normal life for the children.

Although there are no fixed rules as to how long a resident may stay at the Home, the average single-parent family leaves the program after three to five years. For them, their time at the National Home is generally a transitional period during which they prepare themselves for lives outside the Home. Children without parents at the Home usually stay until graduation from high school. There is, however, an after-care program. After graduation, some children live independently on campus for a transitional period or while they attend a community college.

With the chance in life the National Home gives them, many graduates go on to become engineers, lawyers, nurses, farmers, secretaries, homemakers, doctors, businessmen, or other successful members of their communities. Because of their success—and the innovative child care methods at the Home that prepare them for success—the National Home is recognized around the world as an outstanding model of a residential child care facility. Over the years, child care experts from many countries have visited the Home to learn about its techniques.

To many, one of the Home's most astounding achievements is that it operates without any direct

Holly Davis, a resident of Illinois I House, was all smiles at the 1987 Cootie Christmas.

funds from federal, state, or local governments. As it has been since its founding, it is solely supported by contributions from the VFW and its auxiliaries. Approximately one-third of its income comes from the Seals program, the National Home's only annual fund raiser for its daily operation. Through this program, each VFW post and Auxiliary member receives a packet of National Home seals, for which he or she is asked to make a donation. This money is used for the direct support of the children and families at the Home. Other sources of income for the Home include Buddy Poppy sales, investments, Social Security and Veterans Administration entitlements of some children, oil leases, and general donations and bequests. The Home also frequently receives special contributions by the Ladies Auxiliary, Cooties, or others for special projects.

Exactly how the Home spends its income each year is determined by the Home's Board of Trustees, which draws up the annual budget. Although the Home's Board occasionally receives suggestions or criticism from the VFW or its members, the Home is a separate corporation and operates according to the mandates of its own Board of Trustees. With annual budgets exceeding $4 million, many VFW and Auxiliary members question whether the Home has become too expensive to operate. But at least in the opinions of most of the Home's residents, the programs are worth every penny they cost.

The feelings of one mother of four—interviewed by Dr. Marjorie Bottoms at the Home in 1988—are typical. "I remember well," the mother said, "while they were telling me what the Home would provide I was thinking, 'There's got to be a catch. Nobody gives you that much for nothing.'" When she arrived, her disbelief was even stronger. "Food, a house like this to live in, clothing and schooling for the kids for free? I thought there's got to be a catch."

This mother had been in her mid-thirties when she and her husband divorced. Unable to find work because she had not been employed for more than a decade, she had had no alternative but to become a welfare recipient. Then her father, a VFW member, told her of the VFW National Home and initiated the action to get her and her family admitted.

To this woman, the advantages of living at the Home rather than receiving welfare were enormous. "On welfare," she said, "you're stuck in a pit. Here the advantages make it possible to move forward toward achieving a workable family unit and then prepare yourself to make a salary that will enable you to move back into the everyday world and get on with your life."

Another single mother who lived at the National Home expressed similar feelings of gratitude in an open letter to the staff and the entire VFW organization. This letter, reprinted below, gives a better indication of the Home's worth than could be given in a detailed documentary.

AN OPEN LETTER

To everyone who has been so helpful and supportive over the 7½ years we were at the VFW National Home, we would like to express our deepest appreciation for everything you have done for us.

It's not just the financial support, although that helped enormously, but mostly the moral and emotional support we received from all of you. With your help, we've come a long way.

May was 10 years old, shy (very) and unable to walk without falling down every few steps because of muscular weakness. Now she is 18 and almost out of school. She has friends and is able to participate with others. She attends the M.D. Clinic (along with Steve), and is doing much better. Charlie was six years old. He's now 14 and doing great in school. He has grown so much; it's hard to believe he was ever smaller than I am.

Stevie was 10 months old when we came to the VFW Home. At that time he couldn't walk, wouldn't talk to anyone but family and definitely did not want me out of his sight. Now he's eight years old, has girlfriends at school, can move faster than a speeding train, and won't be quiet for more than a minute or two. (He probably even talks in his sleep.) I wouldn't have it any other way!

As for me, I was pretty shy myself. I had no confidence in myself and was scared crazy. Now I have a job that deals with the public on a regular basis, and with my mom, we have a home of our own. Who would have guessed it 7½ years ago?

We work as a family to overcome our problems and hopefully will continue to do so in the future. It was your help and support that enabled us to do so. We'll never forget all that you have done.

Before I close, I would like to thank VFW Post #6034 (Potterville, Michigan) and its Ladies Auxiliary for sponsoring us at the Home; the posts and auxiliaries of the State of Virginia for all the help in supporting the Virginia Cottage; Sue Shoultz, Wilma Bailey, Jo Cox and other members of the Home for being a great friend to me and my family. We will miss you, but then again, we are only a few miles away so we'll be seeing you often.

God Bless,
Georgia Farr
Mary
Charlie
Stevie

Despite the heartfelt appreciation of the Home's residents, the VFW members still question whether the concept of a home for widows and orphans has lived beyond its time. With governmental agencies continually imposing more stringent care requirements, and with inflation pushing the costs of meeting these requirements ever higher, is there a more efficient way to accomplish this same mission?

Balanced against the pride and loyalty that members of the VFW and its auxiliaries have in their Home's accomplishments, it is not a question that will be decided easily or quickly.

CHAPTER NINE

THE AUXILIARIES

THE LADIES AUXILIARY

For as long as men have been going into battle, women have been nursing sick and wounded warriors back to health. Until recently, this was a necessity because governments did not provide adequate medical facilities for their servicemen. In fact, medical care was often so abysmal that more men died of disease and food poisoning than of wounds.

Like many veteran's organizations, the first women's auxiliaries were formed to promote the health and welfare of soldiers and veterans. During the Civil War, groups such as the Women's Relief Corps of the Grand Army of the Republic and the American Sanitary Commission worked to eradicate unsanitary conditions on the battlefield, in military hospitals, or wherever they found them. Many of these units allied themselves with Clara Barton in the North or Sally Thompkins in the South, actively nursing sick and injured soldiers. And during the Spanish American War, the women in the Soldier's Aid Society pleaded for better care of the shiploads of fever-laden soldiers waiting at the piers in New York Harbor. Yet despite notable successes achieved by

these groups over the short term, lasting reform remained elusive. Because the women's auxiliaries—like the veteran's organizations of the time—were formed only to deal with the problems surrounding one conflict, they, too, died out with their generations.

Then in 1914, the recently merged VFW started a new kind of ladies auxiliary. This group differed from earlier women's auxiliaries in two respects. First, because the VFW was open to veterans of all wars and the Ladies Auxiliary was open to the wives of all VFW members, the Auxiliary was designed to outlive its generation. Second, its primary purpose was not to aid servicemen and veterans directly, but to help the members of the VFW aid their comrades. Perhaps because the VFW members feared that the women would usurp their authority, in the beginning they insisted that the Ladies Auxiliary confine itself to planning and orchestrating social activities. Soon, however, the Auxiliary took on programs of its own such as fund-raising and hospital and relief work.

Today, the Ladies Auxiliary is involved in a kaleidoscopic range of activities. While continuing to support the VFW and its causes, the Ladies Auxiliary has developed a social conscience of its own. With the paramount goal of helping families in distress, its members perform community service, fund cancer research, fight drug abuse and illiteracy, advocate for the rights of the elderly, and support the VFW National Home, Special Olympics, and other worthy causes.

Membership has been broadened to include not only wives of VFW members, but also their mothers, widows, sisters, half-sisters, daughters, grandmothers, and granddaughters. Foster mothers and foster daughters are also eligible, provided their relationship with the VFW member predates his military service. With their inexhaustible supply of goals and members, there is no doubt that the Ladies Auxiliary is here to stay.

The History of the Ladies Auxiliary

In 1913, when the American Veterans of Foreign Service and the Army of the Philippines merged to form the VFW, both groups already had their own Ladies Auxiliary. Rather than adopt the existing groups as a VFW auxiliary, Commander-in-Chief Rice Means suggested that the wives of the VFW members form a new national Ladies Auxiliary. At his request, about fifty women, including thirty voting delegates, attended the Women's 1914 National Convention to do just that.

On September 14, 1914, the first president of the new, but not chartered, national auxiliary took office. She was Margaret Armstrong of Pittsburgh. Other officers also elected by unanimous ballot were: Mrs. W.F. (Sadie) Kern, Senior Vice-President; Mrs. Jacob Kolber, Junior Vice-President; Mrs. George (Josephine) Geis, Treasurer; and Mrs. William Walker and Mrs. Gus (Pearle) Hartung, members of the executive committee. Mrs. Joseph Brice was appointed National Secretary. Before they adjourned, the members of the new auxiliary passed a motion to assess a per capita tax of fifteen cents per member. Then with a slate of untried officers and $6.75 in its treasury, the Ladies Auxiliary to the Veterans of Foreign Wars of the United States set out to become a truly national organization.

For its first few years, the Ladies Auxiliary concentrated on recruitment. Using as its nucleus the first six local chapters (in Pittsburgh, St. Paul, Albany, Denver, Camden, and McKeesport, Pennsylvania), the Auxiliary steadily added new members and units. By the 1915 convention, there were thirteen chapters in good standing, and by 1917, there were twenty.

When the United States entered World War I in April 1917, the Ladies Auxiliary shifted its emphasis from membership to the war effort. Together with VFW members, the Auxiliary members sold Liberty Bonds to encourage patriotism and help finance the war. And, as other women's auxiliaries had done in past wars, they tried to assuage the suffering caused by injuries and disease. Many members volunteered to care for sick and wounded servicemen in the hospitals. Others opened their homes and turned them into sewing centers. From these centers poured lap robes, surgical dressings, pillows, and other hospital supplies. From still other home centers, women rolled bandages and directed hospital visitations and efforts to assist needy families of veterans and servicemen.

Although the war united the Auxiliary members in fighting for a common goal, after it was over the national organization was still a rather disjointed organization. At the 1919 convention, for example, one transcription of the Auxiliary's proceedings was titled "Report of 6th Annual Convention Ladies' Auxiliaries—Veterans of Foreign Wars." As Betty Mellicker, author of *Fifty Years of Service,* noted, this was "a convention of 'auxiliaries,' not of *the* Auxiliary." *

What finally cemented the Ladies Auxiliary into one cohesive group was the granting of its charter. This was accomplished at the 1920 VFW Encampment in Washington, D.C. According to Mellicker, "The charter was back-dated to September 1, 1914, a date actually preceding that of the first organizational meeting of the ladies, although informal meetings and

---

*   Betty Mellicker and the Ladies Auxiliary to the Veterans of Foreign Wars, *Fifty Years of Service* (Kansas City, Mo.: Lowell Press, 1964), p. 24.

Following World War I, Ladies Auxiliary members helped process applications for membership in the VFW.

planning sessions had probably taken place before then."* The charter was signed by Commander-in-Chief Robert Woodside and Adjutant General Reuel W. Elton sometime after the encampment had adjourned. Also adopted at this encampment was a new set of by-laws, which changed the Auxiliary's election rules, National Council of Administration terms of office, and other provisions, and changed the name of their annual meeting from "convention" to "encampment." From now on, as Mellicker stated, "There would be no more meetings of 'auxiliaries,' only meetings of a strong, growing, national organization." **

Throughout the 1920s, the Ladies Auxiliary worked hard to become a national organization in fact as well as in name. Although most of its national officers were still from the Spanish American War era, the Auxiliary aggressively recruited new members from the World War I years. These practices stood in stark contrast to those of auxiliaries such as the Malate Auxiliary of Pittsburgh, which became defunct in 1928 when its last members from the Spanish American War era died.

In 1921, the Ladies Auxiliary had approximately 10,000 members in 287 chapters. Over the next year, 132 new units were added, and by 1928 the Auxiliary had expanded to include units in locations as far-flung as Honolulu and Paris. In the final years of the decade, the pace of recruitment picked up even more, thanks to President Bessie Hanken. Upon taking office in 1929, she vowed to add one hundred new units to the Auxiliary. That year this energetic woman traveled 68,000 miles on Auxiliary business. Although she fell four units short of her goal in 1929, 123 local units were added during her second term in office, bringing the total number to 758 units.

As the Ladies Auxiliary grew in size, several administrative changes were made to keep the organiza-

---

*   Mellicker, p. 29.
** Mellicker, p. 25.

tion running smoothly. In 1921, the Auxiliary took the advice of their auditor and put the organization's finances on a commercial basis. Their transactions had become too numerous to be handled by their old management system. The following year, the Auxiliary expanded its Council of Administration at the recommendation of Commander-in-Chief Tillinghast Huston. Seats on the Council were given to the Auxiliary's Senior Vice-President, Junior Vice-President, and Treasurer.

In 1923, the organization started a national newsletter to keep its expanding membership better informed and to tie them more closely together. At the 1923 Encampment, each local unit was asked to contribute five dollars toward the publication of *The VFW Auxiliary Messenger*.

Inevitably, as the Ladies Auxiliary grew in membership and increased in independence, it ran into some friction with its parent organization, the VFW. In 1922, for instance, a local Auxiliary unit refused to admit the National Senior Vice-Commander to a meeting. Shortly afterwards, Commander-in-Chief Tillinghast Huston sent an order that his representatives were to be admitted, at any time, to local Auxiliary meetings. All local units were cautioned to obey the order. There was a bigger uproar at the 1924 Encampment after the Ladies Auxiliary rejected a VFW request to move its national headquarters into the VFW building in Kansas City. The Auxiliary preferred to change the location of its national headquarters each year so that it was always in a city convenient to the national president's home. After the Auxiliary had explained its position to the VFW meeting, a VFW committee arrived at the women's meeting with an announcement. "The Commander-in-Chief has stated that it is the pleasure of the Encampment of the VFW that they will not impose anything on the ladies that the ladies do not desire." (It was not until 1932 that the Ladies Auxiliary finally agreed to move its national headquarters to the VFW building at 34th and Broadway in Kansas City, Missouri.)

During the 1920s, the national officers were not the only Auxiliary members without a permanent home. Because most VFW posts had yet to acquire their own buildings, the Auxiliary units often met in facilities owned by other organizations or by the public. This handicap, however, had little, if any effect, on their enthusiasm. They worked tirelessly to raise funds for their own and VFW projects, often by hosting balls or other social events. In 1920, Madam Ernestine Schumann-Heink, a famous Czecho-slovakian-born opera singer, attended one such ball given by Auxiliary No. 409 of Salt Lake City. Madam Schumann-Heink was so impressed by the Auxiliary's work that she joined the unit and contributed $100 to its treasury. During these years, the Ladies Auxiliary also continued its hospital and relief work, and joined the VFW in working toward acceptance of the "Star-Spangled Banner" as the national anthem. And from the founding of the VFW National Home in 1925, they devoted themselves to its support. They collected both money and clothing for the Home through their National Home Fund, and in 1928 and 1929 raised the money to construct a thirty-five-bed hospital at the Home. At the 1929 National Encampment, the Ladies Auxiliary tendered the key to this new hospital to the VFW Commander-in-Chief. That same year, President Bessie Hanken joined with national officers of the VFW in accompanying the bodies of the "Polar Bears" from their port of entry to their final resting place in Detroit. (See Chapter 3 for the story of the Polar Bear Expedition.)

In the 1930s, the depression gave the Ladies Auxiliary's work a new focus. As women, the Auxiliary members could understand the plaintive cry of a hungry child or the frustration of a husband working at a job far below the level of his skills just to keep his family together. But also as women, they had to accept—willingly or unwillingly—the commonplace of that era that "a woman's place is in the home" (unless, of course, she was doing "women's work" such as nursing, teaching, or working as a secretary). Because the Ladies Auxiliary members were effectively barred from entering the labor market to help their own or other needy families, many of them turned to Auxiliary activities as a means of helping others. As a result, membership in the Auxiliary climbed steeply in the 1930s. In 1932, National President Dora Raffensperger reported a membership of 49,000. In 1941, outgoing President Mabel C. Tanner's report showed: 2510 local units, 77 county councils, 45 state departments, 258 Daughters units, and 96,000 members.

During the depression, the local Auxiliaries worked to keep the families among their own membership off welfare and to see that they had food on the table and a roof over their heads. They held socials, dinners, and balls, and donated the proceeds to those in need. Unfortunately, with each passing month, more of the helpers became the helped. Still, the hard-pressed veterans and their wives generally managed to find a few extra pennies for those worse off than themselves. In one twelve-month period (1932–33), one Auxiliary reported it served 39,103 meals to school children.

Strapped as most Auxiliaries were for funds during the depression, they were still able to find or raise funds with which to assist the VFW in its legislative battles for a cash bonus and expanded medical care for veterans. They also took time off from relief work to write letters to congressmen and to collect signatures for VFW petitions. In 1938, for example, they helped the VFW gather nearly 4 million signatures on the "Keep America Out of War" petition.

The outbreak of World War II heralded yet another change in direction for the Ladies Auxiliary. On the day the Japanese bombed Pearl Harbor, National President Alice Chadwick was attending Denver's Founder's Day Parade. Immediately, she began to consider how best to involve her members in national defense and war service.

At the same time President Chadwick was plotting her strategy for the Auxiliary's participation in the war effort, one of her Auxiliary units was already helping to solve problems on the battle front. Many members of the Honolulu Auxiliary were helping to find shelter for bombed-out and homeless families and providing them with daily meals. For the Honolulu Auxiliary, the transition to wartime service

As part of their "Gifts for the Boys in Service" project, members of the Ladies Auxiliary of Hanover Post No. 2506 sent monthly presents to service members involved in World War II.

was not difficult. Some of its members were giving their assistance to a third war effort.

For most Auxiliaries, of course, wartime service took place not on the battle front, but on the home front. Like the VFW, they were involved in virtually every aspect of the war effort. Auxiliary members donated blood, sold war bonds, collected scrap metal, manned listening posts, drove in motor transportation corps, and made earmuffs and other clothing items for servicemen. They also trained nurses, women aviators, and air wardens. And above all, they raised funds: for the government, for soldiers, for servicemen's families and others in need. At the 1943 National Encampment, for example, outgoing President Marie DeWitt presented $5,000 to representatives of two tobacco companies to purchase 110,000 packages of cigarettes as gifts for servicemen.

After the war ended, the Ladies Auxiliary increasingly embraced the concept of service to "mankind as a whole," introduced in 1947 by President Dorothy Mann. While continuing to help the VFW advocate for the rights and entitlements of veterans, the Auxiliary also instituted a number of programs of its own aimed at helping people of all ages, from all walks of life, both in the U.S. and abroad.

During her 1948–1949 term, President Helen Murphy tried to bring the world a little closer with a good-

PETERSEN · HARNED · VON MAUR

Staffed by members of the Auxiliary to Post No. 2963 of Davenport, Iowa, this Victory Booth sold $2,717.05 worth of war savings stamps and $2,175 worth of war savings bonds in the course of 3 weeks.

will tour to Cuba and a flight into Communist-blockaded West Berlin on one of the airlift planes. Then, as the rift between the western democracies and the Communists widened in the early 1950s, the Auxiliaries pitched in to help fight the Cold War. Because Americans considered themselves vulnerable to strikes from Communist rockets and atom bombs, Auxiliaries offered programs to teach women what to do in case of an attack. Auxiliaries also encouraged their members to learn or update first aid skills. One Auxiliary, No. 8849 of Middle River, Maryland, maintained its own Civil Defense Rescue team.

In 1952, the Auxiliary's contributions to community service received national recognition. As the result of a year-long contest designed to increase post and Auxiliary participation in community service, the Ladies Auxiliary was awarded a gold medal from the Freedoms Foundation. This award was in addition to the one the VFW received that same year. President Ethel Griffith became the first national president to ap-

pear on nationwide television when she accepted the award on a Kansas City talk show.

Over the next few years, many of the Ladies Auxiliary's activities centered around the education of young people. Under the auspices of 1952 to 1953 National President Doris Holm, the Auxiliary launched the "American Trail," a children's radio series about American History. During the several years it lasted, this series earned national attention as well as the endorsement of forty-two state governors. Nationally known figures such as President Dwight D. Eisenhower, General James Doolittle, and singer Bing Crosby took part in them.

In 1957, the Ladies Auxiliary adopted a more "hands-on" approach to education when it instituted program "Classroom Helper." To alleviate the shortage of teachers caused by a surge in enrollment of young children, Auxiliary members took on many of the teachers' non-teaching duties such as playground, hallway, and lunch room supervision. This gave teachers more time to devote to their

Vice President Richard Nixon with Ladies Auxiliary members at the 1960 VFW National Convention

primary function of teaching. Local units continued their assistance as long as it was needed, then phased out their individual programs.

In 1959, the Auxiliary turned its attention back to the Cold War and raised money to help support Radio Free Europe's broadcasts to Communist nations. Its members also presented over 18,000 American flags to individuals and organizations, and helped the VFW finance construction of the VFW Memorial Building in Washington, D.C.

As the sixties dawned, the Ladies Auxiliary found a new cause to champion when National President Gertrude Rhind pointed out that many World War I veterans were of retirement age. Under Rhind and subsequent presidents, the Auxiliaries launched several programs to improve conditions for older Americans. Members visited their older neighbors both in their own homes and in nursing homes, often providing hot meals, laundry services, and transportation to the doctor's office, drug store, grocery store, or church. Auxiliary members also pressed the local and national

governments for assistance for senior citizens, but often it was their simple assistance with daily routines that made life easier for older community members.

At the same time the veteran population was aging, so too was the Ladies Auxiliary. In 1963, the Auxiliary celebrated its Golden Anniversary at the VFW Auxiliary National Convention in Seattle. From the presentation of the golden-gowned past presidents to the sale of the Convention Flower (a golden poppy), it was a convention to remember. A highlight of the celebration was a showing of a professionally produced documentary entitled "First Ladies," which detailed the Auxiliary's first fifty years. Among the honored women in attendance was Past National President (1927–28) and only living founder, Florence Stark.

The year after the fiftieth anniversary festivities was noteworthy for the Auxiliary's response to the 1964 Alaskan earthquake and tidal wave. Thanks to the members' own wave of five-dollar donations, within ten days the Alaskan Relief Fund collected $50,000 to aid VFW families affected by the disaster.

1965 brought a renewed interest in education issues. That year, the Ladies Auxiliary provided the VFW National Home with its first library. Space was made for the library inside the Community Center, which was renovated with funds raised through Auxiliary raffles, food sales, and entertainment. The Ladies also raised funds with which to furnish the library with books and other necessary equipment. Auxiliary No. 7881 of Hammond, Indiana, also embarked on its own library project, collecting text books and dictionaries for a Peace Corps-operated school in Liberia. The Peace Corps volunteers wrote that not only were the Auxiliary's books being used, but the crates had been turned into book shelves.

As America's involvement in the Vietnam War deepened, many of the Ladies Auxiliary's activities naturally centered around the events in Southeast Asia. For example, when American forces in Vietnam launched their biggest offensive in 1967, Auxiliary members across the nation stepped up their voluntary services at VA hospitals. Through the Veterans Administration Volunteer Service program (VAVS), auxiliaries helped make life for the patients in the VA Hospitals a little easier and more enjoyable. Members wrote and read letters for patients, pushed patients in wheelchairs around hospital floors, and assisted with outings and hospital entertainment. That year, the Auxiliary also undertook several projects to aid South Vietnamese civilians. It purchased 63 tons of rice for them, which was then distributed by the Green Berets. It also donated one hundred Singer sewing machines to widows and orphans of the South Vietnamese Veterans Legion, so they could support themselves by sewing uniforms for the Vietnamese army.

The year 1967 also found the Ladies Auxiliary holding its first independent, mid-year conference ever—in Washington, D.C. This and subsequent mid-year conferences allowed the organization to take care of some of its award presentations and organizational business that would otherwise have to be handled at the National Conventions in August. During the 1967

conference, the Ladies Auxiliary presented comedienne Phyllis Diller a Distinguished Service Citation commending her for entertaining the troops during the Bob Hope Christmas tour to Vietnam. Afterwards, President Lyndon B. Johnson's wife, Lady Bird, invited the three hundred plus delegates to the White House. All were invited to shake her hand, and the rule against taking photographs in the White House was lifted. Mrs. Johnson thanked the Auxiliary for its work in helping "Keep America Beautiful" through community service projects.

In 1968, as the Auxiliary's membership topped 400,000, it masterminded a new project to help relieve the homesickness of servicemen separated from their loved ones. Auxiliary members filmed the families, new babies, and pets of some 5,000 members of the armed forces in Vietnam and sent the home movies on to them.

The Ladies Auxiliary wrapped up its wartime activities in 1970 with two ambitious projects. First, Mary Cottone, the 1970 National Auxiliary President, spearheaded a drive to persuade the North Vietnamese government to free American Prisoners of War. That year, Auxiliary and VFW members collected 2 million signatures on a petition requesting their release. With VFW Commander-in-Chief Herbert Rainwater, Cottone flew to Paris to present their petition to the Vietnamese delegation. Unfortunately, the Vietnamese refused to accept the petition. Undaunted, President Cottone asked each Auxiliary member to write to the North Vietnamese premier urging the prisoners' release, but their pleas fell on deaf ears. Cottone's second project met with better success. Under her direction, the Auxiliary raised $32,000 to train Cambodian technicians and furnish material to provide improved artificial limbs to Cambodian amputees.

As the United States military began its slow withdrawal from Vietnam, the Ladies Auxiliary found a host of social, medical, political, and veterans' issues awaiting its attention. Topping its list of concerns in the early 1970s were two killers: cancer and drug abuse. In 1971, the Auxiliary's donations to fund cancer research exceeded its one-dollar-per-member goal.

That year, the organization also contributed $10,000 toward the establishment of the Lurleen B. Wallace Cancer Research Center in Birmingham, Alabama. Alabama Governor George Wallace accepted the donation in behalf of his deceased wife at that year's VFW National Convention. The following year, the Auxiliary began pouring its energies into stamping out the second killer. National President Lola Reed introduced a special program called "Drug Abuse Control," which was designed to educate Americans of all ages about the dangers involved in taking drugs.

In 1974, the Ladies Auxiliary got into several skirmishes with the president of the United States. First, the Ladies Auxiliary refused to soften its position on amnesty for American draft evaders. Although President Gerald R. Ford advocated forgiveness in his address at the opening ceremony of the 1974 VFW National Convention, both the Ladies Auxiliary and the VFW remained totally committed to VFW Resolution 401—the "No Amnesty" policy. The Auxiliary resolved, in part, ". . . not to relinquish, dilute, or compromise this position." Several months later, the Auxiliary again stood up to Ford when he vetoed the Veterans Readjustment Act, which would have increased Vietnam veterans' educational benefits. In fact, the Auxiliary initiated a letter-writing campaign which helped persuade the U.S. Congress to override the president's veto.

Despite its occasional disagreements with the president of the U.S., the Ladies Auxiliary's patriotism remained unshakable. During the nation's two hundredth birthday celebration in 1976, that patriotism rose to a fever pitch. The national Auxiliary gave each of its over 6000 chapters a three-foot by five-foot American flag. Auxiliary members also sold patriotic postcards to help the VFW raise funds for a "Torch of Freedom" monument. This three-story stone monument to veterans and their families is located on the grounds of the VFW Memorial Building in Washington, D.C.

The national Auxiliary capped off the 1970s with a Youth Activities Program designed to assist young students who were interested in pursuing careers in art. During the 1978–79 year, forty-three departments sponsored a Young American Creative Art competition in which entrants competed for a national first-place scholarship of $1,000 and a second-place scholarship of $500.

Also in 1979, a local unit in Richmond Heights, Missouri, made news by sponsoring a "Yellow Ribbon Day" in behalf of the fifty-two American citizens held hostage in Iran by Moslem extremists. Auxiliary No. 3500 flew a large yellow ribbon from its flagpole and decorated the trees and light poles in its hometown with over 9,000 smaller ribbons.

In the 1980s, the Ladies Auxiliary's programs reflected a healthy mixture of old and new concerns. Not only did the Auxiliary tackle perennial problems such as hunger, drug abuse, and the plight of the elderly, but it also began new projects in youth activities, community service, and other areas.

Among the largest of the long-standing problems facing the Ladies Auxiliary in this decade was poverty. Indeed, as a recession forced plant closings and skyrocketing unemployment, it sometimes seemed as if the 1980s were the 1930s all over again. In industrial and rural areas alike, many Americans lost their jobs and sometimes even their homes. To help those hardest hit by the crumbling economy, the Auxiliary pitched in with the person-to-person caring that has always been its hallmark. Uncounted Auxiliary members donated their time to staff local "soup kitchens," maintain emergency food lockers, and collect clothing for needy children and adults.

Drug abuse was another scourge that the Ladies Auxiliary spent long hours fighting in the 1980s. Auxiliary members worked to eliminate the problem through efforts on both the national and local level. On the national level, for example, the Auxiliary donated $10,000 to First Lady Nancy Reagan's "Just Say No" anti-drug campaign. On a local level, an Auxiliary in Florida adopted its own slogan: "Crack Down on Crack." To this day, the Ladies Auxiliary sponsors new anti-drug programs yearly. It oversees "Just Say No" clubs to educate young people and also works to boost parents' drug awareness. In addition,

The VFW and Ladies Auxiliary jointly fight drug abuse.
(Photo courtesy of the Ladies Auxiliary to
the Veterans of Foreign Wars)

many local units offer financial and other assistance to
anti-drug programs sponsored by local government
and concerned citizens' groups.

Other "old" projects that the Auxiliary continued
to work on in the 1980s were designed to aid two
groups of largely forgotten Americans: the elderly and
the POW/MIAs in Southeast Asia. As they had for
decades, many Auxiliary members across the country
devoted themselves to helping senior citizens in their
communities lead happier and healthier lives. In
Nogales, Arizona, for example, the members of
Auxiliary No. 2066 initiated a program called Tele-
Care. Each day its members telephoned older people
living alone to check on their well-being. In another
gesture of caring, the Junior Girls Unit No. 2858 of
Tiffin, Ohio, adopted grandparents in a local nursing
home. In other areas of the country, members donated
countless hours to providing companionship, transportation, and entertainment for senior citizens.

Although the Ladies Auxiliary could not aid the
POW/MIAs as directly as it could the elderly, members could and did bring continual attention to their

dilemma. Alone or working side by side with the National League of Families of American Prisoners and
Missing in Southeast Asia, local units jarred the
nation's conscience with their balloon releases, Races
for Freedom, and candlelight vigils. Although it will
probably never be possible to measure the exact
amount of influence these efforts had in motivating
our government and the North Vietnamese Government to act on the POW/MIA issue, records show that
more was accomplished following these demonstra-
tions than before.

Among the new activities undertaken by the
Ladies Auxiliary in the 1980s was one designed to
recognize youth achievement. In 1980, the Auxiliary
became a contributing patron of the Academy of
Achievement, a non-profit California organization
dedicated to the inspiration of youth. After the
Auxiliary had become a sponsor of the program, the
winners of its Junior Girls Scholarship Competitions
and Patriotic Art Contests, as well as the state winners
of the VFW's Voice of Democracy Program were invited each year to attend the Academy's Salute to Excellence Weekend. During this weekend, gifted
students from across the country share ideas and at-

*Costumed members of the Ladies Auxiliary to Post No. 5729
of Medford, Wisconsin, routinely entertain residents of
nursing homes and veteran's homes.*

Junior Girls
(Courtesy of Ladies Auxiliary to VFW)

tend symposia led by prominent American businessmen, entertainers, artists, athletes, and politicians.

Other new projects included two joint programs of the VFW and the Auxiliary begun in 1981: Hunter Safety and Fire Prevention. With the help of local experts such as game wardens and fire fighters, local units started offering instruction in these areas to all interested members of the community. Using their facilities and personnel coupled with knowledgeable local people, Auxiliary units set about offering these programs to interested parties in their areas. That year, the Auxiliary and the VFW also pledged $500,000 toward the proposed Bob Hope USO Headquarters to be built in Washington, D.C.

After agreeing to help fund the USO headquarters, the Auxiliary proceeded to make another huge contribution—this time to the Statue of Liberty. Over the years, the Auxiliary had already donated a portable stage, redwood benches, a public address system, wheelchairs, drinking fountains, and American flags to the statue. In 1985, the women's organization contributed $221,000 to help finance the facelift she was given for her one hundredth birthday. The Auxiliary also organized the statue's official 100th birthday party, held on her island on October 28, 1987.

A year after the Statue of Liberty's hundredth birthday, the Ladies Auxiliary celebrated its own

Diamond Jubilee. Seventy-fifth anniversary festivities were held at the 1988 VFW National Convention in Chicago amidst a parade of candidates for president of the U.S. Vice President George Bush, Congressman Dan Quayle, and Senator Lloyd Bentsen all spoke at the convention in an attempt to win VFW and Auxiliary support for the 1988 election. Also at the convention, the Auxiliary recognized Mother Clara Hale for her many years of caring for children with AIDs and for infants born addicted to drugs.

In the final year of the decade, the Ladies Auxiliary raised $10,000 for Special Olympics International. National President Mona Longly was honored by being appointed to serve on the 1989 National Awards Jury of the Freedoms Foundation at Valley Forge. And, as the seventy-fifth year of the Auxiliary's service to veterans and mankind ended in September 1989, its membership stood at approximately 750,000 members in 7,110 chapters. Three-quarters of a million strong, the Ladies Auxiliary faced the challenges of the new decade with its customary resolve. In war or in peace, the Ladies

The Hunting Safety Program is sponsored jointly by the VFW and its Ladies Auxiliary.

Auxiliary to the Veterans of Foreign Wars stands ready to assist those in need and to work for the betterment of the nation and its people.

Programs of the Ladies Auxiliary

While always ready to lend a helping hand to the VFW or to those in need, the Ladies Auxiliary also has a variety of other goals. To help channel its members' energies into achieving these goals, the organization has developed many special programs. These programs are supervised on a day-to-day basis by thirteen chairmen or directors. In addition, each department president appoints a chairman or a committee to work with the National Program Director in carrying out that particular program. This section describes a few of the most important of the Auxiliary's current programs.

The VFW National Home

Ever since the VFW National Home was founded in 1925, the Ladies Auxiliary has loyally given it both financial and moral backing. This makes the Home—a residential facility in Eaton Rapids, Michigan, for the families of deceased VFW or Auxiliary members—the oldest of the Auxiliary's ongoing programs.

Over the years, the Ladies Auxiliary has inaugurated many special projects aimed at improving the Home and its residents' quality of life. In addition to raising funds for the day-to-day operation of the Home, the Auxiliary has financed the construction of a hospital, a combination guest lodge and chapel, and several other buildings. Today the Auxiliary maintains an ongoing fund for the National Home called the "Health, Happiness/Christmas Cheer Fund" supported by a 25¢ a member per capita tax. This fund is used to maintain National Home buildings given the Home by the Ladies Auxiliary, to purchase a Christmas present for each child at the Home, and to supply money for each child to buy his parents a present and to take each family out for a Christmas dinner. Local Auxiliaries and departments also directly donate additional funds to the Home. Chapter 8 provides a more in-depth account of the Auxiliary's involvement with the Home.

Hospital Work and VA Voluntary Service

Long before the Ladies Auxiliary was founded, women were humanizing hospitals—volunteering their services to brighten the lives of their "boys" who had contracted diseases or suffered injuries while in the service. They sewed lap robes, rolled bandages, and baked breads and desserts; they assisted hospital workers with administrative, janitorial, and laundry chores; they provided companionship to bedridden patients by talking with them, reading to them, and helping them write letters to loved ones. Most importantly, they reassured patients that they were important and not forgotten. And when the Ladies Auxiliary was founded in 1914, many members of the new organization continued their volunteer service without pause.

Despite the number of hours contributed by Auxiliary members in the organization's early years, the Ladies Auxiliary did not officially recognize its hospital program until 1928. That year, the Auxiliary appointed its first hospital chairperson in an attempt to determine the extent of its members' volunteer services and to coordinate their work. The Auxiliary also began formally backing and recognizing its hospital volunteers. With the support of their organization, by 1940 Auxiliary members were annually donating 600,000 hours of their time and over $335,000 to hospitals.

After World War II, the day of the "amateur" volunteer waned. Many volunteers felt that the influx of school-trained nursing assistants, "Candy Stripers," and Licensed Practical Nurses had made their help unnecessary. To address this problem, Veterans Administration (VA) officials met in April 1946 with representatives of the veteran's organizations, ladies auxiliaries, the Red Cross, and the USO. Together they organized a new system for volunteer services—the VA Volunteer Service (VAVS).

The Auxiliary's role in this VAVS system is to supplement the services provided by the trained

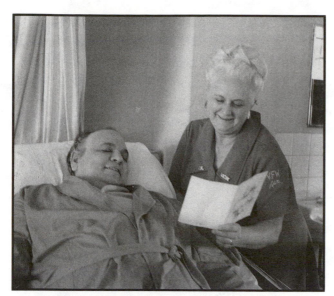

A VAVS volunteer brightening up a patient's day
(Courtesy of Ladies Auxiliary to VFW)

professionals of the hospital's staff. VAVS volunteers move patients in wheelchairs from their rooms to doctors' offices and treatment and testing areas, provide entertainment, write letters for patients, oversee many outside recreational trips, and in general provide the personal touch that a busy staff has little time to give. In VA Hospitals, one or more full-time professionals direct the services provided by VAVS volunteers.

Over the years, the Volunteer Service program has proven itself cost-effective for the hospitals, psychologically healthy for the patients, and emotionally satisfying for the givers. Each year, VA hospitals around the country honor these volunteer workers by recognizing the number of hours donated to the welfare of its patients. Many Auxiliary members have certificates attesting to thousands of hours of volunteer service.

Today, the Hospital and VAVS programs also serve patients in non-VA hospitals, and in nursing and convalescent homes. The challenge faced by these dedicated workers is the growing number of aging veterans who will require long-term care and volunteer support.

Americanism

The Ladies Auxiliary's Americanism program, like the VFW program of the same name, strives to foster love for the United States and loyalty to its institutions and ideals. In the program's infancy, it was closely associated with the VFW's Americanism program. Back then, Auxiliary members and VFW members often worked side by side toward common Americanism goals—for example, the adoption of the "Star-Spangled Banner" as America's official national anthem, and the passage of the "Cash Bonus" for World War I veterans.

As the Auxiliary's Americanism program matured, it began to take on patriotic projects of its own. Among its first was the sponsorship of a nationwide essay contest on the subject of "What the Statue of Liberty Means to Me." This contest, held at the request of the National Park Service, was part of the

The annual Statue of Liberty Birthday Ceremony
(Courtesy of Ladies Auxiliary to VFW)

golden anniversary celebrations for the statue in 1936. The winner of the contest, Edna Falk of Pueblo,

Above, Auxiliary 5735, Slidell, Louisiana, presented twenty American classroom flags to Our Lady of Lourdes School in March 1975.

Below, members of VFW Post 1000 of Independence, Missouri, and its Auxiliary presented classroom flags to students in State School No. 6 for Retarded Children in October, 1970. (Courtesy of Ladies Auxiliary to VFW)

Colorado, was awarded the Auxiliary's gold medal and a trip to Paris provided by the Auxiliary, the Federation of French Veterans of the Great War, and a Paris newspaper. This essay contest was held yearly until 1964. To this date, the Auxiliary continues to hold annual birthday parties for the Statue of Liberty on Liberty Island (formerly Bedloe's Island).

In 1956, one of the Auxiliary's Americanism projects again centered around the Statue of Liberty. That year, the Auxiliary became the first organization to pledge a substantial amount for the construction of a Museum of Immigration in the base of the statue. The Auxiliary delivered the final installment of its $50,000 pledge during the cornerstone-laying ceremonies in 1962.

Through its Americanism program, the Ladies Auxiliary has also supported other patriotic organizations. In 1961 and 1962, the Auxiliary funded construction of the Lucy Knox Evaluation Room at the Freedoms Foundations Center in Valley Forge, Pennsylvania. In this room, juries choose prize-winning examples of Americanism for Freedoms Foundations awards each year. In 1980, the Auxiliary was itself honored by the Freedoms Foundations when it received the Principal Award for a non-profit publication.

Of course, not all the Auxiliary's Americanism activities are on such a grand scale. Many programs are also carried out at the local level. Each year, for example, local units present thousands of American flags to government units, youth groups, schools, and churches. Units also teach proper care of the flag, distribute Americanism literature, sponsor citizenship classes, and otherwise help keep the flame of patriotism burning brightly.

Rehabilitation

The Auxiliary's unpublished and unofficial slogan, "We Take Care of Our Own," is embodied in its rehabilitation programs. Through these programs, Auxiliary members raise money; collect clothing, food, and household goods; arrange for housing; and perform other services for those less fortunate than themselves. Often these good deeds are carried out jointly with other local charitable agencies.

In the beginning, these programs were called "welfare" programs—an apt enough name, as their purpose was to improve the financial, physical, and emotional well-being of veterans, their families, and other members of the community. During the depression, however, the word "welfare" became synonymous with the government handouts given to those who could not support themselves. Consequently, the program's name was changed to the more neutral "rehabilitation" in 1936.

Over the years, Auxiliary units have developed a variety of strategies to raise money for rehabilitation activities in their communities. These include holding benefit suppers, bake sales, ice cream socials, raffles, bingo games, and rummage sales, and catering wedding and funeral meals. Even during the depression year of 1939, local units were able to raise about a million dollars annually with these strategies. Fifty years later, the Auxiliary is raising and donating about $8 million (1988–89 figures).

Youth Activities

The Ladies Auxiliary first became involved in youth activities on a national level in 1935. That year, the VFW National Encampment authorized the formation of the Daughters of the VFW to allow the daughters of VFW members to work alongside their mothers on Auxiliary activities. In 1942, the name was changed to Junior Girls.

During World War II, many Junior Girls units had to be disbanded as members became involved in the war effort. After the war, however, membership rebounded. Today membership is open to girls aged six to sixteen who are the daughters, foster daughters, stepdaughters, granddaughters, sisters, half-sisters, foster sisters, or step sisters of VFW members. Currently there are about 3716 members in 306 units. Many of these Junior Girls will become full-fledged members of the Ladies Auxiliary at sixteen, because they can qualify under the same sponsorship as their mother.

Junior Girls at the annual Statue of Liberty ceremony
(Courtesy of Ladies Auxiliary to VFW)

Besides assisting in activities of their sponsoring Auxiliary, Junior Girls participate in community projects, sell Buddy Poppies, cheer up hospitalized veterans, and celebrate patriotic holidays. While it is voluntary, girls are allowed to wear a distinctive uniform. Junior Girls also compete for two scholarships given each year by the National Auxiliary organization. One candidates is nominated by each Auxiliary department, and is then judged on school grades, patriotism, community activities, Americanism, and friendliness. The first prize winner receives $3000; the second place winner, $2000. All other entrants receive $100.

Although the Junior Girls program is the best known of the Ladies Auxiliary's youth activities, it is by no means the only one. In fact, in 1947 the office of Chairperson for the Junior Girls Program was retitled Chairperson of Youth Activities to reflect the true scope of the Auxiliary's involvement. Over the years, VFW Auxiliary units have provided meeting places, adult leadership, and monetary contributions to hundreds of Girl Scout troops, Camp Fire Girls, Y-Teens, 4–H Clubs, and other youth groups.

Cancer Aid and Research

In 1947, National President Dorothy Mann had an idea for a program the likes of which had never before been contemplated by the Ladies Auxiliary. She proposed establishing a Cancer Fellowship Fund to support research into the causes, prevention, treatment, and possible cure of this deadly disease. Then, during her travels as president, she heard of the

destruction by fire and hurricane of the Roscoe B. Jackson Memorial Laboratory in Bar Harbor, Maine. The Jackson Laboratory was an important center for cancer research. After discussing the matter with National Secretary-Treasurer Grace Davis, Mann recommended using the new fellowship fund to rebuild the laboratory. Mann implored each unit to start raising funds so that "not a precious hour of research was wasted." By the end of her year, almost $63,000 had been contributed.

In 1952, the name of the program was changed to Cancer Aid and Research. This reflected a program expansion that allowed for grants-in-aid to members who suffered from the disease. In 1961, however, membership growth, spiraling costs, and requests for

Through the Cancer Aid and Research program, the national Ladies Auxiliary organization and its departments contribute funds to St. Jude Children's Research Hospital in Memphis, Tennessee. (Courtesy of Ladies Auxiliary to VFW)

Making candy for the disabled veterans in the Soldiers and Sailors Home, Quincy, Illinois—an annual community service project of the Auxiliary to Post No. 2234 of Springfield. Here members get ready for the 1942 distribution.

grants began to endanger the Auxiliary's ability to fund both the cancer research and aid-to-members programs. As a result, the Ladies Auxiliary dropped its grants-in-aid program and replaced it with a low-cost cancer insurance program for its members.

Through the years, the Auxiliary has raised more than 32 million dollars to help individuals, research centers, and specialists in its ongoing crusade against cancer. Currently, the Cancer Aid and Research Committee selects three deserving researchers each year for the Auxiliary's prestigious cancer fellowships. At present, these fellowships amount to $20,000 each.

If past performance is any indication of the tenacity of the Auxiliary's members, they will continue to give both time and money until a cure for this dread disease is finally discovered.

Community Service

A program whose purpose is "to improve the general welfare of the communities" would seem to open the doors of auxiliaries to almost any kind of community activity. Yet, that is the stated purpose of the Auxiliary's Community Service Program. It is deliberately expressed in such broad terms to allow local units a wide latitude in choosing activities to better their communities.

Although it would be impossible to enumerate all of the projects undertaken by local units, here is a sample of the kinds of community service many units perform:

They help newborn babies and their families by transporting mother and baby to visit the doctor or clinic; delivering hot meals, especially in the first days home; ensuring that the proper baby food and medication is available if it cannot be provided by the parents; and providing other services related to newborns' care. They support their local schools by funding the high school band's trip to the Rose Bowl Parade; contributing books to the library; raising funds for computers or other needed equipment; or by donating new uniforms for the athletic teams. They make their city's streets safer by purchasing stop signs, streetlights, or walk signals; offering safe driving courses; checking up on "latchkey" children whose mothers work; and in some areas, acting as school crossing guards. In a typical year, Auxiliary members across the country donate almost a million and a half hours and over a million dollars to community service.

Civil Defense

The Civil Defense Program is a follow up of the National Defense Program begun by the federal government in 1950. At that time, there was great concern about civil defense because of the increasing threat of nuclear missiles and chemical warfare brought about by the "Cold War." The National Auxiliary responded to this threat with a program of its own. Beginning in 1952, many units took the lead in distributing civil defense literature around their communities. Some members completed basic or advanced courses in first aid, and others taught members of the community what to do in case of a bomb or rocket attack. In the year 1962 to 1963 alone, Auxiliary members constructed and equipped 1500 fallout shelters, donated 23,100 pints of blood to the blood banks, assisted 692 communities during peacetime disasters, and distributed 474,780 pieces of civil defense literature. All told, its members contributed 1.4 million hours of work and $1,242,000 to the program that year.

As concerns about civil defense lessened, the Auxiliary's civil defense program increasingly turned its attention to dealing with peacetime disasters such as hurricanes, tornados, fires, and floods. Members took first aid courses to prepare themselves for natural disasters, and rallied to provide food, shelter, and blood when necessary. Eventually, as world tensions continued to ease, civil defense activities were discontinued. Today Auxiliary members still stand ready to combat natural disasters—but through the Community Service, not the Civil Defense program.

Fire-fighting and incendiary bomb extinguishing equipment purchased with the proceeds of two benefit dances sponsored by Post No. 2828 of Los Angeles and its Auxiliary. The equipment was for civil defense of the area.

Awards

Every year, the Ladies Auxiliary presents a variety of awards in recognition of those who have made the world a better place in which to live or have otherwise furthered the aims of mankind. To ensure that the selection of recipients not be encumbered by rules that might impose invalid or ill-timed restrictions upon the judges, there are no set criteria to be met for these awards.

Some of the Ladies Auxiliary's awards are reserved for Auxiliary members. These include awards such as the Community Activities Silver Plate Award for Excellence presented to units as a whole. This award was first presented in 1977, to the Post No. 2926 Auxiliary of Cleveland, Ohio, for its efforts to promote legislation benefitting infants and children with mental and physical disabilities. Other awards, such as the President of the Year Award, recognize individual achievement. This award was first presented in 1960 to June Moore, President of the Department of Louisiana.

In addition to singling out its own members for praise, the Ladies Auxiliary also presents several annual awards to nonmembers in recognition of humanitarian action and civic betterment. Two of these—the Better World Award and a second award whose name changes yearly—are allied with the theme chosen by the National Auxiliary President for that year. For example, in 1972 to 1973, when the Auxiliary's priority was controlling drug abuse, the Better World Award was presented to television personality Art Linkletter in recognition of his personal drug education crusade. In 1986, a special Serve America Award was created and presented to newspaper columnist Abigail "Dear Abby" Van Buren.

Another annual award is the Unsung Heroine Award, given to a deserving woman who is not nationally known. Candidates for this award are nominated by Auxiliary national officers, and the Awards Committee then makes the final selection. The Award consists of $3000 and a large framed citation with the title of the award printed in gold letters upon a red velvet backpiece.

NATIONAL PRESIDENTS

1914	Margaret A. Armstrong
1915	Margaret A. Armstrong
1916	Margaret A. Armstrong
1917	Sadie A. Kern
1918	Margaret A. Armstrong
1919	Lydia Riegel
1920	Lydia Riegel
1921	Pearle W. Hartung*
1922	Lena Panzner
1923	Kate M. Hutcheson
1924	Kate M. Hutcheson
1925	Effie King
1926	Effie King
1927	Margaret J. Oldridge
1928	Florence E. Stark
1929	Bessie Hanken
1930	Bessie Hanken
1931	Ada E. Harrison
1932	Dora E. Raffensperger
1933	Consuelo Peart DeCoe*
1934	Julia L. Pitcock
1935	Winifred D. Toussaint
1936	Winifred D. Toussaint
1937	Gladys Mooney
1938	Laurie Schertle
1939	Anna Mae Shaw
1940	Ida Cohen
1941	Mabel C. Tanner
1942	Alice M. Chadwick
1943	Marie DeWitt

---

* Pearle Hartung, Consuelo DeCoe, and Elfrieda Tice are the only National Presidents whose husbands served as VFW Commander-in-Chief (Gus Hartung in 1915, Darold DeCoe in 1931, and Meron Tice in 1954).

1944	Amelia C. Kane
1945	Hazel Miller
1946	M. Frances Anderson
1947	Sally Cannon
1948	Dorothy Mann
1949	Helen Murphy
1950	Evelyn B. Monaco
1951	Sue Ilg
1952	Ethel M. Griffith
1953	Doris Holm
1954	Rosalie W. Schill
1955	Agnes S. Holz
1956	Hedwig Olson
1957	Beth Kveton
1958	Ruby Godbey
1959	Belle V. Myers
1960	Gertrude Rhind
1961	Frances L. Millican
1962	Beulah A. Adamson
1963	Elfrieda Tice*
1964	Lillian Campbell
1965	Marie Klugow
1966	Sophia Goldstein
1967	Georgia B. White
1968	Ruth K. Cunningham
1969	Lora Waters
1970	Erline Mayberry
1971	Mary Cottone
1972	Frances M. Harmon
1973	Lola Reid
1974	Odie Lee Gossett
1975	Betty Butler
1976	Glenn Grossman
1977	Mary Souders
1978	Grace Minnix
1979	Arlene McDermott
1980	Vona Houtz
1981	Jeannette Frank
1982	Marion Watson
1983	Florence Taylor
1984	Harriett Timmons
1985	Glenneta Vogelsang
1986	Lucille Suchina

1987	Rosemary Mazer
1988	Joan Katkus
1989	Mona Longly
1990	Alice Hutto
1991	Frances Booth

MILITARY ORDER OF THE COOTIE

Consider the official uniform of the VFW's Military Order of the Cootie (MOC): red pants with a white stripe running down each side; ruffled white shirt; lace-trimmed red vest emblazoned on the back with a gold-outlined, bug-like creature with flashing light bulb eyes; red, overseas-style cap worn sideways so that the tassels dangle beside the wearer's ears. Surely whoever designed this outfit must have had in mind the old saying that "clothes make the man." After all, one of the principle objectives of the Cootie auxiliary is for its members to have and provide fun for themselves and others.

The MOC can trace its ancestry to the Imperial Order of the Dragon—a similar fun-loving auxiliary that was affiliated with the United Spanish American War Veterans (USAWV). After World War I, two veterans who were members of both the USAWV and the VFW thought that the VFW might be able to attract more members if it formed an auxiliary modeled on the Imperial Order of the Dragon. These men, Fred Madden and F.L. Gransbury, began recruiting members for the new auxiliary on September 17, 1920, at the VFW National Encampment in Washington, D.C. By the end of the encampment, nearly 300 members had been enrolled, and Fred Madden had become the first Seam Squirrel (commander). Later that year, a complete slate of officers was assembled and ratified at a special meeting held in Cavalry Baptist Church in New York City. Madden developed a constitution and

Cooties at the 1950 VFW National Convention

by-laws while Gransbury authored the ritual. (Together with the official uniform, these were approved in 1924.)

At the 1921 Encampment in Detroit, a VFW committee headed by Commander-in-Chief Robert Woodside met with Supreme Cooties F.L. Gransbury and E.S. Davis to consider whether the MOC should be adopted as an official VFW auxiliary. This committee delivered a favorable report to the VFW National Encampment; on its recommendation, the MOC was made a part of the VFW at approximately 9 p.m. Saturday, September 24, 1921. At midnight of the same day, Acting Assistant Supreme Seam Squirrel Davis (National Commander) called the first Supreme Scratch (National Encampment) to order and conducted the first Supreme Election. William E. Eighmey was elected as the Military Order of the Cootie's first Supreme Seam Squirrel.

In the years after its founding, the MOC took on several special projects designed to bring smiles to the faces of two special groups of people—hospitalized veterans and residents of the VFW National Home. Its involvement with the National Home came first. In fact, as Chapter 3 discusses, the Cooties were the first to back Amy Ross's plan for the Home, and, in 1924, helped persuade the VFW to sponsor the project. Since then, there has never been a period of any extended length in which the Cooties have not been involved in some project for the Home's betterment or for the happiness of those who live there.

Shortly after the Home was established, the Cooties began the tradition of sponsoring the Home's annual Christmas party. They took it upon themselves to make sure the residents had Christmas presents and a Christmas dinner, and also that Cootie volunteers were always on hand to help organize and run the party. Then in 1933, the MOC received permission from the VFW National Encampment to build an athletic field at the National Home. Over the next few years, the Cooties raised $15,000 for the field, which was dedicated in 1941. No sooner had they finished paying for the field than the Cooties took on construction of an outdoor swimming pool. Before this pool was dedicated in September 1950, the Cooties had drummed up over $8,000 more than the $40,000 needed to build it.

The next major Home project was the brainchild of two Cooties, Collin Small and Charles Millard of Ohio's Buckeye Pup Tent (local unit) No. 2. Their "Operation Fire Department" called for the MOC to give the Home a fire truck and a building to house it, then train some of the older boys in firefighting techniques. A Home fire department, they reasoned, could give a much faster response time to Home emergencies than fire departments of the surrounding towns. This operation—described in more detail in Chapter 8—was completed in 1950, during Supreme Commander Ernie Moore's term. Subsequently, the Grand (Cootie equivalent of a VFW state department) of Maryland undertook the continual upgrading of the Home's real Fire Department by raising the necessary

funding through the sale of mythical commissions in a mythical "National Home Fire Department." These fees allow the Grand of Maryland to make contributions towards the National Home Fire Department's needs on an ongoing basis.

In later decades, many of the MOC's Home projects centered once again around the Home's athletic program. During the 1970s, the Cooties began a self-sustaining fund to supply athletic equipment for the VFW National Home's teams. In the eighties, it funded the $41,000 renovation of the Home's swimming pool.

At the 64th Scratch in 1985, the MOC approved the establishment of a Supreme Escrow Account as an incentive for the National Home's children to further their education beyond high school. Upon completion of a four-year college course, a student receives a check for $500 for each year attended. A $250 reward

A Cootie Christmas at the VFW National Home

Jim McGill, the Grand of Minnesota from 1987–88, spear-headed a successful drive for a new fire truck for the VFW National Home. (Danny Layne)

tals and nursing homes. Thousands of Cootie hours and thousands of dollars are donated each year in carrying out this program.

At the same time the MOC is pursuing its own goals, it also supports those of its parent organization. For example, in 1948, the Cooties began a new program called " The VFW Booster Program." Through this program, the Cooties help the VFW to attain its annual membership goals. At the 63rd Supreme Scratch in Los Angeles in 1984, the delegates voted unanimously to support the Veterans of Foreign Wars Political Action Committee with voluntary contributions.

Since 1961, the MOC has itself received support in all its activities from its own ladies auxiliary. Granted the authority to form an auxiliary by the delegates to the 1960 VFW National Encampment, the MOC set about establishing auxiliaries at the Pup Tent, Grand, and Supreme levels. Representatives of these units met in Miami at the 1961 Supreme En-campment. Here the Supreme Auxiliary was instituted and Dorothy Briner was elected as the first Supreme President.

Although MOC and ladies auxiliary members enjoy all Cootie activities—from supporting the Na-

is given for each year courses are completed in a trade school or community college.

As dear to a Cootie's heart as its National Home projects are, auxiliary members support its program for hospitalized veterans with equal enthusiasm. This program got its start in the 1940s, when auxiliary members realized that World War II would soon fill the hospitals with sick and wounded veterans. To help these veterans keep their spirits up, many Cooties took it upon themselves to entertain the patients. Soon Cooties all over the country were visiting hospitalized veterans, pledging to "Keep 'em Smiling in Beds of White." Today this goal is still one of the auxiliary's highest priorities. Many Pup Tents and their Auxiliaries not only work with VAVS Hospital teams, but also perform services of their own at VA Hospi-

Past Department of Iowa Commander Rod Johnson with Cooties from Iowa's Sac Fox's Pup Tent 35 holding a bingo game at a nursing home. A part of the "Keep 'em Smiling in Beds of White" program.

tional Home to visiting hospitalized veterans to helping out the VFW—members also engage in many activities that are designed solely for their entertainment. These include the method by which they govern their meetings and various procedures followed within them. To describe these methods and some of the other ways Cooties have fun would violate their by-laws, but it is possible to provide a glimpse of how Cooties sometimes have fun in public.

Picture Main Street in a midwestern city of about 25,000 residents on a sunny Saturday morning in June. The sidewalks are crowded with shoppers, and traffic on the two-lane thoroughfare is almost bumper to bumper. Three men in Cootie uniforms, the lights on their vests winking, are sauntering down the sidewalk in front of the city's largest department store.

Suddenly, one of the men glances heavenward and mumbles, "Oh, my God." The other two look upward. As if they are watching the descent of a falling leaf, all three slowly lower their heads until they are staring at the ground. Taking small manuals from their hip pockets, the three sit down in a circle on the sidewalk, legs crossed and feet tucked under. Opening the manuals, they begin reading the service for a dead Cootie (most of it ad libbed as they go along).

Gradually a crowd gathers around the men, some of it overflowing into the street. As the crowd grows and traffic comes almost to a standstill, two policemen approach to determine the cause of the blockage.

One of the officers glances at the seated trio, then informs them, "You've got three minutes to get him planted, then move on." As a knowledgeable member of the VFW, the officer has quickly sized up the situation. Shaking his head, the officer mutters, "Crazy Cooties," and walks back to his partner.

Attracted by this offbeat brand of humor and the Cooties' light-hearted approach to problem-solving, at present there are about 37,000 Cooties in 1000 Pup tents. Membership is open to members in good standing in the VFW who have displayed their willingness to work for the parent organization. The Military Order of the Cootie Auxiliary (MOCA) draws its membership from the ranks of women eighteen and

older who have been active members of the VFW Ladies Auxiliary for at least six months and who are the wife, widow, sister, half-sister, daughter, foster daughter, or granddaughter of an active VFW member in good standing. Today there are approximately 17,000 auxiliary members contained in 597 Pup Tents.

THE SONS OF THE VFW

In 1918, the Ft. Lansdale Post No. 67 of Sacramento, California, and its Ladies Auxiliary formed the first group for sons and daughters of VFW members. It wasn't until 1934, however, that the National Encampment passed a resolution establishing the Sons of the VFW as an official auxiliary unit. In sanctioning the organization, the VFW opened auxiliary membership to sons, stepsons, and legally adopted sons of all veterans eligible to belong to the VFW. Applicants were required to be between eight and eighteen years of age.

Early members participated in a variety of activities, depending on the philosophy of their parent units. Some VFW posts formed Sons units to help them perform community service work. Others formed units to indoctrinate members' sons in Americanism or to provide a solid base for the post's other youth programs. A few units were started to strengthen father and son relationships. Most Sons units also socialized among themselves or with their Junior Girls unit.

At first, Sons units were quite popular. Three thousand members joined in its first year of existence, and in 1936, membership climbed to 8,000. In 1939, when the Sons of the VFW began publishing a monthly magazine called *Acorn,* 25,000 members were on its list of subscribers.

As World War II approached, membership in Sons units plummeted. Many units folded when their leadership—the seventeen- and eighteen-year-olds—entered the service. In the early forties, the entire program was abandoned by a national mandate.

After lying dormant for two decades, the Sons of the VFW program experienced a resurgence in the 1960s. Some of the old units were revived and a few new units were formed. Presently, approximately six to seven hundred members belong to forty-two units. These members take part in highly individualized programs usually determined by the Sons units themselves. Activities run the gamut from patriotic programs such as replacing worn-out flags and marching in parades to community service programs such as assisting older people with raking leaves, shoveling snow, and other chores. These activities are inserted in between large doses of fun and sporting activities.

While uniforms and accouterments are available from the VFW National Supply, in most units they are optional.

Despite reawakened interest in the Sons of the VFW, the program has one inherent weakness: following a member's eighteenth birthday, there is no further role for him in the organization. A member cannot go on to an advisory/leadership role at a higher level, since these positions are filled by VFW members, nor can he automatically advance into the VFW. This is as the VFW's founders intended. They were well aware of the failures of previous "one-war" veteran's organizations to attain longevity by admitting sons of qualified members. With James C. Putnam, they believed that "red blooded American boys" could not be happy "living on the laurels of their fathers"—a sentiment shared by members of the VFW and the Sons of the VFW to this day.

CHAPTER TEN

RECOGNIZING THE DEEDS OF OTHERS

Commander-in-Chief Charles C. Ralls awarded the Gold VFW Distinguished Service Medal to General Douglas Mac-Arthur at the 1951 VFW National Convention in New York.

Like the armed forces in which its members so proudly served, the VFW makes a practice of recognizing outstanding achievement through medals, citations, and other awards. Its awards program is designed to honor both members and nonmembers of the VFW who have helped to further the organization's goal of making the world a better place in which to live. Consequently, awards are conferred

not only for meritorious achievement in various fields of endeavor, but also for achievement exemplifying ideals which the VFW holds in high esteem. Each level of the VFW, from national to post level, is authorized to present a variety of awards, as described below.

VFW NATIONAL AWARDS AND CITATIONS

Section 616 of the national by-laws provides for a committee to investigate and recommend to the National Council of Administration all proposed candidates for national awards. This National Awards and Citations Committee is composed of five VFW members, each of whom serves for five years. Every year the Commander-in-Chief (who is an ex-officio member of the committee) appoints a new member to replace the one outgoing member. He also designates the member who will chair the committee for that year.

The National Awards and Citations Committee receives suggestions for award recipients from VFW national officers, VFW program directors, VFW department officers, and interested VFW members. For some awards, the Awards Committee may solicit recommendations from Congressional Committees, the Department of Defense, the National Aeronautics and Space Administration, or other outside sources. The committee meets three or four times annually to consider candidates for major national awards. Recommendations are then forwarded to the Commander-in-Chief and National Council of Administration for approval.

Currently, the VFW presents ten different national awards each year, provided the Awards Committee finds a recipient deemed worthy of each. The awards are: Congressional Award, James E. Van Zandt Citizenship Award, Americanism Award, Dwight David Eisenhower Distinguished Service Award, Hall of Fame Award, Armed Forces Award, Aviation and Space Award, J. Edgar Hoover Award, News Media

Award, and Outstanding Firefighter Gold Medal Award. Eligibility criteria for most of these awards are self-explanatory; guidelines are included here for those that are not.

Congressional Award

The Veterans of Foreign Wars Congressional Award is the highest award given by the organization. For this reason, it carries the simple inscription, "For outstanding service to the nation." It is conferred annually upon a sitting member of the U.S. Congress at the VFW Congressional Dinner in Washington, D.C. The recipient of this non-partisan award may be a member of either the House of Representatives or of the Senate. By custom, the award alternates between the two houses.

By awarding this honor to one of our national legislators, the VFW seeks to dramatize the importance of the role of a freely elected legislature in serving the great ends of the Republic, maintaining allegiance to the United States of America and fidelity to its Constitution and laws, fostering true patriotism, maintaining and extending the institutions of American freedom, and preserving and defending our country from all her enemies, at home or abroad.

There are, of course, many ways in which a Congressman may distinguish himself in serving the American people. The Congressional Award may therefore be presented both for service that is carried out in public view to deserved acclaim and for service which gains little public recognition, but may be of equal or even greater value to the country.

In deciding who should receive this honor, the Committee considers each of the 535 members of Congress with respect to his or her achievement in the following areas:

1. contribution to the preservation and perpetuation of the ideals upon which the American system of government is based;
2. recognition by the Congressman's colleagues of his or her service, whether that

Pictured here, clockwise from upper left: Hoover Award, Van Zandt Citizenship Award, Aviation and Space Award, Gold Medal of Merit (bestowed by National Commander-in-Chief), Firefighter Award, Americanism Award, Armed Forces Award, Hall of Fame Award, News Media Award (center)

service be one of quiet dedication and hard work or one achieving wide publicity, to the best and highest interests of the nation;

3. exemplification of the principles of civic duty shared by the VFW, which emphasize the individual, the community, the state, and the nation;

4. unswerving loyalty to, and active performance in, the defense and security of the nation against its foes whomsoever and wherever they may be;

5. compassionate, practical attention to the needs of the men and women who have selflessly given of themselves to the service of America, not only in its wars, but in peaceful pursuits as well;

6. dedication to legislative responsibilities over a period of years and continuous growth in legislative responsibility and experience, not only in fields of special interest to any particular group in American life but in his or her overall stewardship.

The Veterans of Foreign Wars knows and appreciates that there may be many members of both Houses of Congress who meet these rigorous standards. It is their hope that by granting this distinguished award they will call attention not only to the dedicated service of the recipient, in whichever House he may be serving, but to the other deserving members who share the attributes and accomplishments for which the VFW Congressional Award is made each year.

AWARD

Scroll-type plaque, decorated with gold-plated representation of recipient's state, awarded upon authorization of the National Council of Administration to a sitting member of Congress **FOR OUTSTANDING SERVICE TO THE NATION.** 19 x 25 inches. Approximate value: $950.00.

RECIPIENTS

1964 Carl Hayden, U.S. Senator (D) Arizona

1965 John W. McCormack, U.S. Congressman (D) Massachusetts

1966 Everett M. Dirksen, U.S. Senator (R) Illinois

1967 Wilbur D. Mills, U.S. Congressman (D) Arkansas

1968 Richard B. Russell, U.S. Senator (D) Georgia

1969 Olin E. Teague, U.S. Congressman (D) Texas

1970 Henry H. Jackson, U.S. Senator (D) West Virginia

1971 Leslie C. Arends, U.S. Congressman (R) Illinois

1972 Thomas E. Morgan, U.S. Congressman (D) Pennsylvania

1973 John C. Stennis, U.S. Senator (D) Mississippi

1974 George H. Mahon, U.S. Congressman (D) Texas

1975 Barry Goldwater, U.S. Senator (R) Arizona

1976 F. Edward Herbert, U.S. Congressman (D) Louisiana

1977 Herman E. Talmadge, U.S. Senator (D) Georgia

1978 John J. Rhodes, U.S. Congressman (R) Arizona

1979 Bob Dole, U.S. Senator (R) Kansas

1980 G.V., "Sonny" Montgomery U.S. Congressman (D) Mississippi

1981 Paul Laxalt, U.S. Senator (R) Nevada

1982 Sam Stratton, U.S. Congressman (D) New York

1983 John G. Tower, U.S. Senator (R) Texas

1984 John P. Hammerschmidt, U.S. Congressman (R) Arkansas

1985 Strom Thurmond, U.S. Senator (R) South Carolina

1986 Corrine "Lindy" Boggs,
U.S. Congresswoman (D) Louisiana

1987 Daniel K. Inouye, U.S. Senator (D) Hawaii

1988 Bill Nichols, U.S. Congressman (D) Alabama

1989 Sam Nunn, U.S. Senator (D) Georgia

1990 Bob Traxler, U.S. Congressman (D) Michigan

James E. Van Zandt Citizenship Award

James E. "Jimmy" Van Zandt was Commander-in-Chief of the VFW three times, and a veteran of three wars (World War I, World War II, and the Korean War). He served as an enlisted man in World War I and retired as an admiral following the Korean War. Descended from a pioneer family in Blair County, Pennsylvania, Jimmy worked his way from newsboy to United States Congressman. Recipients of the award named in Van Zandt's honor exemplify his dedication to public service, citizenship, and other admirable qualities.

AWARD

Gold medal and citation awarded upon authorization of National Council of Administration **FOR OUT-STANDING SERVICE CONTRIBUTING TO AMERICAN CITIZENSHIP**. Gold-plated medal (2½ inches diameter) with shadow box and 11 x 14 inch citation, matted and framed. Approximate value: $550.00.

RECIPIENTS

1946 Bob Hope, Entertainer

1953 Judge E.J. Dimock, Jurist

1953 Charles F. Johnson, Jr., Businessman, Philanthropist, and Veteran's Advocate

1957 Walter Franklin George, U.S. Senator (D) Georgia

1958 Sam Rayburn, U.S. Congressman (D) Texas

Commander-in-Chief John W. Mahan presenting Senator Lyndon Baines Johnson with the 1959 Citizenship Award

1959 Lyndon Baines Johnson, Senator, U.S. President (D)

1960 Carl Vinson, Congressman (D) Georgia

1963 Dr. Frances O. Kelsey, American Society of Pharmacology

1965 Gen. James Earl Rudder (ret)

1966 Robert W. Sarnhoff, Radio Corporation of America

1969 Bob Hope, Entertainer

1972 John B. Connally, Jr., Governor of Texas (D)

1974 Gerald Ford, U.S. President (R)

1975 Ronald Reagan, U.S. President (R)

1976 Lowell Thomas, Explorer-Commentator

1977 Hubert H. Humphrey, U.S. Senator (D) Minnesota, U.S. Vice President

1978 Anita Bryant, Singer

1980	Melvin Price, Chairman of House Armed Services Committee
1981	James E. Van Zandt, U.S. Congressman (R) Pennsylvania, Past Commander-in-Chief
1982	Charlton Heston, Actor
1983	Joseph R. "Bob" Kerrey, Governor of Nebraska (D)
1984	Jeane J. Kirkpatrick, Educator, U.S. Ambassador to the United Nations
1984	John & Reve Walsh, National Center for Missing and Exploited Children
1985	Everett Alvarez, Jr., Deputy Director of Veterans Administration
1986	Walter Polovchak, Eighteen-year-old Chicagoan, born in the Ukraine, who requested political asylum in the U.S. at the age of 12 rather than accompany his parents back to Russia.
1987	William J. Bennett, U.S. Secretary of Education
1988	Henry J. Hyde, U.S. Congressman (R) Illinois
1989	Bill Mauldin, Political-Military Cartoonist
1990	No award given

Americanism Award

AWARD

Gold medal and citation awarded upon authorization of the National Council of Administration to an individual **FOR OUTSTANDING CONTRIBUTION TO AMERICANISM PRINCIPLES.** Gold-plated medal (2½ inch diameter) with shadow box and 11 x 14 inch citation, matted and framed. Approximate value: $550.00

RECIPIENTS

1959	George Meany, President of the AFL-CIO Union
1960	Thomas S. Gates, Secretary of Defense
1961	George G. Smathers, U.S. Senator
1962	Hubert H. Humphrey, U.S. Senator (D) Minnesota
1963	J. Edgar Hoover, F.B.I. Director
1966	Raymond Burr, Actor
1967	True Davis, Asst. Sec. Treasury Department
1968	Arleigh Burke, Admiral USN
1969	Reverend Theodore N. Hesburgh, Educator
1970	Spiro T. Agnew, U.S. Vice President
1971	John Wayne, Actor
1973	Pete Rozelle, Commissioner of the National Football League
1974	Richard J. Daley, Mayor of Chicago
1975	Leon G. Turrou, Colonel U.S. Army
1976	Daniel (Chappie) James, Jr., Gen. USAF (ret)
1977	Brian B. Reynolds, Amer. Academy of Achievement
1978	Central Intelligence Agency Federal Bureau of Investigation
1979	Russell B. Long, U.S. Senator (D) Louisiana
1980	Charles T. McMillan II, Captain USAF (posthumously)
	Lyn D. McIntosh, Major USAF (posthumously)
	Joel C. Mayo, T/SGT USAF (posthumously)
	Harold L. Lewis, Jr., Major USAF (posthumously)
	Dewey L. Johnson, SSGT USMC (posthumously)
	John D. Harvey, Sergeant USMC (posthumously)
	George M. Holmes, Jr., Corporal USMC (posthumously)
	Richard L. Bakke, Major USAF (posthumously)
1981	James H. Doolittle, Lt. General Army Air Corps
1982	Richard "Red" Skelton, Comedian
1983	Jan Scruggs, Leader of campaign to build Vietnam Veteran's Memorial
1984	Jeffrey N. Nashton, Corporal USMC
1985	Lee Greenwood, Singer/Songwriter

1986   Frederick B. Lacey, Jurist

1987   Paul A. Volker, Banker/Federal Reserve Board

1988   John O. Marsh, Jr., Secretary of the Army

1989   Silvio O. Conte,
U.S. Congressman (R) Massachusetts

1990   A.F. "Bud" Dudley, Executive Director,
Liberty Bowl Festival Association

Bernard M. Baruch Gold Medal Award

The Bernard M. Baruch Gold Medal was formerly awarded for contributions to the cause of American security, unity, and world peace. In 1970, it was replaced by the Dwight David Eisenhower Distinguished Service Award.

RECIPIENTS

1952   Dwight D. Eisenhower, Gen. USA,
U.S. President (R)

1953   Bernard M. Baruch, Statesman

1953   Francis Cardinal Spellman,
Roman Catholic Clergy

1954   Richard M. Nixon, U.S. Vice President (R)

1955   Rev. Billy Graham, Evangelist

1956   Henry Cabot Lodge, Jr., Historian, Statesman

1957   Harry Truman, U.S. President (D)

1958   John Foster Dulles, Statesman

1960   Allen V. Dulles, Director of the CIA

1961   President John F. Kennedy
(Award given in February)

Lauris Norstad, General USA
(Award given in August)

1962   Dean Rusk, Statesman

1963   Richard B. Russell, U.S. Senator (D) Georgia

1964   Lyman L. Lemnitzer, General USA

1965   David H. Lawrence, Novelist

1966   Lewis B. Hershey, General USA

Vice President Richard Nixon received the Bernard Baruch Award from Commander-in-Chief Wayne E. Richards on August 2, 1954 at the National Convention in Philadephia. Nixon later addressed the 7,000 delegates, outlining a three-point program to "preserve the American way of life" against Communism.

1968   Lyndon Baines Johnson, U.S. President (D)

Dwight David Eisenhower Distinguished Service Award

AWARD

Gold Medal and Citation awarded annually upon authorization of the National Council of Administration to an individual **FOR CONTRIBUTIONS TO THE CAUSE OF AMERICAN SECURITY, UNITY AND WORLD PEACE.** Gold-plated medal

(3 inch diameter) with shadow box and 11 x 14 inch citation, matted and framed. Approximate value: $650.00.

RECIPIENTS

1970   Richard M. Nixon, U.S. President (R)

1971   Melvin Laird, U.S. Secretary of Defense

1972   Bob Hope, Entertainer

1973   Henry Kissinger, Statesman, Secretary of State

1976   James R. Schlesinger, Secretary of Defense

1977   James "Strom" Thurmond, U.S. Senator (R) South Carolina

1978   James B. Allen, (posthumously) U.S. Senator from Alabama

1979   John C. Stennis, U.S. Senator (D) Mississippi

1980   Alexander Meigs Haig, Jr., General USA (ret)

1981   H. Ross Perot, Philanthropist/Businessman

1982   Vernon A. Walters, U.S. Ambassador to the UN

1983   Caspar A. Weinberger, Secretary of Defense

1984   George P. Schultz, Statesman, Secretary of State

1985   Richard G. Lugar, U.S. Senator (R) Indiana

1986   Philip C. Habib, U.S. Ambassador to Korea

1987   Bernard W. Rogers, General USA (ret)

1988   John W. Vessey, General USA (ret)

1989   William J. Crowe, Admiral USN, Chairman of Joint Chiefs of Staff

1990   Thomas R. Pickering, U.S. Ambassador to the United Nations*

Close-up of the Dwight David Eisenhower medal

Al Jolson Gold Medal Award

The Al Jolson Gold Medal was conferred for outstanding contributions in the field of entertainment. In 1973, it was superseded by the Hall of Fame Award.

RECIPIENTS

1952   Bob Hope, Entertainer

1953   Joe E. Brown, Entertainer

1954   Eddie Cantor, Entertainer

1955   Ed Sullivan, TV Personality

1958   Arthur Godfrey, Entertainer

1965   Jerry Colonna, Entertainer

1966   Anita Bryant, Singer

---

*   Ambassador Pickering was scheduled to receive the Eisenhower award at the 1990 National Convention. Because the Iraqi invasion of Kuwait necessitated his presence at the U.N., the award presentation was postponed until later.

1967   Frances Langford, Singer

1968   Martha Raye, Entertainer

1971   Jerome Coray, Colonel, Director of USO

1972   George Jessel, Entertainer

Hall of Fame Award

AWARD

Gold medal and citation awarded upon authorization of the National Council of Administration to an individual **FOR DISTINGUISHED SERVICE RENDERED THROUGH OUTSTANDING CONTRIBUTIONS IN THE FIELD OF ENTERTAINMENT.** Gold-plated medal (2¼ inch diameter) with shadow box and 11 x 14 inch citation, matted and framed. Approximate value: $600.00.

RECIPIENTS

1973   George Foreman, U.S. Olympic Boxer, Minister

1975   Rocky Bleier, Pro Football Running Back, Vietnam Veteran

1976   John F. Bookout, President, Shell Oil Company

1977   Rod Carew, Minnesota Twins Baseball Team

1978   Roger Staubach, Dallas Cowboy Football Team

1979   Archie Manning, New Orleans Saints Football Team

1980   George Halas, Pres. Chicago Bears Football Team

1981   Willie Stargell, Pittsburgh Pirates Baseball Team

1982   Eunice Kennedy Shriver, Children's Programs [Dir. of Special Olympics and other Children's Programs.]

1983   Pete Fountain, Clarinetist

1984   Walter Payton, Chicago Bears Football Team

1985   Willis Reed, Jr., NY Knicks Basketball Player

1987   Eddie G. Robinson, College Football Coach

Entertainer Wayne Newton was the winner of the Hall of Fame Award for 1989.

1988 Richard D. Howser, Manager, Kansas City Royals Baseball team

1989 Wayne Newton, Singer

1990 John C. Unitas, former Baltimore Colts football star

Armed Forces Award

AWARD

Gold medal and citation awarded upon authorization of National Council of Administration to active or retired members of the armed forces FOR OUT-STANDING CONTRIBUTIONS TO NATIONAL SECURITY. Gold-plated medal (2 inch diameter) with shadow box and 11 x 14 inch citation, matted and framed. Approximate value: $600.00.

RECIPIENTS

1964 Harry D. Felt, Admiral USN (ret)

1965 Clavin J. Bowlin, Master Sergeant USA

1966 Michael R. Yunck, Colonel USMC

1967 Harvey G. Barnum, Jr., Captain USMC

1968 Robin Olds, Brig. General

1969 Creighton W. Abrams, General USA

1970 The Prisoners of War (in absentia)

1972 John S. Cain, Jr., Admiral USN

1973 Air Force Aces (Captains: Richard S. Ritchie, Charles B. DeBellevue, and Jeffrey S. Feinstein)

1974 Jeremiah A. Denton, Rear Admiral USN (POW)

1975 George Brown, General USAF

1976 Sydney H. Batchelder, Jr., Colonel USMC

1977 Major Arthur G. Bonifas and Lt. Mark T. Barrett (posthumously)

1978 John Singlaub, Major General USA (ret)

1979 Louis H. Wilson, General USMC (ret)

1980 Daniel O. Graham, Lt. General USA (ret)

1981 William A. Connelly, Sergeant Major, USA

Although former Army Captain Harry S. Truman never received an Armed Forces Award, in October 1949, the president accepted a special VFW award created just for him—a Missouri Mule.

1982 Lieutenants James Anderson, Lawrence Amuczynski, David Venlet, USN, and Commander Henry Kleeman, USN

1983 Albert A. Schaufelberger III, Lt. Commander, USN (posthumously)

1984 Paul X. Kelly, General USMC

1985 Arthur D. Nicholson, Jr., Major, USA

1986 Commanding Officer and Crew of USS *Saratoga*

1987 United States Coast Guard

1988 Colin L. Powell, Lt. General USA

1989 Representative/Navy (Received on behalf of Navy)

1990 Lt. General Carl W. Stiner, USA, Commanding General XVIII Corps and Fort Bragg

Aviation and Space Award

AWARD

Gold medal and citation awarded upon authorization of National Council of Administration to an individual **FOR OUTSTANDING CONTRIBUTION IN THE FIELD OF AVIATION/SPACE.** Gold-plated medal (2 inch diameter) with shadow box and 11 x 14 inch citation, matted and framed. Approximate value: $600.00

RECIPIENTS

1964 Dr. Robert Seamans, Jr., National Aeronautics and Space Administration

1964 Alan Shepard and Project Mercury Astronauts

1965 Virgil I. "Gus" Grissom, Astronaut

1966 Surveyor Team

1967 Presented posthumously to Edward H. White II, Roger B. Chaffee, and Gus Grissom, the three astronauts killed in the Apollo launch pad fire

1968 Dr. George Edwin Mueller, NASA

1969 Colonel Frank Borman, USAF, astronaut

In 1969, Commander-in-Chief Richard Homan presented astronaut Frank Borman with the VFW Space Award, as Defense Secretary Melvin Laird looked on.

1970 Neil Armstrong, first astronaut to walk on moon

1971 Richard L. Roudebush, U.S. Congressman, Past VFW Commander-in-Chief

1972 Chris Kraft, Flight Director NASA

1973 Captain Eugene A. Cernan, USN, astronaut

1974 Dr. Wernher Von Braun, NASA Rocket Specialist

1975 Olin E. Teague, U.S. Congressman (D) Texas

1976 U.S. Apollo-Soyuz Flight Crew (Vance D. Brand, Donald K. Slayton, Gen. Thomas P. Stafford)

1977 James A. McDivitt, Brig. Gen., USAF (ret), astronaut

1978 Dr. Sigurd A. Sjoberg, Deputy Director LBJ Space Center

1979 Voyager I Project

1980 Robert A. Frosch, NASA Administrator

1981 Robert F. Thompson, Dir. Space Shuttle Program

1982 Astronauts of the Columbia Space Shuttle (Special Plaque); Thomas K. Mattingly III, Capt., USN, Space Medal

1983 Dr. William R. Lucas, Director of George C. Marshall Space Flight Center

1984 Space Transportation System (Crew of Flight Number Nine and Crew of Flight Number Ten)

1985 Edwin Jacob "Jake" Garn, U.S. Senator (R) Utah

1986 Presented posthumously to Francis "Dick" Scobee, Michael Smith, Ronald McNair, Ellison Onizuka, Christa McAuliffe, Gregory Jarvis, and Judith Resnick, astronauts killed in the explosion of Space Shuttle Challenger

1987 Dick Rutan and Jeanna Yeager, Voyager pilots

1988 Robert A. Roe, U.S. Congressman (D) New Jersey

1989 Arnold D. Aldrich, Dir. Space Shuttle Program

1990 No award given

J. Edgar Hoover Award

The J. Edgar Hoover Award is presented annually to the nation's most outstanding law enforcement officer. It is presented in recognition of the recipient's preeminent abilities; his knowledge and performance of his duties under the law; his dedication to human rights; his integrity, honor, and compassion; and his devotion to public service. The J. Edgar Hoover award is further presented so that brave and honest men and women in the field of law enforcement might know that their dedication and goodwill are appreciated. Finally, the VFW hopes that in giving such an award, those who would subvert the law and order of the nation might learn that their rights and privileges, too, are protected by those they criticize.

Law enforcement officers, in the interpretation of the National Citations and Awards Committee, include:

1. Municipal Policemen
2. County Officials (commonly known as Sheriffs)
3. County Deputy Sheriffs
4. State Officials (commonly known as Highway Patrolmen)
5. Secret Service Personnel
6. F.B.I. Officers
7. Treasury Department Officers (includes Secret Service Agents)

This award is presented in the name of a man who served his nation in the field of law enforcement from 1917 until 1972, and served with great distinction as director of what is now known as the Federal Bureau of Investigation from 1924 to 1972. Through presentation of the J. Edgar Hoover Award, the Veterans of Foreign Wars of the United States strives to honor nationally the law enforcement officer who best exemplifies J. Edgar Hoover's most admirable qualities. In so doing, the VFW hopes to show the nation the outstanding character of the men and women of our law enforcement agencies; their dedication to justice; their understanding of the plight of others; their devotion to law and order; their sworn objective to protect the rights and property of all the people of our nation. The recipient of this award must therefore be an outstanding member of his community, his state, and the nation; and more, an honored member of his fraternity.

Each year, local, state, and national organizations connected with law enforcement organizations nominate thousands of officers for the J. Edgar Hoover Award. To select the winner, the National Citations and Awards Committee and the National Council of Administration consider the accomplishments and attributes of each candidate, as measured against these criteria:

1. Contribution to the preservation and per-petuation of the ideals of law and justice upon which our government is based;
2. Recognition by colleagues of his or her ser-vice, whether that service be one of quiet dedication or one achieving wide publicity, to the best and highest interest of the na-tion, his community, and law and order;
3. Unswerving loyalty to, and active perfor-mance in, the defense and security of the na-tion against its foes, within and without;
4. Dedication to official responsibilities over a period of years and continuous growth in responsibility and experience, not only in the fields within law enforcement, but in those fields which encompass the com-munity, the state and the nation, and in those fields of human relationship.

In presenting the J. Edgar Hoover Award, the VFW acknowledges that there are many members of law enforcement agencies throughout the nation who meet these rigorous standards. The organization hopes that by granting this distinguished award, it will call national attention not only to the dedicated services of the recipient, but also to all other deserving law enfor-cement officers who share the attributes and ac-complishments for which the J. Edgar Hoover Award is made each year.

AWARD

Gold medal and citation awarded upon authorization of National Council of Administration to an individual **FOR OUTSTANDING SERVICE IN THE FIELD OF LAW ENFORCEMENT.** Gold-plated medal (2 inch diameter) with shadow box and 11 x 14 inch cita-tion, matted and framed. Approximate value: $600.00.

RECIPIENTS

1966 Daniel S.C. Liu, Chief of Police, Honolulu, Hawaii

1967 Don S. Genung, Sheriff, Pinellas County, Florida

1968 James Richard Peva, State Police, Indiana

1969 Frank L. Rizzo, Police Commissioner, Philadelphia, Pennsylvania

1970 Clarence M. Kelley, Chief of Police, Kansas City, Missouri

1971 Wilson E. Speir, Director, Dept. of Public Safety, Texas

1972 J. Edgar Hoover, F.B.I. (posthumously)

1972 Peter Pitchess, Sheriff, Los Angeles County, California

1973 William E. Bjork, Chief of Police, Moses Lake, Washington

1974 Joseph T. Carroll, Chief of Police, Lincoln, Nebraska

1975 Benjamin Gonzales, Capt. PD, San Bernardino, California

1976 Joseph P. Fortunato, Juvenile Division, Union City, New Jersey

1977 Lt. Jimmy T. Sakoda, Los Angeles, California, PD

1978 James M. Flynn, Investigator, Bergen County Narcotic Task Force, New Jersey

1979 Fred R. Boyett, Regional Commissioner of Customs, New York

1980 Edward F. La Tuff, Chief of Police, Anoka, Minnesota

1981 Timothy J. McCarthy, Special Agent, U.S. Secret Service

1982 Edward D. McCarthy, Arvada, Colorado PD

1983 Albert C. McMaster, Metropolitan PD, Washington, D.C.

1984 John H. Norton, Chief of California State Police

1985 David D. Howells, Sr. Chief of Police, Allentown, Pennsylvania

1986 Enrique S. Camarena (posthumously), Special Agent, U.S. Drug Enforcement Administration

1987 Sergeant Michael J. Ganley, Minnesota, Law Enforcement Officer (Community Youth Programs)

1988 William D. Langlois, Patrolman, San Francisco, California, PD

1989 Jerry A. Oliver, Asst. Chief of Police, Phoenix, Arizona

1990 Curtis L. Hibbon, Master Police Officer, Lincoln, Nebraska, Police Department

News Media Award

AWARD

Gold medal and citation awarded upon authorization of National Council of Administration to an individual or organization **FOR OUTSTANDING CONTRIBUTIONS TO A BETTER UNDERSTANDING OF OUR AMERICAN WAY OF LIFE AND ITS INSTITUTIONS AND INTERESTS BY HONEST AND FORTHRIGHT REPORTING.** Gold-plated medal (2½ inch diameter) with shadow box and 11 x 14 citation, matted and framed. Approximate value: $600.00.

RECIPIENTS

1978 Fred Hoffman, Associated Press International

1979 John Crown, the *Atlanta Journal*

1980 Jim Bishop, King Features Syndicate

1981 R.E. "Ted" Turner, Turner Broadcasting System

1982 Helen K. Copley, Chairman and CEO of Copley Press, Inc.

1983 *USA Today*

1984 The McLaughlin Group, TV Forum on Current Events

1985 Sarah McClendon, author, newspaper and radio journalist covering the White House

1986 Jeremiah A. O'Leary, News Media

1987 Cable Satellite Public Affairs Network (C-SPAN)

1988 Bill Kurtis, American Broadcast Journalist (CBS)

1989 Drew Middleton, Reporter, *New York Times*

1990 Patrick Buchanan, Co-Host of CNN's "Crossfire"

VFW Outstanding Firefighter Gold Medal Award

In 1990, the VFW inaugurated a new award to recognize the nation's most outstanding firefighters. This annual award, the Outstanding Firefighter Gold Medal, was first presented that summer at the National Convention in Baltimore. The award is presented in recognition of the officer's preeminent abilities, his compassion for fellow human begins, his knowledge of and performance of his duties, his integrity and honor, and his service to the public, state, and nation. The Outstanding Firefighter Gold Medal Award is presented so that brave and honest men and women in the field of fire safety might know that their dedication and goodwill are appreciated. The VFW also hopes that by making such an award, our fellow citizens will be reminded of the special efforts and sacrifices made by this nation's many firefighters.

Through the establishment of the outstanding Firefighter Gold Medal Award, the Veterans of Foreign Wars of the United States wishes to honor the firefighter who exemplifies all of the best qualities of our firefighters. In so doing, the organization hopes to clearly demonstrate to the nation the outstanding character of the men and women of our firefighting agencies; the dedication to country; the understanding of the plight of others; the devotion to fire safety and community; and their sworn objective to protect the life and property of all the people of our nation. The recipient of this award must therefore be an outstanding member of his or her community, state, and the nation; and more, an honored member of the fraternity of firefighters.

Local, state, and national organizations connected with fire safety may nominate anyone who actively fights fires and provides fire safety as a member of any public or volunteer company. From the nominees, the Awards Committee and National Council of Administration chooses a recipient based on his or her accomplishments in these areas:

1. recognition by colleagues of their service, whether that service be one of quiet dedication or one achieving wide publicity, to the best and highest interest of the nation, the community, and fire safety;
2. unswerving loyalty to, and active performance in, the defense and security of the nation's citizens;
3. dedication to their official responsibilities over a period of years and continuous growth in responsibility and experience, not only in fields of fire safety but in those fields which encompass the community, the state, and the nation, and in those fields of human relationships.

The Veterans of Foreign Wars of the United States realizes that there are many members of fire safety companies throughout the nation who meet these rigorous standards. By granting this distinguished award, the VFW hopes to call national attention not only to the dedicated services of the recipient, but to all other deserving firefighters who share the attributes and accomplishments which the Veterans of Foreign Wars Outstanding Firefighter Gold Medal Award represents.

AWARD

Gold medal and citation awarded upon authorization of National Council of Administration to an individual **FOR OUTSTANDING SERVICE IN THE FIELD OF FIRE FIGHTING**. Gold-plated medal (4 inch diameter) with shadow box and 11 x 14 inch citation, matted and framed. Approximate value $600.00.

RECIPIENT

1990   William H. Clutter, Firefighter, Elizabeth, New Jersey, Fire Department

NATIONAL EMPLOYMENT AWARDS PROGRAM

Each year the VFW bestows national awards on individuals, groups, or companies who have furthered employment opportunities for veterans in some way. These awards are intended not only to recognize the achievements of those who have excelled in providing employment services to veterans, but also to increase public awareness of the advantages of employing our nation's veterans. Currently, three different national awards are presented to recognize three different types of achievement in veterans' employment. First, second, and third place winners are chosen for each award. The national employment awards presented are:

Local Office of Public Employment Service Award

The purpose of this award is to recognize Public Employment Service Offices that have excelled in providing services to veterans. It is presented to Public Employment Service Offices that have exceptional records of assisting veterans beyond what is required by federal, state, or local directives. Each department of the VFW nominates one candidate for national competition.

James C. Gates Distinguished Employment Service Award

The James C. Gates Award recognizes extraordinary, meritorious services that have substantially contributed to advancing meaningful employment for veterans. Any individual, group, or organization that has made such a contribution is eligible for the award.

National Employer of the Year Award

This award recognizes employers whose policies and achievements in hiring, promoting, and training veterans—especially veterans with disabilities—are outstanding. By publicizing the experiences of these employers, the VFW hopes to set an example for other employers to follow. Any individual, corporation, or agency with an exceptional record of employing veterans is eligible for the National Employer of the Year Award. There are separate first, second, and third place awards in each of two categories: 1) Large Employer (more than 250 employees); 2) Small Employer (fewer than 250 employees).

Judging of the nominees for the VFW's three national employment awards is conducted by an impartial panel. The panel consists of professional staff members of the Veterans Employment and Training Service, U.S. Department of Labor.

National first place winners of each award are invited to the VFW's Washington Conference. There they receive their award before the assembled members of the National Civil Service and Employment Committee. First place winners also receive a check for $1000 to offset expenses. Second and third place awards are forwarded to the appropriate department to be presented during that department's convention.

NATIONAL AWARDS AUTHORIZED BY THE COMMANDER-IN-CHIEF

While the Awards Committee and National Council of Administration are responsible for choosing recipients for the ten national awards described above,

On February 5, 1952, Commander-in-Chief Frank C. Hilton (center) awarded Captain Henrik Kurt Carlsen (right) a Gold Medal of Merit for courageous actions aboard the sinking freighter Flying Enterprise. *President Truman (left) witnessed the ceremony.*

the national Commander-in-Chief is empowered to present a variety of other national awards. Nominations for these awards are accepted from departments, districts, and posts. Some of the recipients are VFW members; most are not. At least one award is presented in each category annually; sometimes more than one award in a category may be made during the same twelve-month period. Awards are normally presented at the Annual Convention or the Washington Conference.

The Commander-in-Chief is authorized to present the following awards:

GOLD MEDAL OF MERIT AND CITATION: to an individual in recognition of exceptional service rendered the country, community, and mankind on a national or international level.

SILVER MEDAL OF MERIT AND CITATION: to an individual in recognition of exceptional service rendered the country, community, and mankind on a state level.

BRONZE MEDAL OF MERIT AND CITATION: to an individual in recognition of exceptional service rendered the country and mankind on a local or community level.

DISTINGUISHED SERVICE MEDAL AND CITATION: awarded by the Commander-in-Chief to VFW members for distinguished service to the Veterans of Foreign Wars of the U.S.

CERTIFICATE OF APPRECIATION: awarded by the Commander-in-Chief to individuals or organizations in recognition of outstanding service in keeping with the aims or ideals of the Veterans of Foreign Wars of the U.S.

DEPARTMENT AWARDS

Like the national Commander-in-Chief, department commanders are authorized to confer several awards. These awards are most often presented by the commander personally, and include:

AWARD OF COMMENDATION: to recognize distinguished citizens of the state or community who have furthered the aims or ideals of the VFW.

HEROISM MEDAL: normally presented for heroic acts such as saving someone from drowning or from fire. In 1980, for example, the medal was presented to two high school students in Sioux City, Iowa, who rescued a nun from an attempted mugging.

CITIZENSHIP MEDAL: for presentation to citizens in recognition of their local patriotic activities or outstanding qualities of citizenship.

Medals conferred by the national Commander-in-Chief

DISTRICT, COUNTRY COUNCIL, AND POST AWARDS

At the local level, certificates may be presented recognizing citizens or organizations for their outstanding service to their community or other human beings. For example, one man was cited for rescuing a drowning child. A company was given an award for employing a high percentage of veterans with handicaps. A woman was recognized for her work with homeless children. These awards are generally given by the unit most affected by the deed, although sometimes more than one unit may commend an individual or organization for the same accomplishment.

CHAPTER ELEVEN

VETERANS OF FOREIGN WARS OF THE UNITED STATES COMMANDERS-IN-CHIEF 1899–1990

The men who have attained the highest rank in the VFW have been as diverse as the population of the United States as a whole. They have come from a multitude of different nationalities, ethnic groups, religious backgrounds, and occupations. All, however, have shared two beliefs. First, they have been united in their opposition to war. In the words of General Dwight D. Eisenhower, they have hated it "as only a soldier who has lived it can, only as one who has seen its brutality, its futility, and its stupidity."* Second, they have all subscribed to the tenet—handed down by the founders of the VFW organization—that any man who is sent by his government to endure the hazards and sufferings of war is entitled to fair and equitable treatment by that same government upon his return.

According to the records available, more Commanders-in-Chief have practiced law than any other profession, but businessmen have also been well represented. Other occupations of Commanders have included: physician, journalist, rancher, educator, military service member, policeman, miner, farmer, banker, sign painter, and government employee. Commanders-in-Chief who were Army veterans hold an almost two-to-one advantage over veterans of all other branches of the service combined, and those who served as enlisted men outnumber those who served as officers four to three, even though many of the enlisted men later became officers and are therefore counted in both categories. A composite picture of the "typical" VFW Commander-in-Chief would therefore show an attorney who served in the Army as an enlisted man.

---

*   John Gunther, *Eisenhower: The Man and the Symbol* (New York: Harper, 1952), p.42.

Today, the position of Commander-in-Chief is a powerful one indeed. The Commander-in-Chief is an ex-officio member of all VFW committees, and the presiding officer at all national meetings, whether council meetings or conventions. He represents the VFW in all ceremonial affairs involving the organization, unless he delegates the responsibility to another member. Most importantly, he is "Mr. VFW" to both the members and the outside world. Consequently, he usually spends most of his time traveling inside and outside the country, representing the VFW on a worldwide scale. His trips take him to our military bases around the world and often into "hot, sensitive areas." When he is not traveling, the Commander-in-Chief presides over the administrative organization from an office on the twelfth floor of the VFW National Headquarters in Kansas City, Missouri. In his absence, the Adjutant General oversees the day-to-day administrative operation of the VFW. The daily financial responsibilities of the VFW rest with the Quartermaster General. His staff oversees Accounting, Emblem and Supply, Purchasing, Life Membership, Member Insurance Programs, Building Management, and Data Processing.

Presently, the Commander-in-Chief draws an annual salary of $119,000, plus expenses. His wife's expenses are also paid by the organization when her assistance in visiting or entertaining people on the Commander's itinerary is required. The positions of Senior Vice and Junior Vice Commanders are also paid positions with paid expenses.

The only official requirement for the position of Commander-in-Chief is that the candidate be a member in good standing. Normally, however, the position is filled by a member who has held national committee appointments and who has successfully served in the elective offices of Department Commander, Junior Vice Commander-in-Chief, and Senior Vice Commander-in-Chief. Advancement from Junior Vice Commander-in-Chief to Senior Vice Commander-in-Chief and from Senior Vice Commander-in-Chief to Commander-in-Chief is usually automatic unless the candidate shows ineptitude in performing the duties of

his present office. The election to the office of Junior Vice Commander-in-Chief is the difficult task.

Each year, a candidate for National Junior Vice Commander-in-Chief is elected by one of the four conferences (regions) into which the VFW is divided. These conferences are: 1) the Eastern States Conference, composed of departments in Connecticut, Delaware, Washington, D.C., Maine, Maryland, Massachusetts, New Hampshire, New Jersey, New York, Pennsylvania, Rhode Island, Vermont, and Europe; 2) the Western Conference, composed of Alaska, Arizona, California, Colorado, Hawaii, Idaho, Kansas, Montana, Nevada, New Mexico, North Dakota, Oregon, Utah, Washington, the Pacific Areas, and the Panama Canal; 3) the Big 10 Conference, made up of Ohio, Indiana, Michigan, Wisconsin, Illinois, Minnesota, Iowa, Missouri, South Dakota, and Nebraska; and 4) the Southern Conference, made up of Alabama, Arkansas, Florida, Georgia, Kentucky, Louisiana, Mississippi, North Carolina, Oklahoma, South Carolina, Tennessee, Texas, Virginia, and West Virginia. The nominee is then presented to the other conferences for their approval. Once he secures the nod from his conference, he is almost assured of attaining the desired national commandership. The approval of the other three conferences is normally automatic.

This system of filling the organization's top office has two main advantages. First, the members who associate and work with a candidate within his conference usually have a better idea of his qualifications than do members in the rest of the country. Secondly, each of the four conferences is not of the same size or voting strength. But as long as the candidate is chosen from a different conference each year, members from all areas of the country have the opportunity to rise to the apex of the organization. In any given year, each conference has one member in the hierarchy of the national organization—either as Commander-in-Chief, Senior Vice Commander-in-Chief, Junior Vice Commander-in-Chief, or Immediate Past Commander-in-Chief (who, according to the bylaws, serves in an advisory capacity to the Commander-in-Chief).

VFW COMMANDERS-IN-CHIEF

★

YEAR	COMMANDER	POST	STATE
1913	Rice W. Means	1	CO
1914	Thomas Crago	249	PA
1915	Gus Hartung	1	CO
1916	Albert Rabing	71	NY
1917	William Ralston	4	PA
1918	F. Warner Karling	18	MO
1919	F. Warner Karling	18	MO
1920	Robert G. Woodside	285	PA
1921	Robert G. Woodside	285	PA
1922	Tillinghast Huston	243	NY
1923	Gen. Lloyd M. Brett	unknown	D.C.
1924	John H. Dunn	561	MA
1925	Fred Stover	249	PA
1926	Theodore Stitt	44	NY
1927	Frank T. Strayer	1923	IN
1928	Eugene P. Carver, Jr.	529	MA
1929	Hezekiah N. Duff	701	MI
1930	Paul C. Wolman	193	MD
1931	Darold D. DeCoe, Sr.	67	CA
1932	Adm. Robert E. Coontz	2446	MO
1933	James E. Van Zandt	3	PA
1934	James E. Van Zandt	3	PA
1935	James E. Van Zandt	3	PA
1936	Bernard E. Kearney	2077	NY
1937	Scott P. Squyres	405	OK
1938	Eugene I. Van Antwerp	582	MI
1939	Otis N. Brown	2087	NC
1940	Joseph C. Menedez	6640	LA
1941	Max Singer	1018	MA
1942	Robert Merrill	1087	MT
1943	Carl J. Schoeninger	582	MI
1944	Jean A. Brunner	260	NY
1945	Joseph M. Stack	166	PA
1946	Louis E. Starr	1325	OR
1947	Ray Brannaman	2121	CO
1948	Lyall T. Beggs	1318	WI
1949	Clyde A. Lewis	125	NY
1950	Charles C. Ralls	2995	WA
1951	Frank C. Hilton	6558	PA
1952	James W. Cothran	3096	SC
1953	Wayne E. Richards	1254	KS
1954	Merton B. Tice	2750	SD
1955	Timothy J. Murphy	613	MA
1956	Cooper T. Holt	1289	TN
1957	Richard L. Roudebush	6246	IN
1958	John W. Mahan	1116	MT
1959	Louis G. Feldman	589	PA
1960	Ted C. Connell	9192	TX
1961	Robert E. Hansen	295	MN
1962	Byron B. Gentry	1053	CA
1963	Joseph J. Lombardo	601	NY
1964	John A. Jenkins	668	AL
1965	Andy Borg	847	WI
1966	Leslie M. Fry	9211	NV
1967	Joseph A. Scerra	905	MA
1968	Richard Homan	9666	WV
1969	Ray Gallagher	2755	SD
1970	H.R. Rainwater	9223	CA
1971	Joseph L. Vicites	47	PA
1972	Patrick E. Carr	6640	LA
1973	Ray R. Soden	2149	IL
1974	John J. Stang	3147	KS

1975	Thomas C. Walker	5849	CA
1976	R.D. Smith, Jr.	3346	GA
1977	John Wasylik, Jr.	2529	OH
1978	Eric Sandstrom	969	WA
1979	Howard E. Vander Clute, Jr.	8946	NJ
1980	T.C. Selman*/Art Fellwock	4006	TX
1981	Art Fellwock	1114	IN
1982	James R. Currieo	9972	AZ
1983	Clifford G. Olson, Jr.	8699	MA
1984	Billy Ray Cameron	5631	NC
1985	John S. Staum	9625	MN
1986	Norman G. Staab	6240	KS
1987	Earl S. Stock	3275	NY
1988	Larry W. Rivers	1736	LA
1989	Walter G. Hogan	6498	WI

AMERICAN VETERANS OF FOREIGN SERVICE COMMANDERS-IN-CHIEF

YEAR	NAME	CITY OF ELECTION
1899	James C. Putnam	Columbus, Ohio
1900	William S. White	Columbus, Ohio
1901	William S. White	Columbus, Ohio
1902	James Romanis	Columbus, Ohio

1903	James Romanis	Washington Court House, Ohio
1904	James Romanis	Cincinnati, Ohio
1905	Herbert O. Kelley	Altoona, PA
1906	Charles H. Devereaux	Cincinnati, Ohio
1907	David T. Niven	Norfolk, Virginia
1908	J. Alfred Judge	Lebanon, PA
1909	J. Alfred Judge	Pittsburgh, PA
1910	Robert G. Woodside	Jersey City, NJ
1911	Robert G. Woodside	Buffalo, New York
1912	Robert G. Woodside	Philadelphia, PA

ARMY OF THE PHILIPPINES COMMANDERS-IN-CHIEF

DATE	NAME	CITY OF ELECTION
1900	Gen. Francis V. Greene	Denver, Colorado
1901	Gen. Irving Hale	Salt Lake City, Utah
1902	Gen. Irving Hale	Council Bluffs, Iowa
1903	Gen. Charles King	St. Paul, MN
1904	Gen. Wilder S. Metcalf	St. Louis, MO
1905	Col. Alfred Frost	Chicago, Illinois
1906	Gen. Arthur MacArthur	Des Moines, Iowa
1907	Capt. Hustad A. Crow	Kansas City, MO
1908	Major P.J.H. Farrell	Galesburg, IL
1909	Col. Charles L. Jewett	Pittsburgh, PA

---

*   T.C. Selman suffered a heart attack less than two months after assuming the office of Commander-in-Chief. He never recovered. Upon his death, as is stipulated in the national by-laws, Senior Vice Commander-in-Chief Arthur Fellwock assumed the office.

1910	A.H. Anderson	Chicago, Illinois
1911	F. Warner Karling	Detroit, Michigan
1912	F. Warner Karling	Lincoln, Nebraska

BIOGRAPHICAL SKETCHES

These brief biographies are intended to provide a more rounded view of the men who have served as Commander-in-Chief of the VFW. Because Chapters 1 through 7 cover the Commanders' accomplishments on behalf of the VFW, their achievements while in office are not discussed here. Included below are biographies of James Putnam and James Romanis—the two men instrumental in founding the American Veterans of Foreign Service—and General Irving Hale—the man who was the driving force behind the Army of the Philippines. Although these leaders were not technically Commanders-in-Chief of the VFW, their contributions to the organization were certainly great enough to warrant their inclusion here.

James C. Putnam

JAMES C. PUTNAM

James Carrollton Putnam came from a long line of fighters. As he was prone to say, he could trace his "fighters" down his ancestral tree to the middle of the 17th century. "Probably further than that if I took the time to really get into it." The earliest record of Putnams on this side of the Atlantic is of a man named Puttingham who came to America to escape the penalty for "Political Conspiracy" in his native England. For obvious reasons he shortened the family name to Putnam. This Putnam saw service in the French and Indian Wars as a colonel.

The second Putnam of record was an American soldier of Revolutionary War fame, Major General Israel Putnam. This famous soldier was a member of General Washington's staff. It is said that when Israel heard of the fighting around Concord and Lexington, he unhitched his horse and hurried off to Cambridge, leaving his plow standing in the furrow. Israel's son Jesse fought in the War of 1812 and Jesse's son Riley was a fifer during the Mexican War. William Riley Putnam, son of Riley and father of James C., served in the Civil War. James Putnam himself fought in three Indian uprisings and the Spanish American War. Both James and his brother Ray tried to enlist in World War I and were declared too old for service. James tried enlisting again in both World War II and the Korean Conflict. His son Bill saw service in World War II, Korea, and Vietnam. With the exception of World War I, there has been a Putnam in every one of our nation's wars.

Like his great great grandfather Israel, whenever James Putnam felt his duty called, he left whatever he was doing "standing in the furrow" and answered the call. Not only as a soldier, statesman, and VFW founder, but also as father and farmer, Putnam squeezed the last drop of living out of his eighty-eight years of life.

James Putnam was born at Mt. Ayr (Ringold County), Iowa, on April 23, 1868. His father later moved the family to Smith County, Kansas, and homesteaded three miles from the town of Smith Center. In 1886, after graduating from the Smith Center school system, James Putnam moved to Lincoln, Nebraska, to study law with the firm of Philpott and Field. Abandoning law for business, he graduated from the Bryant and Stratton College of Business in 1898.

On January 2, 1889, Putnam enlisted in the Army. He was first assigned to the Sixth Infantry and then to

Company F of the Sixth Regular U.S. Cavalry. With this unit, he campaigned against the Ute Indians in 1889, the Zuni Indians in 1890, and the Sioux in 1891. During this enlistment he served with both "Buffalo Bill" Cody and John J. Pershing. Pershing later gained fame as the Commander of the Allied Expeditionary Forces in the first World War. While Putnam was scouting along the White River in the Badlands of South Dakota, one of Sitting Bull's braves gave him the first of two wounds he would receive during his military service. The leg wound was severe enough that Putnam was discharged April 1, 1892, only three years into a five-year enlistment. This wound would bother him the rest of his life.

In 1893, Putnam took part in the Oklahoma Land Rush and homesteaded a claim on the South Fork in Grant County. In 1894, he was appointed a Grant County Deputy Sheriff.

On September 7, 1895, Putnam signed for another enlistment in the Army. During the Spanish American War, he served with a medical unit which was part of the 17th Volunteer Infantry Regiment. In the fighting around El Caney, Cuba, he was wounded again, this time in the neck. The wound was serious enough for him to be evacuated to a hospital in New York. Aboard ship, on the voyage to the hospital, he served as a nurse for a war correspondent who was believed to be fatally wounded. According to Ripley's well-known "Believe It or Not" column, the correspondent, Edward Marshall, survived. In later years, he also survived three train wrecks, two ship wrecks, and two hotel fires.

Putnam was discharged in Columbus, Ohio, on October 31, 1898, fifty-four days after the other wounded men in his outfit had been released. His discharge was delayed because his "Descriptive List" (describing his wound and its source) was late in arriving from Cuba. After settling in Columbus, Putnam

found work as a city fireman. It was during this period that the veteran's organization he wished for so fervently became a reality. (See Chapters 1 and 2 for an account of the early years of his American Veterans of Foreign Service.)

From 1900 to 1914, Putnam was employed by the Pennsylvania Railroad. From time to time, he also took leave from the railroad to serve as an organizer, legislative agent, and lobbyist for the A.F.L./C.I.O. In 1915, he moved to Panama to work on the canal project as an air brake inspector. While in Panama, he married Eva Hooper and organized the Starr C. Woodruff VFW Post No. 40 in the Canal Zone.

In 1921, Putnam moved with his new bride to Howell County Missouri. Here he purchased and operated the Evergreen Dairy Farm. Never one to occupy his time with only one interest, he was elected to the Missouri State Legislature for three terms and served as chairman of the local school district for ten years.

Two bills he introduced in the legislature attracted considerable interest (but not enough support to pass). The first bill would have allowed counties to erect whipping posts to punish those who were convicted of wife beating, bootlegging, child abandonment, or drunken driving. In the second bill, Putnam made a tongue-in-cheek proposal that the state furnish for "the health and comfort" of each legislator, each day, a packet of his favorite smoking tobacco. This was to be paid for out of the House Speaker's Discretionary Fund. The Speaker replied with his own brand of humor. He assigned the bill to the Committee on Swamplands.

In August 1939, Putnam moved his family to a farm five miles west of Fayetteville so that his son could attend the highly rated College of Law at the University of Arkansas. While his son and daughter attended the university, Putnam devoted his time to securing a Veterans Administration Hospital and a National Cemetery for that area. In this hospital on October 11, 1956—fifty-seven years and one day after the chartering of the American Veterans of Foreign Service—James Carrollton Putnam, last of the thirteen founders died.*

James Romanis *(See photo on page 6)*

The early life of James Romanis, co-founder of the American Veterans of Foreign Service, is cloaked in obscurity. A quiet, deprecating man, he was not prone to volunteer information about past accomplishments. Consequently, his biography must be pieced together from others' accounts and the written records he left behind.

Following his discharge from the 17th Volunteer Infantry Regiment at the end of the Spanish American War, he held many different jobs. It was while working at a pharmacy in Columbus, Ohio, that he helped found one of the VFW's parent organizations, the American Veterans of Foreign Service. (See Chapter 1.) He was later employed as a Deputy Sheriff of Franklin County, Ohio, a Prohibition Commissioner for the federal government, a member of the Board of Civil Service Examiners, a postal letter carrier, an inspector for the American Railway Express Company, and a licensed steam boiler operator.

Romanis started to write a novel, but never finished it. He wrote one song called "Yankee Victory," which was published by Service Publishing Company—a firm of which he was part owner—and later by Nordyke Publishing Company of Hollywood, California.

When he opted to be, Romanis was an eloquent speaker, but his written ideas about recruiting and organization policy might be considered a more important contribution. A long-time member of the Masonic Lodge who became a Master Mason before his thirtieth birthday, he headed the committee which drew up the by-laws of the Columbus, Ohio, Masonic Lodge. In conceiving and instituting programs for the newly founded veteran's organization, he had no peer. Many years after the establishment of the American Veterans of Foreign Service, Putnam was to say of him, "In my honest opinion Comrade Romanis, our first Adjutant and later Commander-in-Chief, did more to insure the success of our pioneer organization than any other one man."

Besides belonging to the Masons, the AVFS, and later, the VFW, Romanis also supported conservative politics. He was a stanch Republican and a member of the Harding Memorial Association.

Despite Romanis's shyness, there was an aura about him that attracted people's attention. He was tall for his era and slender, and always stood or walked with his back straight and his head erect. Even those who classed his personality as "unimposing" would describe his bearing as "regal."

William Selby, Commander of Buckeye Post 1598 to which Romanis belonged, knew him well. "There was something magnetic about him," he recalled. "In later years, when he would walk into the club, although he had spoken to no one, heads would turn and follow his movements. Normally the seat he chose would be separated from other people. He would sit there quietly preferring his own thoughts to exchanging conversation with others."

It was not only those who gathered at the post who noticed his bearing, as this postcard found among Romanis's possessions attests:

```
July 8, 1915
Mr. James Romanis:
    Would you like to meet a nice young
lady? I have seen you several times as I
```

---

* Technically, Rice Means was the first Commander-in-Chief of the Veterans of Foreign Wars of the United States. James Putnam, however, is often given the honorary title of First Commander-in-Chief because he was the first president of the oldest veteran's organization from which the VFW evolved.

```
am a stenographer in one of the rooms
where you carry mail.

     I would very much like to see you some-
time, if I may. You have appealed to me
ever since I saw you. You seem so manly
and noble.

     Please forgive me for writeing [sic]
to you as I have, won't you? And if you
can find time to meet me sometime, I
would be very glad if only once. Please
send me a card anyhow whether you will or
not.
Yours Truely, [sic] Miss M. Donahue
Please write General Del.
won't you?  Columbus
```

It is not known whether Romanis answered her. If so, nothing serious developed from it, as Romanis never married.

On December 7, 1954, James Romanis died at the age of 76. The day of his funeral was cold and punctuated by periods of rain and sleet. Buckeye VFW Post No. 1598 conducted the service. "Perhaps the weather was the reason for the poor attendance," said Post Commander Selby. "There were not enough present to fill all the stations. I had to carry out both Commander and Chaplain's roles."

A trunk containing all of Romanis's worldly effects was left to Commander Selby. These effects consisted largely of newspapers, letters, and other records of his years of service in behalf of the VFW.

Irving Hale *(See photo on page 10)*

The son of the president of Colorado State University, Irving Hale demonstrated his leadership potential early in life. At the U.S. Military Academy at West Point, he achieved the highest scholastic rating ever awarded there, earning a total of 2070.4 points out of a possible 2075. Hale, commissioned a second lieutenant upon graduation, resigned from the Army in 1888. Working for the General Electric Company (then known as the Edison Electric Company), Hale

installed the first successful electric street railroad in Denver.

During the Spanish American War, Hale was appointed Colonel of the First Colorado Infantry U.S. Volunteers. With the 2nd Brigade, 2nd Division, 8th Army Corps, he fought in twenty-eight engagements in the Philippines, and was promoted to brigadier general for his gallantry in action. In the war against the Philippine Insurrection (1899), he was twice cited for gallantry in action and awarded the Silver Star. He was honorably mustered out of service in October, 1899.

After his discharge from the Army in 1899, Hale was active not only in the Army of the Philippines—the veteran's organization he founded in Denver—but also in community and civic affairs. Both the Colorado School of Mines and Colorado State University awarded him honorary degrees for his professional achievements and scholarship. In addition, he was widely sought on the lecture circuit and as a writer on the subjects of engineering and military science.

Although General Hale had been a strong supporter of the merger of the two associations, after the merger he neither sought nor accepted a leadership role in the VFW. General Hale died in Denver on July 26, 1930, after suffering many years from a paralytic stroke.

Rice W. Means (1913–1914)

Rice W. Means was the first Commander-in-Chief of what is now the Veterans of Foreign Wars of the United States. When his term began, however, the organization was named the Army of the Philippines, Cuba and Puerto Rico, and many local units were dissatisfied with the terms of the

merger leading up to the organization's formation. Under Means's direction, the members chose the name "Veterans of Foreign Wars of the United States" and much of the dissention among local units was quelled.

Means was born in Columbia, Missouri, on November 16, 1877. He moved with his family to Yuma County, Colorado, in 1887 and then to Denver two years later. He received his primary schooling in Denver and his L.L.B. from the University of Michigan.

At the outbreak of the Spanish American War, Means accepted a commission as a second lieutenant in the First Colorado Infantry, United States Volunteers, and served in the Philippine Campaign. Promoted to first lieutenant, Means was awarded the Distinguished Service Cross for gallantry and was recommended for the Congressional Medal of Honor.

During World War I, Lt. Colonel Means commanded the U.S. Fourth Infantry in the Meuse-Argonne offensive and Colorado's Own 157th Infantry on its return to the United States.

Means was Judge of Adams County, Colorado, from 1902 to 1904 and Manager of Safety for the City and County of Denver until September 21, 1923. On November 4, 1924, he was appointed United States Senator for Colorado. Following his term as Senator, Means remained in Washington, D.C., where he was owner and publisher of the *National Tribune* and *Stars and Stripes*.

This distinguished soldier, statesman, and civic official was buried with full military honors in Denver, February 2, 1949.

Thomas S. Crago (1914–1915)

Thomas S. Crago was born in Carmichaels, Green County, Pennsylvania on August 8, 1866. He attended Green Academy and Waynesburg College, graduating in 1892. Later he attended Princeton University for one year before returning to Waynesburg to read for the law at the office of Captain James E. Sayers. He was admitted to the bar in 1894.

Crago served in the Spanish American War as a captain and commanding officer of K Company, Tenth Pennsylvania Volunteer Infantry. His outfit was assigned to the Eighth Army Corps commanded by General Wesley Merritt. Following the capture of Manila, they performed garrison duty. Then, after the outbreak of the Philippine Insurrection, Crago and his men agreed to remain on duty until replacements arrived, even though their terms of enlistment had expired. After his unit's return home, Crago continued to serve in the Guard, attaining the rank of lt. colonel.

As a civilian, Crago led a varied career. He was a vice-president of the Union Deposit and Trust Company of Waynesburg and a trustee of Waynesburg College. He also served honorably in the political arena. In 1910, Crago was elected to the United States House of Representatives, representing Pennsylvania's Twenty-third District. He was defeated in the following election, but in 1914 was again elected to the House, this time as a Representative-at-large from Pennsylvania. Crago held this seat until 1923, two years before his death on September 12, 1925.

Gus E. Hartung (1915–1916)

Gus E. Hartung was born in New York City on June 23, 1880. In 1885, he moved to Denver with his family. Hartung gained his eligibility serving with Company I, First Colorado Volunteer Infantry, during the Spanish American War. After he was discharged from active duty as a sergeant, he continued his service in the Colorado National Guard, retiring as a Lt. Colonel.

In 1899, Hartung helped found the John S. Stewart Camp No. 1, Colorado Society, Army of the Philippines. Hartung was also a prime mover in the 1913 amalgamation of the Army of the Philippines and the American Veterans of Foreign Service.

In addition to his other services to the VFW, Hartung was closely allied with the Colorado VFW Band, a musical group founded in 1888. In 1920, Hartung helped organize the Francis Brown Lowry Post 501 in Denver.

Pearle Hartung, the Commander's wife, served as the first President of the Auxiliary to Post No. 1 and as National President of the Ladies Auxiliary in 1920 to 1921. The Hartung's only child, Major George Hartung, was killed in Europe during World War II.

Past Commander-in-Chief Hartung died at the VA Hospital in Denver on April 30, 1958, following a two-month illness. Graveside services were conducted by a ritual team composed of the Past Commanders of Post 501.

Albert Rabing (1916–1917)

Albert Rabing, an attorney, succeeded Commander-in-Chief Gus Hartung after his election at the National Encampment in Chicago in 1916. Under the leadership of Commander-in-Chief Rabing, the VFW urged the nation to prepare itself industrially and militarily for possible involvement in the war then raging in Europe.

After his term as Commander, Rabing remained prominent in VFW affairs. He belonged to VFW Post 71, a New York post no longer in existence. He helped found the VFW National Home and served as its first president in 1925. He was a long-time member of the Home's Board of Trustees and paid off one of the mortgages when the Home was in dire financial straits.

Albert Rabing and his wife had one child, a son, who died young. When Past Commander-in-Chief Rabing died in 1927, the Home lost one of its strongest advocates.

William E. Ralston (1917–1918)

William E. Ralston was born in Burgettstown, Pennsylvania, c. 1878. During the Spanish American War, Ralston served in the Philippine Island Campaign with Company H of the 10th Pennsylvania Infantry. He graduated from Washington and Jefferson College in 1902 and received his degree in law from Pittsburgh Law School in 1905.

Ralston was the first editor of the VFW's magazine, *Foreign Service*. Elected Commander-in-Chief shortly after the United States entered World War I (the war to end all wars), Ralston died in 1942, shortly after our entry into World War II. He was 64.

F. Warner Karling (1918–1920)

Although he served in four of America's wars, F. Warner Karling was not a native of this country. Karling was born in Uppsala, Sweden, on July 30, 1879. He came to the U.S. with his parents at the age of two. He served in the Spanish American War, the Boxer Rebellion in China, the Philippine Insurrection, and World War I. In 1942, he volunteered to serve in World War II, but was turned down because at age 65, he was considered too old.

In private life, Karling was the owner and operator of the F. Warner Karling Furniture Company located at Fifteenth and Walnut streets in Kansas City, Missouri.

Karling was extremely active in veteran's organizations, serving two terms as Commander-in-Chief of the Society of the Army of the Philippines (1911–1913) and two terms as Commander-in-Chief of the VFW (1918–1920). He is credited with calling for the vote of the delegates that brought the organization's headquarters to Kansas City.

Robert G. Woodside (1920–1922)

Robert G. Woodside was born July 16, 1876, in Brooklyn, New York. In the Spanish American War, Woodside served with Company H, 10th Pennsylvania Volunteer Infantry. Afterwards, Woodside attended law school in Pittsburgh, and was admitted to the bar in 1903. During World War I, he attended Second Officers Training Camp, where one of his instructors was Dwight D. Eisenhower. Upon graduation, he was commissioned a captain in the Army, and eventually awarded the Distinguished Service Cross for bravery, the Silver Star, and the Purple Heart for wounds received in the Meuse-Argonne Offensive of 1918. In World War II, Woodside attained the rank of brigadier general in the Pennsylvania Guard.

With his extensive military service, it was natural that Woodside should become deeply involved in veterans' affairs. In fact, his life history reads like a blueprint for anyone wanting to spend his life serving veterans and veterans' causes. Woodside was a charter member of Malate Camp, Army of the Philippines, which was organized November 12, 1901, in Pittsburgh, Pennsylvania. In 1904, he joined McKinley Post, American Veterans of Foreign Service, and later served as its Commander. He was a charter member and one of the founders of VFW Post 285, Pittsburgh, Pennsylvania, in 1919. In addition, he organized and was first Commander of Allegheny Council, VFW.

Comrade Woodside served in the following capacities:

Adjutant General, American Veterans of Foreign Service (Pennsylvania branch), 1905–06

C-in-C, American Veterans of Foreign Service (3 terms), 1910–13

Sr. Vice C-in-C, Army of the Philippines, Cuba and Puerto Rico, 1913–14

Adjutant General, Veterans of Foreign Wars, 1914–17

National Chief of Staff, Veterans of Foreign Wars, 1919–20

C-in-C, Veterans of Foreign Wars (2 terms), 1920–22

President, Board of Trustees, VFW National Home, 1931–39

Chairman, Management Committee, VFW National Home until 1956

Woodside was equally prominent in Pennsylvania politics. He was elected Sheriff of Allegheny County in 1921, and held that office until 1926. In 1927, he was Disbursing Deputy Auditor General of Pennsylvania. In 1928, he was elected County Controller of Allegheny County, a position he held until his retirement.

Woodside was appointed to the Battle Monuments Commission in 1923 by President Harding and served thirty years as a member or vice-chairman of it. He was presented the Medal of Freedom following his retirement from the Commission.

Commander Woodside died in 1964.

Tillinghast Huston (1922–1923)

Tillinghast Huston was a man of many talents. During the Spanish American War, he raised his own volunteer company in Cincinnati and was commissioned its Captain. In World War I, Colonel Huston received a personal commendation from A.E.F. Commanding General John J. Pershing for his service with the 16th Engineers.

For several years Huston was co-owner of the New York Yankee baseball franchise. During this time, he and his partner, Colonel Jacob Ruppert, purchased Babe Ruth's contract and made the Yankees a proverbial pennant contender. They also built Yankee Stadium at an estimated cost of $2 million. Later, Ruppert bought Huston's interest in the franchise. Huston spent his remaining years on his 1,250–acre estate in Georgia raising prize Guernsey cattle and iceberg lettuce.

Comrade Huston was elected Commander-in-Chief of the Veterans of Foreign Wars at the encampment at Seattle in 1922. Subsequently, Huston secured $20,000 for the establishment of the VFW National Home from the receipts of the tied and disputed seventh game of the 1923 World Series between the Yankees and the Giants. (See Chapter 8.) At the same time he was serving as National Commander, he was also Commander of the Unknown Hero Post No. 243 in New York City. Huston had organized this post shortly after his return from France following World War I. The membership of this post included such notables as Irvin S. Cobb, Herbert Corey, James Allison, George Boothby, Damon Runyon, Grantland Rice, Bugs Baer, Ring Lardner, Martin Green, and Bozeman Bulger.

Past Commander-in-Chief Huston died on March 29, 1938, at the age of 71.

Lloyd M. Brett (1923–1924)

Lloyd M. Brett was a West Point graduate who served more than forty years in the U.S. Army. He was elected to head the VFW at the National Encampment in Norfolk, Virginia in 1923. General Brett dedicated himself to the task of extending the organization into every state in the Union. He declared it his purpose to make the VFW more than ever an organization to which the nation could turn for service in time of peace as much as in time of war. It was during his term that the headquarters was transferred from New York City to its present location in Kansas City, Missouri.

John M. Dunn (1924–1925)

Brigadier General John "Jack" Dunn was one of Massachusetts's most noted soldiers. Known in military circles as "Fighting Jack," he was a veteran of four wars and military campaigns. Dunn joined the old Ninth Massachusetts Regiment in 1888, then served in the Spanish American War, the Philippines Insurrection, the Mexican Border Campaign, and World War I.

Between wars, Dunn received his law degree from Boston University and practiced law in Boston.

Active in civic circles, Dunn was a member of the city street commission from 1909 to 1922, becoming its chairman in 1916. He was a member of the Soldier's Relief Commission from 1922 to 1926, a fire commissioner, acting school commissioner, and acting corporation counsel and assessor.

General John H. Dunn died at the age of 72 and was buried June 5, 1942.

Fred Stover (1925–1926)

Fred Stover was born December 2, 1874, in Emlenton, Pennsylvania. At the outbreak of the Spanish American War, he was serving in the Army. He was sent from Fort McPherson, Georgia, to San Francisco, California, with Company C of the 23rd United States Infantry to bolster the strength of a contingent sailing to the Philippines. As a member of General Arthur MacArthur's Brigade, he participated in the capture of Manila, served during the Philippine Insurrection, and was part of two battalions ordered to relieve the Spanish Garrison and take possession of the Sulu Islands.

Stover spent his professional life in the coal mining industry, first as a miner, then as a mine superintendent, and later as the operator of several coal mines. From 1903 to 1907, Stover was an organizer for the United Mine Workers Union.

During his term as Commander-in-Chief, Stover, a wealthy man, traveled over 42,000 miles in thirty-four states, entirely at his own expense. When he left office, the VFW had $9,000 in the treasury—its first ever surplus.

A strong proponent of the VFW National Home, Stover was the first to propose that one cent from each Buddy Poppy sold be given to the Home. As he said in an interview for the *El Paso Times,* "Haphazard charity and voluntary contributions should not be relied upon to take care of war widows and orphans. . . . Arrangements must be made to provide a stable fund to maintain the veterans home for widows and orphans."

Theodore Stitt (1926–1927)

Theodore Stitt was born in Brooklyn in 1887. After receiving his primary education in the Brooklyn Public School System, Stitt graduated from St. Lawrence Law School and was admitted to the State Bar of New York in 1913. Prior to entering the practice of law, Stitt was a reporter for the *Brooklyn Standard Union* and the *New York Sun*. Later, Stitt served New York City as both an Assemblyman in the State Legislature and Justice of the Domestic Relations Court.

Stitt's military service was with the American Expeditionary Forces in World War I. He returned from France a sergeant.

Past Commander-in-Chief Theodore Stitt passed away at his home in Brooklyn, New York, on August 23, 1952.

Frank T. Strayer (1927–1928)

Frank T. Strayer was a self-made man. Born in 1887 in Indianapolis, Indiana, Strayer was deprived of a normal education during his youth. With his wife's encouragement, however, in adult-hood he spent long hours studying. Eventually, he received an L.L.B. degree from McKinley University and became Wayne County Prosecuting Attorney.

In World War I, Strayer resigned from office to accompany his naval reserve unit to France. While overseas, the naval aerial bombing unit with which he served was attacked by German bombers. Strayer, although severely wounded, was one of only two survivors of his unit.

At the time of his death in 1929, Strayer was serving as Assistant Federal District Attorney.

Eugene Pendleton Carver, Jr. (1928–1929)

Eugene Carver enlisted in Company C, 1st Corps of Cadets, Massachusetts National Guard in 1910. He served on the Mexican Border in 1916 as a private, then as a corporal and sergeant. In 1917, he was commissioned a first Lieutenant in the Eighth Infantry Regiment, Mas-

sachusetts National Guard. He served in France and later in Germany with the Army of Occupation.

Carver achieved high office not only in the VFW, but also in the Masons. In 1957, he was elected a Grand High Priest of the Massachusetts Masons, making him the second ranking Mason in Massachusetts.

Commander Carver passed away on December 13, 1975.

Hezekiah N. Duff (1929–1930)

Hezekiah N. Duff was born in Pittsburgh, Pennsylvania, on March 15, 1876. After graduating from Western University of Pennsylvania in 1894 with a B.A., Duff became a journalist. In the meantime, he began studying law. When the Spanish American War broke out, Duff served during the Puerto Rican Campaign as a private in Battery B, Light Field Artillery, Pennsylvania Volunteers.

From 1909 to 1913, he worked as Publicity Director for the J.C. Post Company. Afterwards, Duff returned to journalism, serving first as managing editor for the *Lansing Press*, then as Capitol Correspondent for the *Detroit Free Press*.

Hezekiah Duff died on April 29, 1947.

Paul C. Wolman (1930–1931)

The son of a merchant who immigrated to the United States in 1877, Paul Wolman was born in Carroll County, Maryland, on March 17, 1896. Following his graduation from Baltimore City College, Wolman enrolled in law courses at the University of Maryland.

In 1917, he enlisted in the Army and served two years, mainly overseas. While Wolman was in Europe, he was awarded a prestigious scholarship to do graduate work at a British University. For four months he took special subjects at the Council of Legal Education (Inns of Court in London). Upon his return home, he completed his law degree.

Wolman never sought an elective office, but served as advisor to several Maryland governors and to President Harry S. Truman. Wolman also participated in several fraternal and civic organizations. In addition to being a VFW member, he was a 32nd Degree Mason and a member of the Jewish War Veterans.

Commander-in-Chief Wolman died October 23, 1978.

Darold D. DeCoe, Sr. (1931–1932)

Darold D. DeCoe worked as an attorney in Sacramento, California, before enlisting in the California National Guard. He served six months on the Mexican Border, then saw service in England, France, and Belgium during World War I. After his discharge, DeCoe resumed his practice of law.

Darold DeCoe led his family's way to the top office in the Veterans of Foreign Wars Organization, but just barely. His wife, Consuelo, was right behind him. She was National President of the Ladies Auxiliary to the Veterans of Foreign Wars just twelve months later (1932–1933).

Past Commander-in-Chief Darold D. DeCoe, Sr., passed away on March 23, 1952.

Robert E. Coontz (1932–1933)

Robert E. Coontz was born in Hannibal, Missouri, on July 11, 1864. He graduated from Hannibal Missouri College in 1880 and from the United States Naval Academy in 1885. Commissioned an ensign in the United States Navy in 1887, Coontz received his first star in 1917. In 1919, he received both his fourth star and his appointment as Chief of Naval Operations.

A recipient of the U.S. Government's Distinguished Service Medal, the Admiral served as Commander General of the Military Order of Foreign Wars from 1920 to 1923. In 1923, he was awarded the American Legion's Distinguished Service medal.

Coontz's son, Lt. Lee Coontz, U.S.N., served as the Commander of the VFW's Department of the District of Columbia in 1923.

Admiral Robert E. Cooontz died on January 26, 1935. He is buried in Mount Olivet Cemetery in Hannibal, Missouri—the town in which he spent his early years.

James Edward Van Zandt II (1933–1936)

To his friends, he was "Jimmy." To others, depending upon the year in which they addressed him, he could have been Commander Van Zandt, Captain Van Zandt, Admiral Van Zandt, Commander-in-Chief Van Zandt or Congressman Van Zandt.

Jimmy never did anything half-way. If he believed in something, he worked at it with gusto. Born December 18, 1898, the descendant of a pioneer family of Blair County, Pennsylvania, Jimmy learned the value of work early. At the age of ten, he became a newsboy. Later, he was an apprentice in the shops of the Pennsylvania Railroad School. Working his way ever upward, he eventually secured a position as District Passenger Agent.

In 1939, Van Zandt was granted a leave of absence to serve as U.S. Congressman from Pennsylvania's 23rd District. He was re-elected eight times, and interrupted his political career only to serve a three-and-a-half-year hitch in the United States Navy during World War II. During his eighteen years in the House, Van Zandt was a strong advocate for veterans' legislation. As a member of various Congressional Committees, he traveled to most regions of the globe, including both poles and behind the Iron Curtain. But one of his best-known exploits occurred right in the House of Representatives.

On January 21, 1954, Puerto Rican Nationalists shot and wounded five Congressmen from a spectator's gallery in the House. Congressman Van Zandt and others rushed to disarm and capture the gunmen. Lee Thomas, chief telephone page of the House of Representatives, was close to the struggle. He later told representatives of the press, "At the right of the struggle, I saw and heard him [Congressman Van Zandt] shouting for handcuffs and asking the Puerto Ricans why they wanted to disturb Congress in such a manner."

In 1962, Van Zandt lost a bid for election to the U.S. Senate by slightly over 100,000 votes out of over 4.4 million cast. Afterwards, Jimmy served three Pennsylvania governors as their special representative in Washington and was Secretary to the Pennsylvania Congressional Delegation Steering Committee.

Van Zandt's military career spanned forty-two years and saw him rise from Apprentice Seaman in the United States Navy during World War I to Rear Admiral, USNR, by his retirement in 1959. He saw service in World War I, World War II, and the Korean Conflict. During World War II, Captain Richard M. Scruggs, USN, Commander of Flotilla 7 (LST), commended James E. Van Zandt as follows: "You have made a record for D-Day participation in troops and cargo carried, that in my opinion, no other flotilla can equal. You have been bombed, shelled and torpedoed, but the fires were extinguished, the holes plugged and NOT A SHIP HAS BEEN LOST."

Van Zandt's military decorations included: Legion of Merit, Combat V; Bronze Star Medal, Combat V; Naval Reserve Medal, four stars; World War I Victory Medal, Transport Clasp; American Defense Service Medal, Bronze A; American Campaign Medal; European-African-Middle Eastern Campaign Medal; Asiatic-Pacific Campaign Medal, one silver star and two bronze stars; World War II Victory Medal; Navy Occupation Service Medal, Asia Clasp; National Defense Service Medal; Korean Service Medal; United Nations Service Medal; Philippine Liberation Ribbon, two bronze stars; Philippine Republic Presidential Unit Citation Badge; and Philippine Legion of Honor.

Among Van Zandt's other awards were: the Veterans of Foreign Wars Distinguished Service Medal; the Freedoms Foundation George Washington Medal (for a magazine article entitled "The United States Is Not a Democracy, It Is a Republic—Long Live Our Republic"); Gold Medal Award from the Altoona Campus of Pennsylvania State University; and the Gold Citizenship Medal by the National Society of the Sons of the American Revolution "in recognition of notable services in behalf of our American principles."

In addition to serving as a three-time National Commander of the VFW (1933–36), Van Zandt also served as a two-time Commander of the VFW's Department of Pennsylvania (1928–30) and as the chairman of numerous national committees of the VFW. Without a doubt, Jimmy Van Zandt was a worker and a believer right up to the time of his death on January 6, 1986.

Bernard W. Kearney (1936–1937)

Born May 23, 1889, in Ithaca, New York, Bernard W. (Pat) Kearney received his education from schools in Schenectady, and from Union University and Albany Law School. After being admitted to the bar in 1914, he served as City Judge of Gloversville, New York (1920–24), Assistant District Attorney for Hamilton County (1924–29) and for Fulton County (1929–31), and District Attorney for Fulton County (1931–42). In 1942, Kearney was elected U.S. Congressman from New York's 31st District. While in Congress, Kearney was active in veterans' affairs and served on the House Committee covering Un-American Affairs and Veterans Affairs.

He was a member of the New York National Guard from 1909 until a service-connected injury forced him to retire in 1940. He saw service not only in his home state, but also on the Mexican Border and the battle fields of France. From a "private in the rear rank," Kearney advanced to the rank of Major General by the time of his retirement.

Scott P. Squyres (1937–1938)

Three years before being elected to head the VFW, Scott P. Squyres was Commander of the Department of Oklahoma. As VFW Commander-in-Chief, Squyres directed most of his efforts to trying to keep America out of another World War. He led the VFW in a campaign to build our nation's defense to a status second to none, in hopes that this would deter aggressors from provoking us as they had during World War I. To this end, VFW posts gathered millions of signatures petitioning Congress to build a defense system strong enough to "Keep America Out of War."

Commander Squyres lived to see America at peace once more before he died in 1946.

Eugene I. Van Antwerp (1938–1939)

Eugene I. Van Antwerp, a descendant of Dutch, Irish, and Swiss immigrants who came to this country in 1656, was a member of a family which has resided in Detroit since 1825.

Born in Detroit July 26, 1889, Van Antwerp was educated in Detroit's schools and later at the University of Detroit. He worked as an engineer for the Michigan Central Railroad and before and after World War I with the Grand Truck Railroad. Later he opened his own Civil Engineering practice. Active in civic affairs, he was a member of the Detroit City Council for four terms (1931 to 1939). In 1939 he was elected the city's mayor.

As Commander-in-Chief of the VFW, Van Antwerp followed in Squyres's footsteps by advocating for a strong defense to keep the United States out of world problems. He personally informed President Franklin Roosevelt of the VFW's demands for increased national security efforts.

Commander Van Antwerp died on August 5, 1962.

Otis N. Brown (1939–1940)

Otis Brown was a native of Greensboro, North Carolina, and received his early education from its schools. Almost all of his adult life was spent working for the state's railroads. He was a charter and lifelong member of Greensboro's VFW Post 2087.

Commander-in-Chief Otis Brown and the other members of the VFW were wearing big smiles as they prepared to celebrate the organization's 40th year. The smiles, however, were destined to be short lived. Brown took over the leadership reins on September 1, 1939, the day that Hitler's armies swept into Poland, signifying the official start of World War II. A few days later, President Roosevelt proclaimed a limited national emergency to meet the threat of war. Although he had been in office only a few days, Commander-in-Chief Brown called for a program of constant education to expose the propaganda of subversive groups operating within the borders of the United states.

Joseph C. Menedez (1940–1941)

Born of Spanish-French parents in New Orleans on September 20, 1894, Joseph C. Menedez received his primary education in that city's schools. He earned his degree in medicine at Tulane

University, from which he graduated with high honors.

In 1918, Dr. Menedez entered the Army Medical Corps. He was assigned to a unit that assumed charge of a hospital in Italy and performed primarily field hospital and evacuation work. In recognition of his contributions, the Italian government awarded Menedez several decorations.

Following the war, Dr. Menedez practiced medicine in his home city. With another physician, he organized St. Rits's Surgical Infirmary in New Orleans. From 1919 until 1924, he was an instructor in surgery at the Loyola post-graduate School of Medicine. Dr. Menedez passed away on October 28, 1985, at the age of ninety-one.

Max Singer (1941–1942)

Max Singer was born in New York on February 11, 1888, and moved to Massachusetts in 1914. He enlisted in the Navy in November 1917. After his discharge, Singer worked as a detective for the Boston Police Department. Like many other officers serving on the Boston PD, he belonged to VFW Post 1018, the Boston Police Post.

There is no doubt that Max was a policeman through and through. Legend has it that during the parade in Philadephia preparatory to his swearing in as Commander-in-Chief, he was escorted by twenty Boston policemen of Boston Police Post 1018 and the Boston Police Department's "Black Maria." While riding in the parade, Max spotted a pickpocket plying his trade. Jumping out of the moving car, Max collared the thief and turned him over to a local officer who was assigned to the parade.

As Commander-in-Chief, Singer pledged the strength of the VFW in support of all-out national defense objectives and a militant campaign of education against the forces of totalitarianism. After the attack on Pearl Harbor, he immediately established telephone contact with National Headquarters in Kansas City and the VFW offices in Washington, D.C. He issued instructions placing the VFW on a war emergency basis and offered President Franklin Roosevelt the total resources of the organization.

Past Commander Singer died on November 8, 1968.

Robert T. Merrill (1942–1943)

A native of Great Falls, Montana, Robert T. Merrill was born February 23, 1896. He enlisted in the United States Army Signal Corps on December 11, 1917, and served overseas with the 306th Aero Squadron. Upon his return to Montana, Merrill pursued a degree in law from the University of Montana. He was admitted to the Montana Bar in 1922, after which he practiced law in Havre, Montana. He also served as a special referee during the wage scale hearings of the United States Department of Labor.

Now retired, Merrill resides in Escondido, California.

Carl J. Schoeninger (1943–1944)

Carl J. Schoeninger was born in Defiance, Ohio, on September 25, 1895. Following his graduation from St. Mary's Parochial School, he attended the University of Detroit. Later he graduated from Cass Technical School, also in Detroit, with a degree in electrical engineering.

From May 23, 1917, to May 20, 1919, Schoeninger served with the 16th Engineers, A.E.F. After his discharge, he became a charter member of the 16th Engineers Post No. 582 in Detroit.

Schoeninger was a member of the Wayne County Board of Supervisors from 1934 until 1943, President of the Michigan Association of Electrical Inspectors in 1935, and later was employed as Associate Electrical Engineer in the Department of Buildings and Safety Engineering in Detroit.

He was elected Commander-in-Chief at the 44th National Encampment in New York on September 30, 1943, just five days after his 48th birthday. He died on June 28, 1980.

Jean A. Brunner (1944–1945)

Jean A. Brunner was born in Pont-a-Mousson, France, on October 31, 1893. The following year, his parents brought him to the United States. Brunner was reared and educated in New York City, and, except for a brief stint in the military, lived in that city his entire life.

On September 24, 1918, Brunner enlisted in the Army. Shipped overseas following his basic training, he was promoted to sergeant while in France.

Besides belonging to the VFW, Brunner was an active member of New York City's "Old Guard" (an honorary, quasi military group), holding the rank of Major. He served as its Commandant during 1948 and 1949.

At the time of his death on May 21, 1951, Brunner was the manager of a real estate company in New York City.

Joseph M. Stack (1945–1946)

Joseph M. Stack was born in Pittsburgh, Pennsylvania, on May 15, 1895. He enlisted in the Army in June 1918, and saw service in the St. Mihiel and the Muese-Argonne Campaigns with the 90th Infantry Division. Following the cessation of hostilities, Stack continued his overseas service with the Army of Occupation in Hillesheim, Germany. He returned to the United States in July 1919.

At the time of his election, he was the Chief of the Allegheny (Pennsylvania) County Detectives. Commander Stack died on March 7, 1952.

Louis E. Starr (1946–1947)

Born at Frazeysburg, Ohio, on March 17, 1897, Louis E. Starr was a direct descendent of Dr. Comfort Starr, who came to America in 1620. Starr received his early education in Ohio and graduated from Northwestern University in Illinois with an L.L.B. degree. Subsequently, he practiced law in Portland, Oregon, and also served as Secretary-Commissioner of the Oregon State Boxing Commission.

This Commander's military career began with his enlistment in the Oregon National Guard in March 1917. For eighteen months, Starr served with the infantry in France, where he was wounded in combat. In October 1918, he returned to the U.S. as a sergeant. Starr was commissioned a second lieutenant in 1926, and transferred to the Officers Reserve Corps. There he served as an instructor and attained the rank of captain of infantry. In World War II, Starr was denied active service because of the injury he had sustained in World War I.

Ray H. Brannaman (1947–1948)

Ray H. Brannaman was born on January 15, 1892, in Lisbon, Iowa, a small town just east of Cedar Rapids. He graduated from Washington High School in Cedar Rapids, where he was senior class president and editor of the school's newspaper and yearbook. At graduation, he had won more athletic letters than anyone else in his class.

Following his graduation from high school, Brannaman served as the athletic director for the Iowa State Reformatory at Anamosa, Iowa. When World War I began, he left this position to attend officer's training at Fort Snelling, Minnesota. As the commanding officer of Aero Squadrons 231 and 657 in France, he received personal commendations for their performances from A.E.F. Commander General John Pershing.

After the war, Brannaman and his family homesteaded in the Colorado Mountains. While ranching, he continued his education, earning his B.S. degree from Colorado A&M College and a master's in Educational Administration from Colorado State University. He also devoted his time to assisting veterans and advocating for labor and road safety.

The Brannamans were parents of a son and daughter. The son, Ray Jr., was killed in action on Saipan during World War II on the first anniversary of his enlistment.

Brannaman's most cherished decoration was a miniature horse collar presented to him by his Colorado comrades. The horse collar symbolized his willingness to "put his shoulder to the collar and work whenever there was an organization task that needed to be done," according to National VFW Commander's-in-Chief biographic files. Because he wore this unique decoration at all official VFW functions, he became affectionately known as "Horse Collar Brannaman." He died on November 6, 1977.

Lyall T. Beggs (1948–1949)

Wisconsinite Lyall T. Beggs earned his eligibility for the VFW while serving with the infantry in France during the First World War. After enlisting at seventeen, Beggs was promoted to the rank of corporal. During his service, he had the misfortune to suffer an attack of German mustard gas.

In civilian life, Beggs was a practicing Wisconsin attorney. For six years, he held a seat in the Wisconsin Legislature and also served the people of Dane County as their District Attorney. As VFW Commander-in-Chief, Beggs had the honor of leading the VFW during its Golden Jubilee Anniversary Year.

Commander Beggs passed away on May 14, 1973.

Clyde A. Lewis (1949–1950)

Clyde A. Lewis was born in Hoquiam, Washington, on June 20, 1913, and attended school in South Bend, Washington. He received his B.A. from Notre Dame University and the J.D. (Doctor of Laws) from Harvard Law School in 1939.

In April 1942, Lewis enlisted in the Army Air Corps as a private. After being appointed an aviation cadet, he earned his wings in March 1943. Lewis served twenty-one months overseas with the 401st Bomb Group as a pilot, and was successively a Flight Commander, Squadron Operations Officer, and Squadron Com-

mander. Having completed one tour of duty earlier, by V.E. Day Beggs had almost completed his second. During this second tour, he flew as a Group and Wing Commander. His decorations include the Distinguished Flying Cross with two Oakleaf Clusters, the French Croix de Guerre, the Air Medal with four clusters, the Distinguished Unit Citation with one cluster, the European-African-Middle East campaign ribbon with six battle stars, and the American Theater ribbon.

Following his discharge, Lewis practiced law in Plattsburgh, New York.

When Lewis was elected Commander-in-Chief at the Golden Jubilee Convention in Miami in 1949, he became the first World War II veteran to hold this, the highest office, in the Veteran of Foreign Wars.

Commmander Lewis, now retired, maintains his residence in Plattsburg, New York.

Charles C. Ralls (1950–1951)

The late Charles C. Ralls knew the military both in times of peace and war. He served as an enlisted man during the pre-World War II days and as a combat line officer with the U.S. Marines Fifth Amphibious Corps in World War II.

Born in Missoula, Montana, on March 29, 1904, Ralls attended both high school and Gonzaga University in Gonzaga, Washington. While attending the university's School of Law in 1928 and 1929, Ralls was a star halfback on the football team.

A Washington attorney, Ralls married the former Alice O'Leary, another attorney. Later he served as Chairman of the Washington State Census Bureau and Special Assistant Attorney General for the state. He died during the first week in January, 1979.

Frank C. Hilton (1951–1952)

Frank C. Hilton was born in Pittsburgh on October 12, 1908. He received his education in public schools and at Springfield College in Springfield, Massachusetts.

Enlisting in the Army as a private in March 1942, he saw active service with Allied Force Headquarters in Italy. Hilton was honorably discharged with the rank of captain.

Back home in Meadville, Pennsylvania, Hilton was active in local, state, and national affairs. He was chairman of the Young Republicans of Pennsylvania and vice chairman of the Young Republicans National Federation. Hilton belonged to the Rotary International, Moose, Grange, and was a 32nd degree Mason. Often urged to be a candidate for appointive or elected office, he preferred to devote his time to the affairs of veterans.

Past Commander Hilton presently resides in Meadville, Pennsylvania.

James W. Cothran (1952–1953)

Lawyer, civic leader, and active church worker is the way people of Bishopville, South Carolina, described James W. Cothran. A South Carolina native, he was born in Cartersville on January 6, 1915. After graduation from Timmonsville High School, he attended the University of South Carolina, receiving his law degree from that institution in 1939. He began his law practice in Bishopville in 1940.

During World War II, Cothran served aboard the USS *Charles J. Badger* as its Communications Officer. He saw action at Matsuwa, Kurabu Zaki, Paramushire, and the Kurile Islands. He also participated in the initial landings and occupation of Leyte, Luzon, and Okinawa.

James Cothran became active in the VFW immediately upon his return to South Carolina and remained so for the rest of his life. He died on August 3, 1982.

Wayne E. Richards (1953–1954)

Wayne E. Richards was born at Newkirk, Oklahoma, on November 19, 1910. He received his primary education in the Arkansas City (Kansas) school system and later attended junior college in the same city.

He enlisted in the U.S. Army Air Corps in July 1942 and was commissioned a pilot in October 1943. He served his overseas time in the Pacific in the New Guinea, Philippines, Biak, Okinawa, and Japanese campaigns.

After his release from active duty, Richards returned to Arkansas City, Kansas. There he sold farm machinery and automobiles as owner and operator of Farmer's Enterprises, Inc.

Following his term as Commander-in-Chief, Richards served as Arkansas City's Postmaster. He died August 23, 1970.

Merton B. Tice (1954–1955)

Merton Baird Tice was a real native of South Dakota, as his parents were home-steaders of that state. He was born December 7, 1909, in Mitchell, South Dakota, and received his primary education from its schools. During his school years, Tice was an outstanding athlete and achieved prominence as an all-state and all-conference player both in basketball and football on both levels. He also received his letter in tennis, and participated in the boxing program at the University of South Dakota.

Following his graduation from the USD law school, Tice served for six years with the U.S. Treasury Department in Washington, D.C., New York, and Chicago.

On October 3, 1941, Tice accepted a commission as a first lieutenant in the United States Army Infantry. By the time of his discharge on January 26, 1946, he had risen to the rank of lieutenant colonel. A gliderist with the 18th Airborne Corps, he saw service in Holland, the Battle of the Bulge, the crossing of the Rhine, the Ruhr Pocket cleanup, and the crossing of the Elbe. In addition to his campaign ribbons, he received four battle stars and two general commendations.

"Da Judge," as he was affectionately known around VFW circles, was an attorney in his hometown of Mitchell, South Dakota, and former judge of its Municipal Court. He maintained his membership in Post No. 2750 in Mitchell.

Judge Tice died August 31, 1988.

Timothy J. Murphy (1955–1956)

Tim Murphy was born in Dorchester, Massachusetts, one of eleven children. He was educated in the Dorchester school system and graduated from high school at sixteen. At nineteen, he became a licensed electrician. Later, he received his law degree from Northeastern University School of Law and was admitted to the bar in 1933. Murphy was elected to the state legislature in 1934, and reelected in 1936 with the highest vote ever given a candidate from that ward. From 1938 until 1944, he served as Assistant District Attorney for Suffolk County, Massachusetts.

In 1944, Murphy enlisted in the U.S. Navy. During his tour, he served as a line officer aboard a small aircraft carrier in the South Pacific. Tim was one of ten brothers who saw service during World War II. Three of them were killed in action.

Murphy was elected to the highest office of the VFW at the 56th National Convention in Boston, the city in which he had a law firm, had been council for the Port Authority, and had represented several large labor unions.

Now retired, Past Commander-in-Chief Murphy spends his winters in Naples, Florida, and the balance of the year in his native Massachusetts.

Cooper T. Holt (1956–1957)

Holt, who is known throughout the VFW as "Cooper T," spent his early years in Chattanooga, Tennessee, attending public school and the Edmondson School of Business there. At nineteen, he enlisted in the Army and earned his Infantry Combat Badge with the 164th Infantry in the Asiatic-Pacific Theater.

Upon his return to civilian life, Holt worked as a business executive and post office appointee in Chattanooga. He was elected Commander-in-Chief at the age of thirty-two, making him the youngest man ever to hold that office.

In August 1963, Holt took over as Assistant Adjutant General and Director of the VFW Washington Office. He held this position until he retired on September 1, 1989.

Richard L. Roudebush (1957–1958)

Richard L. Roudebush was born on a farm near Noblesville, Indiana, and received his formal education in that city. He went on to earn a B.S. degree in Business Administration from Butler University in Indianapolis. For several years he was a partner in the Roudebush Commission Company, handling livestock at the Indianapolis Stockyards.

Roudebush served in World War II with the Army ground forces and its air corps as a demolition specialist for the Ordinance Department. He received five battle stars for service in the Middle East, North African, and Italian campaigns.

On November 8, 1960, Roudebush was elected to serve his home state as a United States Congressman from the 6th Congressional District. On October 12, 1974, he was appointed to serve as Administrator of the Veterans Administration.

Still an active member of the VFW, Past Commander Roudebush is also a member of the National Civil War Centennial Committee. He is a past recipient of the American Academy of Achievement's Golden Plate Award.

Past Commander-in-Chief Roudebush spends his winters in Naples, Florida, and his summers in Indiana.

John W. Mahan (1958–1959)

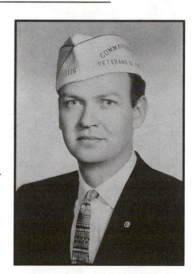

Born in Missoula, Montana on June 24, 1923, John W. Mahan came from a family that was active in veterans' and military affairs. His father, John Sr., had been a brigadier general and Adjutant General of the Montana National Guard at the age of forty-one, the youngest man ever to occupy that position. The senior Mahan was also a leader in the Veterans of Foreign Wars and the American Legion, and was National Commander of the Disabled American Veterans in 1924–25. John's younger brother served as a captain in the 27th Regiment, 25th Division during the Korean Conflict. John himself saw service as a pilot with a Marine dive-bomber squadron in the Pacific during World War II.

Following his discharge from the Marines in 1945, Mahan returned to Montana and completed his degree in law. With his brother as a partner, he set up a practice in Helena, Montana. Mahan twice served as special attorney general for the State of Montana and later left the state to accept an appointment from President Lyndon Johnson to the Subversive Activities Control Board in Washington, D.C.

Since leaving the office of Commander-in-Chief, Mahan has frequently been appointed by the Commander-in-Chief to chair one of the VFW's national committees.

He maintains his residence in Montana.

Louis G. Feldmann (1959–1960)

Born and educated in Wilkes-Barre, Pennsylvania, Louis G. Feldmann received a Bachelor of Science degree in Economics from the University of Pennsylvania. Later, he pursued graduate studies at both the University of Pennsylvania and Duquesne University in Pittsburgh, receiving a degree in law from the latter.

During World War II, Feldmann enlisted as a private in the Marine Corps. Following his basic training and a tour as a drill instructor, Feldmann served in the Asiatic-Pacific theater of operations with the 9th Regiment of the 3rd Marine Division.

Upon his release from active duty, Feldmann entered the field of law. From 1951 to 1955, he was District Attorney for Luzerne County, Pennsylvania. Today he maintains a law office in both Hazelton and Wilkes-Barre, Pennsylvania.

Ted C. Connell (1960–1961)

Ted C. Connell was born in Hamlin, Texas, on December 5, 1924. He served with the field artillery of the U.S. Army during World War II, then returned to Texas and entered the automobile business. Connell also became active in numerous civic programs in and around Killeen, Texas, ably demonstrating how VFW members continue their service to their country by working to make their little "niche in the world" a better place in which to live.

Some of Connell's activities and accomplishments include: member of the Sam Rayburn Foundation's Board of Development, member-at-large of the National Executive Council of the Boy Scouts of America, member and chairman of the Texas Veterans' Affairs Commission, member of the Texas Veterans' Land Board, President of the Greater Killeen Chamber of Commerce, member of the Fort Hood Commanding General's Civilian Advisory Committee, and two-term Mayor of the City of Killeen. Like former Commander-in-Chief Roudebush, Connell is a recipient of the Academy of Achievement's Golden Plate Award.

In recognition of his services, Connell was awarded the VFW's Distinguished Service Medal. In 1966, Texas Governor John B. Connally also presented him with the first Carl L. Estes Award as the outstanding citizen of Texas. He was chosen twice (1958 and 1961) as "Outstanding Citizen of the Year" by the citizens of Killeen, and in 1970 he received the Golden Deeds Award from the Exchange Club of the Greater Killeen area.

Connell makes his home in Killeen, and is still active in local and national affairs.

Byron B. Gentry (1961–1962)

Byron B. Gentry was born October 20, 1913, and received his first national recognition while attending the University of Southern California. An outstanding member of the university's football team, Gentry played in two Rose Bowl Games before going on to play professional football with the Pittsburgh Steelers. Selected as a member of the United Press All-American Professional Team, he participated in two professional bowl games, and, as a member of the All-American Stars, toured Japan in 1935.

In 1942, Gentry enlisted in the service as a private, then rose through the ranks to captain. He graduated from both the Air Intelligence School at Harrisburg, Pennsylvania, and the British Intelligence School at Highgate, England. He served as Combat Intelligence Officer for the 161st Tactical Reconnaissance Squadron and was assigned to the Army Air Corps and attached to both the Third and Ninth Armies. As an additional duty, Gentry defended 150 enlisted men in military courts, losing fewer than ten cases. His service took him to England, Belgium, France, Luxembourg, Holland, and Germany. He was awarded six battle stars, a Presidential Citation, the Belgian Fourragere, and three commendations.

After World War II, Gentry resumed his career as a lawyer. He maintained a limited civil law practice and served as Pasadena City Prosecutor. He also served as a Deputy City Attorney of Los Angeles. Gentry is currently a member of the California Supreme Court and Pasadena Bar Association.

Among Gentry's many interests is a passion for veterans' affairs. (He states his politics as "Veterans.") In addition to his VFW service, he has served as Chairman of the California Veterans Employment Committee, a member of the California Veterans Board, and a member of Directors of the Los Angles County Veterans Service Center.

Gentry also supports a variety of civic organizations, serving as a member of the Board of Directors, American Gold Star Mothers Home Corp.; member, Los Angeles County Committee for the Aging; Board of Directors, Pasadena Committee for the Employment of the Physically Handicapped; co-founder and two-time President, Pasadena Committee for Education on Alcoholism; co-founder and former president, Pasadena Committee for Narcotics Education.

A gifted luncheon and after dinner speaker, Gentry is also an author. He has published both a book of poetry, *Voices of the Airways,* and a book of prose, *The Way the Ball Bounces.*

This two-time winner of the Distinguished Service Award for District Commanders and Captain of the All American Team of Department Commanders was elected to the organization's highest office at the 63rd National Convention in Minneapolis.

Robert E. Hansen (1962–1963)

Robert E. Hansen was born in South St. Paul, Minnesota on January 28, 1926. He is a graduate of South St. Paul High School and the American Aeronautical Institute of St. Paul. During World War II, he served as an enlisted man in Alaska and the Aleutian Islands with the U.S. Naval Air Transport.

After completing his military service, Hansen joined his father, a thirty-year VFW member, and his mother, a twenty-five-year Auxiliary member, in the veterans' affairs arena. As Minnesota Department Commander for 1961–62, he successfully led the fight for passage of the Korean Bonus legislation in the Minnesota Legislature. As VFW National Loyalty Day Chairman, Hansen saw President Nixon sign into law legislation proclaiming May 1st as Loyalty Day.

After his election at the 62nd National Convention in Miami, Hansen's first order of business was a fact-finding trip to Europe to observe the NATO forces deployed there. Upon his return, he discussed his findings with President John F. Kennedy. Hansen also took trips to the Far East and to Cuba, where he inspected the "Cactus Curtain."

Past Commander Hansen, an insurance agent, lives with his wife in Mendota Heights, Minnesota. He remains active in both state and national veterans' affairs.

Joseph J. Lombardo (1963–1964)

A native of Brooklyn, New York, Joseph J. Lombardo was born on September 30, 1914. He received his primary education in the New York City public school system, and his law degree from St. John's University. During World War II, Lombardo served with the Fleet Marine Force in the South Pacific. Following his discharge, he joined the VFW's Sgt. Harry William Steneck Post 601 in Brooklyn, New York.

Lombardo practiced law in metropolitan New York until he was elected a Justice on the New York Supreme Court. He continued to serve on that court until his death on February 13, 1990.

John A. Jenkins (1964–1965)

John A. Jenkins, or "Buck" as he was called by his friends, was a native of Geneva, Alabama. He attended Marion (Alabama) Military Institute, Washington and Lee University, Birmingham Southern College, and Birmingham Law School before being admitted to the Bar of Alabama.

In 1942, Jenkins enlisted in the U.S. Army as a private. He later graduated from Field Artillery Officer Candidate School and served overseas. He was discharged as a Captain.

After returning to civilian life, Jenkins continued his practice of law. He served as an instructor at the Birmingham School of Law and as city attorney for Vestavia Hills, a suburb of Birmingham.

In addition to his involvement with the VFW, Jenkins has supported many other civic and fraternal groups, serving terms on the Board of Directors of the Alabama Anti-Tuberculosis Society, and as Vice President of Marion Institute Alumni Association.

Commander Jenkins died during the 71st National Convention on August 23, 1970.

Andy Borg (1965–1966)

Andy Borg was born on May 17, 1911, and raised in Superior, Wisconsin. He completed his undergraduate studies at Wisconsin State University and received his L.L.B. from the University of Minnesota. During World War II, Borg served overseas with the U.S. Navy. He was elected a district attorney while still in the service. Later, Borg practiced law with the firm of Borg, McGill and Moodie in Superior Wisconsin.

Past Commander Borg was active in community, civic, and VFW work. In 1970, he was sworn in as Chairman of the U.S. Section, Permanent Joint Board on Defense, United States and Canada. The board was established in 1940 to conduct studies relating to the defense of the North American continent.

Today Past Commander Borg resides in a nursing home in Duluth, Minnesota.

Leslie M. Fry (1966–1967)

Leslie M. Fry was born in Louisiana, Missouri, on March 13, 1913. He attended the University of Missouri and the University of Louisville, receiving his L.L.B from the latter in 1939. In World War II, Fry left his law practice in Hartford, Kentucky, to serve with the 136th Field Artillery of the 37th Division in New Zealand, Fiji, Guadalcanal, Bougain-

ville, and Luzon, P.I.. He advanced to the rank of major and was awarded the Bronze Star, Philippine Liberation Medal, Asiatic-Pacific Service Medal, American Defense Service Medal, and the World War II Victory Medal.

Following his release from the service, he and his wife, Jean, moved to Reno, Nevada. There, in addition to attending to his legal work and VFW duties, Fry served as national president of the Future Farmers of America and president of the Nevada Area Council of the Boy Scouts of America. Currently, Mr. Fry serves on the American Battle Monuments Commission under the chairmanship of General Mark W. Clark.

Joseph A. Scerra (1967–1968)

Joseph A. Scerra (Share-ah) was born in Gardner, Massachusetts, on July 9, 1914. During World War II, he served with Company B, 415th Infantry of the 104th (Timberwolf) Infantry Division. Scerra was awarded the Combat Infantryman's Badge, EAME Ribbon with two battle stars, and German Occupation and Victory ribbons. While still in Europe, he joined the Ovila Case VFW Post No. 905 in Gardner.

A career employee of the United States Postal Service, Scerra held positions as Station Superintendent, Delivery and Vehicle Service Officer, and Veterans' Affairs Officer for the Postal Department on a nationwide basis. After retiring in 1971 with thirty-five years of service, Scerra worked for three years as the Assistant Veterans Agent for the City of Gardner. In July 1974, he was appointed State Adjutant of the Department of Massachusetts, a position he still holds.

Richard W. Homan (1968–1969)

A native son of West Virginia, Richard W. Homan was born in Sugar Grove, West Virginia, on January 14, 1923. Following his graduation from Franklin High School in Franklin, West Virginia, Homan attended Bridgewater College in Bridgewater, Virginia, where he received a B.A. in mathematics.

Homan was inducted into the Army in 1944, then sent to the European Theater in February 1945. There he participated in the Rhineland and Central Germany Campaigns with the 610th Tank Destroyer Battalion. During these actions he was promoted to sergeant. Following the cessation of hostilities, Homan was assigned as noncom officer in charge of billeting and messing of military personnel to the International Military Tribunal at the Nurnberg war trials.

After returning home in mid–1946, he opened a flour and feed processing mill and assisted in the management of a family-owned Hereford cattle ranch in Rockingham County, Virginia, and Pendleton County, West Virginia. Homan also became active in civic affairs, serving on his area's school board, Area Advisory Committee to West Virginia University, Pendleton County Board of Health, and the Veteran's Council of the West Virginia Department of Veterans Affairs. Currently a bank executive in Sugar Grove, West Virginia, he maintains his residence in Franklin, West Virginia.

Raymond A. Gallagher (1969–1970)

Raymond A. Gallagher was born in Sioux Falls, South Dakota, on July 29, 1921. He attended Millsaps College in Jackson, Mississippi, and the University of South Dakota, receiving an L.L.B. degree from the latter. In World War II, Gallagher served on LST duty with the U.S. Navy in the Pacific Theater.

In addition to his service to the VFW, Gallagher has served as President of the Redfield (South Dakota) Chamber of Commerce, Chairman of the Redfield Community Fund (which he founded), President of the Spink County Mental Health Division, Chairman of the Sioux Falls Diocesan Aid Program, and member of the South Dakota Veterans Commission. He served as Chairman of the VFW National Finance Committee during the 1989 to 1990 year. He is a partner in the law firm of Gallagher and Battey of Redfield, South Dakota.

Herbert R. Rainwater (1970–1971)

Herbert R. "Chief" Rainwater of San Diego, California, was born in Morrilton, Arkansas, on April 15, 1919. During World War II, he served as an artilleryman with the U.S. Army in China. Later, during the Burma-India campaign, he helped to build the Burma road.

After his discharge, Rainwater became a professional veterans' advocate. He worked for veterans' rights in several capacities, including as a State of California and Federal Government representative overseeing the VA entitlements program for veterans of Southern California.

Past Commander-in-Chief Rainwater and his wife reside in Sun City, California.

Joseph L. Vicites (1971–1972)

Joseph L. "Joe" Vicites, a native of Uniontown, Pennsylvania, was born in 1925. He earned his eligibility as a soldier during World War II. A deeply religious man, he was active in many civic and fraternal associations in addition to the VFW, including the Catholic War Veterans, American Legion, AMVETS, Knights of Columbus, Sons of Italy, the Heart Association, and the American Cancer Society.

During his year as Commander-in-Chief, Vicites continually called on each post to become a "Citadel of Patriotism." His year also became known for his no-retreat stand against the draft dodgers and deserters of the Vietnam era. He led the fight against amnesty. Appearing before a Congressional Subcommittee he summed up his position: "The real gut question is do we countenance self-serving indulgence at best or cowardice at its worst?"

In professional life, Vicites served the people of his state as Clerk of Courts for Fayette County, Pennsylvania, and State Director of Selective Service. He was an assistant auditor in the office of the State Auditor General at the time of his death, July 10, 1987. He was sixty-two.

Patrick E. Carr (1972–1973)

Patrick E. Carr was born on October 2, 1922 in Paulding, Mississippi. He enlisted in the Army Air Corps on June 12, 1942 and flew as a gunner on a B-24 Liberator in Italy with the 464th Bomb Group, 778th Bomb Squadron. While flying their 40th mission over Budapest on August 9, 1944, he and his crew were shot down. A prisoner of war until April 26, 1945, Carr was discharged later that same year. In addition to his campaign ribbons, Carr was awarded the Air Medal with Oak Leaf Cluster and a Purple Heart, and shared in a Presidential Unit Citation.

After his release from active duty, Carr moved to New Orleans, enrolled in Loyola University, and earned a law degree. He practiced law in New Orleans from 1950 to 1975, when he was appointed to his present position of Federal District Judge.

Ray R. Soden (1973–1974)

Born March 26, 1924, Ray R. Soden was a graduate of Steinmetz High School in Chicago. As a young man, he worked as a musician. He sang on the "National Barn Dance," a network radio program over WLS in Chicago, and shared the mike with such future notables as George Gobel, Lulubelle and Scotty, Homer and Jethro, and Andy Williams.

Soon after the attack on Pearl Harbor, Soden enlisted in the Navy. Initially, he was assigned to sing with banjo player Eddie Peabody and pianist Eddie Duchin. Because he had joined the service to fight, not sing, however, Soden applied for sea duty. By war's end, he had earned both European and Asiatic campaign ribbons with seven battle stars, as well as shares in two Presidential Unit Citations. He took part in the invasions of North Africa, Okinawa, Leyte Gulf, Guam, Saipan, Guadalcanal, and Iwo Jima.

After World War II, Soden became a staff engineer for the Illinois Bell Telephone System. He never forgot his early background in music, however. At one National Convention in Chicago, his impromptu singing (without any musical accompaniment) entertained a convention hall full of delegates for forty-five minutes while they awaited the late arrival of presidential candidate Ronald Reagan.

Besides supporting VFW activities, Soden has served on many civic and fraternal committees including Advisory Committee to the Senate Foreign Affairs Committee and Advisory Committee to SETA.

Now retired, Soden serves on the Executive Board of the Boy Scouts of America and is active in numerous civic organizations, including the Lions and Kiwanis. He lives in Wood Dale, Illinois.

John J. Stang (1974–1975)

Kansan John J. Stang was born in 1928. After high school graduation, in 1946 Stang enlisted in the Army. Following his discharge as a staff sergeant, he entered the University of Kansas School of Business and enrolled in the Reserve Officers Training Corps. Stang was commissioned in 1950 and immediately recalled to serve with an artillery battery

in the Korean War. During the Berlin crisis in 1961, he was again recalled. He was discharged as a major. Stang is a graduate of the Command and General Staff College at Fort Leavenworth, Kansas.

In 1957, Stang received his degree in law from the University of Kansas and later a Juris Doctorate from that same institution. Afterwards, he served the community of La Crosse, Kansas, as City Commissioner, Mayor, and County Attorney for Rush County. From 1963 until 1966, he served on the Kansas Governor's Veterans Commission. Presently, he is an attorney in La Crosse.

Thomas C. Walker (1975–1976)

Thomas C. "Pete" Walker is a native of New London, Connecticut. A veteran of both World War II and the Korean War, he served a total of eleven years with the United States Army. He enlisted in the Connecticut National Guard as a private in 1940 and was commissioned a lieutenant of infantry after attending Officer Candidate School at Fort Benning, Georgia. Later, he underwent pilot training and served as a fighter pilot during World War II in the South Pacific. Recalled for service during the Korean War, Walker fought with an anti-aircraft unit.

In civilian life, Walker was a safety compliance officer for Pfizer Inc., a pharmaceutical company. For many years, he also acted as a baseball and softball official in local leagues around New London and served as president of the Thames Valley Baseball Officials, the Eastern Connecticut Board of Baseball Umpires, and the New London Softball Umpires Association. In addition, Walker was a long-time member of the Allen Hook and Ladder Volunteer Fire Department and vice-chairman of the New London Selective Service Board. "Pistol Pete" currently resides in Daly City, California.

"Pete" Walker is also one of the most quoted men in the Veterans of Foreign Wars. About him, his comrades have long testified, "When Pete has something to say, he spits it out." Below are just a few of his short and to-the-point thrusts.

"I believe that never again, comrades, and I mean never, should we embark on a war and not attain victory in the shortest time possible."

"I believe the American Congress is so mired in internal procedures that the security needs of our country play second fiddle to personal ambition."

"Both Greece and Turkey have been rebuffed and affronted by American policy, and our Central Intelligence Agency is hamstrung, hampered, and hassled by Congressional 'show-boating.'"

"I believe that this might well be the time that the United States start rethinking its position relative to the United Nations General Assembly. Frankly, in my book, the U.N. has been a disappointment and at best all we should pay is our pro rata share of that 'Cavern of Winds.'"

"My words on the travesty called 'amnesty' will be brief. It was 'no' yesterday, it is 'no' today and it will be 'no' forever. We will fight any Presidential candidate who chooses to run on a 'pro-amnesty' platform in 1976."

flew the last bombing missions of World War II.

For most of his adult life, Bulldog has worked for the federal government. He began his career by working as a page in the United States House of Representatives. In 1951, he was appointed to the House Un-American Activities Committee Staff by its chairman, Congressman John S. Wood. Today, "Bulldog" serves as the Assistant Veterans Employment Representative for the U.S. Department of Labor.

He and his wife, Betty, reside in Toccoa, Georgia.

John Wasylik (1977–1978)

John Wasylik was born June 28, 1927, in Chester, Pennsylvania. He grew up in Dover, Ohio, and moved to Sandusky, Ohio, in 1958 where he lives today.

During the Korean War, Wasylik served as the sergeant of a machine gun section with the 17th Infantry, Seventh Division. Wasylik earned the Combat Infantry Badge and the Bronze Star, and shared in a Unit Citation.

A practicing optometrist, "Doc" has served on the Ohio State Board of Examiners for Optometry and was named Optometrist of the Year in Ohio in recognition of his civic and optometric achievements.

R.D. Smith (1976–1977)

R.D. "Bulldog" Smith is a native of Georgia. He served his military time in the Army with the 50th Air Engineers Service Group, attached to the B-29 Heavy Bombardment Group of the 20th Air Force. This group

Eric G. Sandstrom (1978–1979)

Eric G. Sandstrom earned his eligibility for the VFW with the 21st Regiment of the 3rd Marine Division during World War II. He fought at Guadalcanal, Bougainville, Guam, and Iwo Jima, and was awarded the Silver Star and two Purple Hearts.

Born in Mankato, Minnesota, on September 22, 1920, Sandstrom is a graduate of the Mankato school system and the Industrial Art School in Minneapolis, Minnesota. He owns and operates his own sign company in Tacoma, Washington.

Howard E. Vander Clute, Jr. (1979–1980)

Howard E. Vander Clute, Jr., was born in Hackensack, New Jersey, on October 27, 1929. He served as an enlisted man with the United States Army in Germany.

At the age of thirty-nine, Vander Clute shed his blue collar and overhauls, the uniform of his masonry construction business, and donned the white collar and business suit of a salesman for the Celotex Corporation. In the corporation's most recent fiscal year, his sales totaled over $4.3 million, exceeding his quota by one million dollars.

In 1972, former Governor William Cahill of New Jersey appointed Vander Clute as State Veteran's Day Chairman. Later, New Jersey Governor Brendan

Byrne appointed him to two successive four-year terms as chairman of the State Veteran's Service Council.

Before ascending to the highest office in the VFW, Vander Clute rose through the chairs of his post, county council, and department (he has served in every elective office of these units). In 1981, Past Commander-in-Chief Vander Clute succeeded Julian Dickennson as the National Adjutant General and is presently serving in that capacity.

T.C. Selman (1980–1980)

T.C., as he was known to his comrades, was born in Magnolia, Texas, on October 6, 1920. He was a graduate of Palestine High School and Nixon Business College in Palestine, Texas.

Selman earned his battle stars and veteran status with the United States Marine Corps. During World War II, he saw action in the campaigns that secured Guam, the Solomon Islands, Saipan, and the Marianas Islands for the U.S. After the invasion of Guam, he was promoted from First Sergeant to Sergeant Major. As a Sergeant Major, he supervised marines who had been First Sergeants longer than he had been in the Marine Corps.

Following his discharge in September 1945, Selman returned to his home state of Texas and his managerial position with the J.C. Penney Company. From 1964 until 1972, he served as the Mayor of Freeport, Texas. He was also actively involved with the Chamber of Commerce, civic projects, and patriotic activities.

Elected Commander-in-Chief at the 81st National Convention in Chicago, Illinois, August 21, 1980, Selman suffered a heart attack at his VFW Homecoming celebration and died shortly after. He was succeeded in office by Senior Vice Commander-in-Chief Arthur J. Fellwock.

Arthur J. Fellwock (1980–1982)

A lifelong resident of Evansville, Indiana, Arthur J. Fellwock was born July 3, 1926. He holds a Bachelor of Science from the University of Evansville.

Fellwock became eligible for VFW membership by serving in the Navy during World War II. He took part in the landings on Guam, New Guinea, Iwo Jima, and the Philippines.

Fellwock served almost two complete terms, assuming the Commandership upon the death of newly elected Commander-in-Chief T.C. Selman in October of 1980.

Today, Fellwock is Vice President of Sales for the Universal Corporation, a company which specializes in production controls for large corporations. Commander Fellwock continues his VFW activities from his home in Evansville, Indiana.

James R. Currieo (1982–1983)

Born in Denver, Colorado, on May 12, 1934, James R. "Bob" Currieo is a career military man. A former instructor at Fort Huachuca in the Combat Surveillance School, he retired from the Army as a sergeant major with twenty-two years of service.

Currieo holds both bachelor's and master's degrees from the University of Arizona. In 1966 he was named one of Arizona's outstanding young men by the Junior Chamber of Commerce. Bob has served successive terms on the Arizona Governor's Veteran's Advisory Council. Currently Currieo is serving as the Director of the VFW Political Action Committee in Washington, D.C.

Clifford G. Olson, Jr. (1983–1984)

Clifford G. Olson, Jr., was born in the Dorchester section of Boston and graduated from Hyde Park High School. He entered the Navy at the age of seventeen and became an air crewman and a hydraulic specialist. His "hitch" lasted from 1951 to 1959. His wartime missions (Korean War) were performed with Patrol Squadron 7, flying PV2 aircraft, which provided air cover for the 7th Fleet and worked extensively carrying out anti-submarine patrols, weather reconnaissance, and intelligence sorties.

Following his year as Commander-in-Chief of the Veterans of Foreign Wars, Olson returned to his position with the City of Boston's Transit system. He maintains his residence in Bryantville, Massachusetts.

Billy Ray Cameron (1984–1985)

Billy Ray Cameron, born February 6, 1944 in Sanford, North Carolina, was the first Vietnam veteran to become the Commander-in-Chief of the Veterans of Foreign Wars. Cameron joined the VFW from his hospital bed in Camp Lejeune, North Carolina.

Billy Ray, as he is called by most all who know him, served with the First Marine Division in the Da Nang area from August 1967 to March of 1968, earning two meritorious combat promotions and becoming a squad leader. He was awarded a Purple Heart with Oak Leaf Cluster.

In 1972, Cameron, a graduate of Wingate College, Wingate, North Carolina, won the honor of being selected North Carolina Disabled Veteran of the Year. In 1976, Governor James E. Holshouser, Jr. appointed him to a four-year term on the North Carolina Veteran's Commission, a position he was reappointed to by the succeeding Governor, James B. Hunt, Jr. Cameron also served as Chairman of the North Carolina Veteran's Council for the term 1976–77.

Past Commander Cameron and his family live in his hometown of Sanford, North Carolina, where he is Emergency Management Coordinator (formerly called Director of Civil Defense) for the City of Sanford.

John S. Staum (1985–1986)

Minneapolis native John S. Staum attended St. Olaf College in Northfield, Minnesota, as a pre-seminary student for two years. During the Korean War, he gave up his student deferment to join the Marine Corps. He served in the Marine Corps detachments aboard both the heavy cruiser *USS Bremerton* and the aircraft carrier *USS Princeton*.

After his discharge, Staum worked for the Glenmar Company, a sub-contracting and building supply firm in Minneapolis, retiring as president. At fifty-four, he assumed the reins as Commander-in-Chief of the VFW. Staum is also a member of the American Legion and the Marine Corps League.

Commander Staum lives in Minneapolis.

Norman G. Staab (1986–1987)

Norman G. Staab was born in Catherine, Kansas, on December 27, 1929. He attended St. Joseph's Military Academy and graduated from Hays (Kansas) High School.

Staab served forty months with the 16th Infantry in the Army of Occupation in Germany. In 1950, he played guard on the EUCOM (European Command) championship football team.

For the past thirty-four years, Staab has been associated with LTV Energy Products Company and has managed its Russell, Kansas store for twenty-two. In December, 1986, he was named "Man of the Year" in Russell County, Kansas. This honor was bestowed on him in recognition of his outstanding services, duties, and honors.

Besides serving as a VFW National Chair Officer, Past Commander-in-Chief Staab has also personally recruited more than 400 VFW members and 350 Life Members. These recruits contributed to the total of 1,177 members and 1,041 Life Members that Post 6240, his home post, now shows on its roster.

Staab currently lives in Hays, Kansas. He is serving as the 1990 to 1991 Chairman of the National Finance Committee.

Earl L. Stock, Jr. (1987–1988)

A lifelong resident of New York, Earl L. Stock, Jr., was born March 27, 1924, in Johnstown, New York. Stock served his country with the 11th Airborne Division, taking part in five Pacific Campaigns during World War II. He joined the VFW within a month after his discharge. The reason he selected the VFW, he recalls, is the assistance the organization gave his parents following the death of his brother in World War II.

After leaving the Army, Stock worked as a dairyman, then was elected a township supervisor of Herkimer County, New York. Later he became executive director of Herkimer County's Civil Service Commission. Stock served two terms as president of the New York State Civil Service Officers Commission. He also served three Governors as a Commissioner on the New York State Division of Veterans' Affairs.

Now retired, Commander Stock lives near Fort Plain, New York. Even in his retirement, Commander Stock is serving the VFW on the VFW National Home Board of Trustees. In October, 1989, he was elected to a six-year term representing the Sixth National Home District (New York, New Jersey, and Europe).

Larry W. Rivers (1988–1989)

Larry W. Rivers was born in Beaumont, Texas, on November 6, 1946. He entered the Marine Corps in June 1968 and remained on active duty through June 1971. As an infantry officer in Vietnam, Rivers earned the Combat Action Ribbon, the Vietnamese Cross of Gallantry, and the Bronze Star.

Before entering the military, Rivers attended Northwestern State University of Louisiana, receiving a B.A. in government. Following his discharge, he went on to earn a Juris Doctor degree from Loyola University of the South in 1974. He was a partner in the Alexandria, Louisiana, law firm of Rivers & Beck.

After his year as Commander-in-Chief, Rivers was appointed to replace retiring Assistant Adjutant General Cooper T. Holt as Director of the Washington, D.C., Office.

Rivers holds the distinction of being the youngest person ever to have been elected to serve as department commander in his native state of Louisiana. He was thirty-three when elected to that office. He is the second Commander-in-Chief from the Vietnam era.

Walter G. Hogan (1989–1990)

Commander Hogan earned his VFW eligibility during the Korean War as a squad leader of Fox Company, Seventeenth Regiment of the Seventh Infantry Division. Wounded by mortar fragments, "Wally" was given a medical discharge in July of 1953. He was awarded the Purple Heart, Combat Infantry Badge, and the Korean Service Medal with two battle stars.

Born in Green Bay, Wisconsin, on January 8, 1932, Commander Hogan received his early education from elementary schools in Green Bay, and graduated from high school in Milwaukee, Wisconsin. He holds a Bachelor of Arts degree from Milwaukee's Spencerian College.

Following his military service, he was employed by Rexnord, Inc., rising to the position of plant manager. Hogan retired in 1987 after thirty-two years with the company.

Wally and his wife, the former Shirley Goll of Milwaukee, are the parents of five children. The Hogans reside in Greenfield, Wisconsin.

CHAPTER TWELVE

PROGRAMS OF THE VFW

Both the VFW and its immediate predecessors were founded for one primary purpose: to care for and protect the veteran and his entitlements. Today the organization's paramount goal is still to look after the well-being of veterans and their families and to champion their cause whenever and wherever necessary. But the VFW has also adopted a number of other goals aimed at strengthening the fabric of our society as a whole. The organization's members are dedicated to making the United States a better place to live by instilling patriotism and love of country in her citizens, fostering growth and learning in young people, and helping communities solve their problems.

To reach its many goals, the VFW has developed many programs. Some programs—particularly those concerned with veterans' education and rehabilitation or with securing legislation favorable to veterans—require the organization to work closely with the federal government. These programs *for* veterans are handled by the VFW's Washington, D.C., office under the guidance of the Assistant Adjutant General and Director of the Washington office. The balance of the programs—primarily those *by* veterans—are administered by the National Headquarters staff in Kansas City, Missouri. Programs relating to veterans' education, legislation, and rehabilitation were covered in earlier chapters, since many of them were begun or modified only after years of lobbying the federal government. This chapter discusses those programs established by the VFW itself and governed solely by the organization.

THE BUDDY POPPY PROGRAM

From its inception, the Buddy Poppy program has helped the VFW live up to its motto, "to honor the dead by helping the living." The Buddy Poppy—a small red flower symbolic of the blood shed in World War I by millions of Allied soldiers in defense of freedom—was originally sold to provide relief for the people of war-devastated France. Later, its sale directly benefitted thousands of disabled and down-and-out American veterans.

National Home resident Ellen Sunday presenting a Buddy Poppy to J. Edgar Hoover, Director of the F.B.I., circa 1945

The poppy program actually got its start on the other side of the Atlantic Ocean. Shortly after World War I, Madame E. Guerin, founder of the American and French Children's League, became concerned that the free world was "forgetting to [sic] soon those sleeping in Flanders Fields."* Inspired by Colonel John McCrae's poem, "In Flanders Field," which spoke of poppies growing in an Allied graveyard "between the crosses, row on row," Guerin decided on the poppy as the most appropriate memorial flower. She began attending the conventions of any serviceman's organization that would allow her to speak. Her request was always the same—to enact the following resolution: "Be it resolved that every member, if possible, and his or her family shall wear a silk red poppy on Decoration Day in memory of those who gave their lives for humanity."

The poppy program was quickly embraced by the people of France, and also secured the sponsorship of the Prince of Wales, the Governors General of Canada, Australia, and New Zealand, and the President of Cuba. In each of these countries, veteran's organizations and their auxiliaries agreed to sell memorial poppies for the benefit of the children of France.

In April 1919, the "Poppy Lady," as Madame Guerin was now known, arrived in the United States. She came to speak in support of the "Victory Loan"—financial assistance to help France's homeless and jobless get back on their feet. While stateside, she asked

---

* From a letter to VFW Adjutant General Robert Handy, February 8, 1922.

the newly formed American Legion to sponsor the poppy program in the United States. At their second national convention in Cleveland in September 1920, the American Legion passed a resolution making the poppy their official flower. At the next year's convention, however, the delegates repudiated the poppy and instead adopted the daisy as the organization's official flower. Subsequently, Madame Guerin reported that her "deception was great on the 23rd of January [1922] to hear that the American Legion Auxiliary had taken the Idea to sponsor FOR THEMSELVES the Poppy Day of the U.S."

When the Poppy Lady turned to the VFW for help, the organization readily agreed to take over from the American Legion. In May 1922, the VFW conducted the first nationwide distribution of poppies in the United States. Then, at its National Encampment in Seattle in August 1922, the organization adopted the poppy as the official memorial flower of the VFW.

Following the success of the VFW's first poppy sale, the American Legion had second thoughts about its withdrawal from the program. On June 3, 1922, the *Ohio Legionnaire* printed this editorial:

"It is a matter of sincere regret to The American Legion that another service men's organization should take it upon itself to appropriate the Flanders Poppy without consent or approval.

"The motives that prompted the Veterans of Foreign Wars to stage a Poppy Day are without question, but the appropriation of an emblem belonging so distinctly to The Legion by an organization that does not represent in any appreciable degree, the veterans of Flanders Fields, was an act that should have been given great consideration.

"It should be borne in mind that the membership of the V. of F.W. is not limited to World War veterans, and that it is limited to men who served "overseas" in any American War."

The July 1922 issue of the VFW's *Foreign Service* magazine reprinted the editorial under the heading "Poppies and Poppycock," together with a scathing rebuttal. The VFW called the American Legion's editorial "a misstatement of facts," and termed the charge that the VFW "does not represent, in any appreciable degree, the veterans of Flanders Fields" "particularly offensive." The VFW went on to ask, "And what is this about 'consent' and 'approval'? Since when has it been necessary for the Veterans of Foreign Wars to ask the American Legion or any other organization how they shall assist their disabled comrades? That is gross effrontery and presumptuous arrogance." The VFW further condemned the American Legion for attempting "to gather undeserved praise and unearned funds by besmirching an organization the members of which have added more glorious pages to American history than the American Legion ever will."

A disgruntled American Legion was not the only problem to plague the VFW's poppy program in the early years. The American and French Children's League (sometimes referred to as the Franco-American Children's League) had been dissolved shortly before the VFW's 1922 poppy sale. Much of the poppy supply went with it. Consequently, the VFW had great difficult obtaining enough poppies for the 1923 sale.

From the frustrations of the 1923 sales year evolved a plan to pay disabled and needy American veterans to make the poppies. This plan was presented to the 1923 National Encampment for approval. Immediately following the plan's adoption, a VFW poppy factory was set up in Pittsburgh, Pennsylvania. All veterans who would be manufacturing poppies for the 1924 sale were sent to a training workshop by the U.S. Veterans Bureau regional manager in Pittsburgh.

It was from these early disabled poppy makers that the name which would be the flower's trademark came. The name just "grew" out of the poppy makers' remembrances of their buddies who never came back from war. Undoubtedly, because it expressed so simply the deepest significance of the Poppy Plan, the

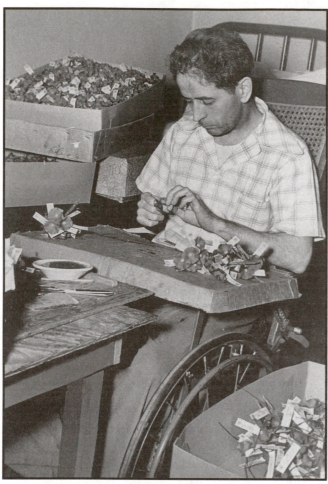

A veteran assembling Buddy Poppies

name stuck. All over the country, the little red flower became known as the "Buddy Poppy."

In February 1924, the VFW registered the name "Buddy Poppy" with the U.S. Patent Office. On May 20, 1924, a certificate was issued granting the VFW, under the classification of artificial flowers, all trademark rights to the name of "Buddy." No other organization, firm, or individual can use the name "Buddy Poppy." The VFW has made this trademark a guarantee that all poppies bearing that name and the VFW label are the work of bona fide disabled and needy veterans.

After the 1924 sale, some of the larger state departments of the VFW suggested that it might improve local sales if the poppies used were made by hospitalized veterans from their own area. The delegates at the 1924 National Encampment agreed. They ruled that poppies would now be made throughout the U.S. by disabled veterans in government hospitals and by needy veterans in workshops supervised by the VFW. Currently the little red flowers of silk-like fabric are assembled in eleven different locations.* The VA Facilities in which they are made are located in: Leavenworth and Topeka, Kansas; Biloxi, Mississippi; Temple, Texas; Martinsburg, West Virginia; Hampton, Virginia; Milwaukee, Wisconsin; Dayton, Ohio; and White City and Grand Rapids, Michigan.

From the start of the VFW's poppy program, the U.S. Veterans Bureau, the Administrator of Veterans Affairs, and other federal agencies have supported the Buddy Poppy. And beginning with Warren G. Harding, U.S. presidents have also been staunch supporters of the program. Each year, a Poppy Girl or Poppy Boy selected from the National Home's residents starts the annual campaign by presenting the first poppy to the president of the United States. (The sole departure from this tradition occurred in 1975, when President Gerald Ford failed to invite the Poppy Child to the White House.) These presentations are not without peril for the adult VFW members who accompany the Poppy Child. One year, President Franklin Roosevelt pointed to the miniature figures of a donkey and an elephant on the edge of his desk. Turning to that year's Poppy Girl, he asked, "Which one do you like better?" Everyone present held their breath until the child, after moments of serious consideration, reached for the donkey. During Harry Truman's term of office, there was a similar tense moment when the Poppy Girl made a rather unusual request. "Please," she asked Truman, "would you play the piano for me?" With a look of surprise rapidly giving way to a large grin, the

---

* This special fabric was first used in 1989. Prior to that, Buddy Poppies were made of paper.

department service work or other programs for the relief or well-being of VFW members.

Posts receive their profits from direct sale of the poppies to the public. National by-laws require that the profits from these sales be placed in the post's Relief Fund to be used only for the following purposes:

> "For the aid, assistance, relief, and comfort of needy or disabled veterans or members of the Armed Forces and their dependents, and the widows and orphans of deceased veterans.
>
> "For the maintenance and expansion of the VFW National Home and other facilities devoted exclusively to the benefit and welfare of the dependents, widows, and orphans of disabled, needy, or deceased veterans or members of the Armed Forces.
>
> "For necessary expenses in providing entertainment, care, and assistance to hospitalized veterans or members of the Armed Forces.
>
> "For veterans' rehabilitation, welfare, and service work.
>
> "To perpetuate the memory of deceased veterans and members of the Armed Forces, and to comfort survivors."

With help from the VFW, the "Little Red Flower" continues to benefit the needy just as the Poppy Lady believed it was capable of so many years ago. In 1989, for example, 17,894,684 poppies were sold for an average donation of 55 cents. To date, the VFW has sold over three quarters of a billion Buddy Poppies. As long as Americans continue to spill their blood in defense of freedom, sales of these blood-red poppies will undoubtedly continue strong.

Vice President Richard M. Nixon posed with the Buddy Poppy Girl in 1953.

President told her, "I'd be glad to, but there is no piano here. I'm sorry."

Today, there are strict rules governing how profits from Buddy Poppy sales are to be used at different levels within the organization. The National organization assesses a tax of three and one-half cents on every poppy sold to a state department. This tax is added to the cost of manufacturing and distributing the poppy. Tax revenues are allotted as follows: one and one-half cents to the service fund of the department that purchased the poppy, one cent to the VFW National Home, and one cent to the Veterans Service fund of the National Headquarters.

At the department level, an additional tax is normally added to the cost of the poppies it sells to the posts in its jurisdiction. This profit is used to fund

MEMBERSHIP PROGRAM

The membership program is the lifeblood of the VFW. Without members, there would be no people to carry out the other programs and no money with which to fund them. And without *enough* members to give the VFW its political clout, it would have little chance of successfully grappling with veterans' problems and needs.

To guide the membership program, each national Commander-in-Chief sets his personal recruitment quota for the VFW as a whole. In arriving at this quota, the Commander-in-Chief takes into consideration the number of members who will be lost each year due to death or to failures to renew membership ("back-door losses"). Currently, this number averages about 7 percent of the total membership each year—about 140,000 members in 1989. In order to show any *gain* in membership, the quota must therefore be set at greater than 7 percent of the present membership.

Once a national recruitment goal has been decided upon, each department, district, county council, and post is given an individual quota. These quotas are based on the units' total membership the previous year. Smaller units—posts of one hundred members, for example—may be asked to increase their membership to 125 percent, while a larger post of one thousand members may only be assigned a 101 percent objective. If units meet or exceed their quotas, they receive recognition from their department and/or the national organization. Units that win national recognition are given All American status, and those that win department recognition are given All State status. Along with this recognition, units and their

commanders may win gifts or nationally sponsored trips.

The actual method of recruiting varies from unit to unit and commander to commander. What motivates one recruiter or team of recruiters may not encourage others. Each unit commander designs his own program or agrees to one designed by his membership chairman. Usually, individual recruiters are given small awards as tokens of the commander's thanks and to reward them for their success. For example, a recruiter who signed up three new or reinstated members might receive the Commander's Pin. For ten members, he might earn a special recruiting pin, and for twenty-five, a jacket personalized with his name, the VFW Emblem, and name of his post. For fifty members, the recruiter receives a national designation as "National Aide de Camp, Recruiting Class," a VFW Cap bearing that designation, and has his or her name listed in the National General Orders published in the *VFW Magazine*.

The success of the VFW's membership program is reflected in the organization's steady growth over the years. Since 1899, membership has grown from the original 13 members to over 2 million. The most recent tally, in 1990, showed 10,513 posts as of April and approximately 2,100,000 members by National Convention time in August. (Of this total, 52 percent had received campaign ribbons in World War II, 21 percent in the Korean War, 24 percent in the Vietnam War, and 3 percent from occupation duty and expeditionary service in twenty smaller campaigns.) In reaching this total, each of the VFW's fifty-four departments had surpassed its previous year's membership.* This marked the thirty-fifth consecutive year in which the VFW has increased in size. No other major organization can make that claim.

---

*   In January 1991, the VFW created its fifty-fifth department, the Department of Puerto Rico and Virgin Islands.

NUMBER OF MEMBERS

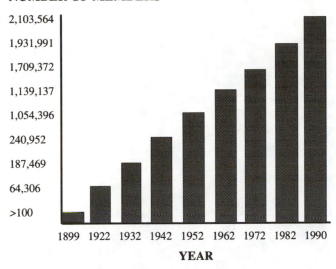

(Until 1922, no exact membership records were kept.)

AMERICANISM PROGRAM

"Americanism is an unfailing love of country: loyalty to its institutions and ideals; eagerness to defend it against all enemies; undivided allegiance to the flag; and a desire to secure the blessings of liberty to ourselves and posterity."

This was the definition adopted during the late 1920s or early 1930s by the Commanders-in-Chief of the VFW and national commanders of four other veteran's organizations. But long before these leaders agreed on this definition, the VFW had founded its own Americanism program based on the principles of its constitution.

The program got its start under Captain Walter I. Joyce on March 1, 1921. As Chairman of the Committee on Americanization, Joyce embarked on an aggressive campaign to stir up patriotism across the United States. His early efforts were aimed at furthering the goals of the VFW Creed he had developed himself. This creed, adopted by the National Council of Administration in January 1921, declared that the VFW would:

"1. Do everything within its power to eliminate the hyphen in organizations composed of residents or citizens of the United States." [That is, that there should be no Irish-Americans, German-Americans, Italian-Americans, etc., only Americans.]

"2. That this organization endeavor to bring about the speaking of the language of our country at all times and in all places within the boundaries of the United States.

"3. That this organization emphatically favor publication of the newspapers of our country in the language of our country and positively discourage as an act of disloyalty the publication of our newspapers in the language of any other country or race.

"4. That we use our utmost efforts through legislation and other means to insist that the alien population of this country prepare to become citizens or prepare to leave the country until they change their minds, and furthermore that all aliens who for cause have been refused citizenship be deported at once.

"5. Resolved, that the above declared principles be spread broadcast by the VFW in carrying out its principles of Americanism."

As part of their Americanism activities, VFW posts and their Ladies Auxiliaries distribute American flags in their communities. Pictured here, members of VFW Post No. 4667 of Marion, Virginia.

This creed was distributed to members throughout the country, as well as to other military, fraternal, and veteran's organizations. Eventually, 150,000 signatures were obtained on a petition urging the adoption of this program to "Americanize America."*

During the early 1920s, a second Joyce campaign, to "Buy American," and a third, to take "Un-American Textbooks out of the schools," followed closely behind the first. Close to a million copies of Joyce's booklet, "Etiquette of the Stars and Stripes," were also distributed to schools, posts, and other organizations during this period.

Joyce's crowning achievement was to lead the VFW in the campaign to have the "Star-Spangled Banner" proclaimed our national anthem. For years, the "Star-Spangled Banner" had been our unofficial anthem, and in 1916 President Woodrow Wilson had declared that it was, indeed, our national anthem. But the song could not be our *official* anthem until Congress approved a bill declaring it so.

At Joyce's request, New York Congressman Hamilton Fish introduced a bill into the 69th Congress to make the "Star-Spangled Banner" our national anthem, but to no avail. Fish reintroduced the same bill into the 70th Congress. Again no action was taken. On January 30, 1930, representatives of the VFW and more than sixty veteran and patriotic groups met in a conference in Washington. They urged passage of the Star-Spangled Banner Bill, then pending in Congress. Hearings on this bill, which had been introduced by Congressman Charles Linthicum of Maryland, were to begin the next day. At this hearing, VFW petitions bearing more than 5 million signatures were presented to the House Judiciary Committee. In addition, the

---

* Often the VFW's early Americanism program is referred to as the "Americanization" program. The misnomer undoubtedly came from this era, possibly from the petition drive.

Today VFW posts sponsor over 1,200 Boy Scout troops. Pictured here, the troop sponsored by VFW Post 3755 of Ogallala, Nebraska.

VFW presented favorable endorsements from organizations totalling over 15 million in membership. Still, there were objections to the bill. Pacifists complained that the words were too military. Others said the tune was too hard to sing. To help overcome these objections, Joyce arranged for the U.S. Navy Band and soprano Elsie Reilly, a member of the Ladies Auxiliary to Post 824 of Washington, D.C., to perform the song for the committee. Her rendition must have been particularly stirring because the bill made it out of committee and was approved by the House on April 21, 1930.

In the Senate, the bill was held up in the Library Committee until February of the following year. Joyce and other members of the VFW Legislative Committee called on the senators opposed to the bill and secured their agreement not to block passage. Finally, the Star-Spangled Banner Bill made it to the floor of the Senate on March 3, 1931. This time it fared well. Just hours before Congress adjourned it

was passed unanimously and signed into law by President Hoover.

In the mid 1930s, Victor Devereaux followed Joyce as Director of the Americanism program. As Devereaux instilled his own beliefs into the program, it gradually became more right wing. The new director guided the program's efforts to expose radical elements and subversive organizations operating inside our country. These activities reached their peak in World War II. During the war, the Department of Americanism cooperated with the F.B.I. in reporting subversive groups and acts of sabotage.

Devereaux also began the VFW Youth Activity program in 1935. The following year, the National Encampment passed a resolution requiring that a national director of Youth Activities be appointed and instructing each department and post to appoint a director of these junior activities. Through this program, many Sons and Daughters of the VFW units were formed. These groups reached a membership peak of 50,000 to 65,000 before the outbreak of

World War II. Later, many sons' units were disbanded when their members joined the service, and the Junior Girls units were absorbed into the Ladies Auxiliary. Other youth projects included a National Softball Tournament, rifle shooting tournaments, Bicycle Safety Clubs, sponsorship of Boy Scout and Cub Scout troops, and a model airplane building club with over 50,000 members. So successful would these youth activities become that in 1945 youth activities were made into a separate program with their own director. (See below.)

Another of Devereaux's accomplishments was to found a speaker's club whose members presented prepared speeches about America, veterans, youth activities, and other topics to groups and social gatherings across the nation. Through this club, 300 to 400 speakers each gave about a dozen speeches a year.

Upon the resignation of Devereaux in 1945, Mark Kinsey, an Iowa newspaperman and radio writer, became Americanism director. His primary contribution to the program was to compile, evaluate, and distribute information on Americanism and to speak for the VFW on Americanism matters. Under his direction, the Americanism Department prepared scripts that were used by 500 radio stations across the country, as well as articles that were published in 120 magazines and newspapers. He also set up a section to answer requests from organizations and individuals for information concerning VFW policies and general patriotic subjects. In 1947, the Americanism Department mailed over 5,600 "Speak Up for Democracy" scripts and press releases, 4,300 sets of articles and speeches, and 3,500 personal letters.

In 1949, the Americanism Department began a long fight to have May 1st designated as "Loyalty Day." In doing so, it hoped to counteract the messages of hate which the Communists broadcast during their annual May Day celebrations. For many years, the VFW struggled to get Congress to consider the bill. Finally, in 1954, Congressman and three-time National Commander-in-Chief James E. Van Zandt of Pennsylvania introduced a House Joint Resolution calling for the declaration of Loyalty Day. His bill passed the

House, but not the Senate. Undaunted, he reintroduced the bill in 1955. This time, Congress passed the bill, but designated only May 1st of that year as "Loyalty Day." Not satisfied, the VFW continued its push to have May 1st of each year proclaimed as "Loyalty Day." This date was finally given official recognition in 1958 when Congress adopted Public Law 529 designating May 1st as Loyalty Day. Although never recognized as a major national holiday, Loyalty Day is still celebrated by posts, county councils, and districts all across this nation. To demonstrate their loyalty to our nation, its ideals, and its flag these units sponsor parades, hold dinners to honor wartime and peacetime heroes, and donate and ceremoniously replace worn and tattered flags flying in their community.

Shortly after the campaign for Loyalty Day was concluded, the Americanism Department succeeded in achieving another long-standing goal. For twenty years, the VFW had been working for the admission of Hawaii into the union; in fact, it had been the first patriotic organization to propose admission. On August 21, 1959, Hawaii became the fiftieth state.

Just as the VFW Creed had set the tone for the Americanism Department's activities in the 1920s, in the 1960s the Americanism Department was guided by a new manifesto. During the 1961 to 1962 year, the national Americanism committee approved the following Code of Ethics for The Veterans of Foreign Wars Fight Against Communism.

CODE OF ETHICS

1. We will support the principles of freedom and justice, law and order upon which our country, the United States of America, is founded.
2. We will support and seek to strengthen our institutions, public or private, which preserve, protect and defend our American freedoms.
3. We will initiate steps and work with others to solve local problems by means of positive, constructive community action, no matter how small or large the problem.

4. We recognize that it is our duty as loyal, active citizens to vote intelligently, based on careful consideration of issues and candidates, and to follow through by keeping elected officials informed of our views on all issues affecting the interests of all the people.

5. We accept as a basis for action that Communists—whatever they profess at any given moment—are seeking by any and all means to subvert and destroy our ideals and national security. We will seek to defeat Communist objectives by the use of all legitimate means within the framework of our free society.

6. We will not resort to gossip-mongering, name-calling tactics, or characterize any individual or organization as Communist on our own authority. We will regard such actions as threatening the basic freedoms which we are striving to defend.

7. We will carry our fight against Communists and at their objectives on the basis of issues rather than personalities relying upon the persuasiveness of our position, rather than upon any form of intimidation or force, to bring success to our cause.

8. We will test every issue two ways: (1) on the basis of whether action stemming from it will strengthen or weaken the free institutions and national security of the United States, and (2) on the basis of whether such action will strengthen or weaken the Communist cause in our country or abroad.

9. We recognize that one of the greatest needs in our country today is education against Communism. We will initiate and support efforts to more fully enlighten all the people concerning Communist principles, objectives and techniques, and follow through by emphasizing the attributes of our American way of life.

10. Our objective in supporting American ideals and in defeating Communist aims is not to act alone in order to win honor for ourselves; rather it is to work with like-minded citizens for the security, for the increased unity, and for the continuing improvement of our country.

Throughout the 1960s, the Americanism Department worked to foster support for our troops fighting Communism in Vietnam. With the help of the Ladies Auxiliary, VFW members gathered and sent relief supplies such as food, clothing, and medical supplies to our soldiers in Vietnam for distribution among the Vietnamese civilians whose way of life had been devasted by the war.

While it was supporting the players in the current conflict, the VFW did not forget those who had served in earlier wars. After learning that nowhere in France was there a memorial to World War I American Expeditionary Forces Commander and VFW member John J. Pershing, the VFW set about rectifying that oversight. In February of 1967, with another VFW member, Dwight D. Eisenhower, heading the memorial committee, an impressive statue sculpted by world-famous artist Felix W. de Weldon was erected. Because of the high regard the French veterans had for their American counterparts, the city of Paris approved $10,000 for landscaping the site.

As the 1960s gave way to the 1970s, the Americanism Department and its activities had become such an integral part of the organization as a whole that less and less distinction was made between what was a VFW project and what was an exclusive project of the Americanism Department. Certainly in reporting activities to the media, it was less cumbersome to say that something was done by the VFW, rather than as as Americanism Project of the Veterans of Foreign Wars of the United States. It was the same work, done in the same way, by the same people, only the credit was given in a different way. Inside the organization, however, the work was still accredited and reported and judged by the same people in the same way.

*Commander-in-Chief Thomas C. Walker welcomed
the throng that witnessed the dedication of the
VFW Torch of Freedom.*

During the nation's bicentennial year, the VFW and its Ladies Auxiliary unveiled yet another monument—the "Torch of Freedom" monument. Located on the grounds of the VFW Washington Office in our nation's capital, this thirty-six-foot-high, three-sided marble and bronze sculpture features three-dimensional plaques recalling America's battles for freedom. At the top is a simulated flame which is lighted at night. The monument bears the inscription: "Out of the past so great to build a greater future in honor and memory of the veterans of all America's wars who by their service kept the Torch of Freedom burning. This monument is dedicated by the Veterans of Foreign Wars and the Ladies Auxiliary to the VFW in honor of all who have served, their parents, wives and children."

Over the next years, recognition of those who had kept the Torch of Freedom burning remained a high priority of the VFW and its Americanism Department. At the VFW National Convention in August 1982, Jan Scruggs, president of the Vietnam Veterans Memorial Fund paid tribute to the VFW's part in helping the Vietnam Veterans Memorial become a reality. Scruggs recalled that in 1969 he recommended to Congress that a monument be erected to Vietnam veterans. When Congress backed away from the project, he elected to undertake the project himself. "I needed money to stimulate the necessary interest, and the VFW was the only organization to come forward with some money. Then I had to go to Congress to get two acres near the Lincoln Memorial. Cooper T. Holt, the Executive Director of the VFW Washington Office, got personally involved. Then the VFW had fund raising dinners and everywhere I went the VFW was right in the middle of it. They actually contributed $300,000. Even during the arguments over the style of the monument, the VFW stood with us."

During the Vietnam Memorial Monument Dedication on November 10 to 14, 1982, the VFW was well represented by its Jr. Vice Commander-in-Chief and Vietnam veteran Billy Ray Cameron of North Carolina. Cameron participated in all of the events and was one of the principal speakers for the actual dedication ceremony of November 23rd. Cameron told the 250,000 assembled for the dedication, "The VFW has always held, and will continue to hold to the ancient wisdom that says, 'Hate War, Yet Honor The Warrior.'"

Two years later, on Memorial Day 1984, the VFW helped win another struggle for the Vietnam veterans. After years of advocating by the VFW and other veteran's organizations, the body of an unknown Vietnam veteran was interred in Arlington National Cemetery alongside his comrades-in-arms from the First and Second World Wars and the Korean War.

In 1989 and 1990, the VFW again manned the ramparts, this time in a war with the Supreme Court and the Congress over the "Desecration of the American Flag Issue." On June 11, 1989, the Flag Act of 1989—which prescribed penalties for the desecration or burning of the American Flag—had been declared unconstitutional in a 5:4 decision by the Supreme Court. The VFW announced it would keep the heat on Congress until it passed a constitutional amendment to resolve this controversial issue. In a hurried, but massive effort, the VFW and other patriotic organizations attempted to force Congress into calling for and ratifying a constitutional amendment. Although their effort came to naught, they vowed to keep the issue alive until some adequate protection is given our national banner.

In another emotional area, the VFW took a leading role in prompting Congress and the nation in remembering the virtually forgotten veterans of the Korean War. Putting its money where its mouth was, the VFW surpassed its fund-raising commitment by tendering $550,000 toward the Korean War Memorial Fund. The Ladies Auxiliary contributed an additional $97,000.

The top ten contributors to the Korean War Memorial were:

1. Hyundai Motor America and U.S. Distributors: $1,204,000
2. Veterans of Foreign Wars of the United States: $550,000
3. Disabled American Veterans: $520,000
4. Korean War Veterans Association: $500,000
5. Paralyzed Veterans of America: $175,000
6. VFW Ladies Auxiliary: $97,000
7. AFL/CIO Affiliates: $80,000
8. American Legion: $75,000
9. Ford Motor Company: $50,000
10. Pohang Steel America: $50,000

To drum up further recognition for those who fought in Korea, the VFW helped convince Congress to pass a resolution honoring veterans of the Korean War. The resolution declared that June 25, 1990, would be known as Korean War Veterans Recognition Day. On that day, VFW posts worldwide offered special recognition to those who had served in that worthy effort.

Obviously, the Department of Americanism is charged with a staggering responsibility. It is the conscience of the VFW, and, to a lesser degree, of the nation. The department takes direction from the Commander-in-Chief and the National Encampment, and on occasion remind both of what that direction should be. Americanism and the VFW are so closely intertwined that they cannot be separated.

YOUTH PROGRAMS

In 1945, the VFW decided to increase its commitment to the youth of this country. That year the National Encampment directed the organization to take the lead in providing a constructive outlet for teenagers' energies. After the encampment, the VFW released the following statement about its proposed plan for a youth program:

"The VFW is face to face with an opportunity. It is an opportunity to render real and vital service to our nation. . . . It is not a call to face an enemy from without, but to overcome an enemy within our own nation that is presenting a more serious threat to the continuance of our Democracy than any alien power. . . .

"The enemy has always been with us, but in the last few years the forces have multiplied to the point where they are now an immediate and definite threat to the continuance of our form of government. The weak spot in our American system is that we have never paid any attention to the older boy and girl.... We give the youngsters free schools and force them to obtain a minimum of education—and then we turn them loose.... Worse, most of our splendid youth organizations, the things upon which we depended to implant the fundamentals of democracy—organizations such as Boy Scouts, the 4–H Clubs, the junior church societies, and other organizations—are all set up for the younger boy and girl...."

A former colonel, Lawrence A. "Buck" Rogers was selected to direct the Department of Youth Activities (originally called the Department of Athletics and Recreation). Rogers had extensive experience in managing recreation programs, having been responsible for the athletic programs of forty-three separate Air Transport Command bases during World War II.

Rogers moved rapidly to get the VFW's youth program up and running. He notified the posts that the VFW would sponsor national tournaments in seven different sports: bowling, basketball, marbles, swimming, softball, rifle shooting, and boxing. Most of these tournaments were for teenagers only. The softball tournament, however, was open to juniors aged nine to seventeen and was sanctioned by the National Amateur Softball Association. In 1979, the rifle shooting program was changed and placed under the auspices of the National Rifle Association (NRA). It, too, was then opened to anybody eighteen years old or younger who belonged to a sanctioned rifle club or a Sons of the VFW Unit. Currently, NRA youth shooting groups are sponsored by 306 posts in 45 states.

Today, the national organization no longer sponsors any sports tournaments, but many departments maintain statewide programs and offer their own tournaments and prizes. The Department of Minnesota, for example, sponsors an annual hockey program. In addition, over 8,000 posts sponsor one or more sports.

Other youth activities instituted over the years have included "Take a Kid Fishing" clubs, horseshoe tournaments, hockey leagues, model aviation clubs, swimming, golf, boating, camping, fund raising for the Special Olympics, Junior and Senior ROTC Programs, musical groups, American Youth Soccer Teams, Boys Clubs, Cub Scout packs, and Boy and Girl Scout troops. At present, VFW posts sponsor over 1,200 Boy Scout Troops, making the VFW one of the country's largest sponsors of Boy Scout programs.

A final youth activity worth a special mention is the Lite a Bike program. This program, begun in 1962, is aimed at reducing the number of bicyclists struck by motor vehicles during the hours of darkness. Participating VFW posts around the world purchase and apply reflective tape to children's bicycles to make them more visible at night. More than 30 million bicycles have been provided with this reflective tape since the program's inception. The program has been especially welcome in Taiwan, where bicycles are more commonly used for transportation than in the United States. Although better reflective devices on bicycles are making this program less necessary, many posts still continue it. Others have expanded the

A young participant in the VFW's Lite a Bike program

program by offering to apply the tape to the costumes of trick-or-treaters on Halloween.

VOICE OF DEMOCRACY

In 1946, the National Association of Broadcasters began sponsoring an annual speech competition for high school students. This Voice of Democracy competition was run with the help of the VFW, and offered prizes for speeches that were well conceived and well delivered. Each year, four regional winners were selected and awarded a $500 savings bond and a wristwatch.

In 1960, the National Association of Broadcasters decided it could no longer sponsor the program on a national basis, so the VFW assumed sole sponsorship of it. With its network of 10,000 posts and 8,000 Auxiliaries, the VFW was soon able to make the competition a truly nationwide undertaking. By 1974, Edward Burnham, then Director of the Voice of Democracy (VOD) Program, noted that each year students from some 7500 public and parochial high schools were taking part in the VOD program.

Today, the Voice of Democracy competition is open to high school sophomores, juniors, and seniors across the country. Each contestant is required to write and record a three to five minute script on the subject selected as that year's topic. Some past topics have included "What Freedom Means to Me," "Freedom's Challenge," "My Responsibility as a Citizen," "New Horizons for America's Youth," and "Why I Am Proud of America." The recordings are then judged at post or school, district, and state levels. Winners at each level receive prizes and recognition. State winners are given an all-expense paid trip to Washington, D.C., where the final judging and awards presentation take place.

JUDGES SCORE SHEET														
CRITERIA	SCALE	\multicolumn{13}{l}{Contestants Code Numbers}
		1	2	3	4	5	6	7	8	9	10	11	12	
1. DELIVERY														
a. Enunciation & Pronunciation	1-15													
b. Expressiveness	1-15													
c. Sincerity of Tone	1-10													
MAX. SCORE	40													
2. ORIGINALITY														
a. Positive Approach	1-10													
b. Use of Imagination	1-5													
c. Individualistic Approach	1-5													
d. Human Interest Appeal	1-5													
MAX. SCORE	25													
3. CONTENT														
a. Relates to Subject	1-15													
b. Logical Development of Ideas	1-10													
c. Clarity of Ideas	1-10													
MAX. SCORE	35													
TOTAL MAX. SCORE	100													

Contest Location _____ Date _____

Judge's Signature _____

(Please sign your score sheet)

Additional judges score sheets are available on request.

The judging sheet used at all levels in the VFW-sponsored Voice of Democracy competition

During their five-day stay in Washington, the state winners visit many sights, including the Smithsonian, Mount Vernon, the White House, the Library of Congress, and Arlington National Cemetery. Throughout these tours, the VOD participants are highly visible, each wearing a special jacket awarded by the VFW. Most often, these jackets are decorated with Commander's Pins from each of the VFW's departments. Each department gives its participant enough of that year's pins to trade with the other fifty-four contestants.

At the end of their visit, the state winners are guests of honor at the VFW's Congressional Banquet. Each winner is introduced individually, and seated at the head table with fifty dignitaries from the VFW, the armed forces, the federal government, and the Ladies Auxiliary. During this program, the names of the winners are announced. Each of the national winners receives his or her award, and then the first-place winner delivers his or her winning speech.

Prizes currently total $60,000, and consist of scholarships of $18,000 for the first place winner, $13,000 for second place, $9,000 for third place, $5,500 for fourth, $4,000 for fifth, $3,000 for sixth, $2,000 for seventh, $1,500 for eighth, and $1,000 for ninth places through twelfth places.

After their return home, the state winners are invited to take another all-expense paid trip—this time to the Academy of Achievement. This unique California-based program selects a different city each year in which to hold its seminar. The winners' three-day trip is normally paid for by the sponsoring departments. While at the Academy, the VOD winners, together with several hundred other academically gifted students, attend symposiums led by some of the nation's leaders in business, entertainment, art, sports, and government. VFW participation in the Academy of Achievement started in 1972.

Throughout the history of the VOD competition, there have been many notable winners, including television journalist Charles Kuralt, singer/activist Anita Bryant, actress/TV personality Mariette Hartley, and John Ashcroft, the present Governor of Missouri. Since the VFW began sponsoring the Voice of Democracy competition, over 6 million students have participated, and awards totalling more than $6 million in scholarships, savings bonds, and other prizes have been given winners at the various levels.

COMMUNITY ACTIVITIES

"Community Service" is the term applied to the many deeds which VFW posts undertake to: improve their city, town or neighborhood; aid individual families or people; better recreational and educational opportunities for everyone; assist schools, churches, and other organizations. But the Community Service program goes far beyond this textbook definition. The time and energy that VFW and Ladies Auxiliary members donate to their communities is nothing short of an affirmation of their love and concern for the well-being of their fellow Americans and their country.

As the strength and influence of posts have grown since World War II, so too has the VFW's role in the community. This is because the majority of work for the betterment of communities goes on at the local level. As Past Commander-in-Chief Lyall Beggs declared, "No matter how many brilliant ideas the national officers concoct—no matter how hard they are willing to work—nothing happens until local units go into action."

To list even a small percentage of the Community Activity Projects accomplished by the VFW posts and their Auxiliaries would be impractical as well as impossible. Instead, here are just a few of the thousands of more recent projects that members have taken the time to report.

- Post 1857, Okalahoma City, Oklahoma, provided eighty students with nearly $80,000 in scholarships between the years of 1964 and 1979.

- In 1980, Post 1326 contributed $18,000 to be used in providing two automatic sliding doors for students at the Jamestown, North Dakota School for Crippled Children.

- Incoming Post Commander Anthony Power of Blairstown, New Jersey Post 10600 decided the post should involve itself in a community activity project. When Isabelle Dodd suggested helping to restore the Statue of Liberty, Commander Power said, "Let's get the whole town involved." A fund-raising ball was planned. Kids colored posters. The city's firemen offered their facilities and help while the businessmen had the tickets printed. Another veteran's organization hung the posters and furnished the prizes. In the end, the project raised over $6,000 to assist in the renovation of the Statue of Liberty.

- McKenna-Frye Post 6626 and the Eastern Paralyzed Veterans Association banded together with volunteers from New York Telephone and members of the Castle Point VA Medical Center staff to inaugurate a program that provided bedside phones on which patients with spinal cord injuries could call home. The program, dubbed "PT PHONE HOME" (PT is the hospital abbreviation for patient), has been so successful that the Bell Telephone System is now researching the feasibility of installing voice-activated computers for patients with spinal cord injuries. The computer would not only dial the phones for patients, but would write letters and perform other activities without the assistance of the hospital staff.

- Post 8586 of Perrysville, Ohio, raised $4,100 to provide lights for the Kettering-Mohican Area Medical Center's helicopter landing

Members of Klossner-Dietzler Post No. 5729 laying a walkway on the future site of the Veterans of Foreign Wars and Auxiliary Memorial Park in Medford, Wisconsin

pad. The lights enabled the helicopter to land at the center after dark.

Obviously, community projects are as individual as the communities themselves. *Many* if not most VFW posts around the world have done at least one of the following:

- provided special tutoring, plastic surgery, wheelchairs, and TVs for children with disabilities;
- saved many lives by sponsoring blood, bone, and skin banks;
- donated playgrounds, lighted athletic fields, swimming pools, clubhouses, recreational centers, and athletic funds to their schools and community;
- hosted thousands of needy children and orphans at VFW Post Picnics, Christmas parties, and other special events;
- coached thousands of aliens to help them become U.S. citizens;
- aided National Guard units by providing them with training quarters and boosting their enlistment campaigns;
- given liberally to community chests, the Red Cross, and charity fund drives;

- provided new homes, clothing, and food for families stricken by fire, flood, or other disasters.

Overall, the VFW posts and Ladies Auxiliaries annually donate a staggering amount of time and money to the betterment of their communities. In a survey conducted in 1985, Community Activities Director Ray Price and Publications and Public Relations Director Wade LaDue found the figures "beyond comprehension." Very conservative estimates put the number of hours donated by the men and women of the VFW toward its Community Activity Program at in excess of *500 million* hours each year. And in an average year, the worth of the VFW's community services is valued at more than *$450 million.*

In making these contributions to community welfare, the VFW often works with others within the community. Civic officials, businessmen's service clubs, women's groups, educators, the press, radio and television stations, and local leaders all help to make the VFW Community Service Program possible. And in turn, the Community Service Program ensures that the veteran's fight to make his "little corner of the world" a safer and better place in which to live will continue indefinitely.

VFW MAGAZINE

From its earliest days, the VFW has recognized the need to communicate with its members about organizational and veterans' issues. In the beginning, the group was small enough that communication could be accomplished by word of mouth. But as membership swelled and posts were established all across the country, the organization had to turn to written communication to keep its members informed.

The first publication of what is now the VFW was published by the American Veterans of Foreign Service and took its title from that organization. Because early issues were not always given a volume or serial number, it is difficult to pinpoint exactly when the first issue was released. Most likely, however, the first issue of the *American Veteran of Foreign Service Magazine* was released about October 1904.

James Romanis was the first editor of this early publication and also one of the owners of the Service Publishing Company of Columbus, Ohio, which printed it. As Chapter 2 discusses, Romanis relied heavily on articles in this magazine to drum up support for the merger of the eastern and western branches of the AVFS. After the merger was successfully completed, the magazine folded. The magazine was later resurrected and renamed *The American Veteran of Foreign Service Journal.* Because this publication was sold on a subscription plan to a very limited number of members, it was constantly in financial troubles. In 1910, it was discontinued once again, only to be resurrected in September 1912, with William E. Ralston as editor. This magazine lasted until the AVFS merged with the Army of the Philippines a year later.

Shortly before the merger, the Army of the Philippines also got into the publishing act. Early in June 1912, National Historian Julian E. Duvall of Norton, Kansas, started publishing a newspaper titled *The Philippine Veteran.* This publication, billed as the "Official Publication of the Army of the Philippines," was short-lived. After the merger, it continued for several months as *The Veteran,* then ceased with the January 1914 issue.

When the fifteenth Annual Encampment assembled in Pittsburgh on September 14, 1914, the newly combined memberships of the AVFS and the Army of the Philippines adopted the name Veterans of Foreign Wars of the United States. To keep its members informed, the group appointed Julian Duval editor and publisher of its new official publication: *Foreign Service* magazine.

From the start, this revived *Foreign Service* was plagued with problems. It depended upon subscriptions for support, but only a small number of the members were interested enough to subscribe. In addition, the paper's limited and special circulation made it difficult to find advertisers. Soon Duvall began to lose money on the venture.

To bail out the floundering magazine, the VFW worked out an agreement with the *American Standard,* a newspaper published by the National Tribune publishing company and already distributed to many other veteran's groups. At a cost of 20 cents per member per year, the *American Standard* agreed to send a copy of the paper once a month to each VFW member in good standing. In each issue, the VFW was to have two pages to itself, edited by William E. Ralston.

Within a few months, it was apparent that this was not to be a happy association. In order to continue to appeal to its older readers, many of them Civil War veterans, the *Standard* started editing the VFW news down to the bone. The *Standard's* editorial staff did not seem to understand what the VFW members wanted to see in print and often ignored what editor Ralston sent in. Highly dissatisfied, the VFW severed its arrangement with the *Standard* and once again began publishing *Foreign Service* on its own. The first issue of the new *Foreign Service* appeared in September 1915 as Volume V, No. 1. Shortly after the printing of *Foreign Service* was resumed by the VFW itself, the required subscription payment was dropped and the publication was sent free to each member in good standing.

Ralston continued as the publication's editor until August 1919, when he was succeeded by W.W. Ward as editor and Walter Joyce as manager. In June 1920, Ward was replaced by a trio of assistants handling the writing and editorial duties: J.N. Calvert, Julius Berg, and Norman Shannon Hall. In July of that year, Charles S. Pemburn was added to the editorial staff, and after October 1920, Julius Berg's name no longer appeared on the editorial page.

From December 1920 until December 1926, *Foreign Service* went through five different editors: W.N. Morell, Norman Shannon Hall, Fred J. Dimes, Robert Christenberry, and Lt. Col. Charles A. Messerve. Among these, according to a brief history written by National Historian J.I. Billman in 1933, Hall gave the magazine a literary value it had not attained since James Romanis had served as editor of the *American Veteran of Foreign Service.* In Billman's words, "James Romanis, in 1904–05, was somewhat partial to 'literary' material, poetry as well as prose. Not until the time of Norman Shannon Hall was this again true. He was a poet and writer who could, on occasion, turn out very credible work. . . ."

According to Billman, *Foreign Service* really came into its own after Barney Yanofsky assumed the editorial reins. Yanofsky, a native of London who came to this country as a child, had previously worked as a reporter and managing editor with the Fremont, Nebraska, *Tribune.* In December 1926, he was named editor, director of publications and publicity with the national staff of the VFW. While editor of *Foreign Service,* his editorials "set a new standard for veterans publications"—at least in Billman's opinion.

In 1949, publicity functions were separated from the publications department. Yanofsky continued, however, as editor and director of publications. During Yanofsky's editorship, subscriptions to the national magazine grew from 60,000 to over 1.3 million, as did the VFW's membership. During the 1952 to 1953 year, the name of the magazine was changed from *Foreign Service* to *VFW Magazine.*

Upon Yanofsky's death on January 30, 1962, John Smith, the VFW's Director of Public Relations, was assigned the additional duties of editor and publisher of the *VFW Magazine.* In 1982, the positions of Director of Publications and Director of Public Relations were again separated. John Smith continued as publications director, while Wade W. LaDue, a retired army officer, took over as public relations director. When Smith retired in April 1986, LaDue took on both jobs.

In December 1986, James K. Anderson became editor of the *VFW Magazine.* After his retirement in 1989, Richard L. Kolb, a former freelance writer and editor, replaced him.

Editor Barney Yanofsky (seated, far right) helped mold the VFW Magazine into one of the nation's most authoritative and respected veterans' publications. Robert B. Handy, Jr., long-time VFW Quartermaster General, is seated second from the left.

Today the magazine's circulation exceeds 2.1 million, with approximately 30 percent of its cost covered by the sale of advertising. Despite its vastly expanded readership, the mission of this "house organ" has remained the same since the magazine's beginning: to entertain its readers, inform them about current veterans' issues and entitlements, assist in finding former comrades-in-arms, and publish dates of units' reunions.

POLITICAL ACTION COMMITTEE

After many years of working to influence federal legislation on behalf of the veterans it represented, in 1979 the VFW established a political action committee (VFW-PAC). A political action committee is the only legal way that the VFW, as a group, can take an active role in federal elections. Through the PAC, members can express support for, contribute to, or spend money on behalf of candidates for election to the offices of President of the United States, United States Senator, and United States Representative. Funding is entirely by voluntary personal contributions sent directly to the PAC or through VFW posts and auxiliaries. At present, there are over a million active VFW-PAC donors.

Through its role in federal elections, the VFW-PAC strives to accomplish two goals: 1) the defense and promotion of veterans' entitlements; and 2) support of national defense issues. Because of its special concerns about these issues, the PAC has been labeled a "special interest" group. Many consider special interest groups to be unethical or even illegal. The VFW-PAC is neither. All PACs are under constant scrutiny by the Federal Election Commission, and their activities and contributions are closely monitored. Violations of election laws are quickly and severely acted upon.

Some prospective PAC members worry that the PAC engages in "vote buying." But contributions go only to legislators who have already proven that they support the PAC's positions. When a candidate has no voting record to indicate his position on the issues, the PAC asks for a written position statement from the candidate. Financial support and endorsement is then based upon his or her response.

PACs in general, and the VFW-PAC in particular, often reveal a legislator's true stand on an issue by monitoring every vote taken in Congress. Based on roll call, or recorded votes (some are taken by voice only), the VFW-PAC rates every senator or representative on his or her record pertaining to veterans' benefits and national defense issues. Releases containing the information about each legislator's vote are then distributed throughout the entire VFW network. Endorsements are made according to the following policy:

Endorsement Policy, 1990

I.

Members of Congress must show support of both: (a) Veterans Legislation and (b) strong National Security. The procedure for scoring shall be based on roll call votes in the respective houses of Congress. Abstentions shall be considered a vote against VFW interests unless special considerations are approved by the Board of Directors.

II.

Members of Congress running for re-election who have a total score of 70 percent or higher in VFW-PAC endorsement scoring may receive the PAC endorsement for a given election year. This endorsement may consist of a monetary contribution to be determined by the VFW-PAC Board of Directors.

III.

Members of Congress running for re-election who achieve a total score of 60 percent or higher in VFW-PAC endorsement scoring may be eligible for a monetary contribution to retire campaign debts and other fund raisers after the election, provided they win re-election. The total contribution to any individual in this category shall be determined by the VFW-PAC Board of Directors. Contributions will be made by the PAC Director only in response to formal solicitations.

IV.

VFW Department Commanders and VFW-PAC State Chairmen will be asked to present recommendations, in writing, to the Board of Directors as to whether or not the VFW-PAC should endorse candidates running for Congress from their respective states. Final decisions will be made by the VFW-PAC Board of Directors.

V.

VFW Department Commanders and VFW-PAC State Chairmen may be asked for endorsement recommendations, in writing, when an incumbent member of the House of Representatives is running for the Senate or there is an open seat in either House of Congress. Final decisions will be made by the VFW-PAC Board of Directors.

VI.

Each member of Congress shall be rated based on his or her previous term in Congress (2 years for the House of Representatives and 6 years for the Senate members).

VII.

Final determinations and actions on all issues and endorsements shall be the responsibility of the VFW-PAC Board of Directors.

Legislators who score the highest on VFW issues receive an Honor Roll Endorsement. They receive a contribution from the VFW-PAC and a VFW-PAC news release timed for maximum benefit to their campaign for election. So, too, do Second Tier endorsees. Non-incumbent candidates are considered for endorsement if the congressional seat has been vacated or if the incumbent's voting record is unsatisfactory. The following table gives an indication of how successful the VFW-PAC's endorsements have been:

VFW-PAC ELECTION ACTIVITY

Election Year	Candidates Endorsed	Candidates Elected	Percent Elected
1980	251	223	89
1982	306	277	91
1984	380	358	92.3
1986	234	224	95.7
1988	340	333	97.9

Other VFW-PAC Activities

Besides endorsing candidates, the VFW-PAC also encourages other programs designed to involve VFW members and their local posts in the political process. These include:

1. Generating VFW attendance at senators' and representatives' "Town Hall Meetings" throughout their states and districts.
2. Hosting U.S. Senators and Representatives at VFW functions.
3. Registering the VFW community to vote.
4. Setting up candidate forums.
5. Distributing information to VFW members on voting procedures and on where the candidates stand on the issues.
6. Getting the VFW members involved in political action.
7. Providing absentee ballots to disabled members.
8. Getting VFW members to the polls on Election Day, whether by a reminder call or transporting them by car.

Politics being what it is and voters being what they are, the future of VFW-PAC will likely depend on how many of its detractors join the ranks of the believers. If most VFW members supported the program, it would truly become a powerful force in the political scene. But if assistance or contributions drop, the VFW-PAC could become just another program that failed.

SAFETY PROGRAM

In 1966, Commander-in-Chief Leslie M. Fry pointed out the need for dynamic programs. "The morale of any organization is based on its achievements," he proclaimed. "Without worthwhile programs, we have no reason to exist."

Taking Fry at his word, the National Council of Administration approved an increase in the budget and then founded the VFW Safety Program. To bring home its message that each individual must do his share in promoting safety, the committee quickly adopted the slogan, "SAFETY BEGINS WITH ME."

This committee's first undertaking was to encourage the posts to sponsor a National Safety Council course in driver improvement for licensed drivers. By 1968, twenty-five departments were offering the course to both VFW and Ladies Auxiliary members.

To assist younger drivers (the bicycle pedalling crowd), the Safety Committee took over the popular "Lite a Bike" program established by the Youth Activities program. The 3–M Company furnished free reflective tape to posts who conducted Lite a Bike rodeos and roundups during which bicycles were given safety inspections. By 1968, well over 16 million bicycles had been marked with reflective safety tape. As more manufacturers began offering bicycles with reflective paint and reflective disks on the spokes, this program began shifting its emphasis to teaching safe riding habits to bicyclists. The program then became known as the "Veterans of Foreign Wars Bicycle Safety Program."

In 1968, the Ladies Auxiliary adopted the Safety Program as one of its major projects. With their help, that year the VFW supported the nationwide drive for reflective license plates. State police, county sheriffs, city police, and concerned citizens from all over the nation also joined in the campaign. Eventually, some state legislatures adopted the idea, while others did not.

In 1970 the Defensive Driving Course was replaced by the "Drive to Survive" program. In addition, the Safety Program developed citations to be presented to law enforcement agencies and officers for outstanding service to their communities in safeguarding the lives and property of citizens. A special award to recognize individuals who have helped law enforcement officers maintain law and order was also established. By 1971, forty-seven departments were participating in the commendation program.

In 1973, the Safety Program started a new program titled "Veterans of Foreign Wars Drug Abuse Program." This program, which was renamed

VFW Post 10273 of Stratford, Connecticut, supports junior rifle safety.

"Veterans Fight Drugs Program" in the 1989 to 1990 year, encourages posts and auxiliaries to sponsor seminars and distribute anti-drug literature.

In 1982, the National Convention added a new program—hunter safety. The purpose of the Hunter Education Program is to promote responsible, ethical hunter conduct; to emphasize the importance of wildlife management, laws, and regulations; and to provide instruction in the safe handling of hunting equipment. Hunters who successfully complete the course have a better understanding of their outdoor obligations to landowners, to natural resources, to other hunters, and to themselves.

The Home Protection Program became part of the Safety package in 1985. The Home Protection package consists of two parts: fire safety and home safety. Through education in home safety, the VFW helps homeowners reduce their vulnerability to burglars and other intruders. Participants in the program learn about the use of safer locks, window stops that do not allow windows to be raised high enough to permit entry, and proper lighting for the grounds surrounding the house. Participants in the fire safety program learn about the proper type and placement of fire extinguishers, the importance of pre-planning escape routes, how to seal off a room if escape is not practical, and how to avoid fire hazards around the home.

Also in 1985, Bicycle Safety and Lite a Bike were combined into a single program. That left the Safety Program with the six programs that it sponsors to this day: Fire Prevention and Home Security, Drive to Survive, Bicycle Safety, Recognition and Public Commendation Certificates, Veterans Fight Drugs, and Hunter Safety.

Making the world a better place in which to live has long been the dream of our nation's veterans. The VFW Safety Program is just another extension of those dreams.

CHAPTER THIRTEEN

IN THE PUBLIC EYE

Many of the VFW's members are better known for their contributions to our society in areas other than veterans' welfare. Presidents, justices, governors, congressmen, authors, astronauts, actors, admirals, generals—they are the "movers and shakers" who shape the destiny of our nation and its citizens.

It would be impossible to list all of the prominent Americans who have belonged to the VFW. First, because their sheer numbers would make this a formidable task. And second, because the organization has upheld its founders' decree that no member should receive special treatment based on past rank or social standing. The national roster of membership lists names only, without reference to members' past or present occupations or status. To compile a list of famous members of the VFW therefore entails considerable research and records checking.

Despite the VFW's policy of treating its members as equals, many believe that having prominent citizens as members enhances the organization's power, credibility, and stature. Here, then, is a partial listing of famous Americans from all walks of life who have chosen to belong to the VFW.

PROMINENT MEMBERS OF THE VFW

NAME	TITLE/PROFESSION	DEPARTMENT
Albert, Carl	Speaker U.S. House	Oklahoma
Alford, Dale T.	Doctor/U.S. Senate	Arkansas
Baldwin, Raymond E.	U.S. Supreme Court	Connecticut
Barrow, Robert H.	General, Marine Corps	Louisiana
Bradley, Omar	General, U.S. Army	Missouri
Britt, Maurice L.	Lt. Governor	Arkansas

Brown, Grady	Director, VA	Arkansas
Brown, Hank	U.S. House	Colorado
Buckley, Mayo	General, U.S. Army	Georgia
Bumpers, Dale	Governor/U.S. Senate	Arkansas
Bush, George	U.S. President	Texas
Byrne, Brendan T.	Governor	New Jersey
Callaway, Howard (Bo)	Secretary of the Army	Colorado
Callihan, Michael	Governor	Colorado
Chennault, Claire Lee	General, U.S. Army	Louisiana
Conte, Silvio	U.S. House	Massachusetts
Coontz, Robert E.	Admiral/Gov. of Guam	Missouri
Crago, Thomas	U.S. House	Pennsylvania
Curley, James M.	U.S. House/Mayor	Massachusetts
Davis, Charlie	General, U.S. Army	Georgia
Derwinski, Edward J.	U.S. Sec. of Veterans Affairs	Illinois
Dole, Bob	U.S. Senate	Kansas
Dumas, W.W. (Woody)	Mayor of Baton Rouge	Louisiana
Early, Joseph	U.S. House	Massachusetts
Edmondson, J. Howard	Governor/U.S. House	Oklahoma
Edwards, Ellis	State Treasurer	Oklahoma
Eisenhower, Dwight D.	U.S. President /General, U.S. Army	Kansas
Evans, Diane Carlson	Co-organizer, Vietnam Women's Memorial Project	Wisconsin
Faubus, Orville	Governor	Arkansas
Fish, Hamilton, Sr.	U.S. House	New York
Floyd, James H.	U.S. House	Georgia
Ford, Gerald R.	U.S. President	Michigan
Fraiser, Joe E.	General, U.S. Army	Georgia
Freeman, Orville	Governor	Minnesota
Frenzel, William	U.S. House	Minnesota
Garn, Jake	U.S. Senator	Utah
Gavin, John	General, U.S. Army	Massachusetts
Gentry, Byron	Lawyer/Athlete/Author	California
Glenn, John	Astronaut/U.S. Senate	Ohio
Goldwater, Barry	U.S. Senate	Arizona
Gordan, Nathan	Lt. Governor (M.O.H.)	Arkansas
Gremillion, Jack R.	State Attorney General	Louisiana
Griffin, Marvin	Governor	Georgia

Griffin. W.E.B.	Author	Alabama
Hammerschmidt, J.P.	U.S. House	Arkansas
Hathaway, Stan	Governor	Wyoming
Herschler, Ed	Governor	Wyoming
Hickey, J.J.	Governor	Wyoming
Hines, Frank	General, U.S. Army	Washington
Ichord, Richard	U.S. House	Missouri
Ingersol, Royal	Admiral, U.S. Navy	Indiana
Jones, Jimmy "Red"	State Auditor	Arkansas
Jones, Sam	Governor	Louisiana
Johnson, Donald	VA Administrator	Iowa
Johnston, J.B.	U.S. Senate	Louisiana
King, Bruce	Governor	New Mexico
King, Ernest J.	Admiral, U.S. Navy	Ohio
Kingston, Robert	General, U.S. Army	Massachusetts
Kennedy, Edward M.	U.S. Senate	Massachusetts
Kennedy, John F.	U.S. President	Massachusetts
Kerrey, J. Robert	U.S. Senate	Nebraska
Knowles, Warren G.	Governor	Wisconsin
Lautenberg, Frank	U.S. Senate	New Jersey
LeBlanc, John	Physician	Louisiana
LeMay, Curtis E.	General, U.S. Air Force	Louisiana
Loehr, Al	Mayor of St. Cloud	Minnesota
Lounge, John M.	Astronaut	Colorado
Love, John A.	Governor	Colorado
Lucy, Patrick	Governor	Wisconsin
Luief, Steve	State Senator	Arkansas
MacArthur, Douglas	General, U.S. Army	California
Mason, Harold (Buss)	Educator	Colorado
McClellan, John L.	U.S. Senator	Arkansas
McKeithen, John J.	Governor	Louisiana
McMath, Sidney	Governor	Arkansas
McNichols, Stephen L.R.	Governor	Colorado
McNichols, William H.	Mayor of Denver	Colorado
Means, Rice W.	U.S. Senator/Publisher	Colorado
Mills, Wilbur	U.S. House	Arkansas
Montgomery, G.V. (Sonny)	U.S. House	Mississippi
Moore, Arch A., Jr.	U.S House/Governor	W. Virginia

Moakley, Joseph	U.S. House	Massachusetts
Mowbray, John C.	Judge	Nevada
Murphy, Audie	Actor/World War II hero (M.O.H.)	Texas
Nigh, George	Governor	Oklahoma
Nimitz, Chester	Admiral, U.S. Navy	California
Nixon, Richard M.	U.S. President	California
O'Brien, Lawrence	U.S. Postmaster	Massachusetts
O'Callaghan, Donal	Governor	Nevada
O'Neill, William A.	Governor	Connecticut
Patton, George	General, U.S. Army	California
Pearson, George O.	General, U.S. Army	Wyoming
Pershing, John J.	General, U.S. Army	Pacific Area
Randall, William	U.S. House	Missouri
Rarick, John	U.S. House	Louisiana
Ray, Robert D.	Governor	Iowa
Richardson, Elliot	Secretary of Health, Education and Welfare	Massachusetts
Riley, Bob	Governor	Arkansas
Robinson, Arthur	U.S. Senate	Indiana
Rogers, Bernard	General, U.S. Army	Kansas
Roncalio, Teno	U.S. House	Wyoming
Rooney, Mickey	Actor	Nebraska
Rutan, Dick	Copilot of *Voyager*	Kansas
Schirra, Walter M.	Astronaut	Colorado
Scott, Robert	General, U.S. Army	Wyoming
Simpson, Alan K.	U.S. Senate	Wyoming
Singlaub, John K.	General, U.S. Army	Colorado
Stimson, Theron	General, U.S. Army	Wyoming
Swainson, John B.	Governor	Michigan
Swigert, Jack	Astronaut	Colorado
Talmadge, Herman	U.S. Senate	Georgia
Thompson, Carl	Governor	Wisconsin
Truman, Harry S.	U.S. President	Missouri
Vandenberg, Hoyt S.	General, U.S. Air Force	Wisconsin
Vanderhoof, John D.	Governor	Colorado
Van Zandt, James	U.S. House	Pennsylvania
Vessey, John	General, U.S. Army	Minnesota
Walt, Lewis W.	General, Marine Corps	Colorado
Westmoreland, William C.	General, U.S. Army	South Carolina

Yarbrough, George M.	State Sen./Lt. Governor	Mississippi
York, Alvin C.	World War I hero	Tennessee
Ziehlsdorf, Arvin R.	Sheriff/General, U.S. Army	Wisconsin

In addition to the famous Americans listed above, many movie actors belong or belonged to the VFW. They include: Caesar Romero, Victor Mature, James Stewart, Robert Montgomery, Melvin Douglas, Clark Gable, Robert Taylor, Spencer Tracy, Adolphe Menjou, Dick Arlen, Paul Lucas, and many others. Walt Disney, the pioneer of animated cartoons, was also a member.

Other notables for whom information about the department of membership is not available are: President Theodore Roosevelt; author and poet Carl Sandburg; radio commentator H.V. Kaltenborn; Generals of the Army George C. Marshall, Walter Bedell Smith, and Lewis B. Hershey; Vice Admiral John S. McCain; Commander Harold Stassen; and Supreme Court Justices Frank Murphy and Harold H. Burton.

General Omar N. Bradley, Administrator of Veterans Affairs

President John F. Kennedy, one-time Commander of the Joseph P. Kennedy, Jr., Post 5880 of Brockton, Massachussetts

Republican presidential nominee George Bush saluting the Joint Opening Session of the 89th National Convention of the VFW. Bush belongs to VFW Post 4344 of Houston, Texas.

Famous members from the days before the Army of the Philippines and the American Veterans of Foreign Service merged to form the VFW include: Generals Francis V. Greene, Charles King, Wilder S. Metcalf, and Arthur MacArthur (father of General Douglas MacArthur); and Colonel Alfred S. Frost.

INTERNATIONAL RECOGNITION

Not only do individual members of the VFW attract public attention, but the organization as a whole is frequently singled out for recognition of its contributions. This recognition does not just come from individuals and organizations in the United States, but also from veteran's groups around the world. Foreign supporters of the VFW and its goals include veteran's associations from Taiwan, the Netherlands, and South Korea.

The VFW has had a particularly long and amicable relationship with the Vocational Assistance Commission for Retired Servicemen, Republic of China (Taiwan). Its friendship goes back to the early 1970s when President Richard Nixon attempted to normalize trade relations with mainland China to the detriment of Taiwan. Condemning the U.S. government for the "selling out of long time friends and dealing with Communists," the VFW stood fast in its defense of its friends in Taiwan. As an expression of solidarity, in 1971 the VFW invited the chairman of

Two long-time VFW members, General Douglas MacArthur and Admiral Chester Nimitz discussing strategy for some Pacific action during World War II

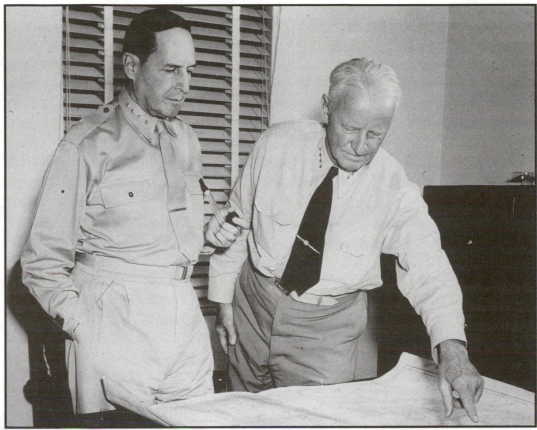

Four Star General, Presidential Advisor, and VFW member George C. Marshall

United States Army Captain and most decorated soldier of World War II, Audie Murphy

Colonel (later President) Theodore Roosevelt joined the VFW during World War I.

President Harry S. Truman was a Life Member and former Commander of VFW Post 35 in Kansas City, Missouri.

the Taiwanese veteran's group to the 72nd National Convention. This invitation was renewed every year until in 1980, the Vocational Assistance Commission for Retired Servicemen and the VFW signed a proclamation of brotherhood between the two organizations. This signing, according to Chairman T.Y. Chao, was "more than just a signing. It is an indication that. . . the Veterans of Foreign Wars of the United States and its Ladies Auxiliary, still continue to support the Republic of China, regardless of the change in the diplomatic relations as set forth by the present administration, they have our undying love and support,

and will continue to have it for their courageous battle against communism."

The Vocational Assistance Commission for Retired Servicemen (VACRS) of the Republic of China, Taiwan, was established November 1, 1954. The present operations of the VACRS include employment, schooling, medical care, and home care. VACRS also provides education, training, and child care. All veterans are assured that the able-bodied will be employed; the learned made use of; the ill hospitalized; children nursed; the aged, the widowed, the orphaned, the childless, and the disabled, cared for. Toward these ends, the VACRS maintains operations

General William C. Westmoreland,
pictured here with the author

Sergeant Alvin C. York (left), the most decorated soldier of
World War I, with Secretary of the Navy Frank Knox. York
was a member of VFW Post No. 1848 of Jackson, Tennessee.

in agriculture, forestry, fisheries, and animal hus-
bandry. Current membership is approximately
594,000.

Another foreign veteran's organization with
which the VFW has allied itself is the Foundation of
the Legion of Ex-Servicemen of the Netherlands (Oud
Strijders Legioen). On March 5, 1984, Prosper J.G.A.
Ego, Chairman of the Netherlands servicemen's organization, and VFW Commander-in-Chief Clifford
G. Olson, Jr., signed a Joint Declaration pledging the
two organizations' cooperation toward similar goals
and their common stand against world Communism.

The Oud Strijders Legioen was founded in 1958
for the purpose of uniting all Dutch ex-servicemen,
regardless of their religious, ideological, or political
ideas—left-wing Socialists, Communists, and Fascists
excluded. Since then, the Veteran's League has become involved in political activities. These activities
led to the League's division into two separate founda-

tions: the Foundation of Ex-Servicemen and the Foundation for Freedom and Security. The goals of both of
these foundations are to maintain the freedom and parliamentary democracy of the Netherlands and to
promote awareness that this aim can only be achieved
through close international cooperation with allies and
other friends with common interests. Currently the
League is the largest non-profit organization in the
Netherlands and accepts no subsidies from government or elsewhere.

Yet a third foreign veteran's organization with
which the VFW has signed a joint agreement is the
Korean Veterans Association (KVA). This association was established on February 1, 1952, and now
boasts a membership of approximately 4.2 million.
The purpose of the association is to promote
friendship and the rights and interests of members
through mutual assistance and help; to protect the free

democratic system; and to contribute to the national development and public interest of Korean society. The KVA maintains friendly ties not only with the VFW, but also with twenty-four other veteran's associations around the world.

The Joint Declaration signed by the VFW and the Legion of Ex-Servicemen of the Netherlands

The VFW's Joint Proclamation with the Vocational Assistance Commission for Retired Servicemen of Taiwan

INDEX

AFTERWORD

As I write these closing paragraphs of the history of the Veterans of Foreign Wars of the United States, I am aware that we have now come full circle. In 1898, the enemy was Spain and the theaters of operation were Cuba and the Philippines. Today the United States and its allies are battling the Iraqis in the Middle East, our battleships even now shelling the aggressor. Once again the United States is struggling to free the conquered from his oppressor.

Once again we will have veterans who will need care and whose sacrifices must be remembered. It is upon us that President Abraham Lincoln laid the mantle of responsibility "to care for him who shall have borne the battle and for his widow and for his orphans." We, in a country of citizen soldiers, only exchange one uniform for another. We only exchange one type of battle for another.

The VFW will, of course, welcome these new veterans into its folds just as it did the veterans of World War I, World War II, Korea, Vietnam, and twenty-odd other skirmishes. To remain evergreen—to accomplish all its goals—the organization must continue to grow in numbers. And yet, there is within the VFW an unspoken desire to see the end of this organization. The end of the Veterans of Foreign Wars, however, could only result from a lack of eligible men and women. The lack of eligible veterans would signify, in turn, the lack of suffering and dying caused by war. No one in the VFW would dispute the wisdom of trading one for the other. Those who do the actual fighting in any war have the greatest hatred for war. They have the most to lose.

Even after ninety-one years of service to our nation and its veterans, our philosophy remains steadfast.

WE ARE THE SAME, YET WE HAVE CHANGED;
WE HAVE CHANGED, YET WE ARE THE SAME.

Bill Bottoms
Eau Claire, Wisconsin
February 6, 1991

ABOUT THE AUTHOR

Bill Bottoms, a life member of the VFW and the Military Order of the Cootie, served as Commander for the VFW Department of Iowa in 1981–1982 and All-American Chairman of the VFW Big Ten Conference in 1983–1984. As a writer and editor, he's contributed to many VFW publications, including *VFW Magazine*. Currently, he's editor of *Wisconsin VFW News* and associate editor of *Messenger,* a newsletter published by VFW Post #305. Mr Bottoms lives in Eau Claire, Wisconsin.

MAIL TO: SUPPLY DEPARTMENT
VETERANS OF FOREIGN WARS
406 WEST 34TH STREET
KANSAS CITY, MISSOURI 64111

DATE _____

POST NO. _____

SHIP TO	**SOLD TO**

NAME_____ NAME _____

STREET _____ STREET _____

CITY _____ STATE_____ CITY _____ STATE_____

YOUR ZIP NO. _____ YOUR ZIP NO. _____

DAYTIME PHONE # (   ) _____ DAYTIME PHONE # (   )_____

Quantity	Stock Number	Catalog Description of Merchandise	Price Each, Set, 100, etc.	Total
	4428	**The VFW: An Illustrated History of the Veterans of Foreign Wars of the United States**	**$24.95 ea.**	

METHOD OF PAYMENT
For your protection, do not send cash or stamps.

Make check or money order payable to Veterans of Foreign Wars of the U.S.
OR Charge it to your MC or Visa.

NO C.O.D.'S

Total for Merchandise Ordered	
Missouri Residents Only—Add 6.475% Tax	
Balance Due From Previous Order Be Sure to Show Invoice No.	
Total Amount	

MC ☐ **(16 numbers)**

VISA ☐ **(13 or 16 numbers)**

DISCOVER ☐

Expiration Date: Month _____ Year _____

Signature_____

Money Order No. _____ Post Check No. _____

TO HELP US SERVE YOU BETTER, PLEASE PROVIDE US WITH YOUR FULL MAILING ADDRESS.
WHENEVER POSSIBLE, AVOID USING P.O. BOX NUMBERS OR ROUTE NUMBERS.

PUBLISHED BY: WOODBINE HOUSE, 5615 FISHERS LANE, ROCKVILLE, MD 20852